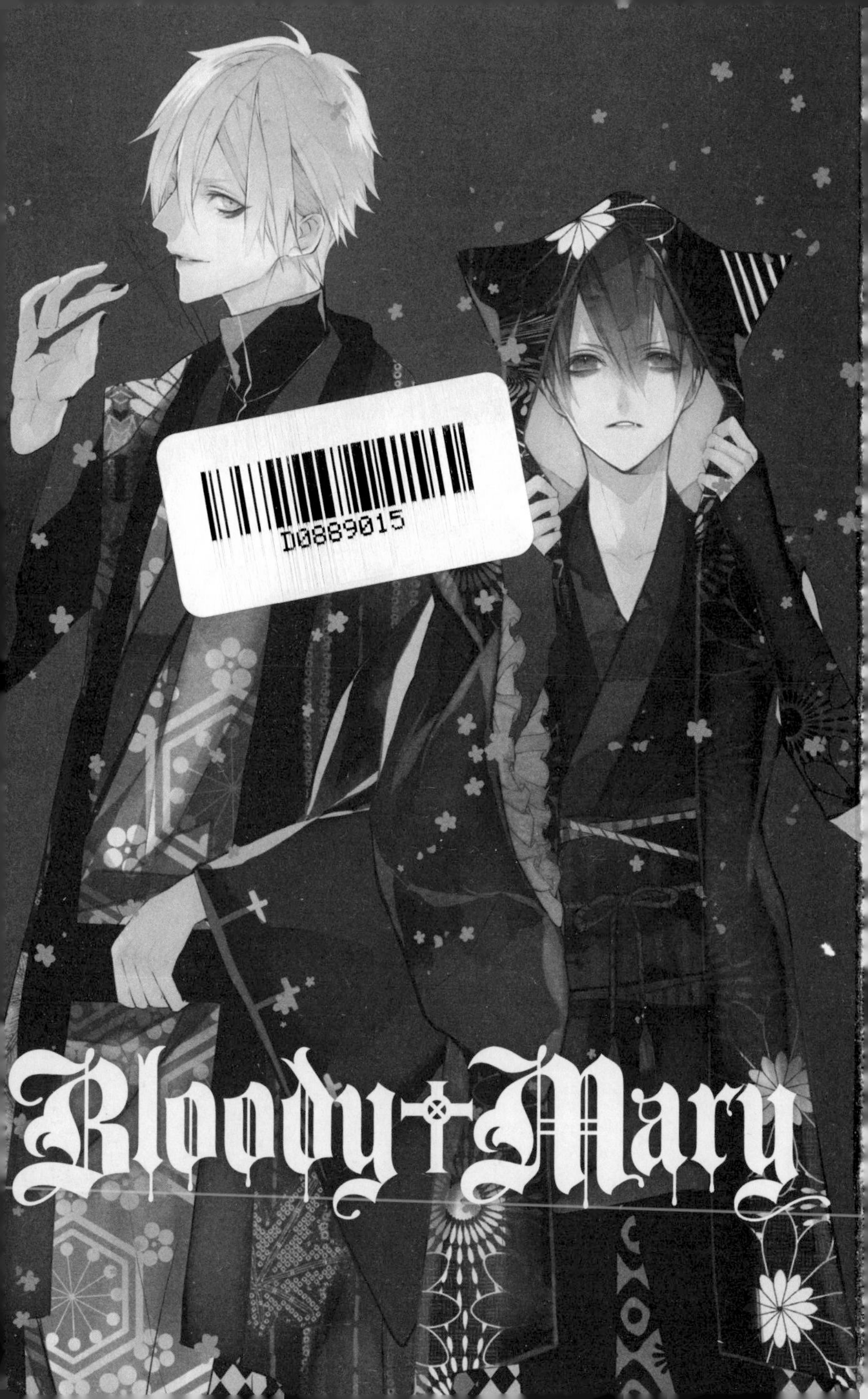
Bloody+Mary

# Bloody✝Mary

## 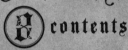 contents

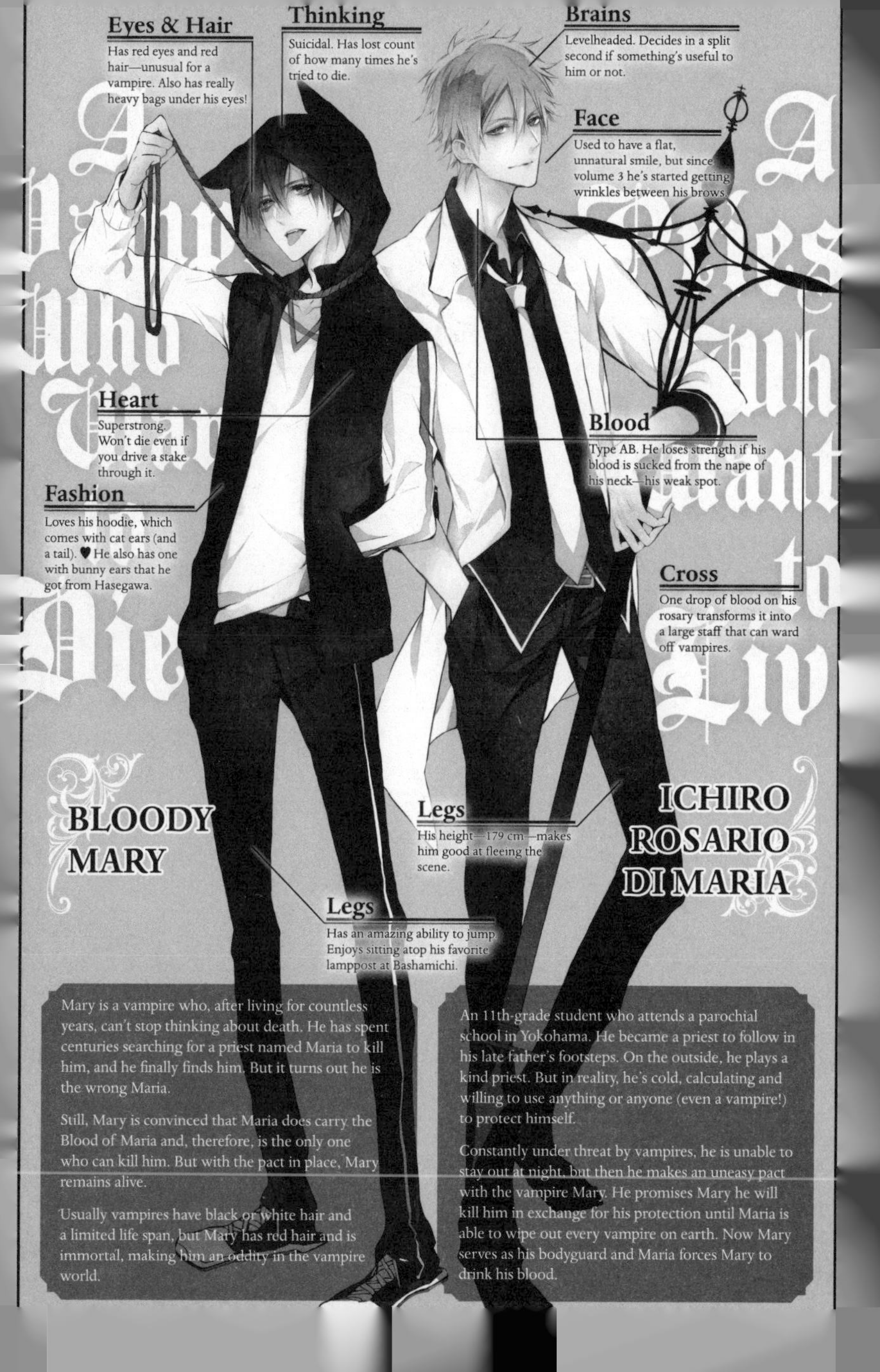
Eyes & Hair
Has red eyes and red hair—unusual for a vampire. Also has really heavy bags under his eyes!
Thinking
Suicidal. Has lost count of how many times he's tried to die.
Brains
Levelheaded. Decides in a split second if something's useful to him or not.
Face
Used to have a flat, unnatural smile, but since volume 3 he's started getting wrinkles between his brows.
Heart
Superstrong. Won't die even if you drive a stake through it.
Blood
Type AB. He loses strength if his blood is sucked from the nape of his neck—his weak spot.
Fashion
Loves his hoodie, which comes with cat ears (and a tail). ♥ He also has one with bunny ears that he got from Hasegawa.
Cross
One drop of blood on his rosary transforms it into a large staff that can ward off vampires.
BLOODY MARY
Legs
His height—179 cm—makes him good at fleeing the scene.
ICHIRO ROSARIO DI MARIA
Legs
Has an amazing ability to jump. Enjoys sitting atop his favorite lamppost at Bashamichi.

Mary is a vampire who, after living for countless years, can't stop thinking about death. He has spent centuries searching for a priest named Maria to kill him, and he finally finds him. But it turns out he is the wrong Maria.

Still, Mary is convinced that Maria does carry the Blood of Maria and, therefore, is the only one who can kill him. But with the pact in place, Mary remains alive.

Usually vampires have black or white hair and a limited life span, but Mary has red hair and is immortal, making him an oddity in the vampire world.

An 11th-grade student who attends a parochial school in Yokohama. He became a priest to follow in his late father's footsteps. On the outside, he plays a kind priest. But in reality, he's cold, calculating and willing to use anything or anyone (even a vampire!) to protect himself.

Constantly under threat by vampires, he is unable to stay out at night, but then he makes an uneasy pact with the vampire Mary. He promises Mary he will kill him in exchange for his protection until Maria is able to wipe out every vampire on earth. Now Mary serves as his bodyguard and Maria forces Mary to drink his blood.

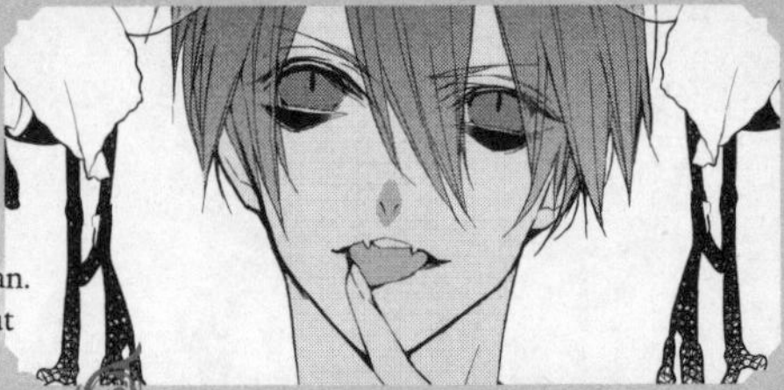

## "MARY"

He was the twin brother of Mary (the masochist) when they were both still human. It's not clear how he became a vampire, but the skeleton of "Mary" was locked away in Hydra's castle for a long time. But then she set it aflame, reducing it to ashes.

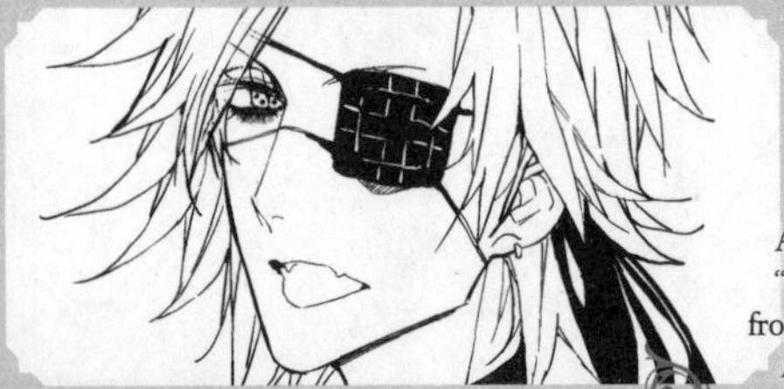

## ALDILA

A guy with an eye patch who's interested in "Bloody," the bloodstained vampire. Orders from "you-know-who" are communicated via Aldila. This volume will reveal how the eye patch isn't just a whimsical character design!

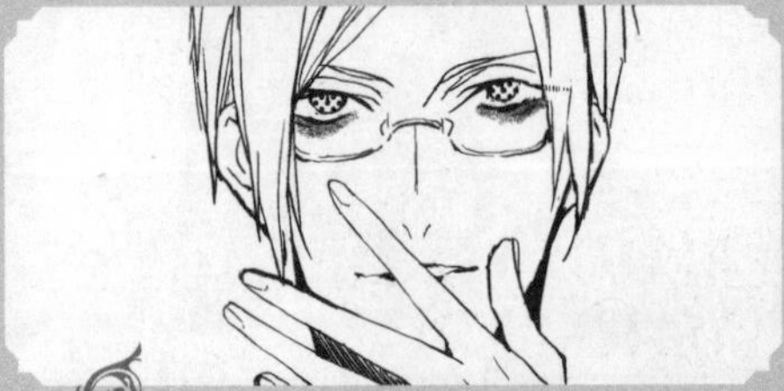

## VESPER

A guy with glasses who's interested in "Bloody," the bloodstained vampire. He seems to share a history with Bloody and freaks out when anyone brings up what happened "back then." What went down? You might find out in this volume…

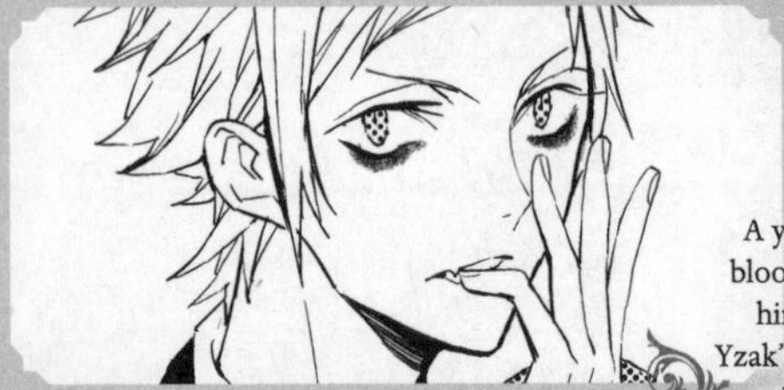

## CARDINAL

A young boy who's interested in "Bloody," the bloodstained vampire. "You-know-who" orders him to capture Yzak, and he sucks up a lot of Yzak's blood to keep himself nubile. Later, there will be a battle between him and Hydra, who has lost her position as the heroine, maybe…!

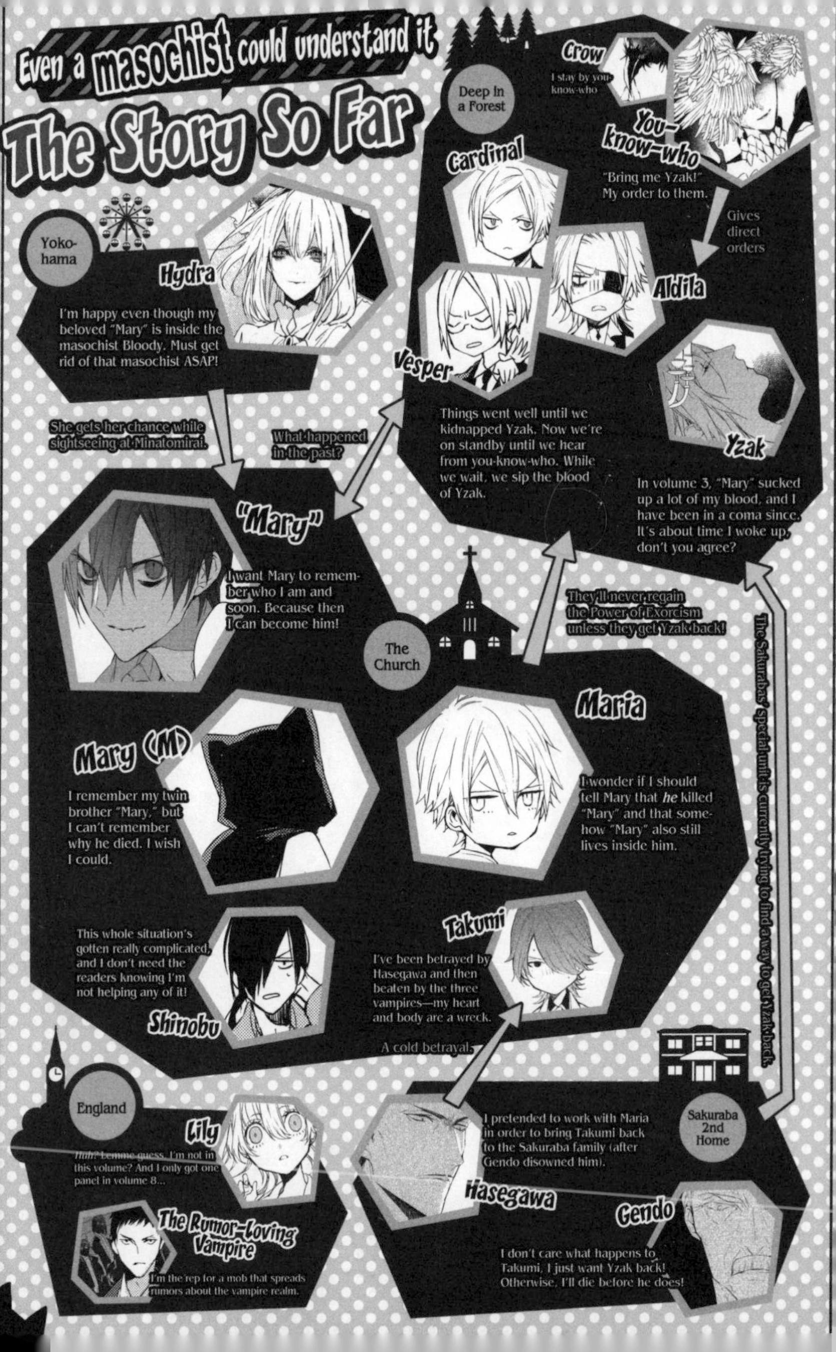

Even a masochist could understand it
The Story So Far
Deep In a Forest
Crow
I stay by you-know-who
You-know-who
"Bring me Yzak!" My order to them.
Gives direct orders
Cardinal
Aldila
Vesper
Things went well until we kidnapped Yzak. Now we're on standby until we hear from you-know-who. While we wait, we sip the blood of Yzak.
Yzak
In volume 3, "Mary" sucked up a lot of my blood, and I have been in a coma since. It's about time I woke up, don't you agree?
Yoko-hama
Hydra
I'm happy even though my beloved "Mary" is inside the masochist Bloody. Must get rid of that masochist ASAP!
She gets her chance while sightseeing at Minatomirai.
What happened in the past?
"Mary"
I want Mary to remember who I am and soon. Because then I can become him!
The Church
They'll never regain the Power of Exorcism unless they get Yzak back!
The Sakurabas' special unit is currently trying to find a way to get Yzak back.
Maria
I wonder if I should tell Mary that *he* killed "Mary" and that somehow "Mary" also still lives inside him.
Mary (M)
I remember my twin brother "Mary," but I can't remember why he died. I wish I could.
This whole situation's gotten really complicated, and I don't need the readers knowing I'm not helping any of it!
Shinobu
Takumi
I've been betrayed by Hasegawa and then beaten by the three vampires—my heart and body are a wreck.
A cold betrayal.
England
Lily
*Huh?* Lemme guess. I'm not in this volume? And I only got one panel in volume 8...
The Rumor-Loving Vampire
I'm the rep for a mob that spreads rumors about the vampire realm.
Sakuraba 2nd Home
I pretended to work with Maria in order to bring Takumi back to the Sakuraba family (after Gendo disowned him).
Hasegawa
Gendo
I don't care what happens to Takumi, I just want Yzak back! Otherwise, I'll die before he does!

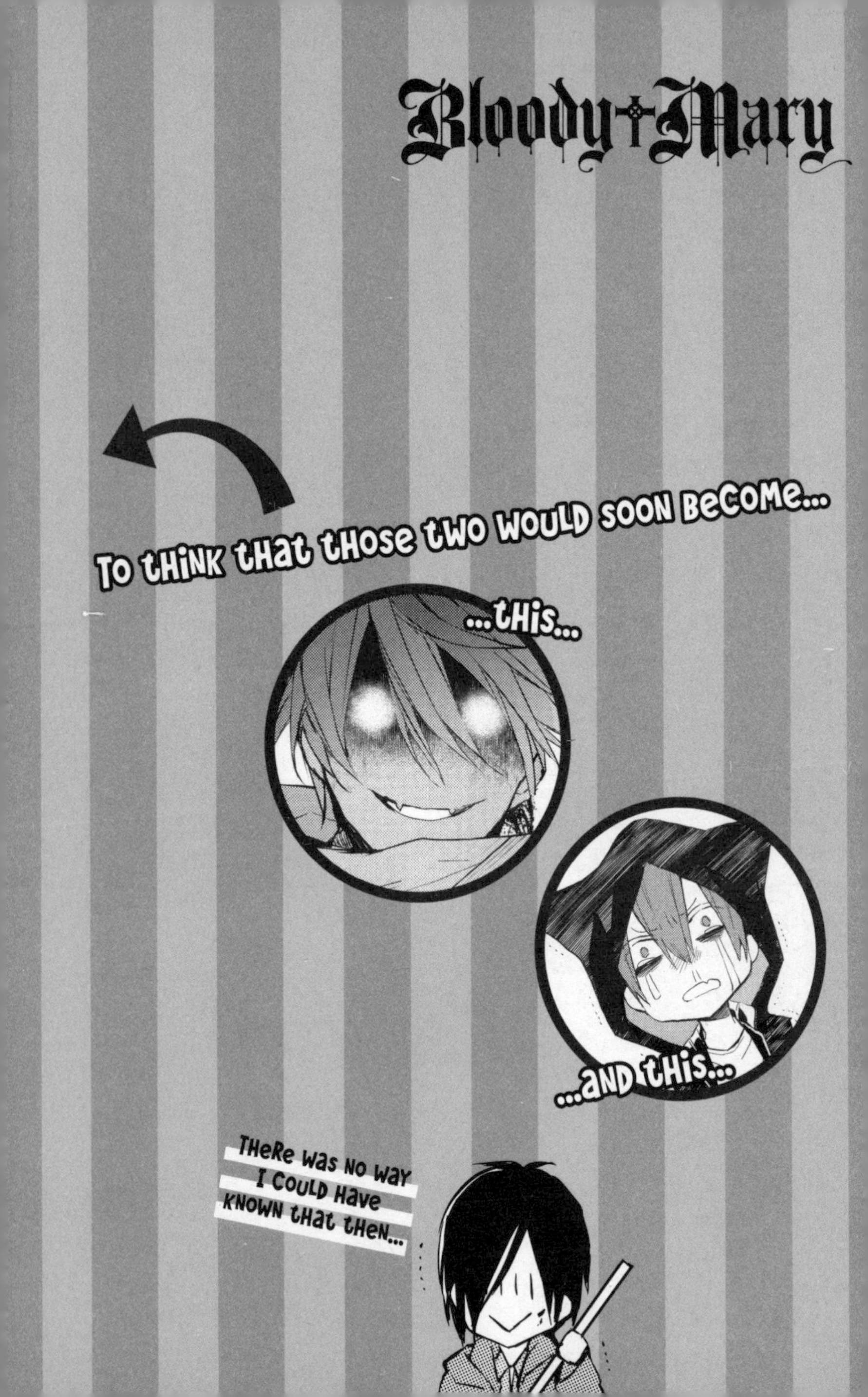
Bloody+Mary
To think that those two would soon become...
...this...
...and this...
There was no way I could have known that then...

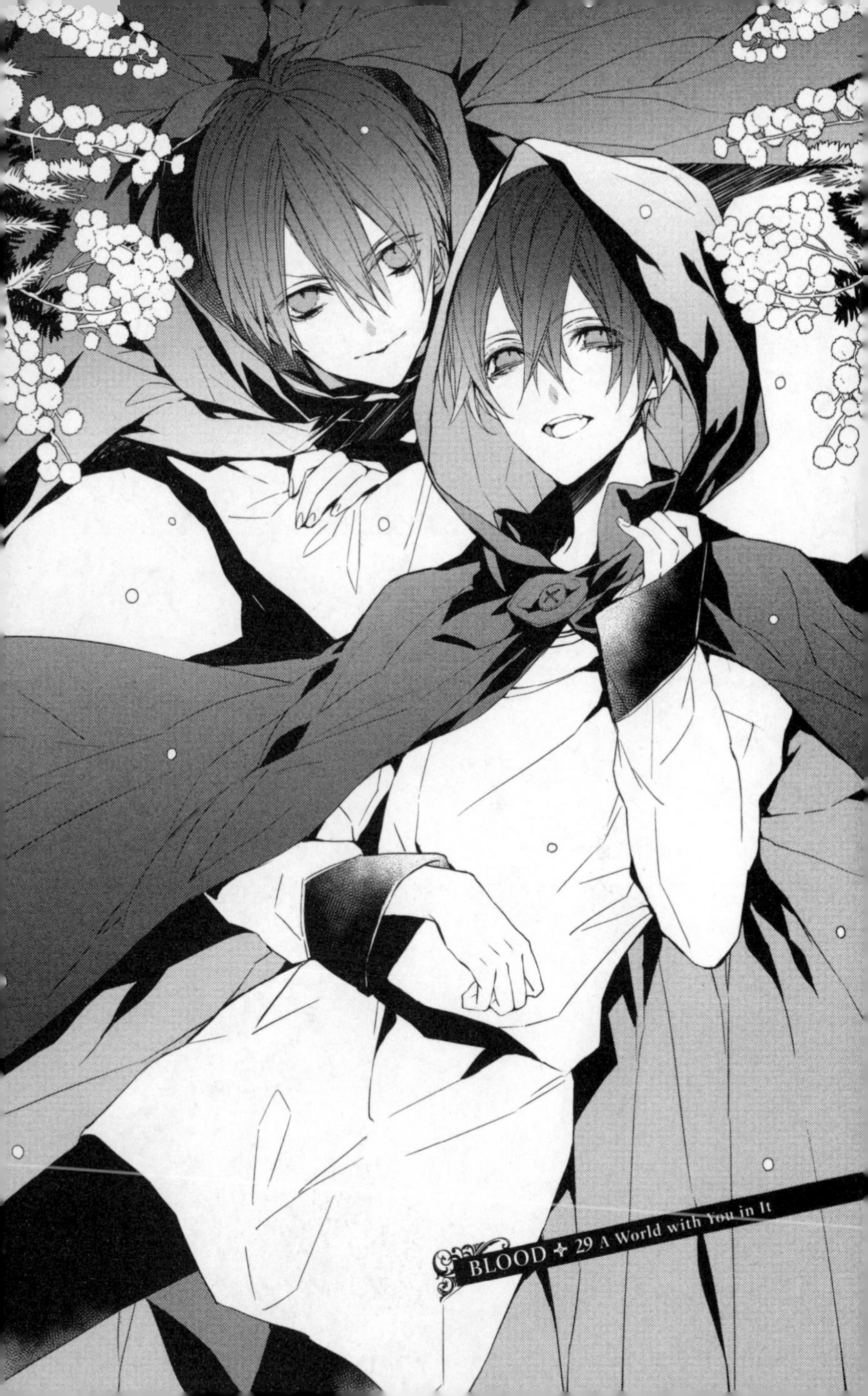
BLOOD ✦ 29 A World with You in It

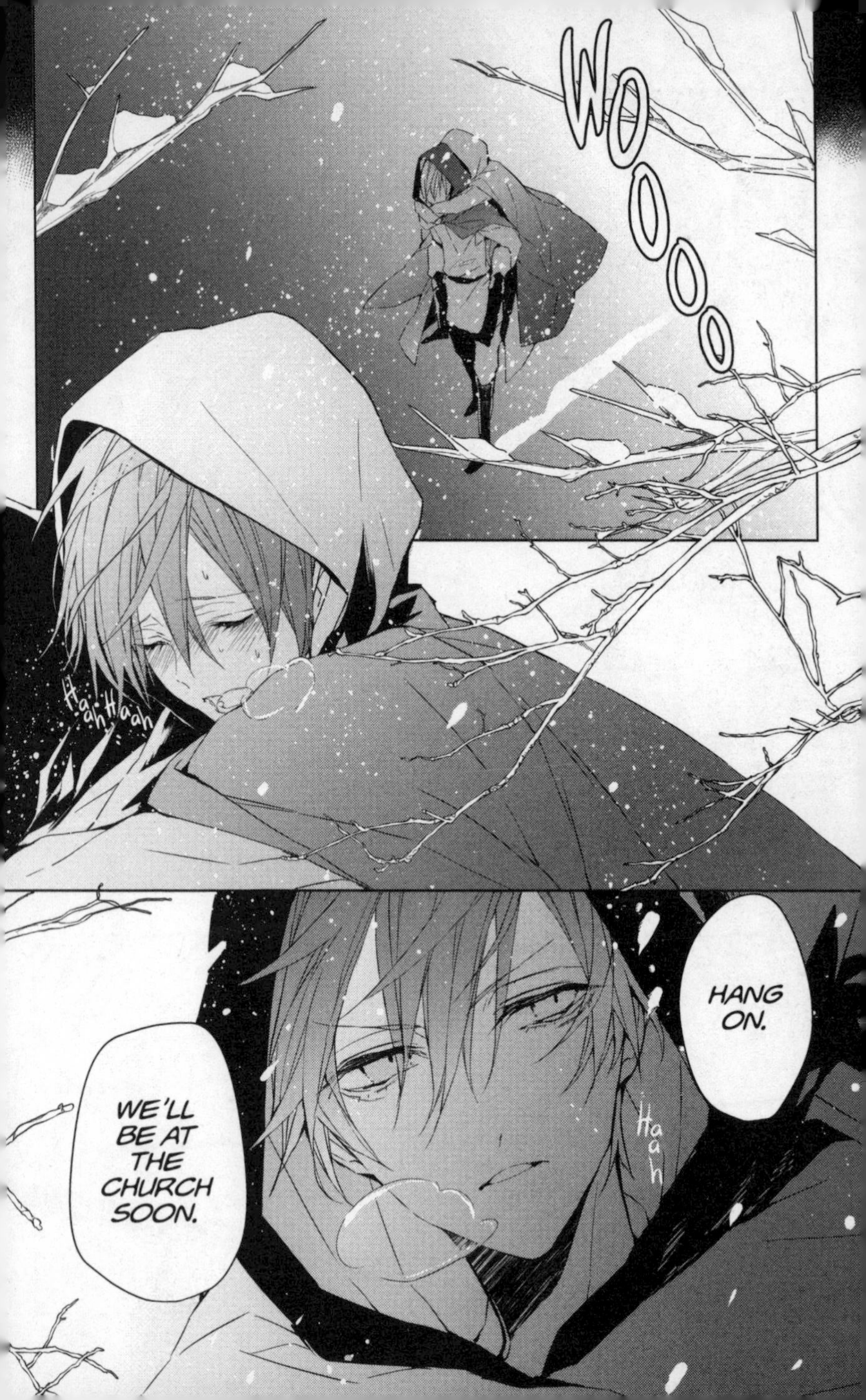
WOOOOO
Haah Haah
HANG ON.
Haah
WE'LL BE AT THE CHURCH SOON.

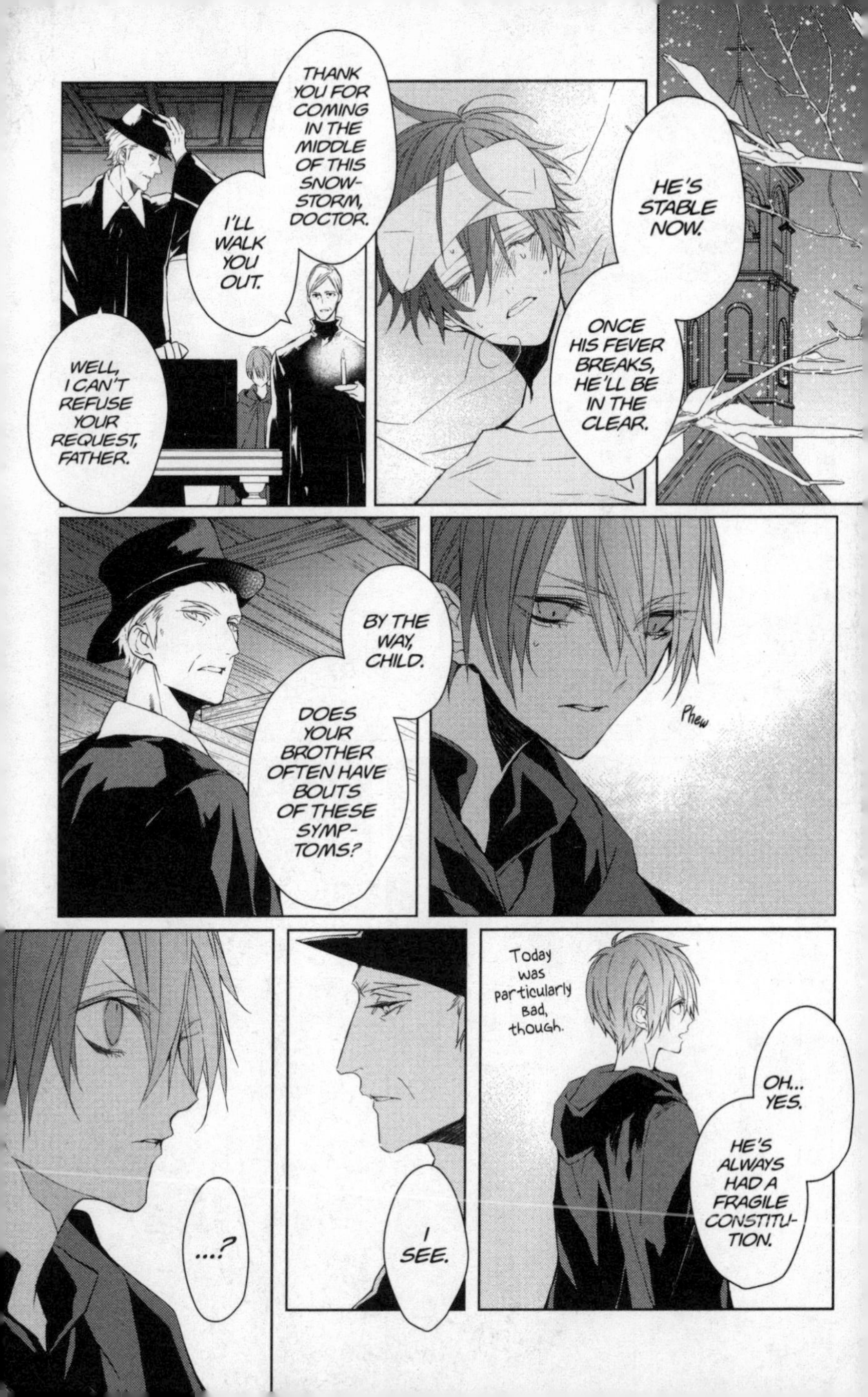
HE'S STABLE NOW.
ONCE HIS FEVER BREAKS, HE'LL BE IN THE CLEAR.
THANK YOU FOR COMING IN THE MIDDLE OF THIS SNOW-STORM, DOCTOR.
I'LL WALK YOU OUT.
WELL, I CAN'T REFUSE YOUR REQUEST, FATHER.
Phew
BY THE WAY, CHILD.
DOES YOUR BROTHER OFTEN HAVE BOUTS OF THESE SYMP-TOMS?
OH... YES.
HE'S ALWAYS HAD A FRAGILE CONSTITU-TION.
Today was particularly bad, though.
I SEE.
...?

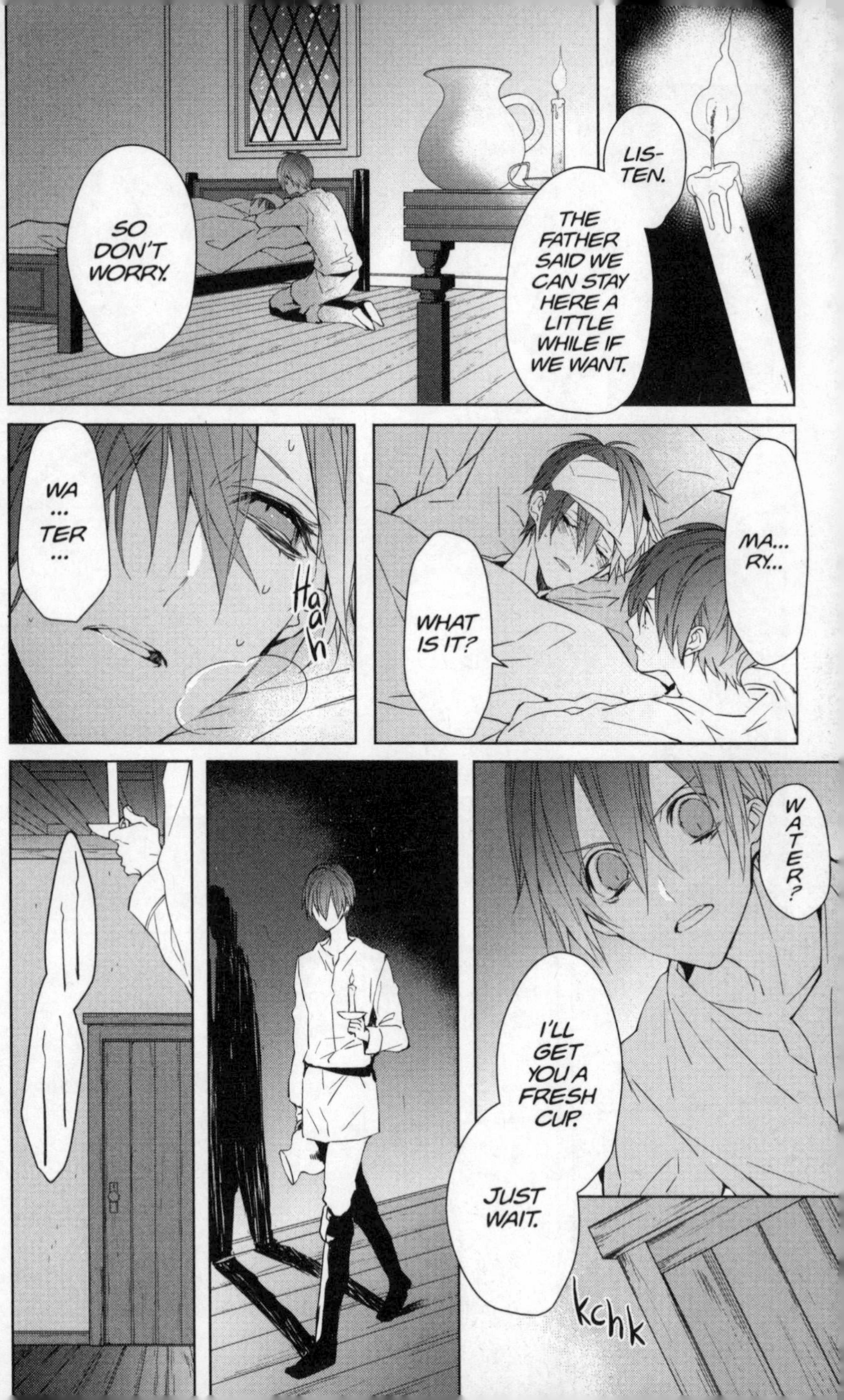
LIS-TEN.
THE FATHER SAID WE CAN STAY HERE A LITTLE WHILE IF WE WANT.
SO DON'T WORRY.
MA... RY...
WHAT IS IT?
WA... TER...
Haah
WATER?
I'LL GET YOU A FRESH CUP.
JUST WAIT.
kchk

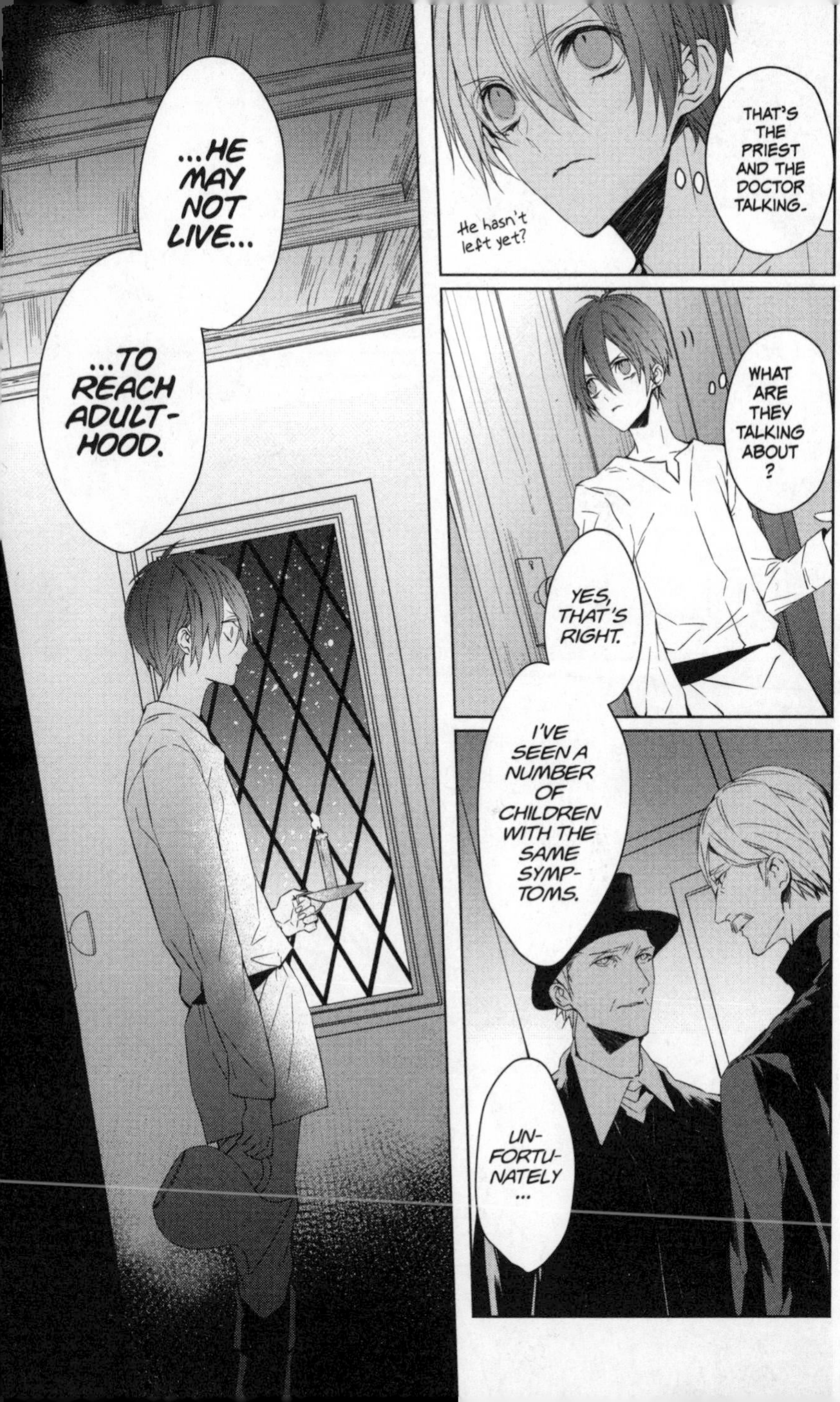
THAT'S THE PRIEST AND THE DOCTOR TALKING.
He hasn't left yet?
WHAT ARE THEY TALKING ABOUT?
YES, THAT'S RIGHT.
I'VE SEEN A NUMBER OF CHILDREN WITH THE SAME SYMPTOMS.
UNFORTUNATELY...
...HE MAY NOT LIVE...
...TO REACH ADULTHOOD.

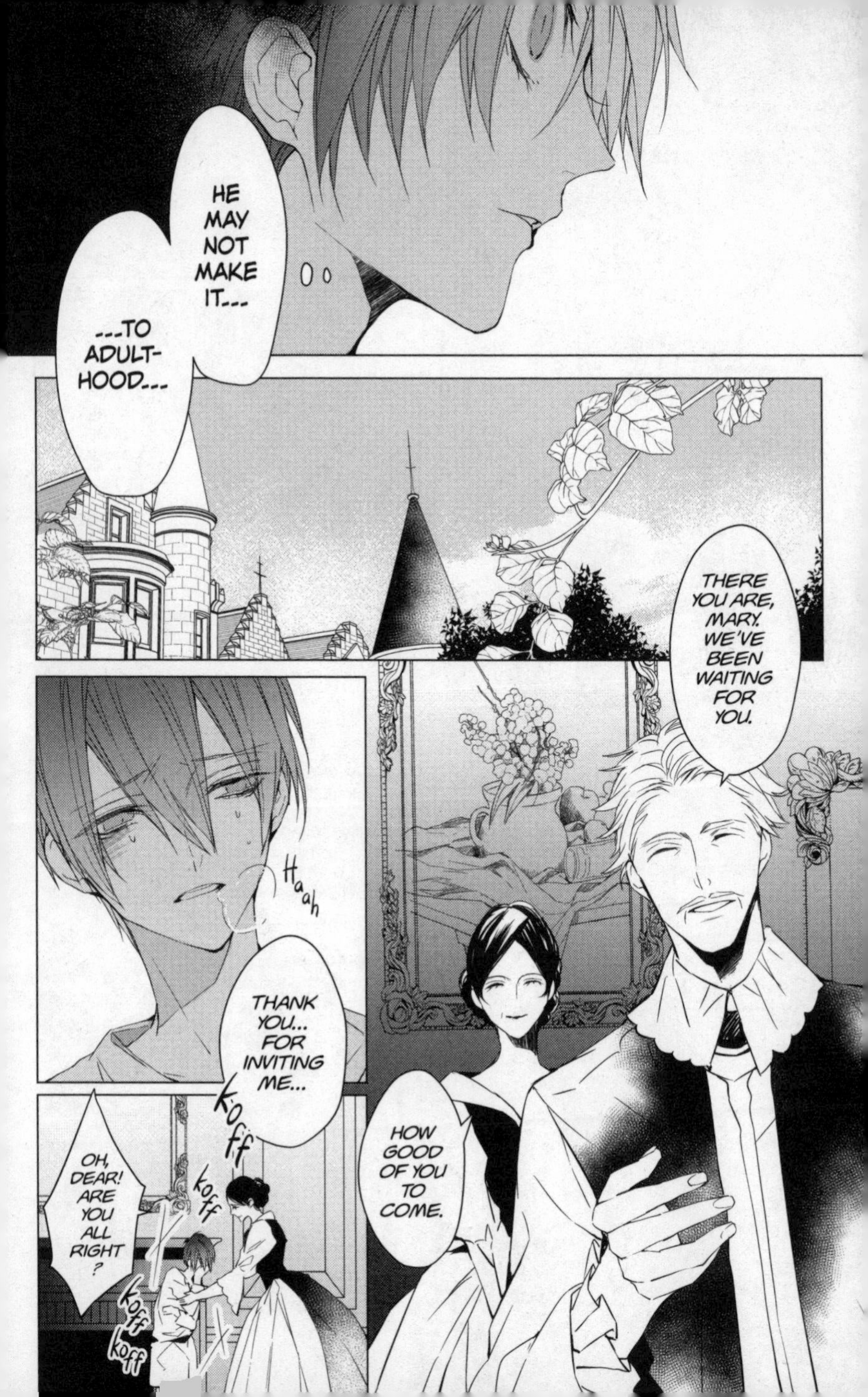
HE MAY NOT MAKE IT...
...TO ADULTHOOD...
THERE YOU ARE, MARY. WE'VE BEEN WAITING FOR YOU.
Haaah
THANK YOU... FOR INVITING ME...
HOW GOOD OF YOU TO COME.
KOFF
KOFF
OH, DEAR! ARE YOU ALL RIGHT?
KOFF KOFF

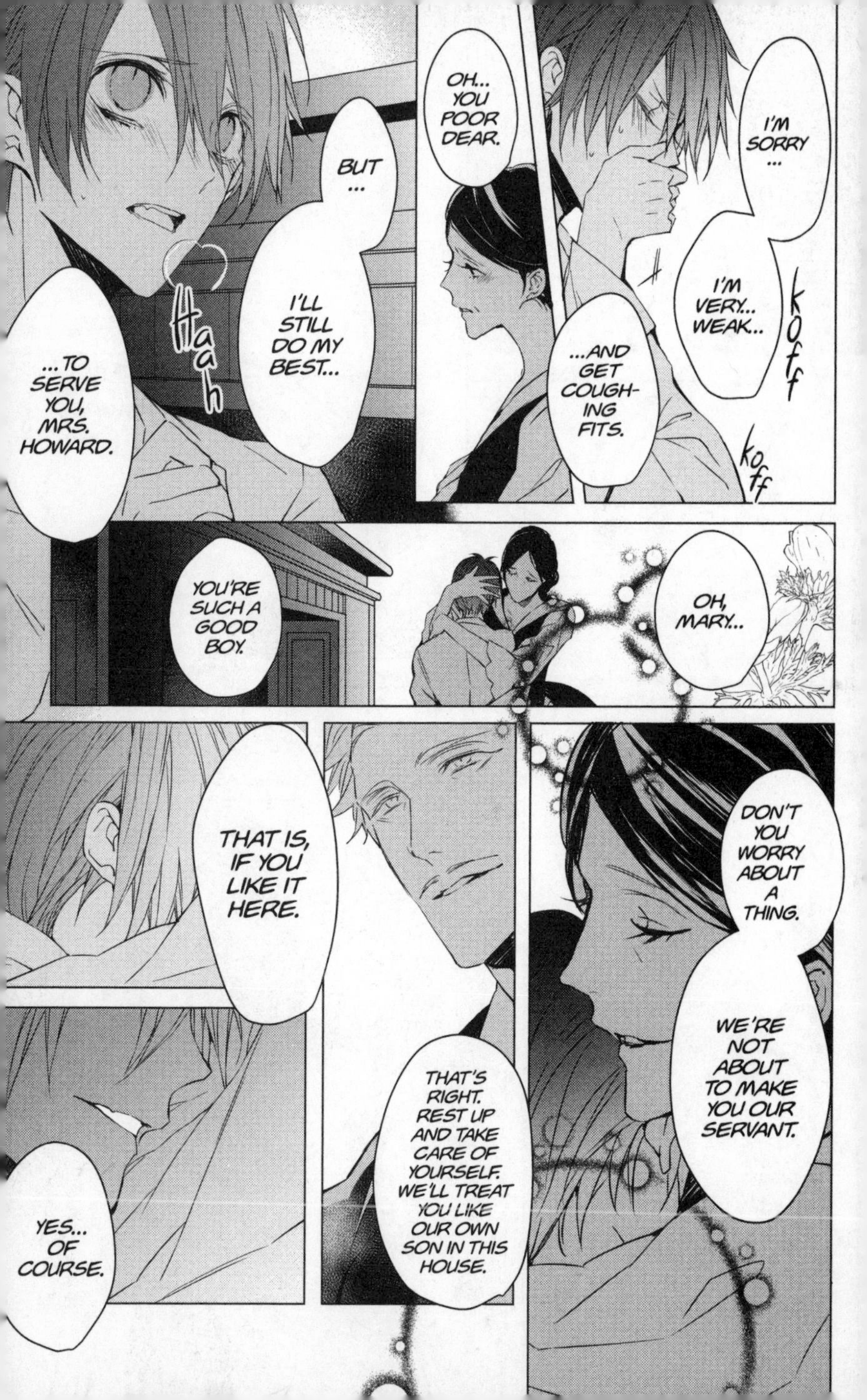
I'M SORRY ...
I'M VERY... WEAK...
koff
koff
...AND GET COUGH-ING FITS.
OH... YOU POOR DEAR.
BUT ...
I'LL STILL DO MY BEST...
Haah
...TO SERVE YOU, MRS. HOWARD.
OH, MARY...
YOU'RE SUCH A GOOD BOY.
DON'T YOU WORRY ABOUT A THING.
WE'RE NOT ABOUT TO MAKE YOU OUR SERVANT.
THAT'S RIGHT. REST UP AND TAKE CARE OF YOURSELF. WE'LL TREAT YOU LIKE OUR OWN SON IN THIS HOUSE.
THAT IS, IF YOU LIKE IT HERE.
YES... OF COURSE.

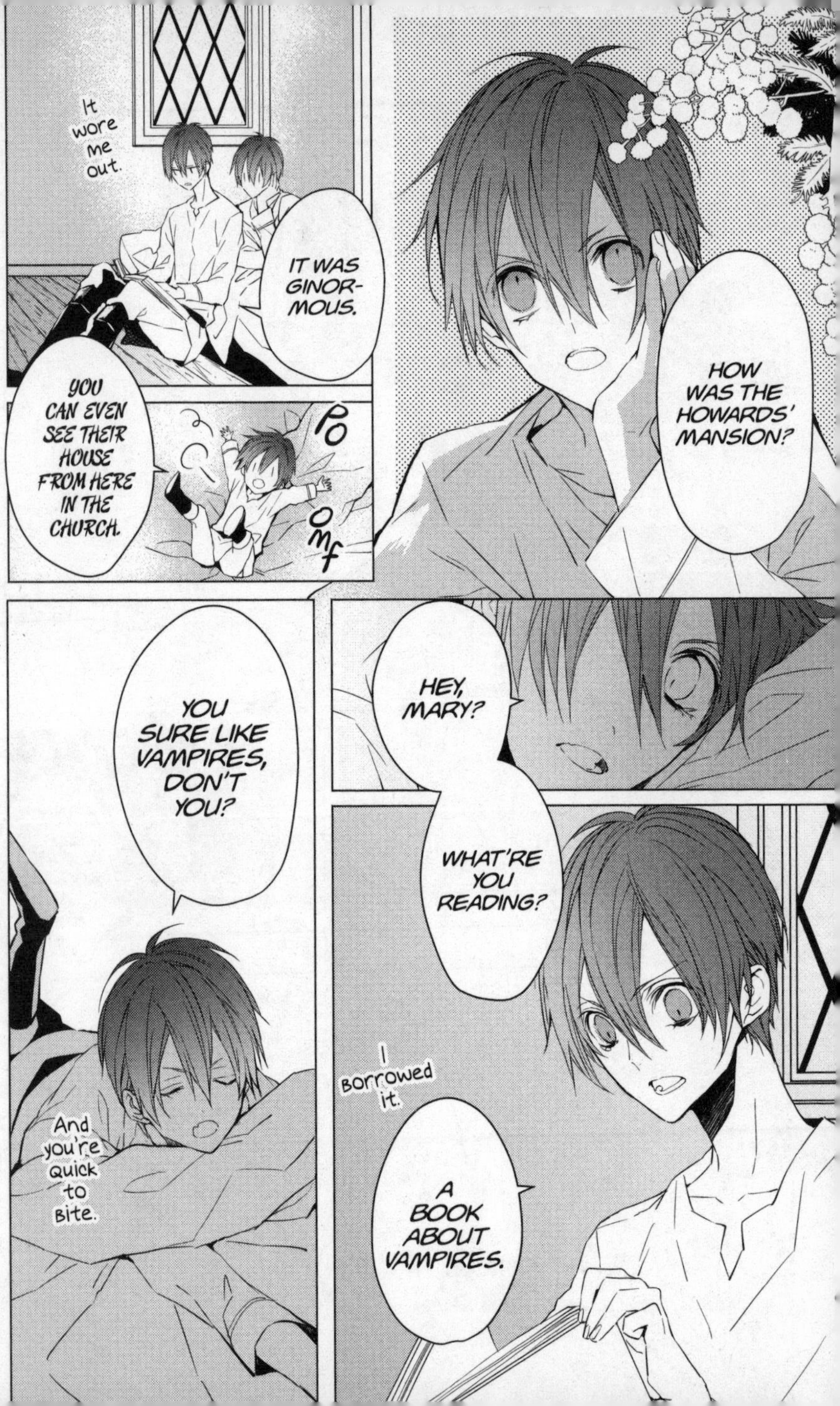
HOW WAS THE HOWARDS' MANSION?
IT WAS GINORMOUS.
It wore me out.
PO
OMF
YOU CAN EVEN SEE THEIR HOUSE FROM HERE IN THE CHURCH.
HEY, MARY?
WHAT'RE YOU READING?
A BOOK ABOUT VAMPIRES.
I borrowed it.
YOU SURE LIKE VAMPIRES, DON'T YOU?
And you're quick to bite.

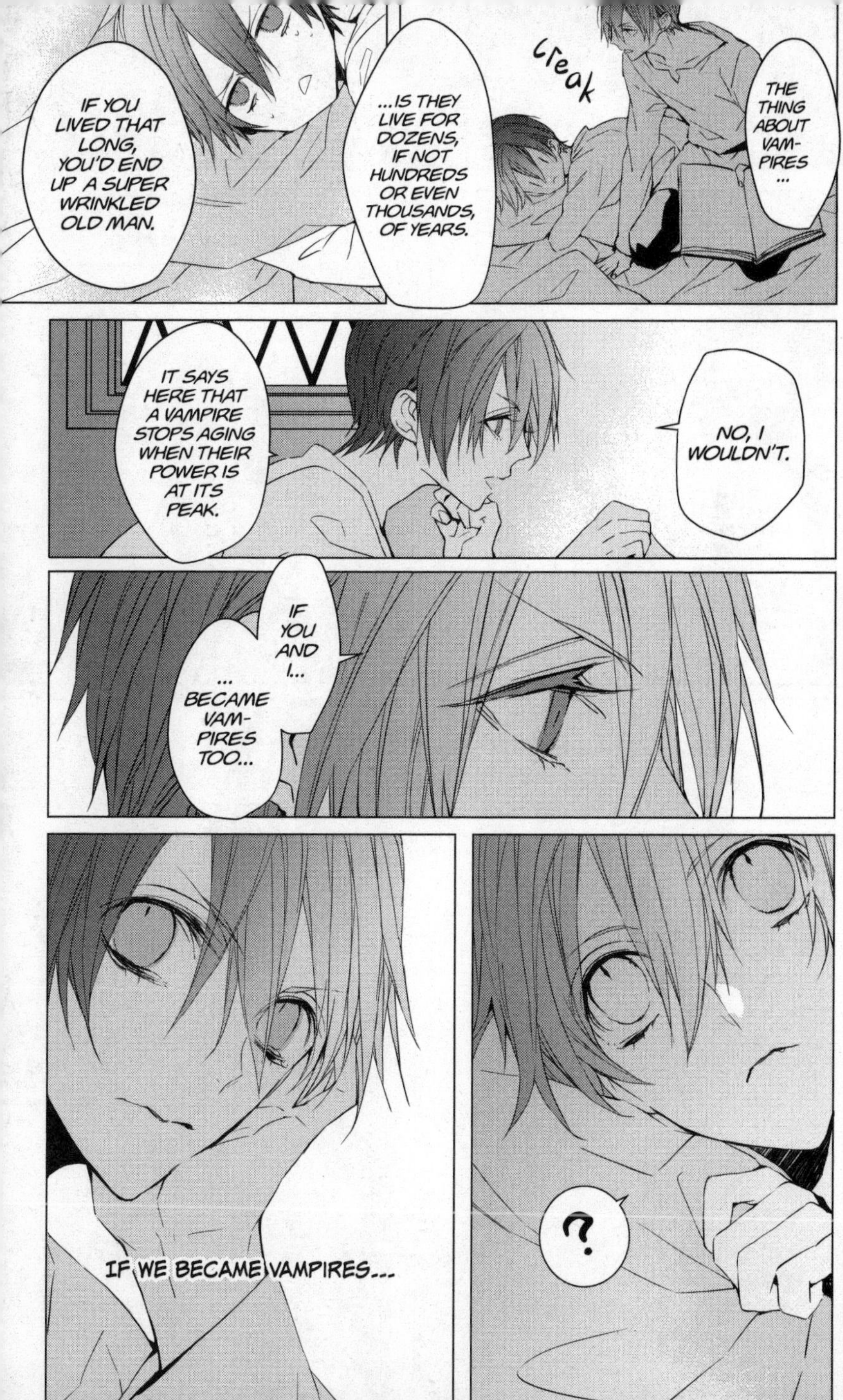
THE THING ABOUT VAM-PIRES ...
creak
...IS THEY LIVE FOR DOZENS, IF NOT HUNDREDS OR EVEN THOUSANDS, OF YEARS.
IF YOU LIVED THAT LONG, YOU'D END UP A SUPER WRINKLED OLD MAN.
NO, I WOULDN'T.
IT SAYS HERE THAT A VAMPIRE STOPS AGING WHEN THEIR POWER IS AT ITS PEAK.
IF YOU AND I...
... BECAME VAM-PIRES TOO...
?
IF WE BECAME VAMPIRES...

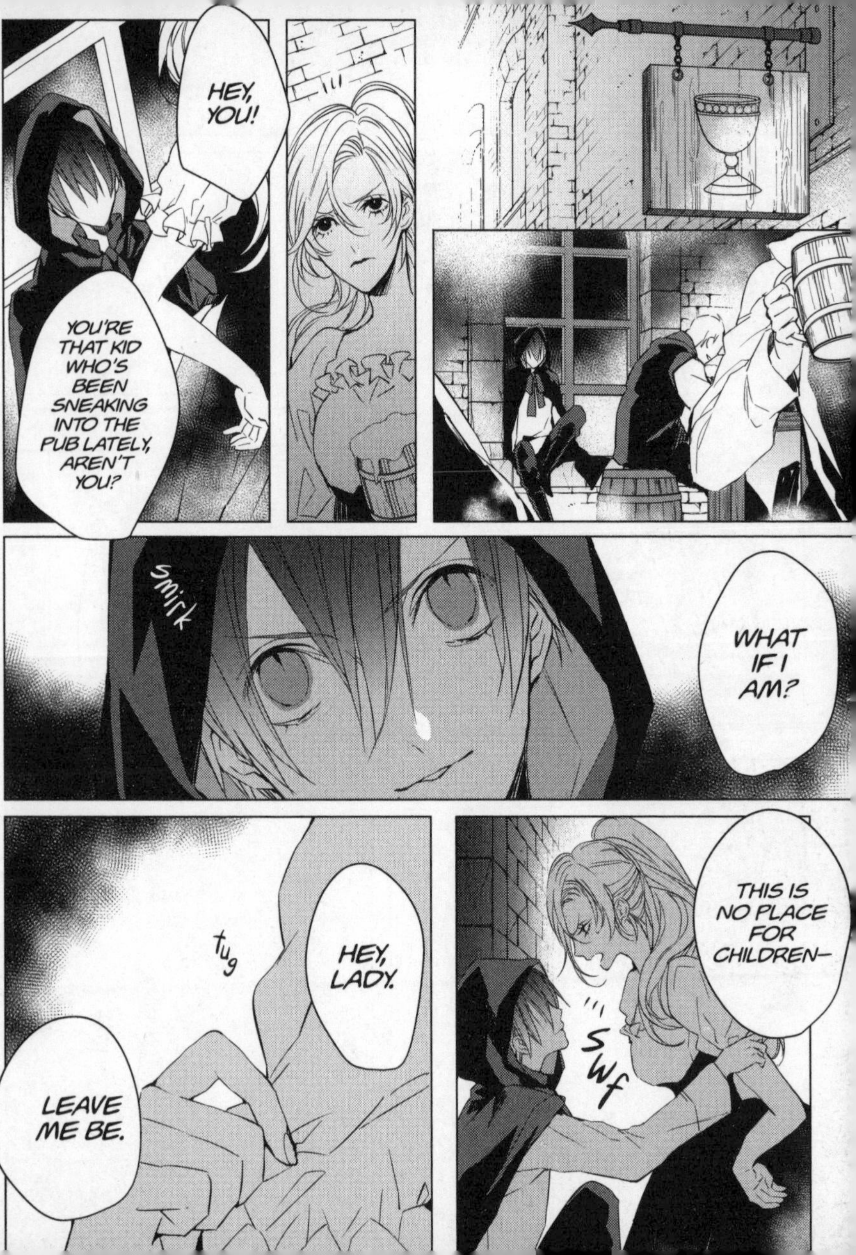
HEY, YOU!
YOU'RE THAT KID WHO'S BEEN SNEAKING INTO THE PUB LATELY, AREN'T YOU?
WHAT IF I AM?
smirk
THIS IS NO PLACE FOR CHILDREN—
SWf
HEY, LADY.
tug
LEAVE ME BE.

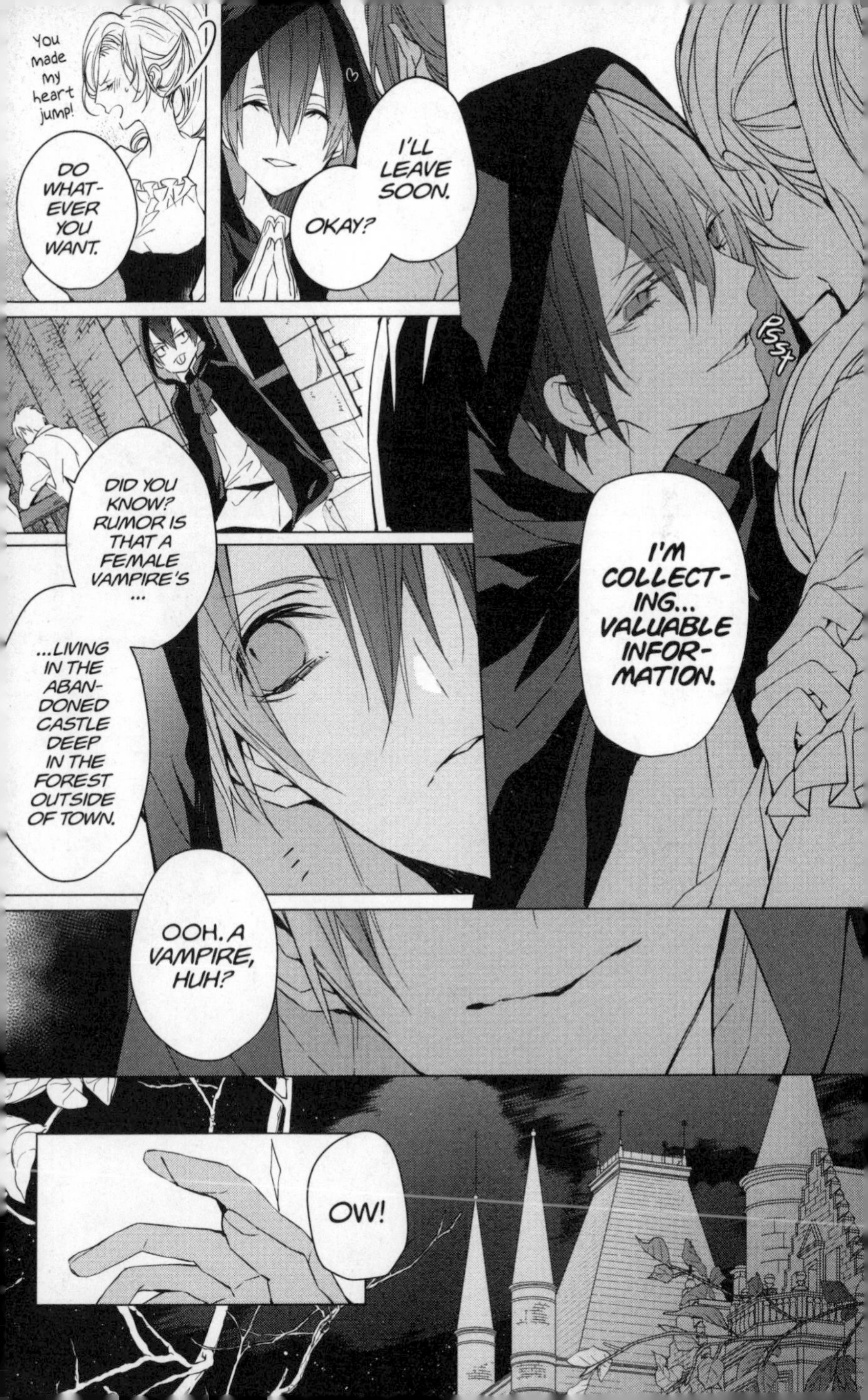
Psst
I'M COLLECTING... VALUABLE INFORMATION.
I'LL LEAVE SOON.
OKAY?
You made my heart jump!
DO WHATEVER YOU WANT.
DID YOU KNOW? RUMOR IS THAT A FEMALE VAMPIRE'S ...
...LIVING IN THE ABANDONED CASTLE DEEP IN THE FOREST OUTSIDE OF TOWN.
OOH. A VAMPIRE, HUH?
OW!

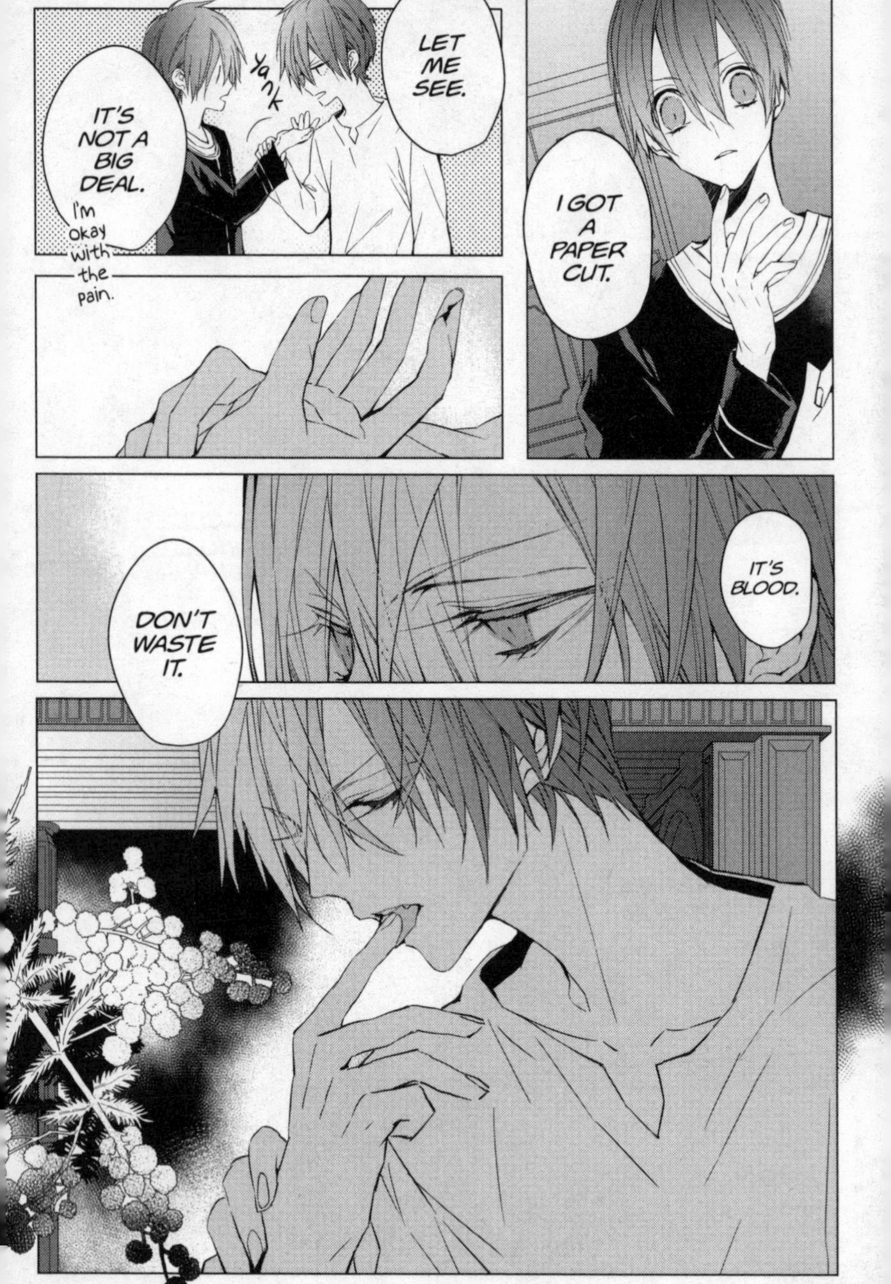
I GOT A PAPER CUT.
LET ME SEE.
Yank
IT'S NOT A BIG DEAL.
I'm okay with the pain.
IT'S BLOOD.
DON'T WASTE IT.

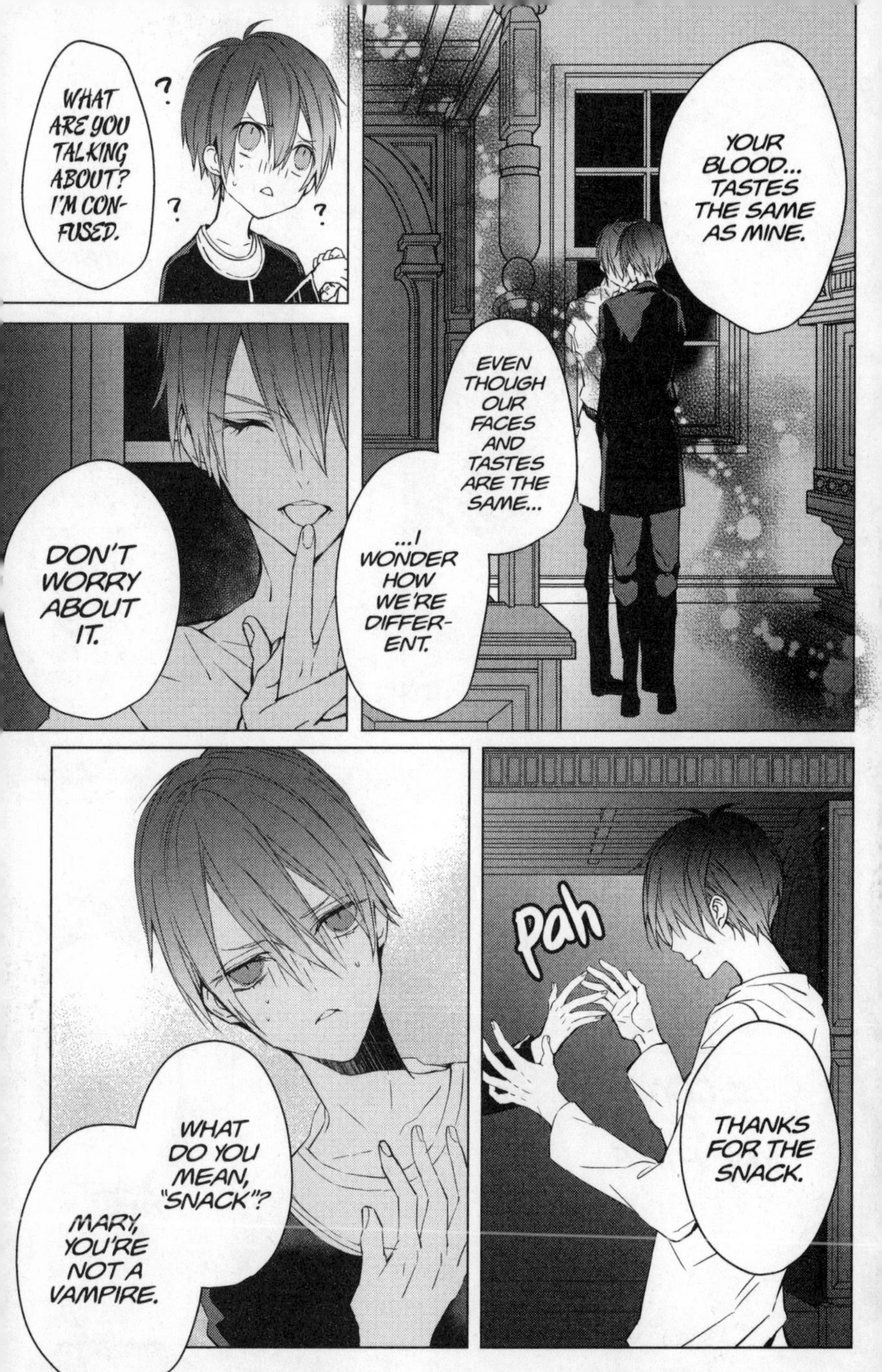
YOUR BLOOD... TASTES THE SAME AS MINE.
EVEN THOUGH OUR FACES AND TASTES ARE THE SAME...
...I WONDER HOW WE'RE DIFFER-ENT.
WHAT ARE YOU TALKING ABOUT? I'M CON-FUSED.
?
?
?
DON'T WORRY ABOUT IT.
pah
THANKS FOR THE SNACK.
WHAT DO YOU MEAN, "SNACK"?
MARY, YOU'RE NOT A VAMPIRE.

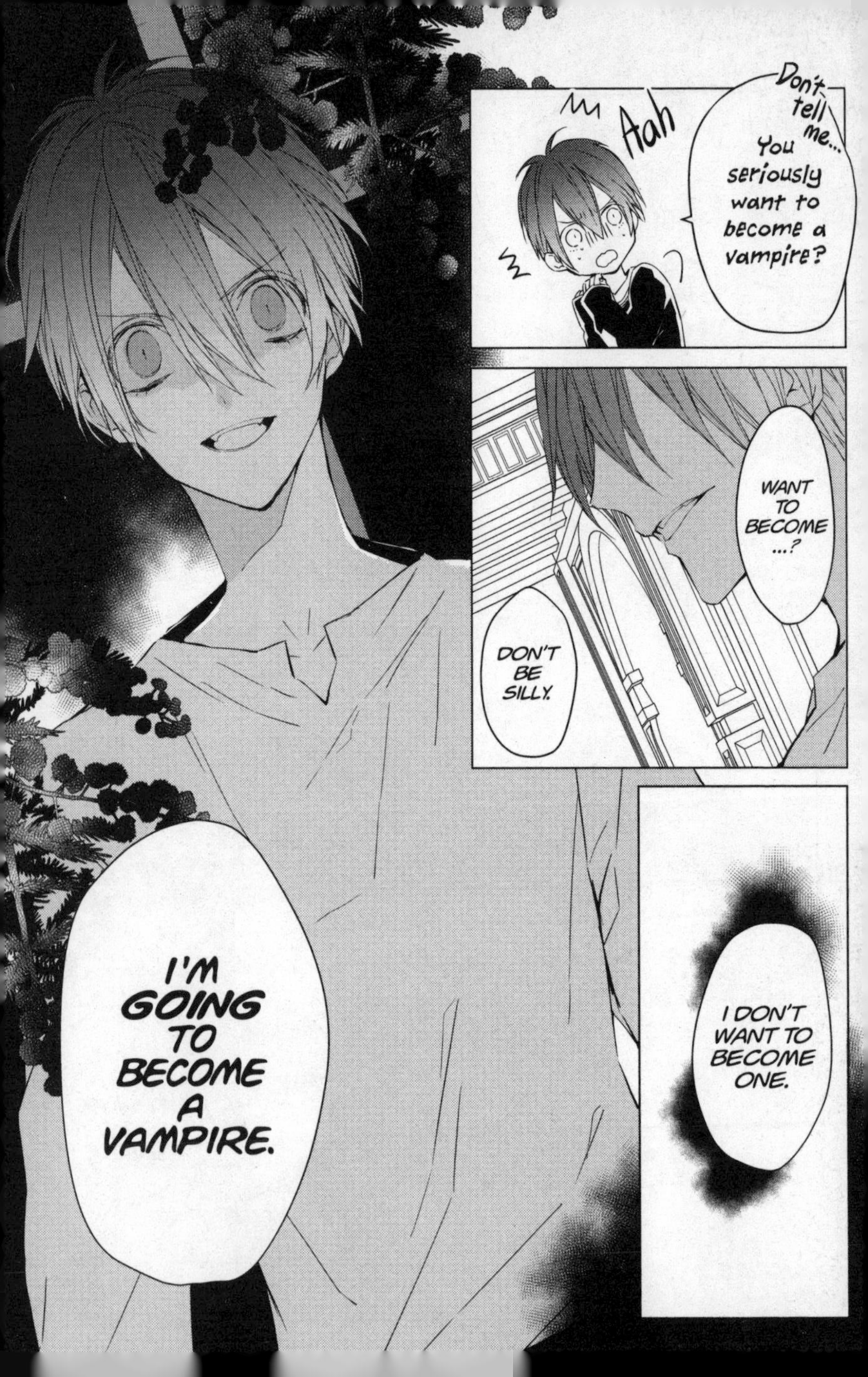
Don't tell me... You seriously want to become a vampire?
Aah
WANT TO BECOME ...?
DON'T BE SILLY.
I DON'T WANT TO BECOME ONE.
I'M GOING TO BECOME A VAMPIRE.

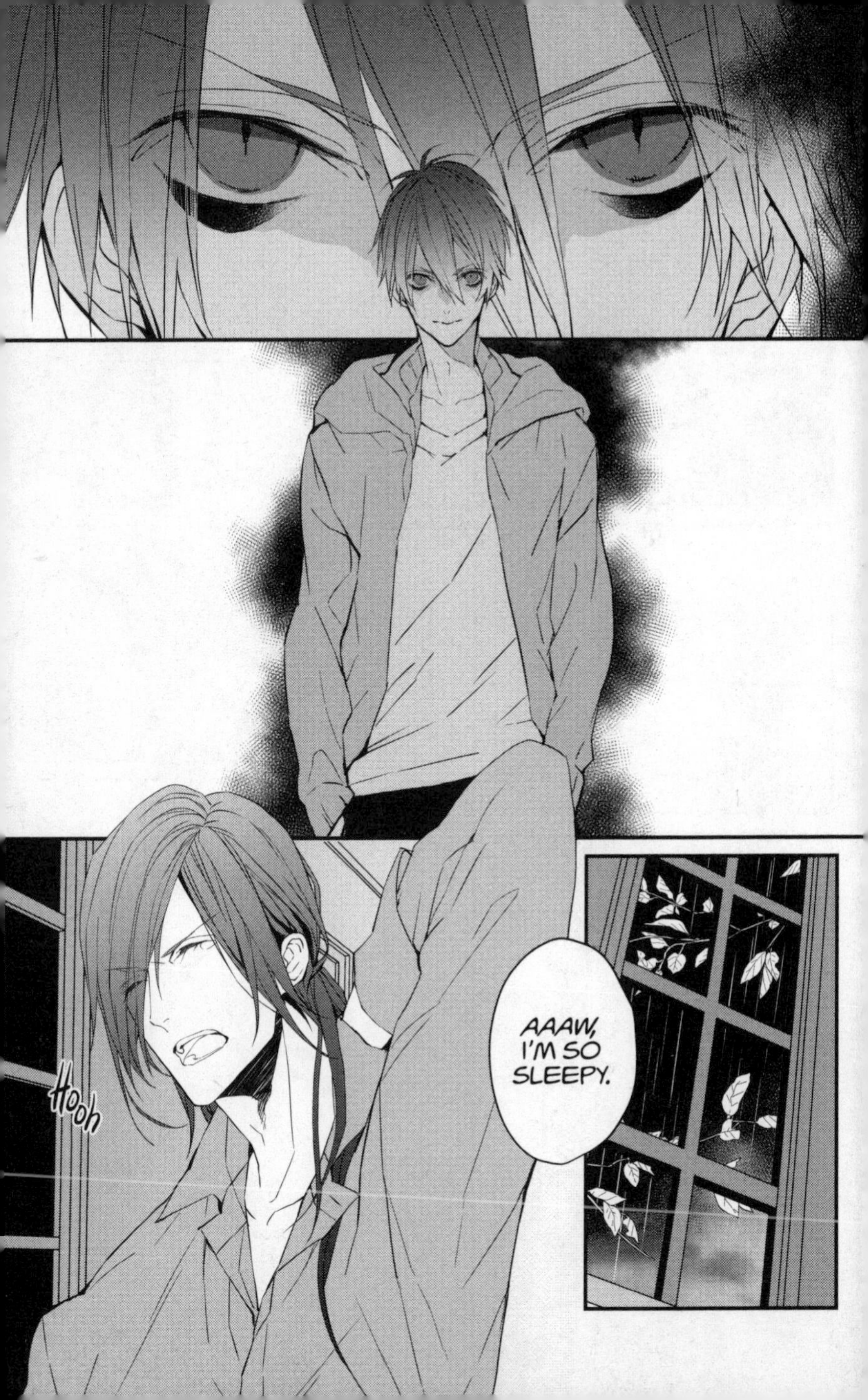
AAAW, I'M SO SLEEPY.
Hooh

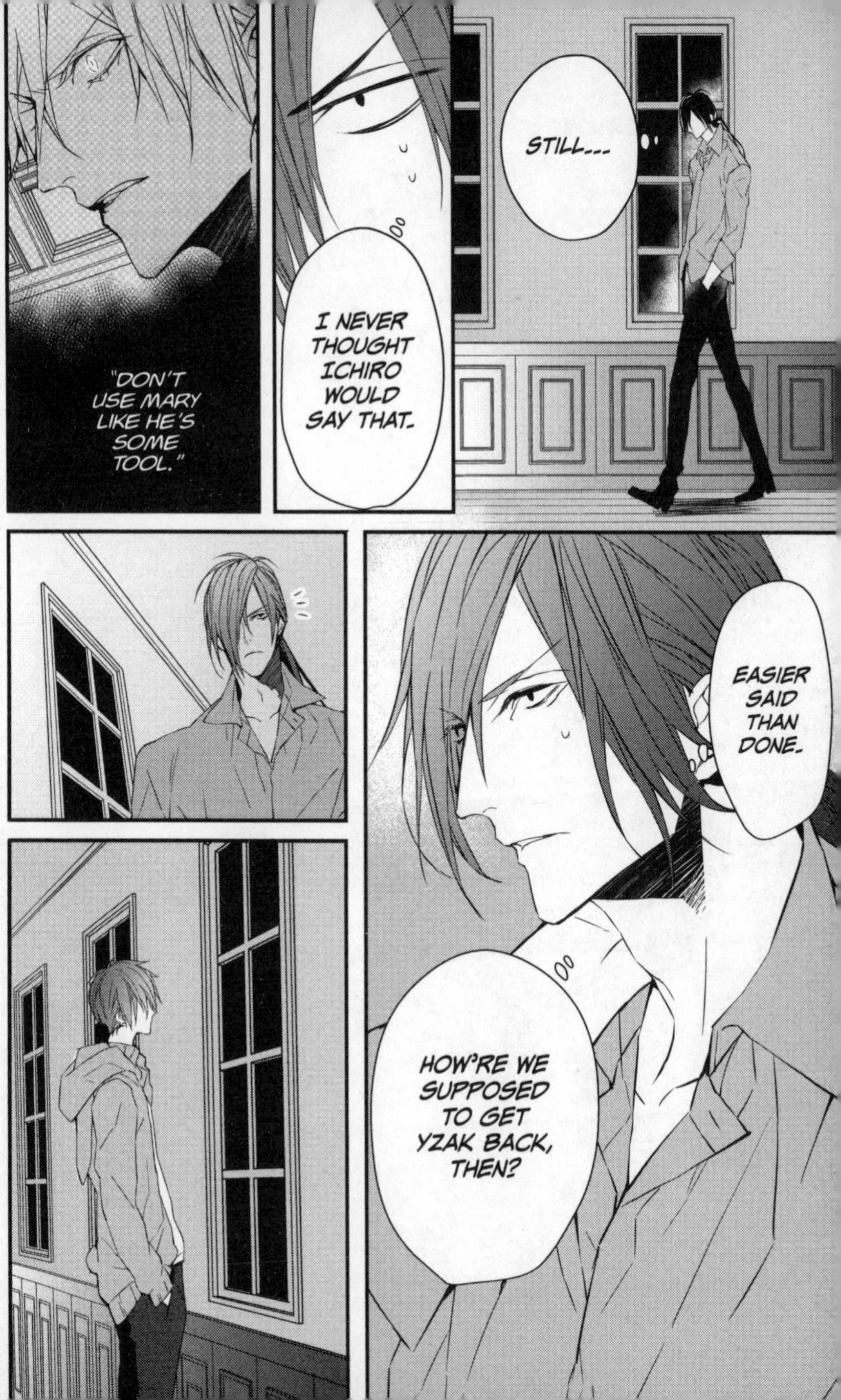
STILL...
I NEVER THOUGHT ICHIRO WOULD SAY THAT.
"DON'T USE MARY LIKE HE'S SOME TOOL."
EASIER SAID THAN DONE.
HOW'RE WE SUPPOSED TO GET YZAK BACK, THEN?

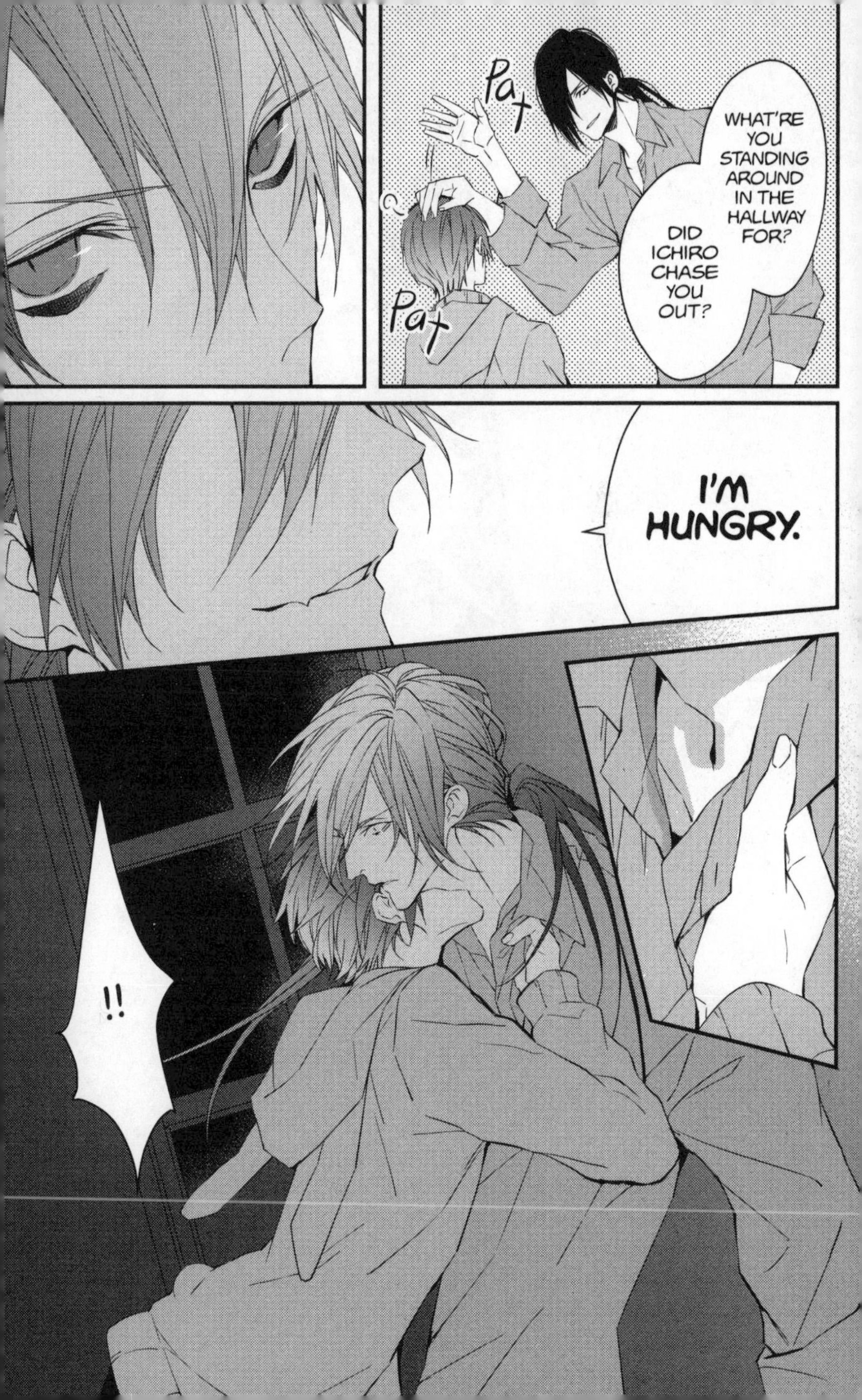
Pat
Pat
WHAT'RE YOU STANDING AROUND IN THE HALLWAY FOR?
DID ICHIRO CHASE YOU OUT?
I'M HUNGRY.
!!

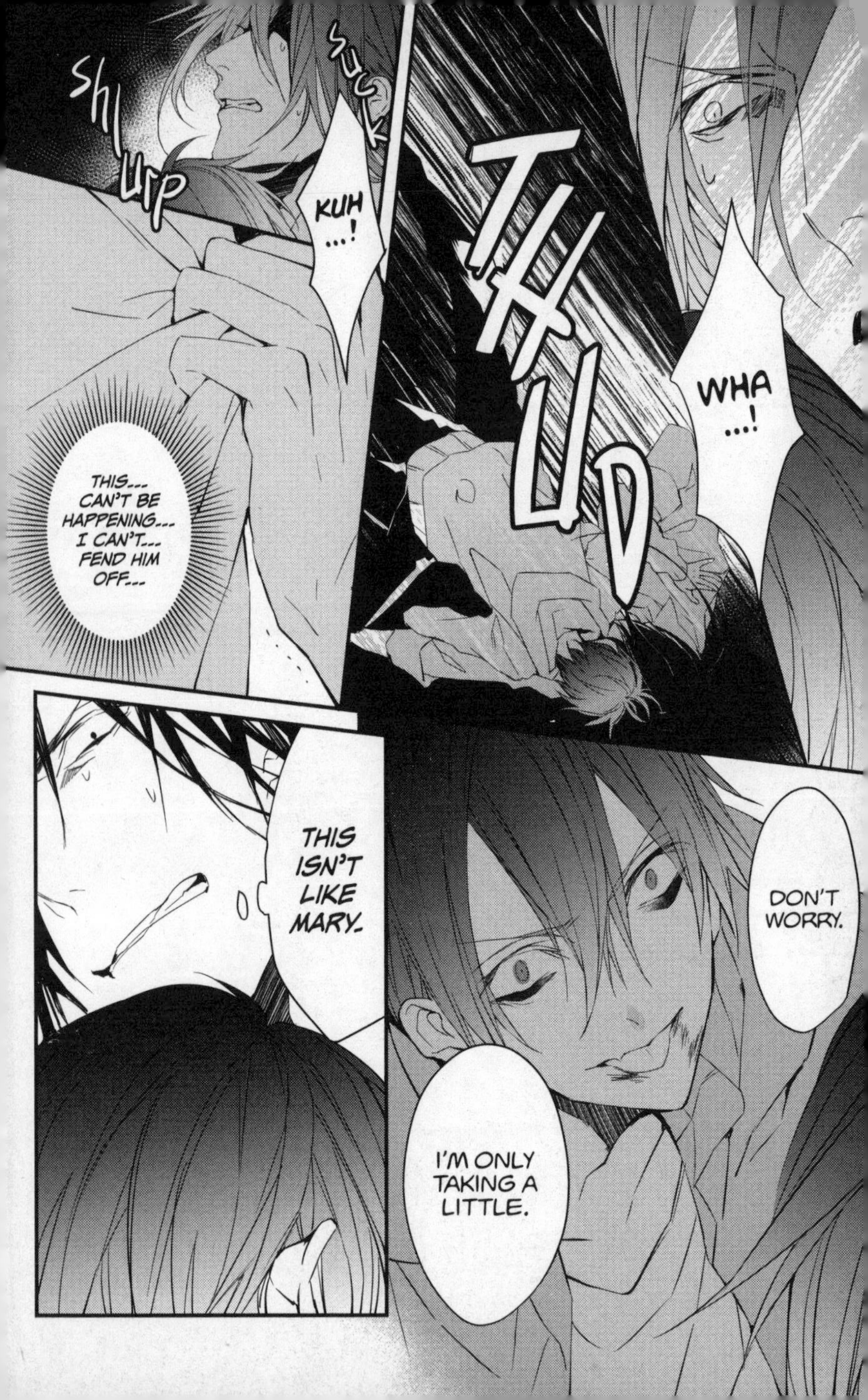
WHA ...!
THUD
SHLURP
SUCK
KUH ...!
THIS... CAN'T BE HAPPENING... I CAN'T... FEND HIM OFF...
DON'T WORRY.
I'M ONLY TAKING A LITTLE.
THIS ISN'T LIKE MARY.

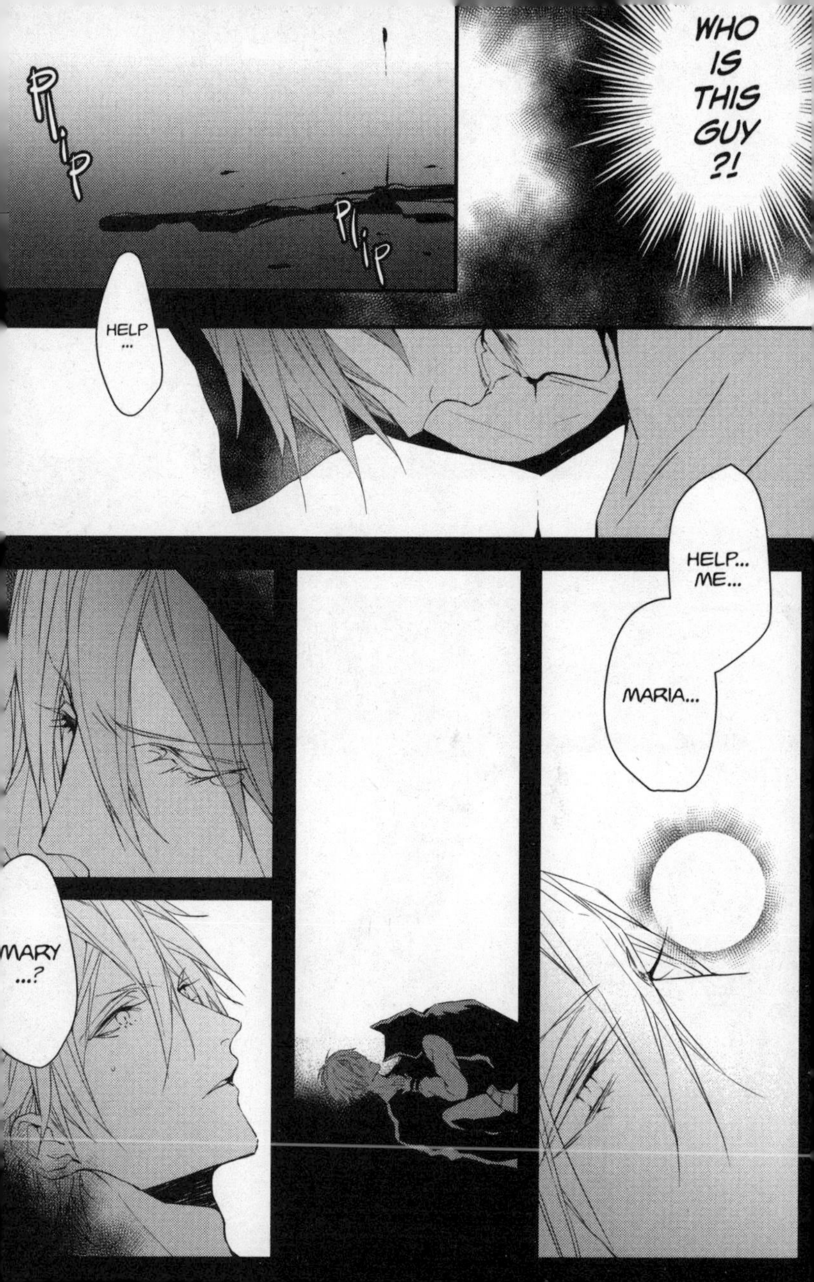
WHO IS THIS GUY ?!
Plip
Plip
HELP ...
HELP... ME...
MARIA...
MARY ...?

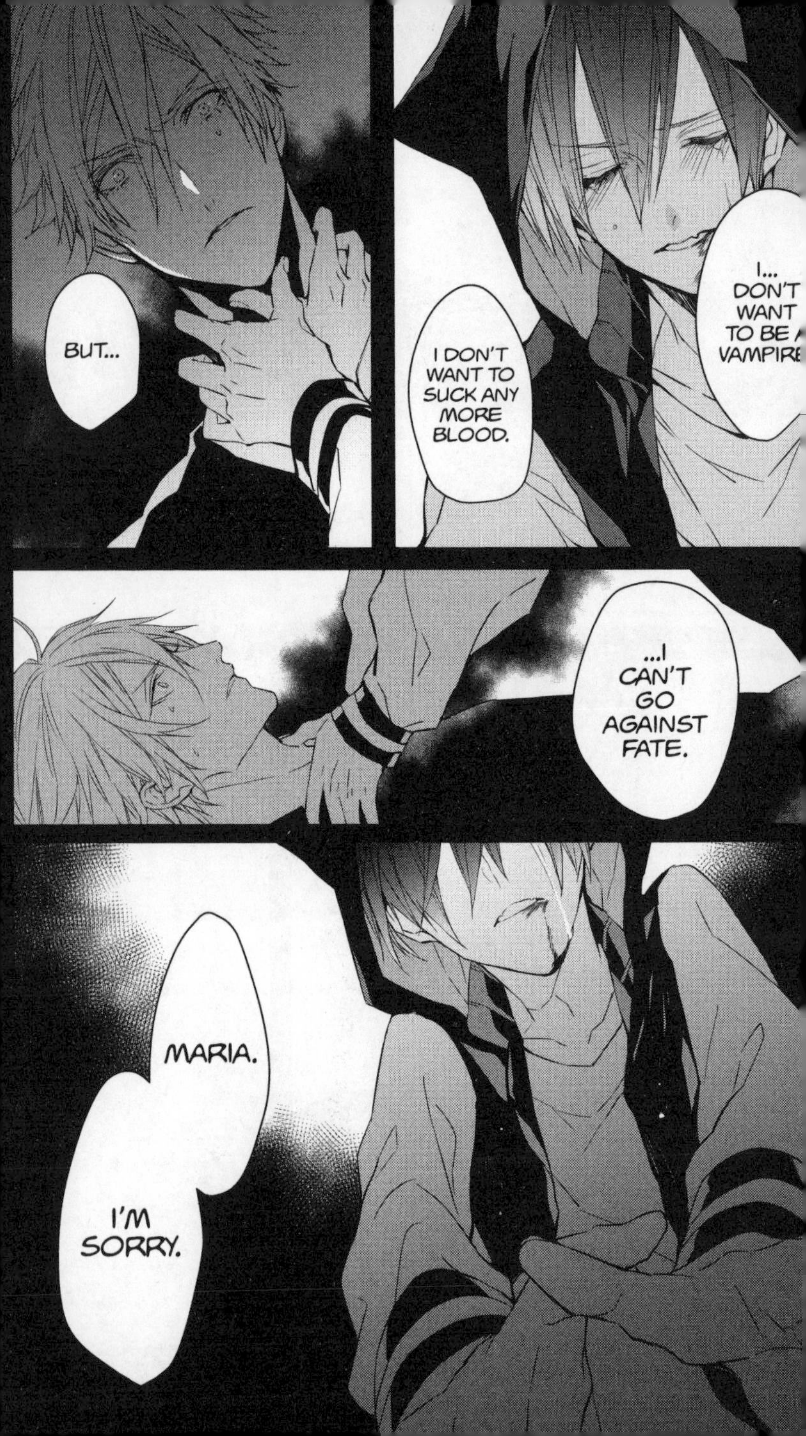
I... DON'T WANT TO BE A VAMPIRE
I DON'T WANT TO SUCK ANY MORE BLOOD.
BUT...
...I CAN'T GO AGAINST FATE.
MARIA.
I'M SORRY.

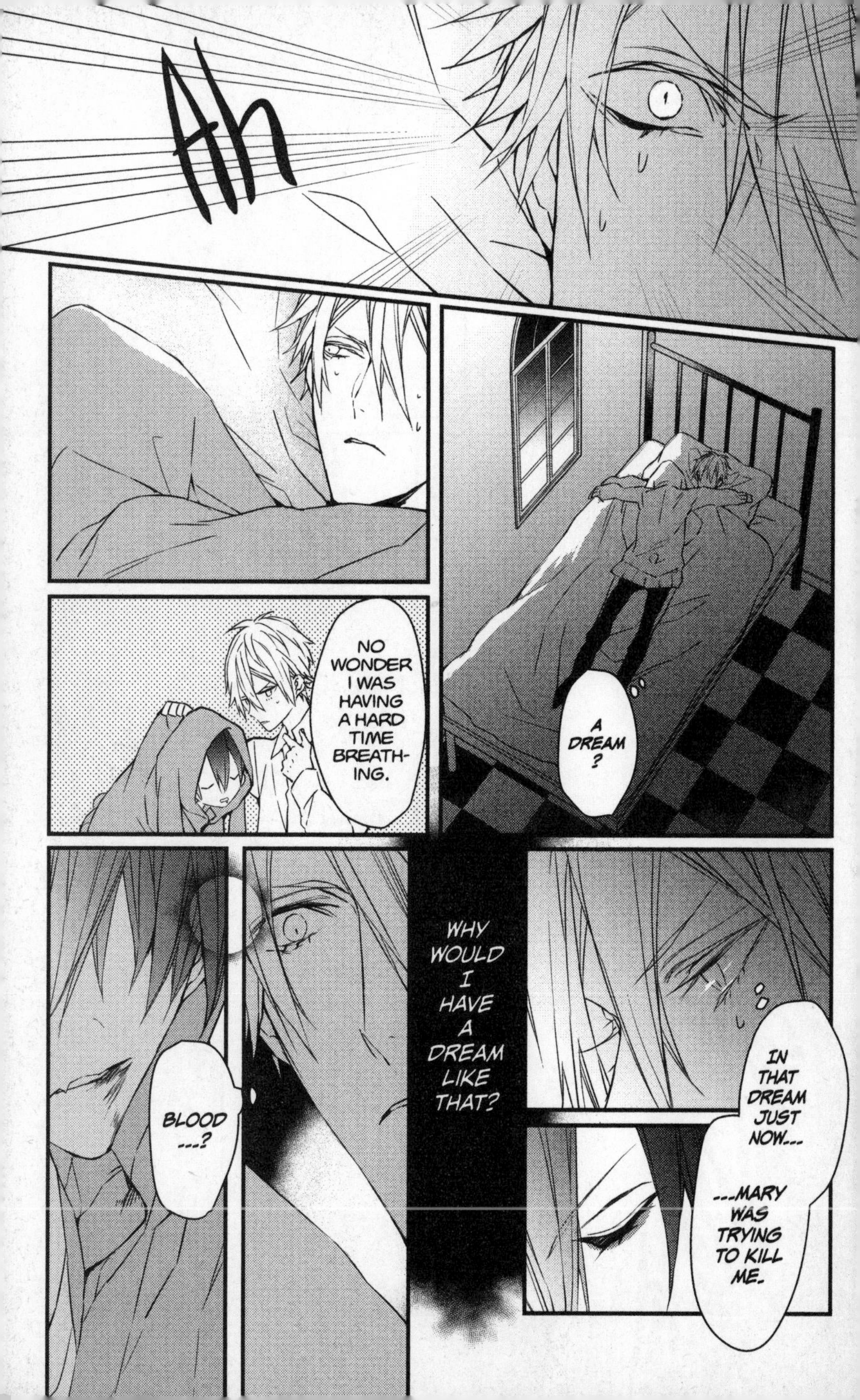
Ah
A DREAM?
NO WONDER I WAS HAVING A HARD TIME BREATH-ING.
IN THAT DREAM JUST NOW...
...MARY WAS TRYING TO KILL ME.
WHY WOULD I HAVE A DREAM LIKE THAT?
BLOOD...?

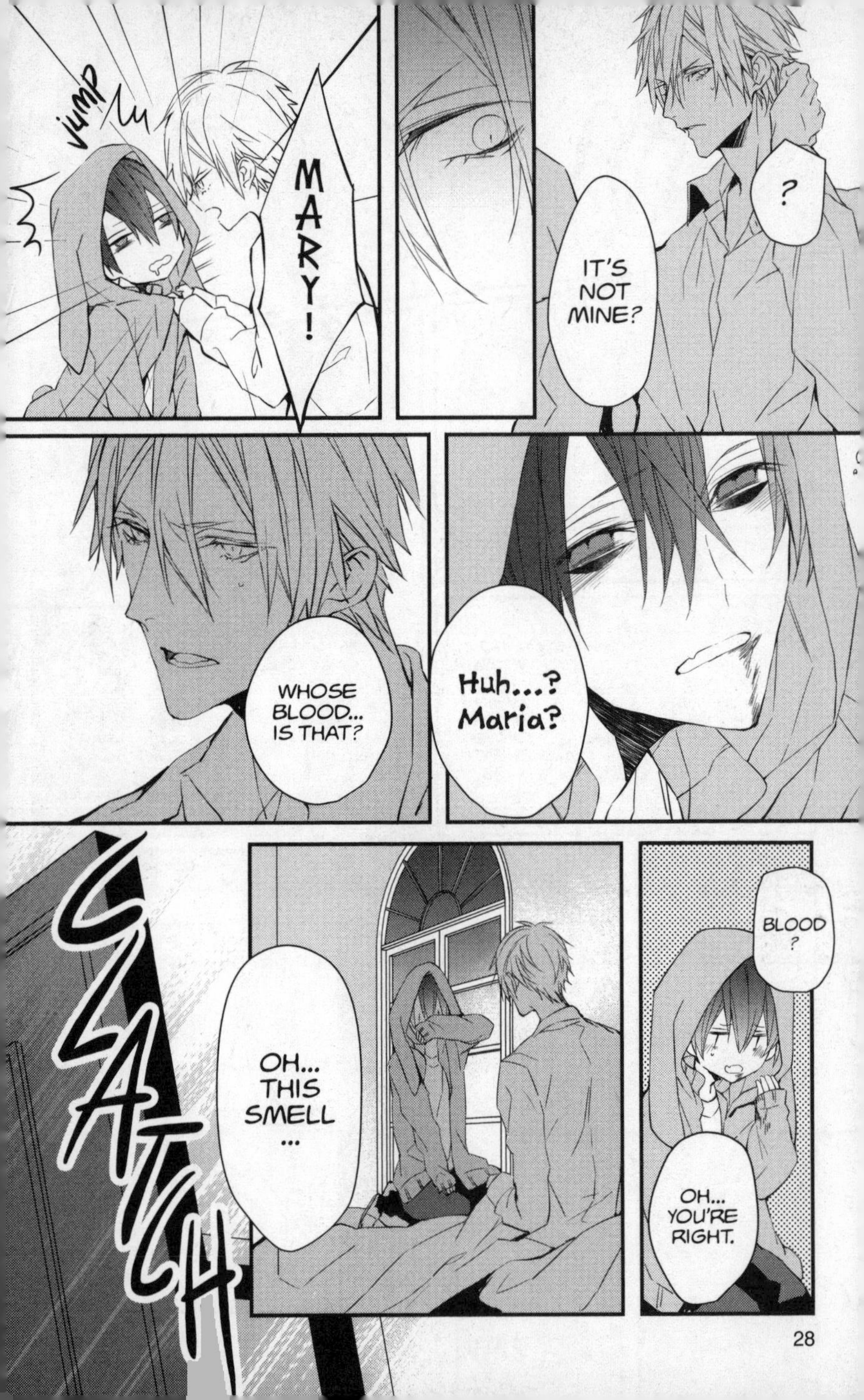
?
IT'S NOT MINE?
MARY!
jump
Huh...? Maria?
WHOSE BLOOD... IS THAT?
BLOOD?
OH... YOU'RE RIGHT.
OH... THIS SMELL ...
SLATCH

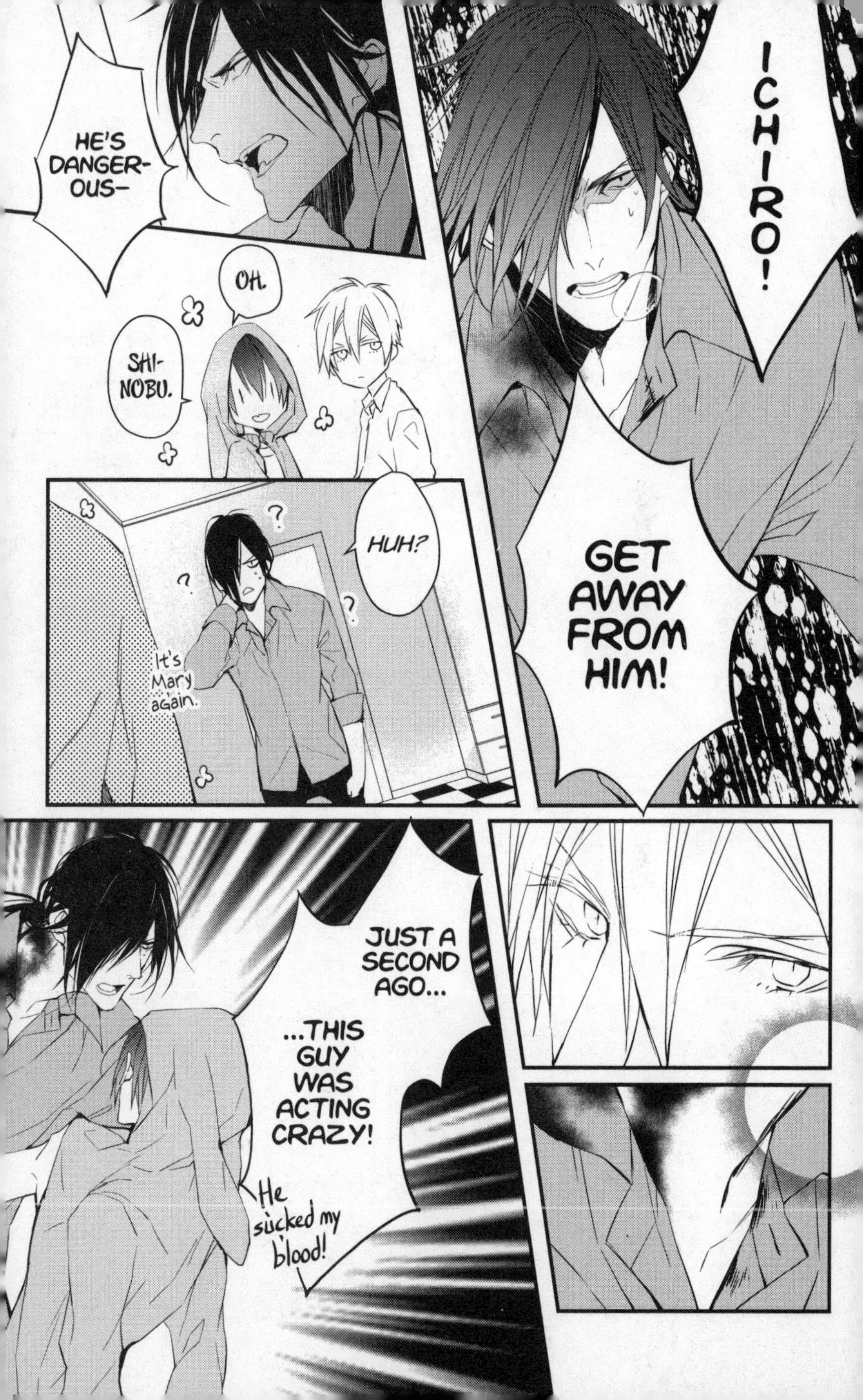
ICHIRO!
GET AWAY FROM HIM!
HE'S DANGER-OUS–
OH.
SHI-NOBU.
HUH?
It's Mary again.
JUST A SECOND AGO...
...THIS GUY WAS ACTING CRAZY!
He sucked my blood!

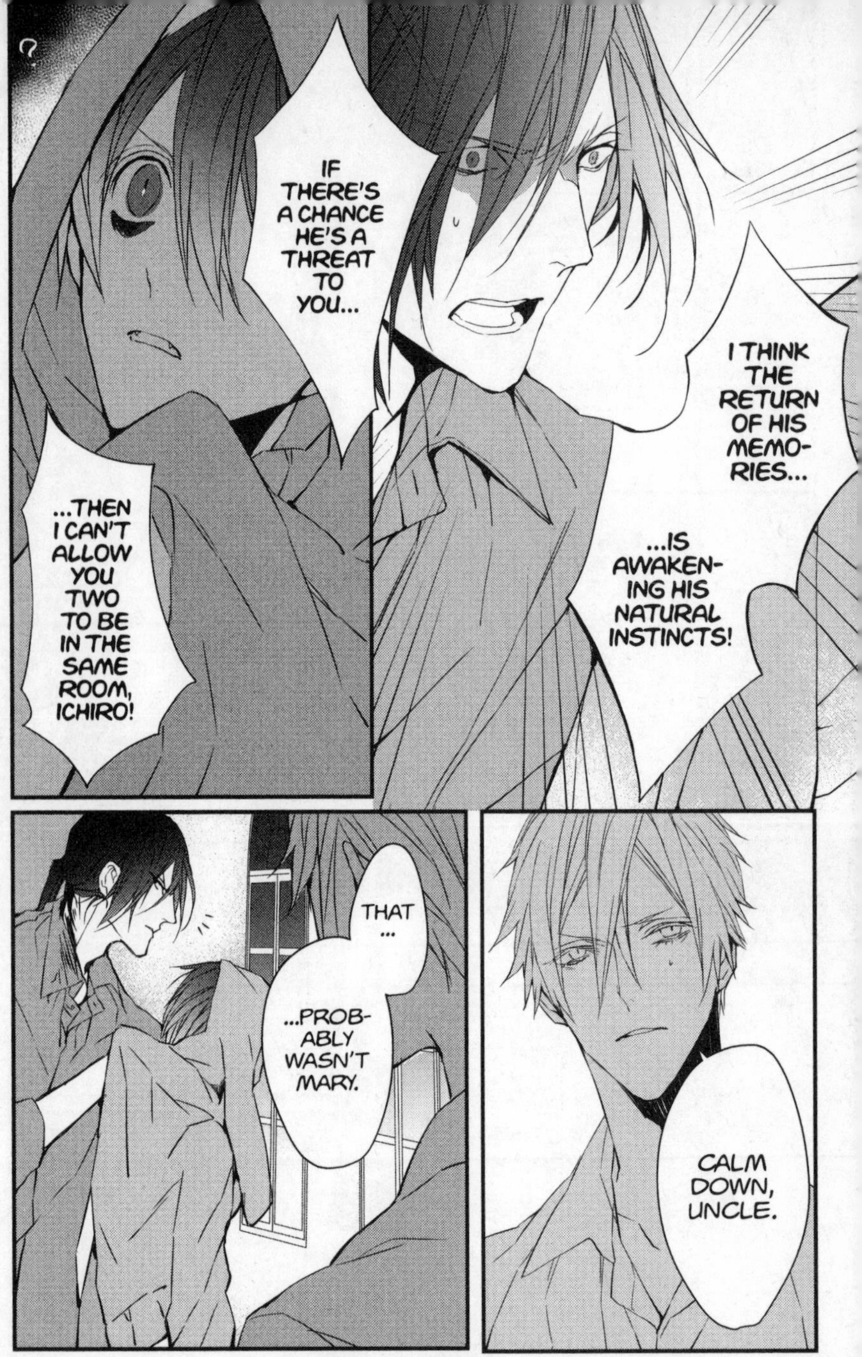
I THINK THE RETURN OF HIS MEMORIES...
...IS AWAKENING HIS NATURAL INSTINCTS!
IF THERE'S A CHANCE HE'S A THREAT TO YOU...
...THEN I CAN'T ALLOW YOU TWO TO BE IN THE SAME ROOM, ICHIRO!
CALM DOWN, UNCLE.
THAT...
...PROBABLY WASN'T MARY.

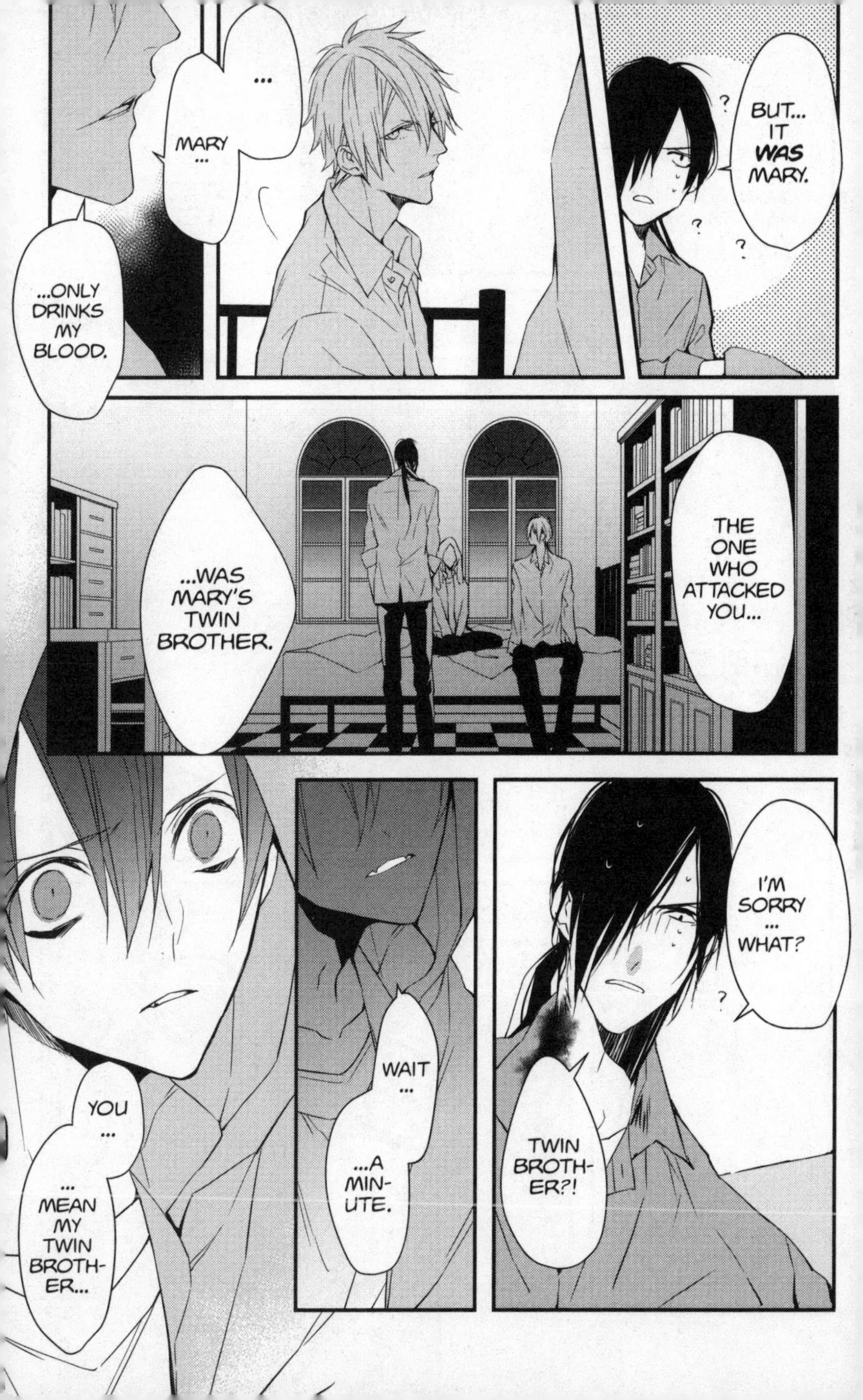
BUT... IT WAS MARY.
...
MARY ...
...ONLY DRINKS MY BLOOD.
THE ONE WHO ATTACKED YOU...
...WAS MARY'S TWIN BROTHER.
I'M SORRY ... WHAT?
TWIN BROTH-ER?!
WAIT ...
...A MIN-UTE.
YOU ...
... MEAN MY TWIN BROTH-ER...

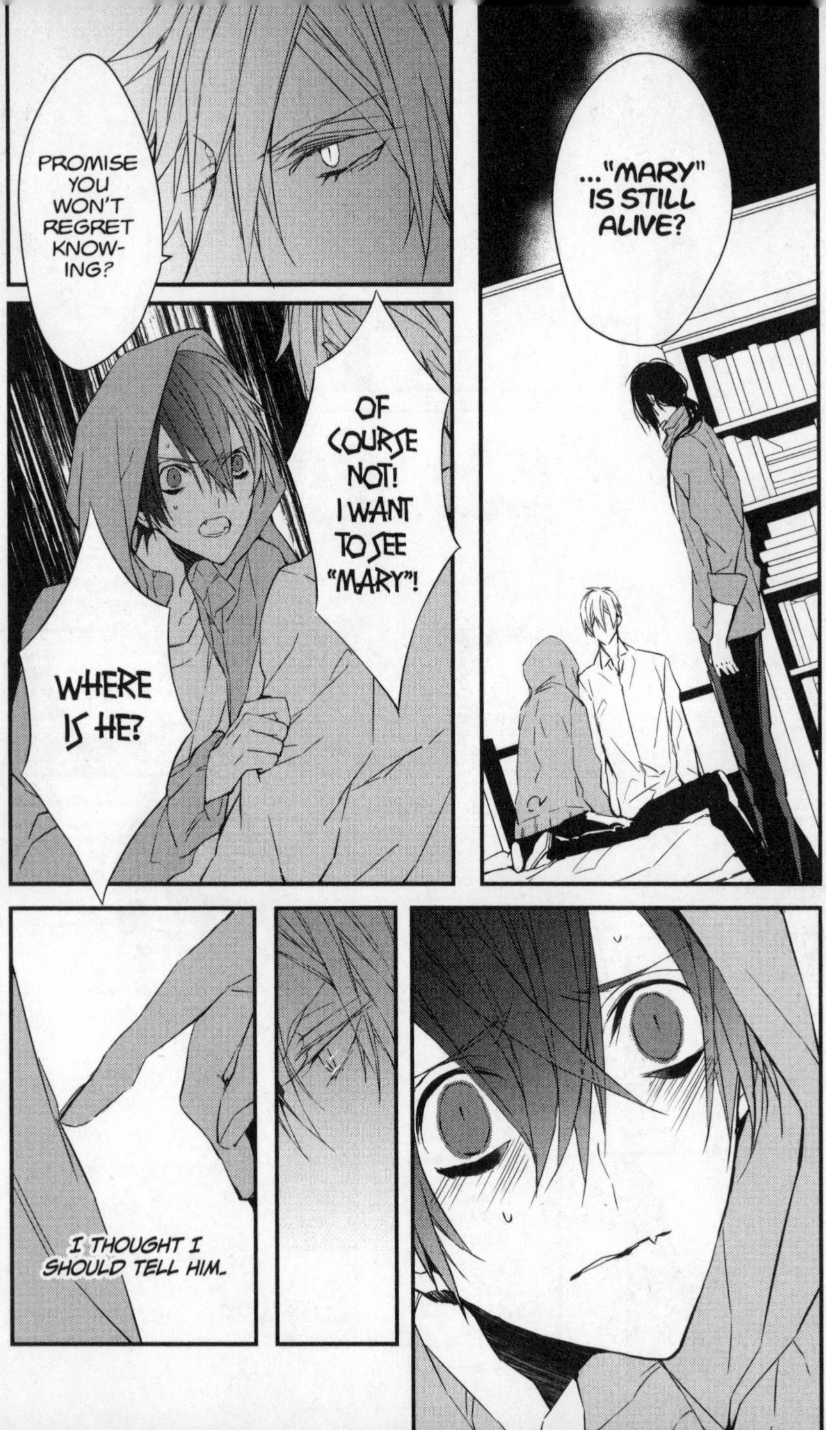
..."MARY" IS STILL ALIVE?
PROMISE YOU WON'T REGRET KNOWING?
OF COURSE NOT! I WANT TO SEE "MARY"!
WHERE IS HE?
I THOUGHT I SHOULD TELL HIM...

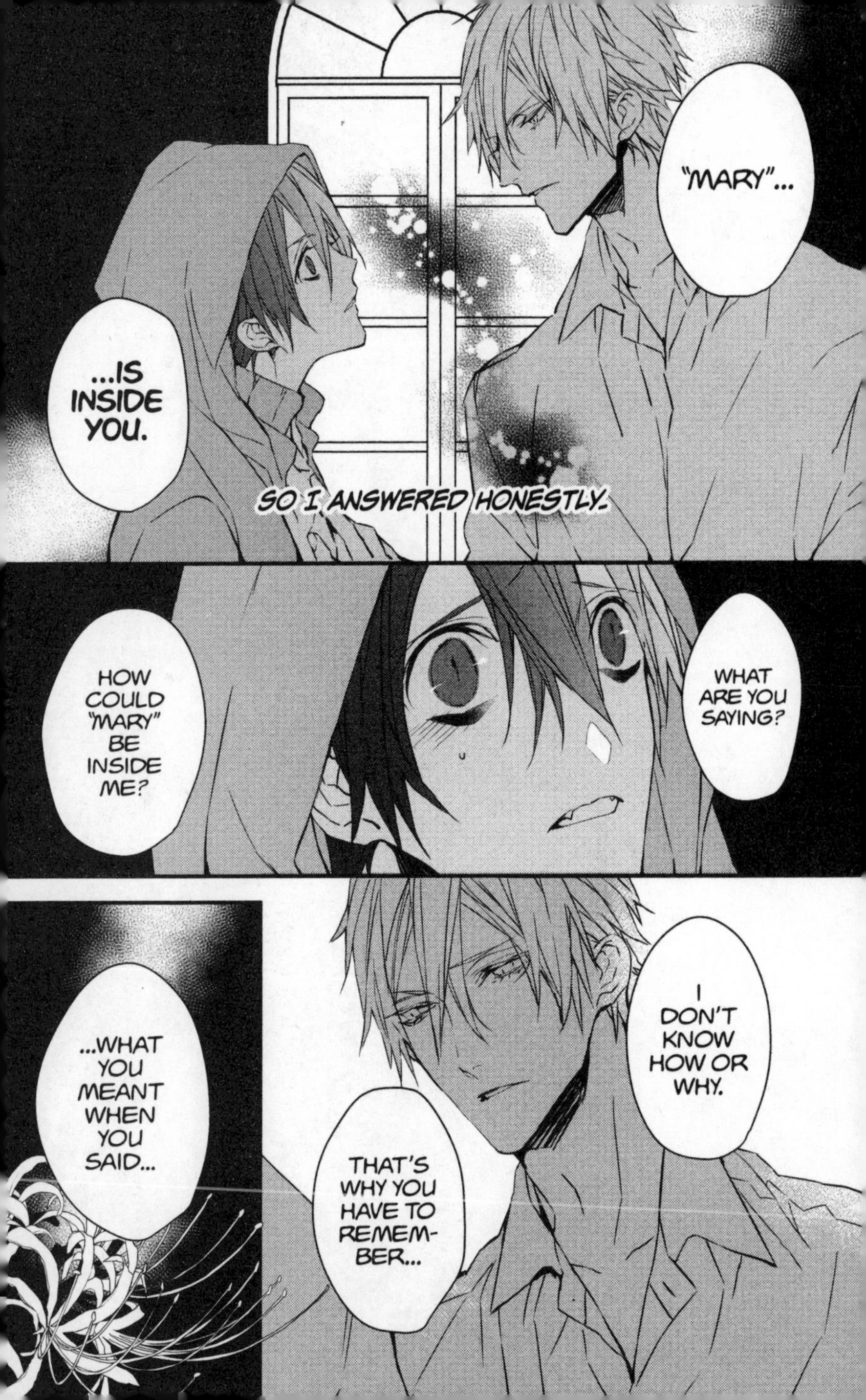
"MARY"...
...IS INSIDE YOU.
SO I ANSWERED HONESTLY.
WHAT ARE YOU SAYING?
HOW COULD "MARY" BE INSIDE ME?
I DON'T KNOW HOW OR WHY.
THAT'S WHY YOU HAVE TO REMEMBER...
...WHAT YOU MEANT WHEN YOU SAID...

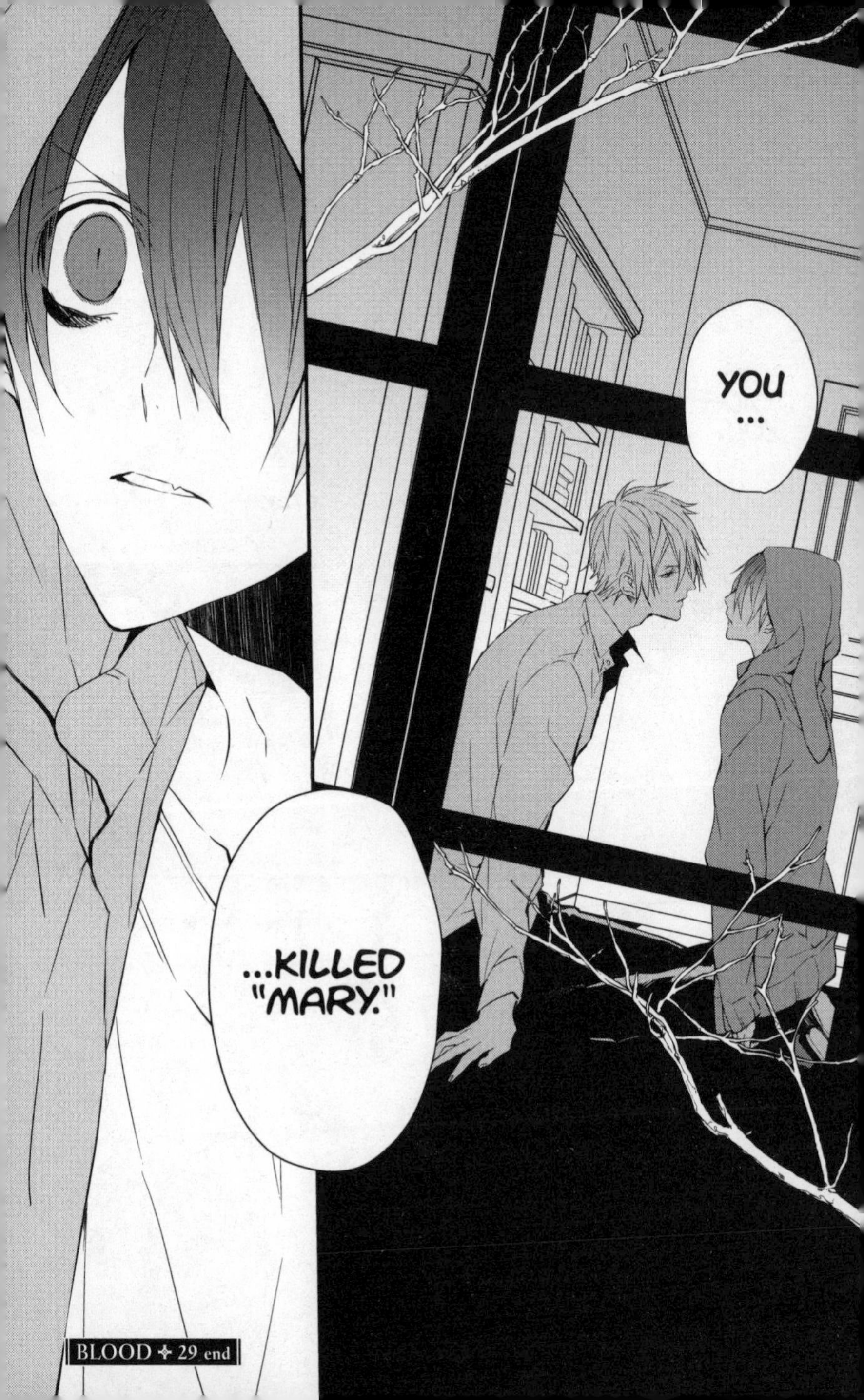
YOU ...
...KILLED "MARY."
BLOOD ✦ 29 end

# Bloody†Mary

He's the
ONLY ONE
WHO
DOESN't
KNOW

↑
HIM

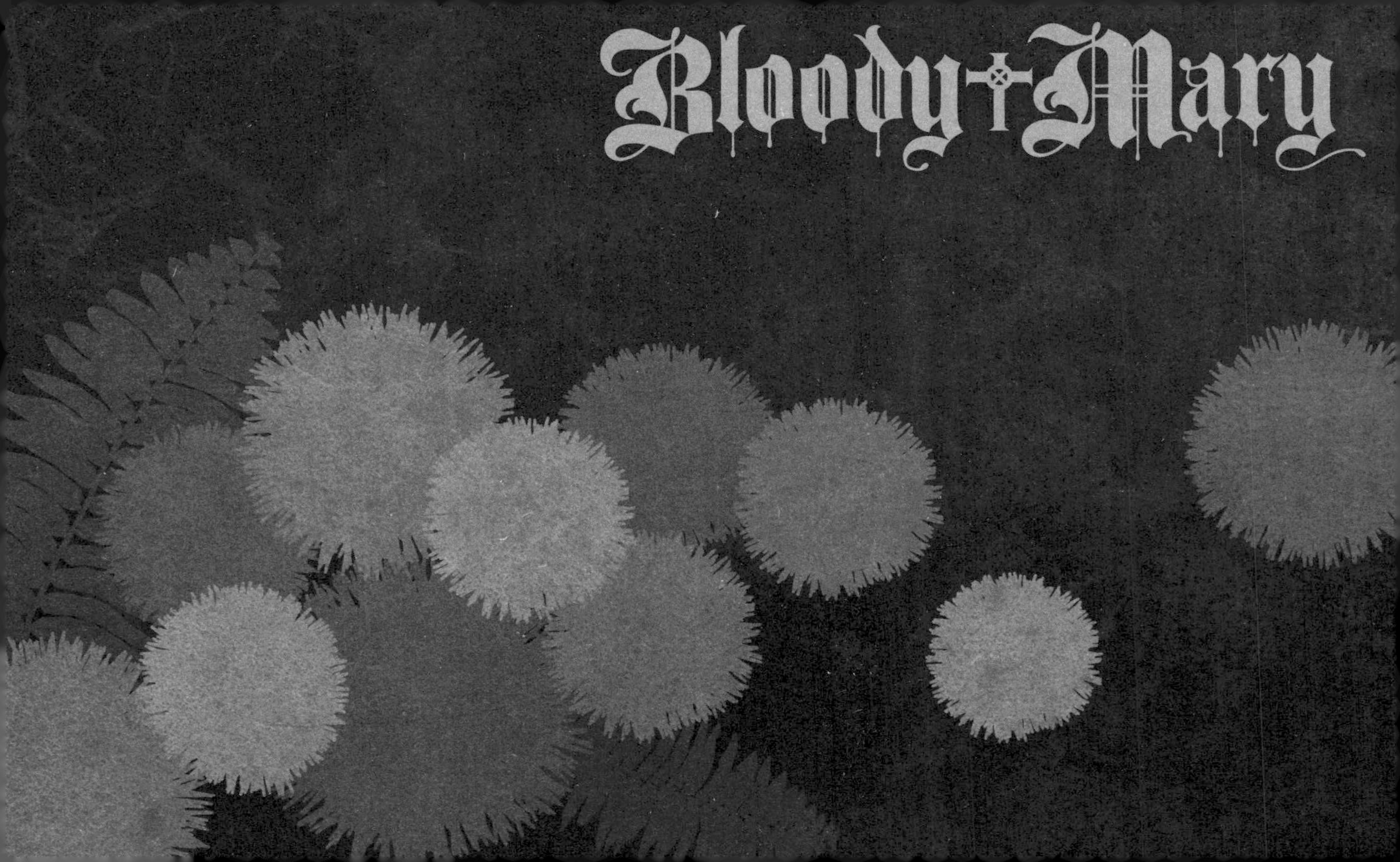
Bloody+Mary

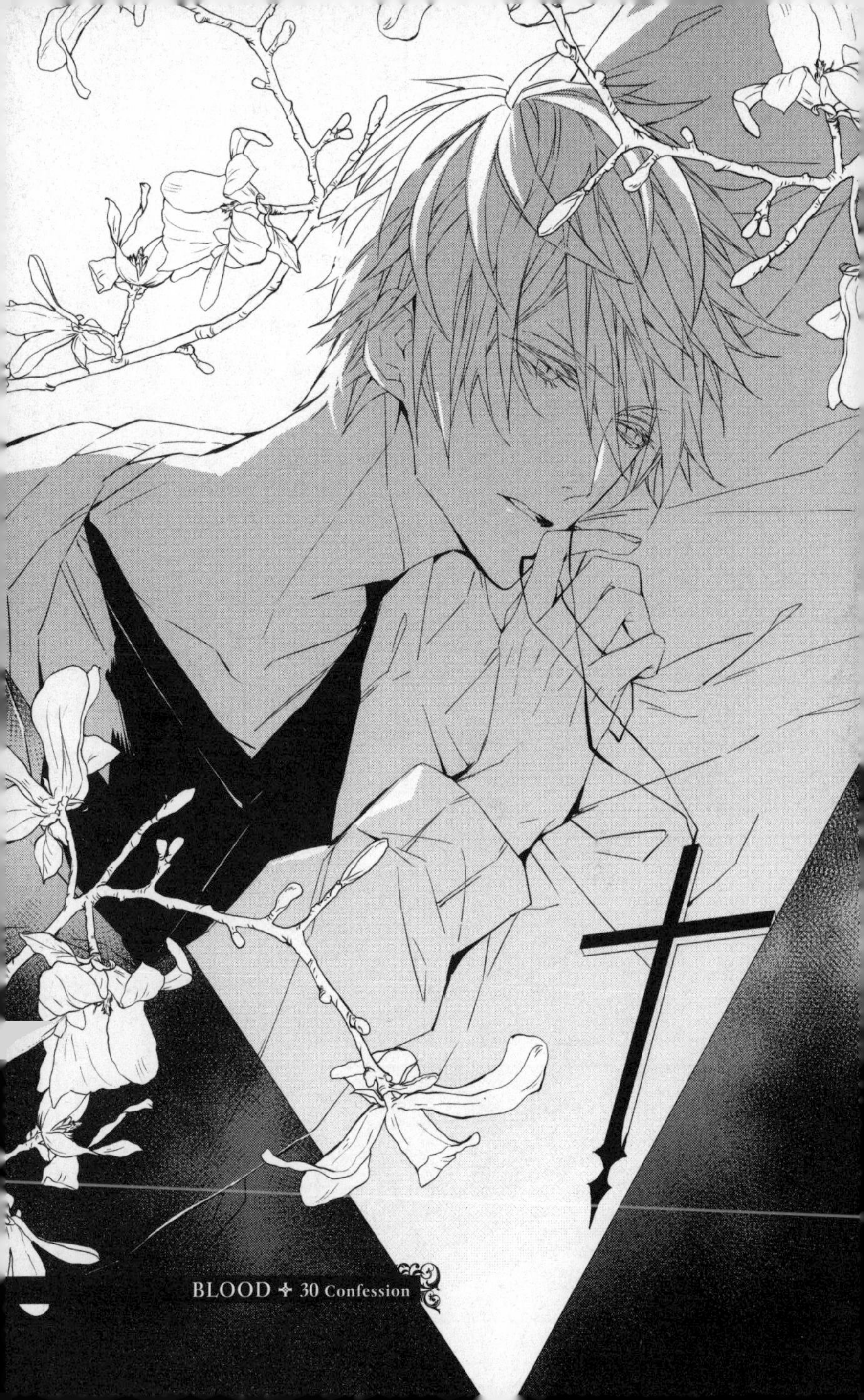
BLOOD ✦ 30 Confession

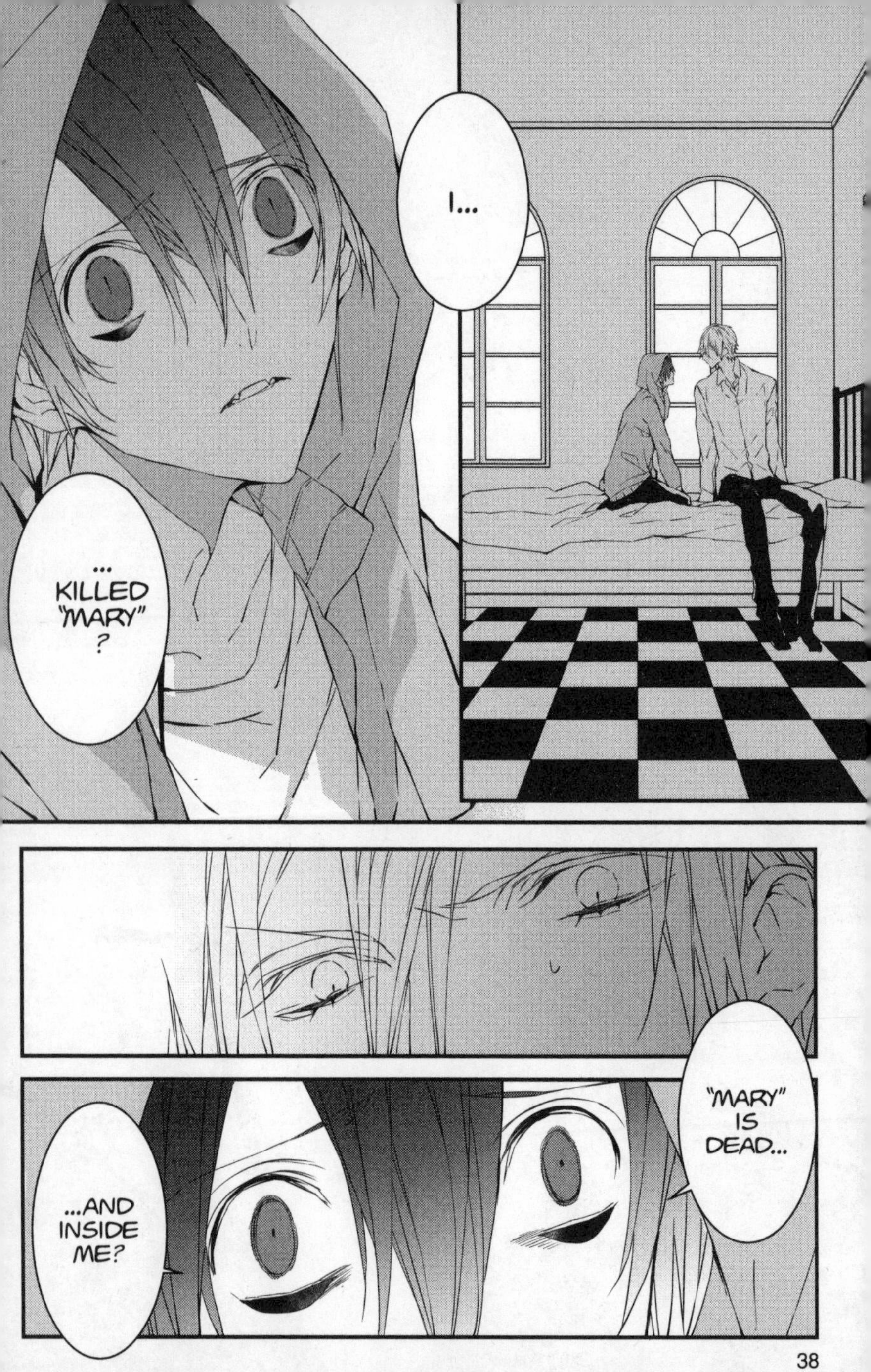
I...
...KILLED "MARY"?
"MARY" IS DEAD...
...AND INSIDE ME?

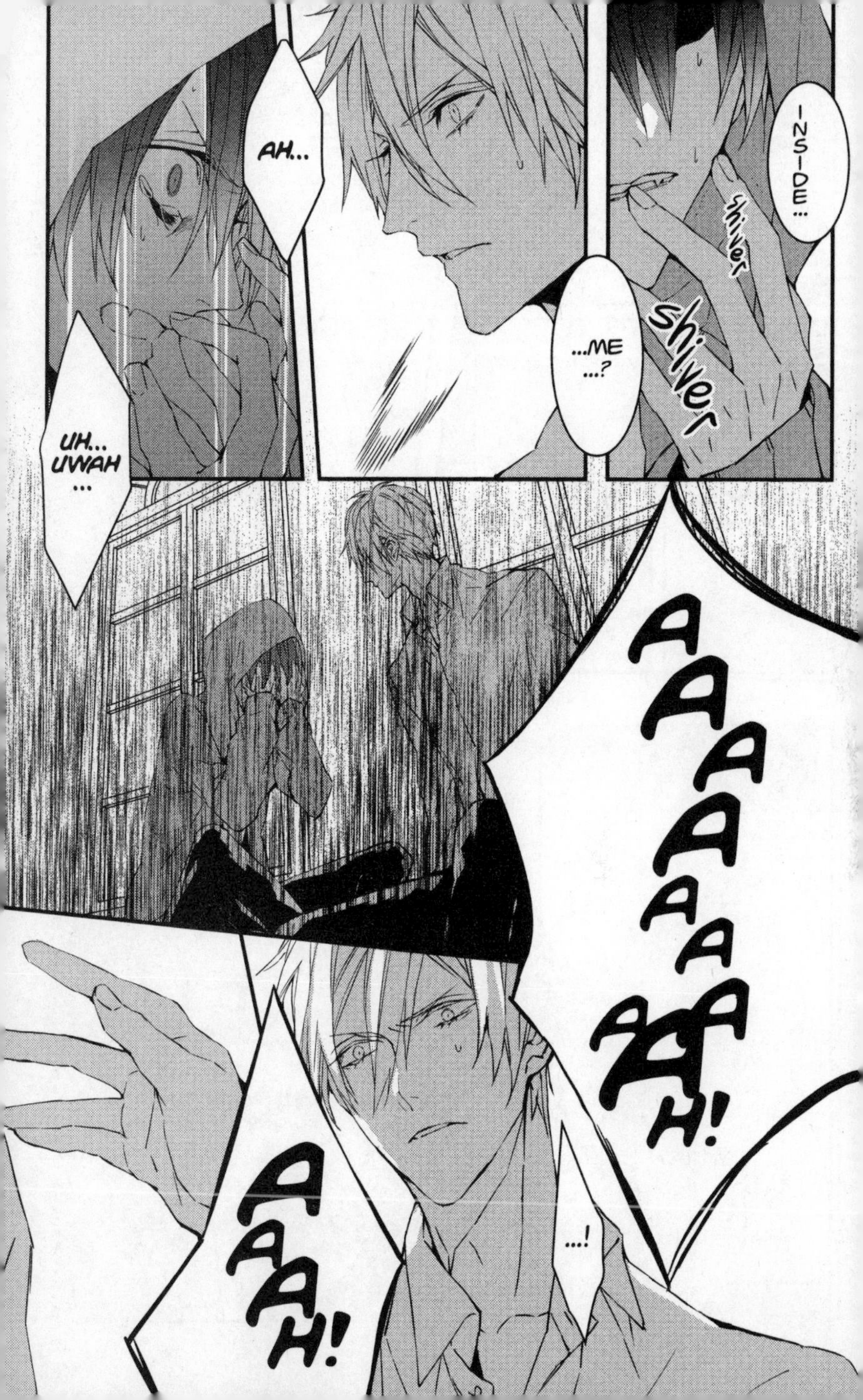
INSIDE...
shiver
shiver
...ME ...?
AH...
UH... UWAH ...
AAAAAAAAAH!
...!
AAAAH!

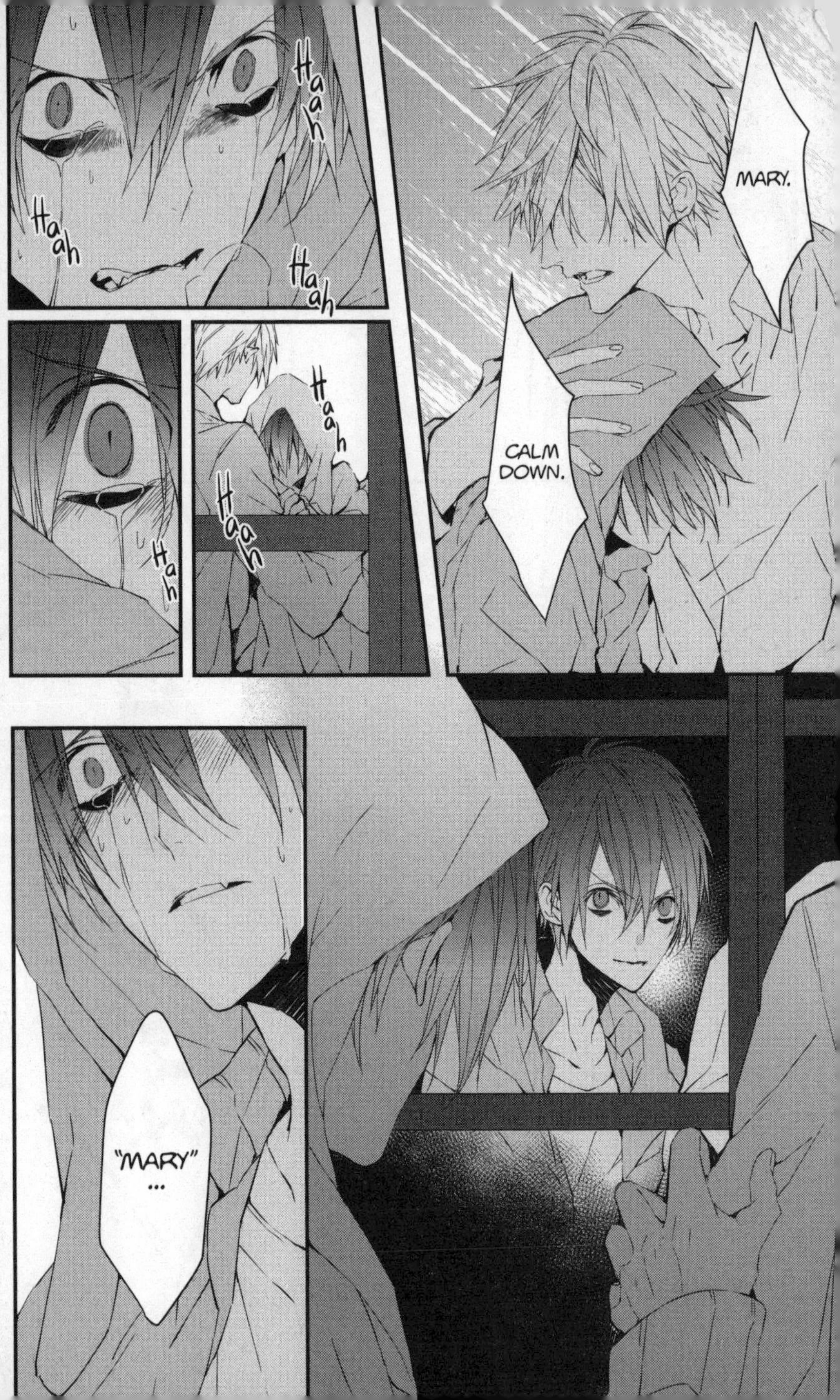
MARY.
CALM DOWN.
Haah
Haah
Haah
Haah
Haaah
Hah
"MARY"
...

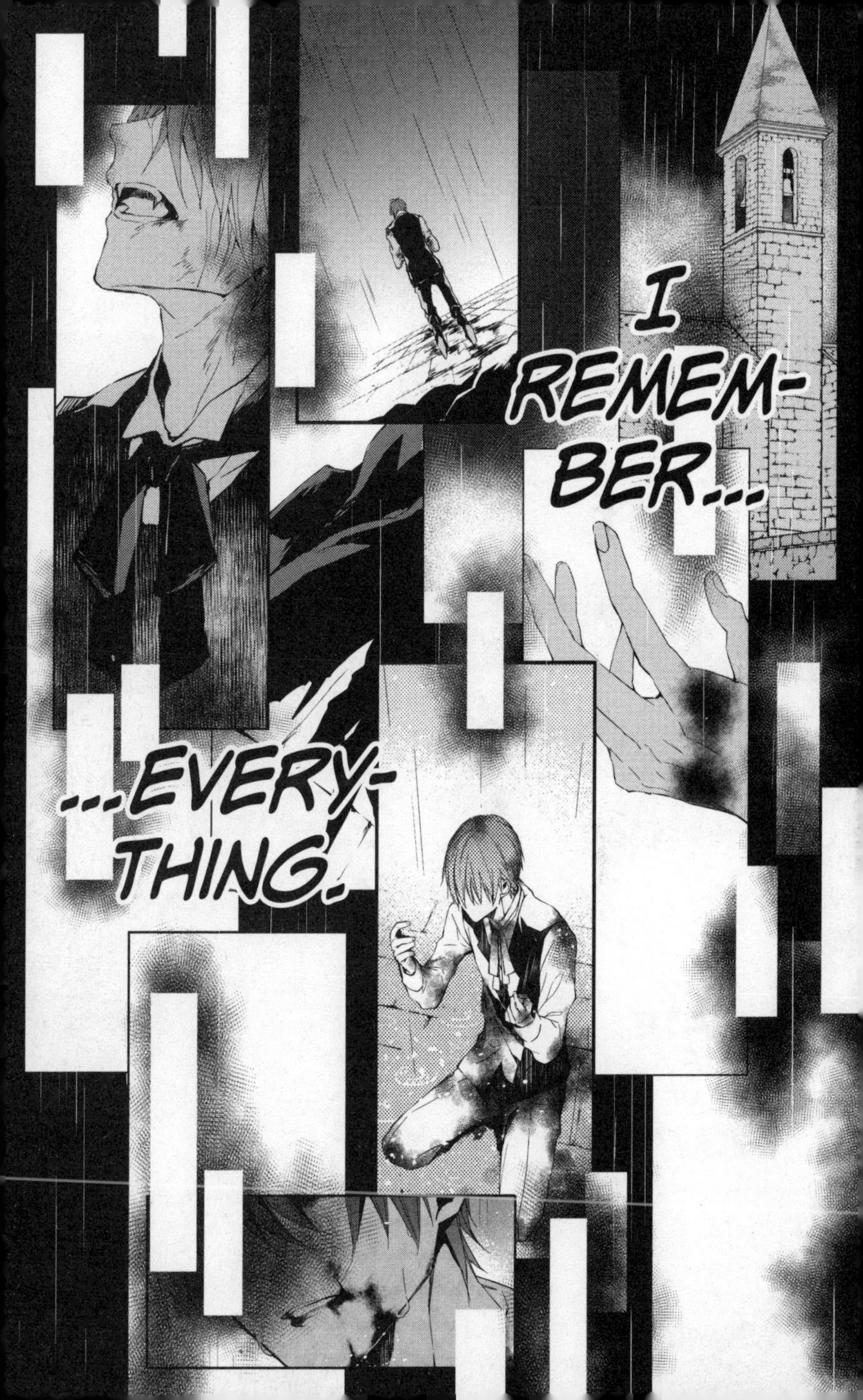
I REMEMBER...
...EVERYTHING.

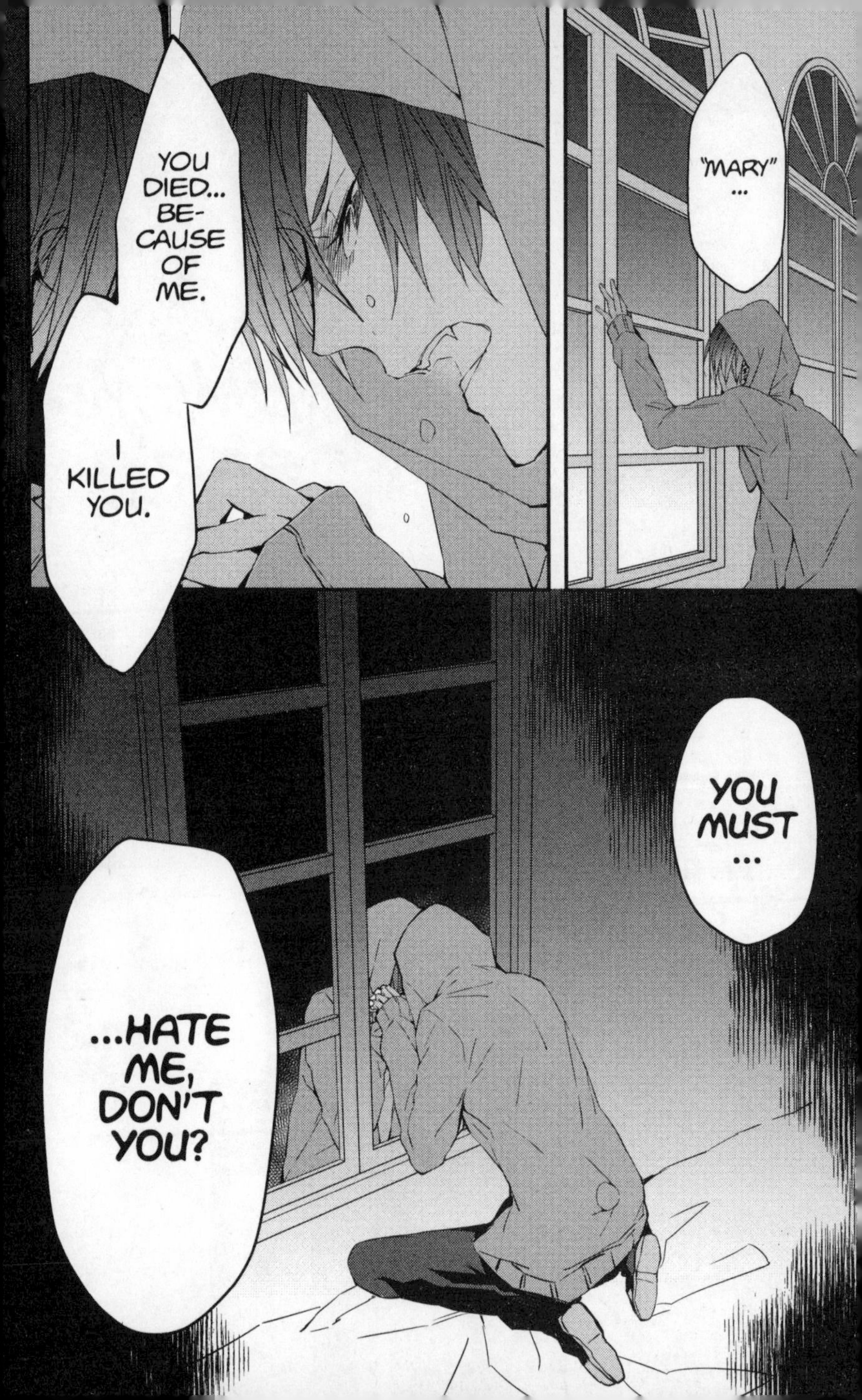
"MARY" ...
YOU DIED... BE-CAUSE OF ME.
I KILLED YOU.
YOU MUST ...
...HATE ME, DON'T YOU?

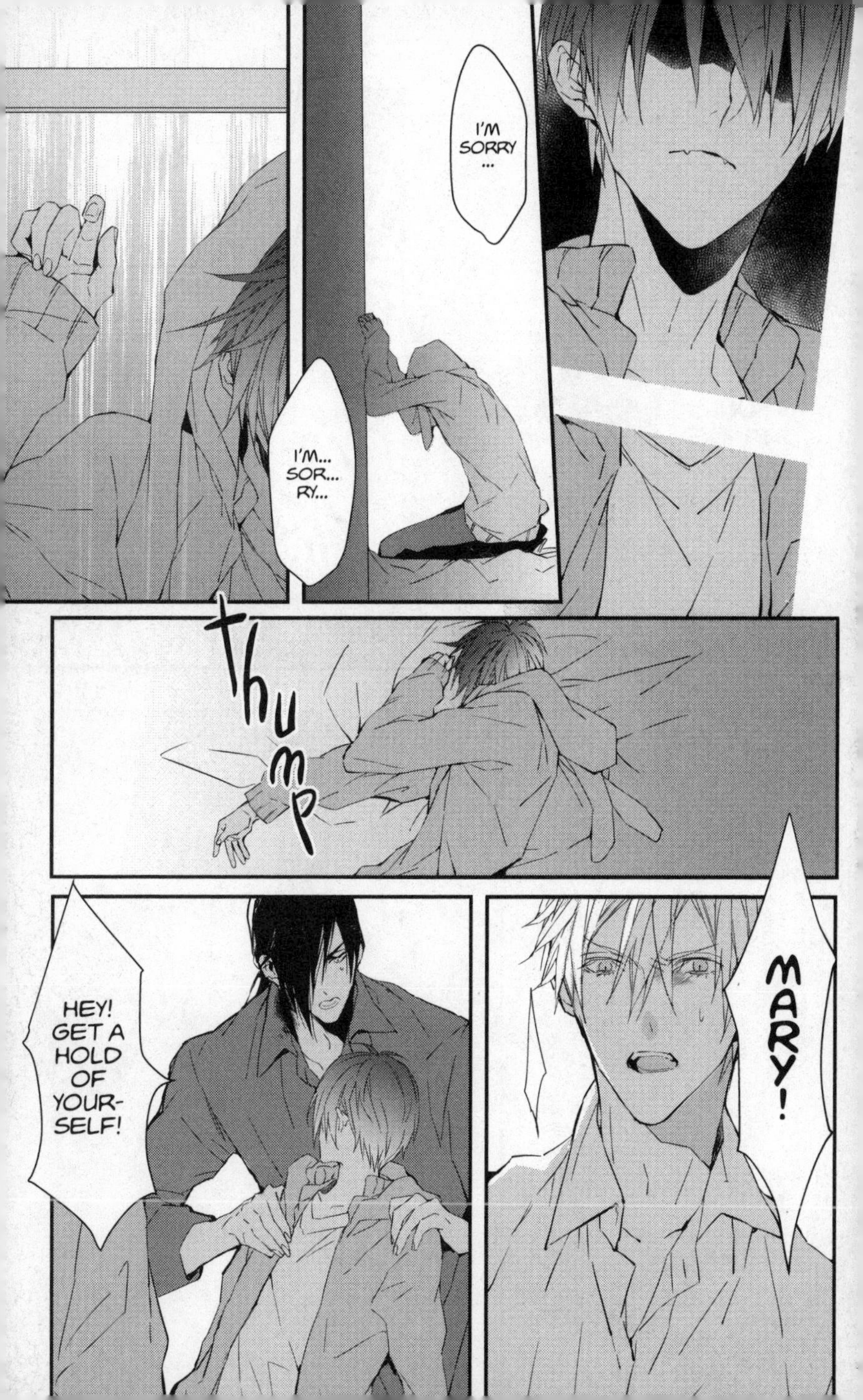
I'M SORRY...
I'M... SOR... RY...
thump
MARY!
HEY! GET A HOLD OF YOURSELF!

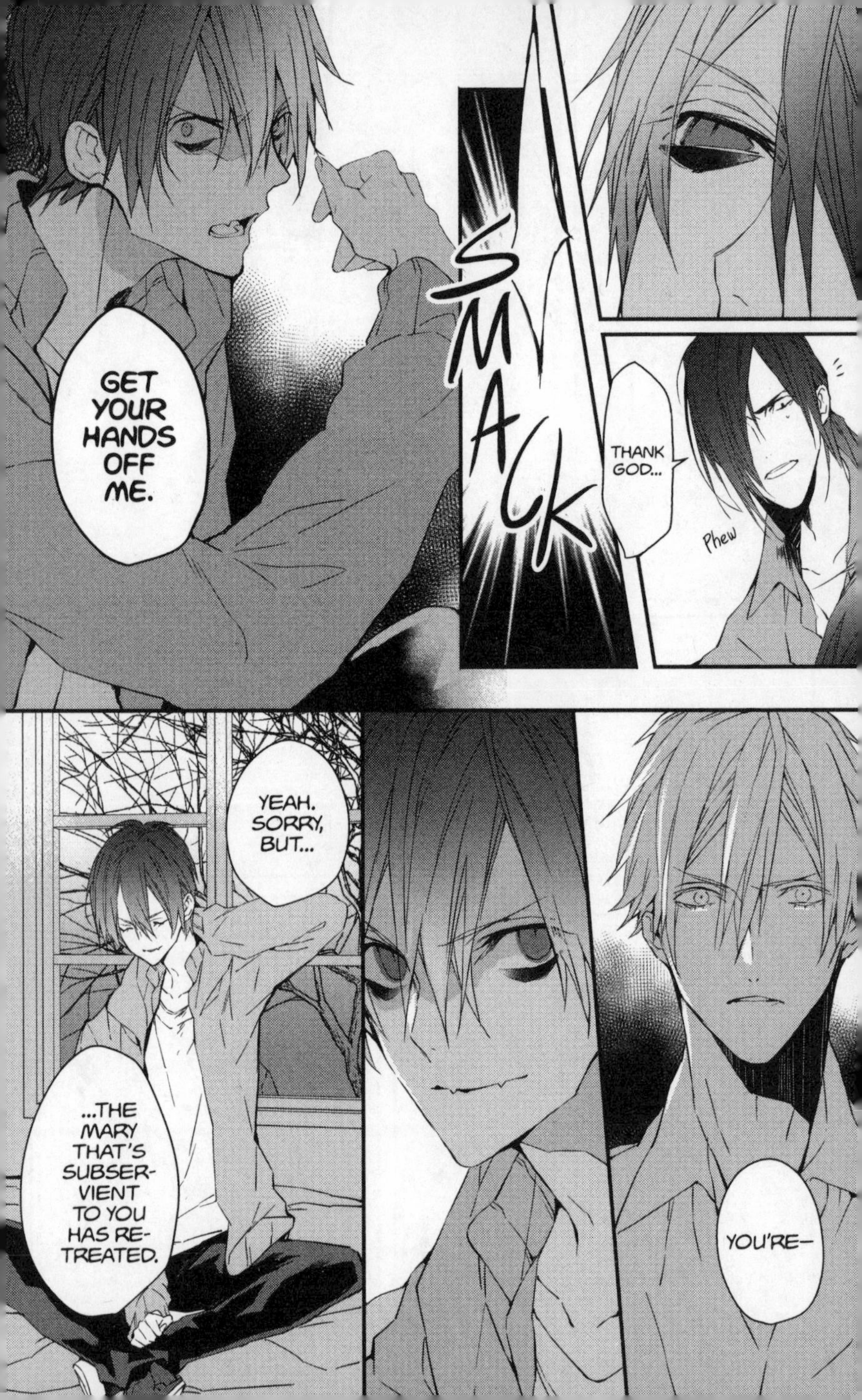
THANK GOD...
Phew
SMACK
GET YOUR HANDS OFF ME.
YOU'RE—
YEAH. SORRY, BUT...
...THE MARY THAT'S SUBSER-VIENT TO YOU HAS RE-TREATED.

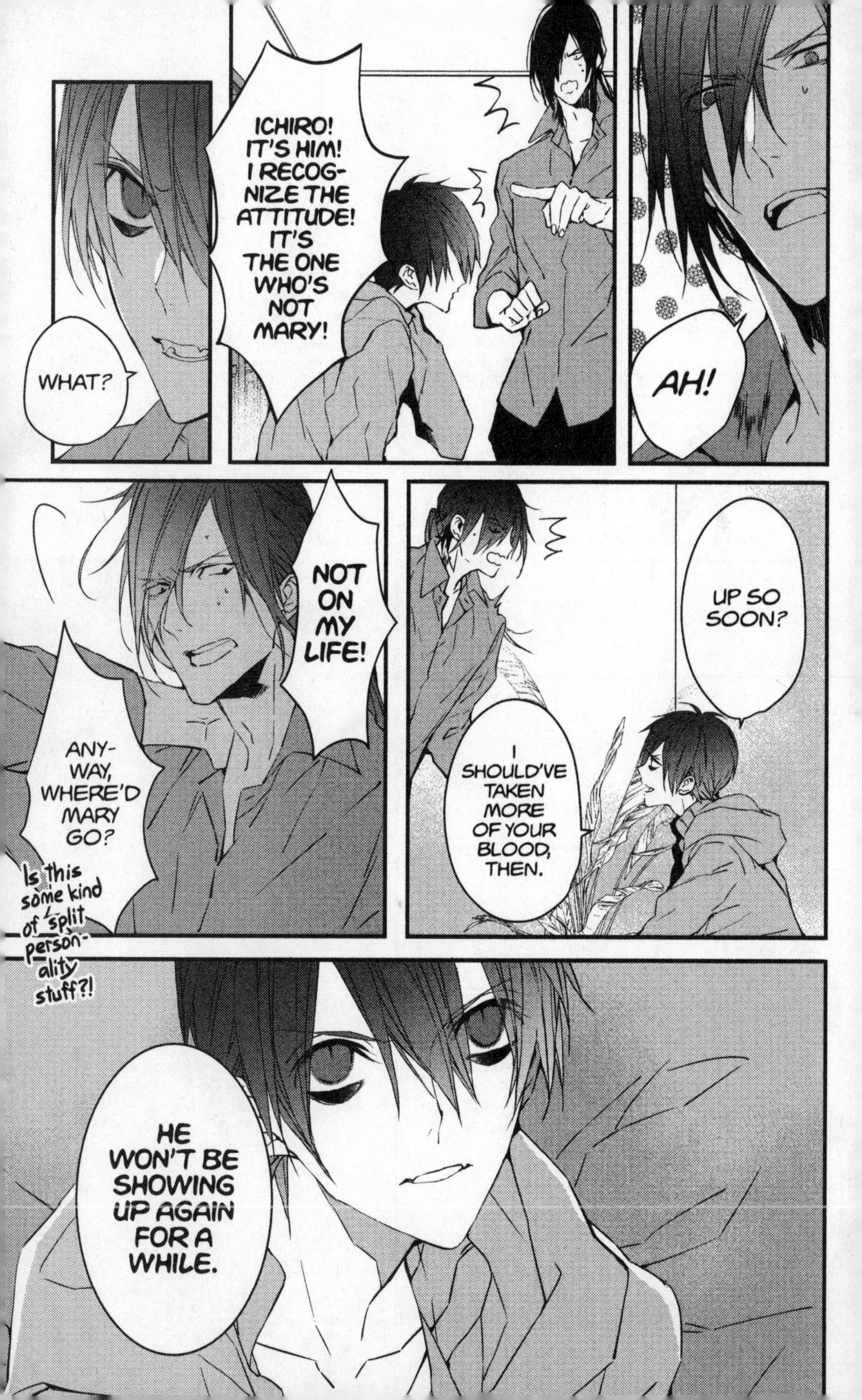
AH!
ICHIRO! IT'S HIM! I RECOGNIZE THE ATTITUDE! IT'S THE ONE WHO'S NOT MARY!
WHAT?
UP SO SOON?
I SHOULD'VE TAKEN MORE OF YOUR BLOOD, THEN.
NOT ON MY LIFE!
ANYWAY, WHERE'D MARY GO?
Is this some kind of split personality stuff?!
HE WON'T BE SHOWING UP AGAIN FOR A WHILE.

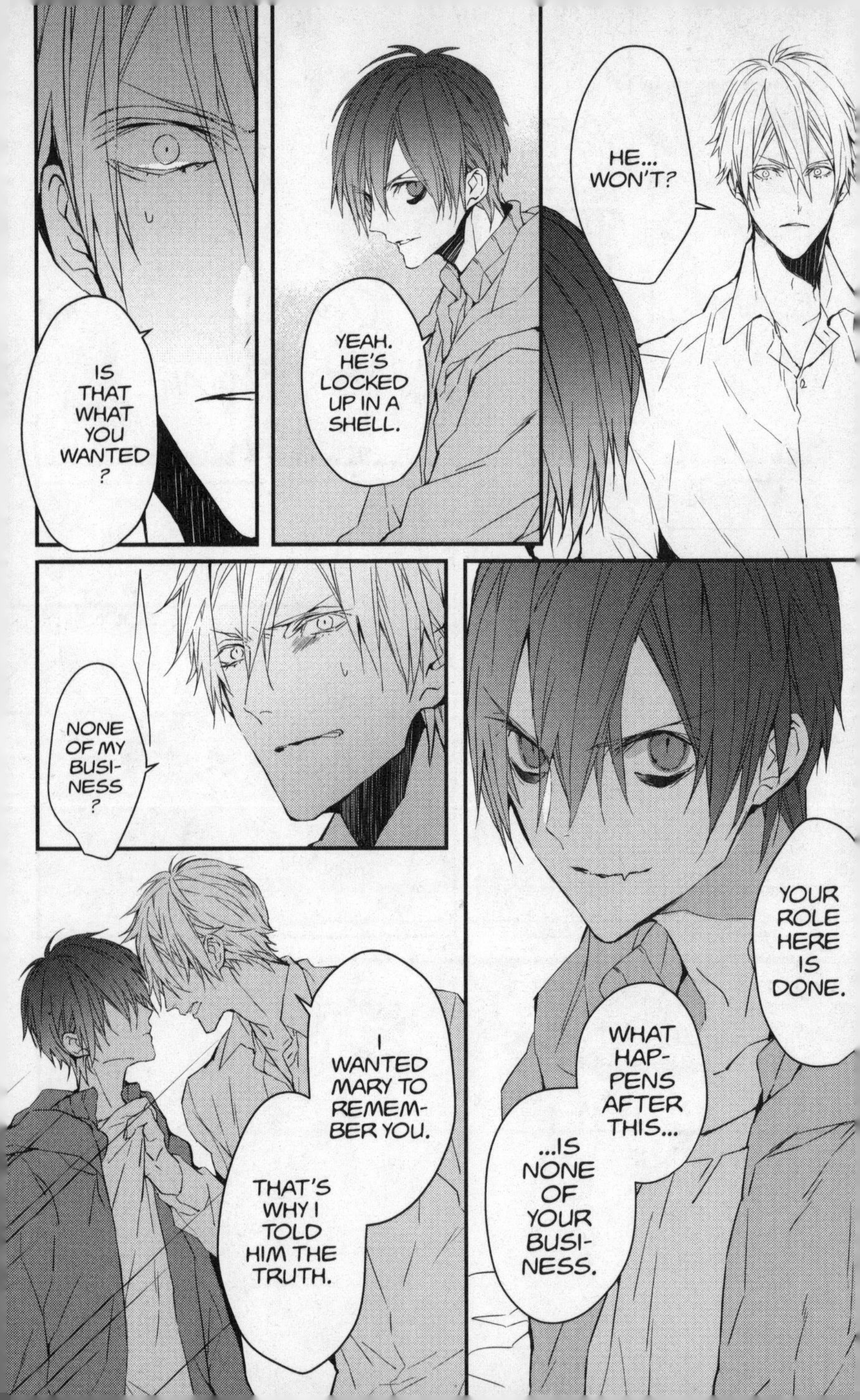
HE... WON'T?
YEAH. HE'S LOCKED UP IN A SHELL.
IS THAT WHAT YOU WANTED?
YOUR ROLE HERE IS DONE.
WHAT HAPPENS AFTER THIS...
...IS NONE OF YOUR BUSINESS.
NONE OF MY BUSINESS?
I WANTED MARY TO REMEMBER YOU.
THAT'S WHY I TOLD HIM THE TRUTH.

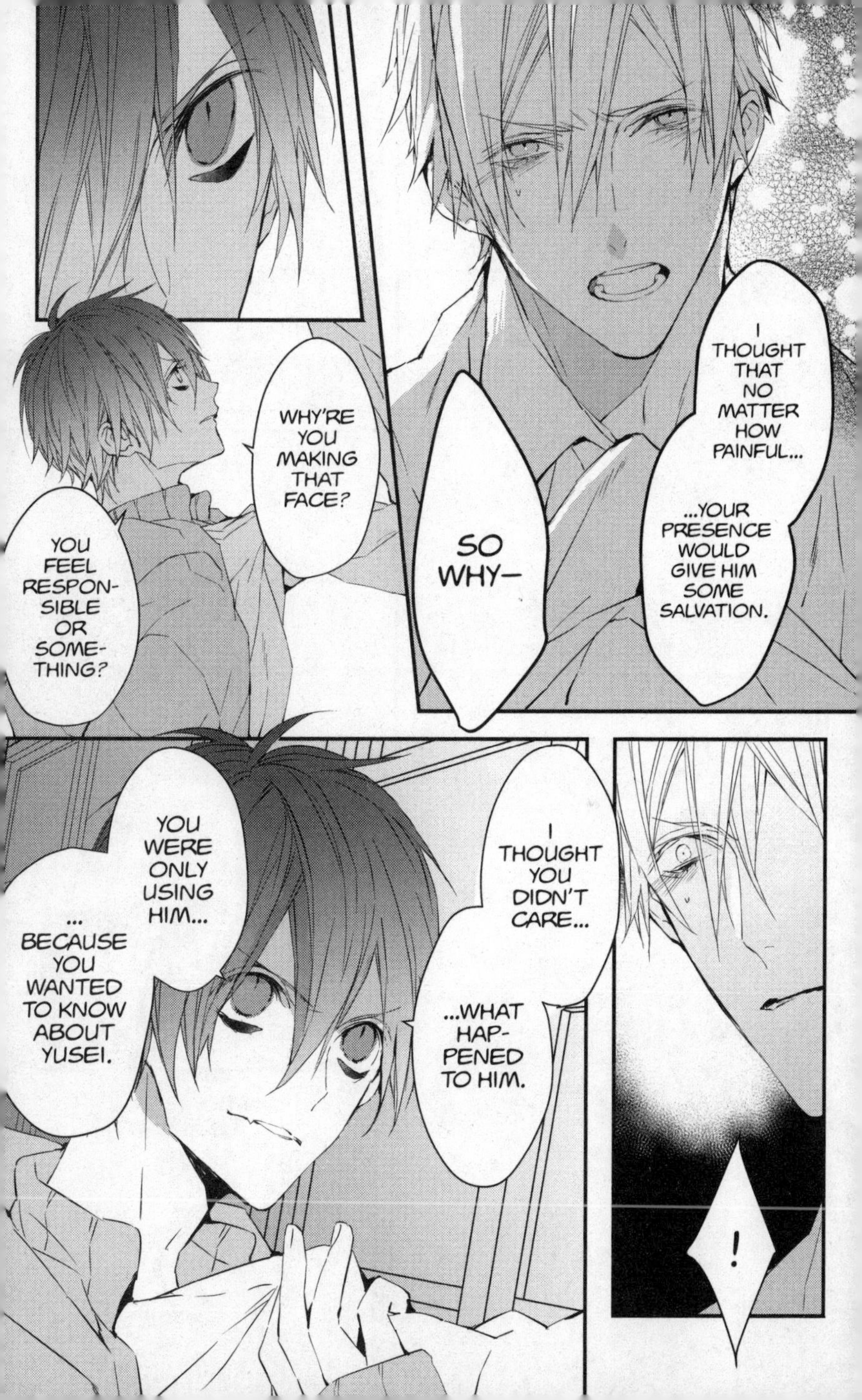
I THOUGHT THAT NO MATTER HOW PAINFUL...
...YOUR PRESENCE WOULD GIVE HIM SOME SALVATION.
SO WHY—
WHY'RE YOU MAKING THAT FACE?
YOU FEEL RESPONSIBLE OR SOMETHING?
!
I THOUGHT YOU DIDN'T CARE...
...WHAT HAPPENED TO HIM.
YOU WERE ONLY USING HIM...
...BECAUSE YOU WANTED TO KNOW ABOUT YUSEI.

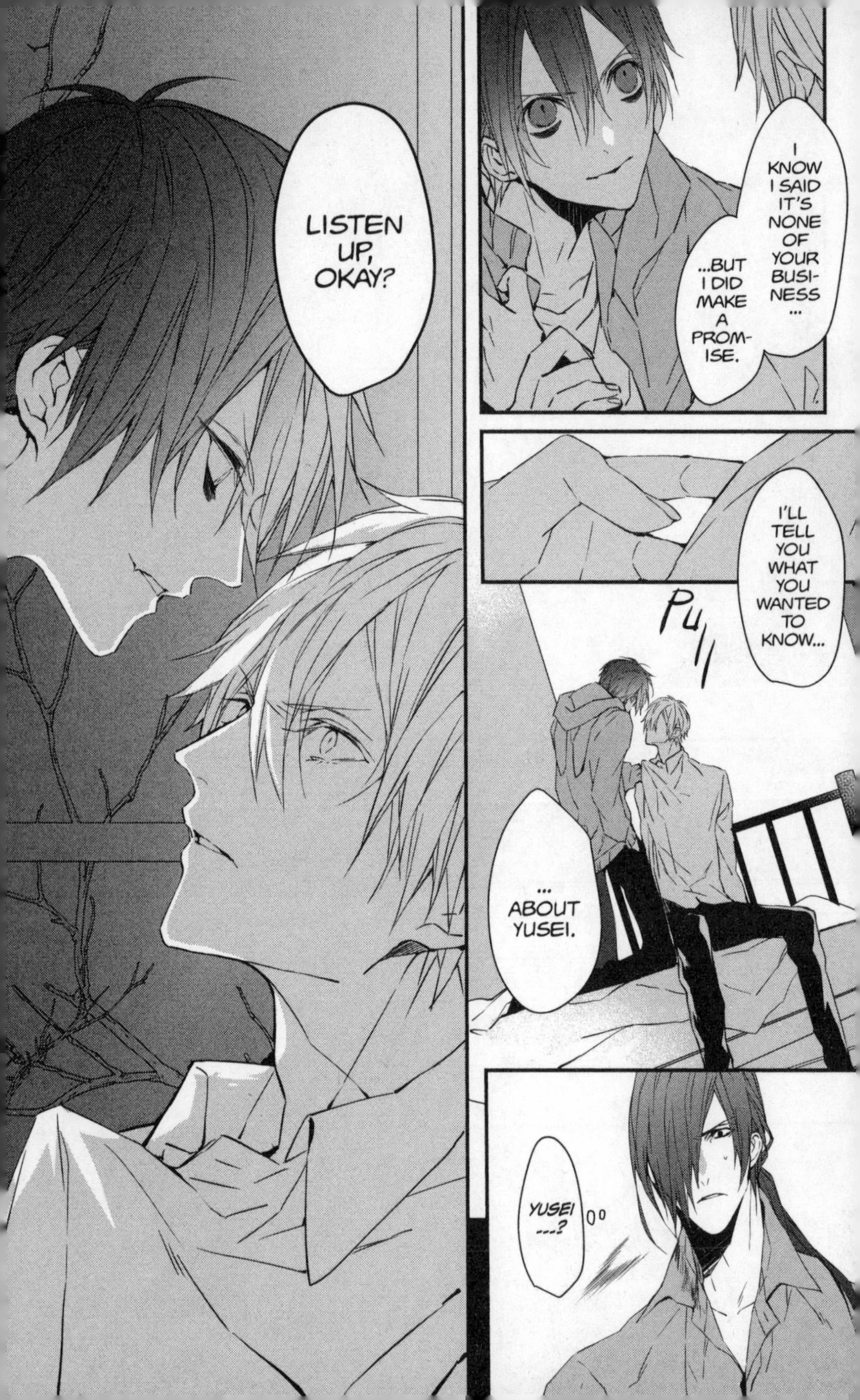
I KNOW I SAID IT'S NONE OF YOUR BUSINESS...
...BUT I DID MAKE A PROMISE.
I'LL TELL YOU WHAT YOU WANTED TO KNOW...
PULL
...ABOUT YUSEI.
YUSEI---?
LISTEN UP, OKAY?

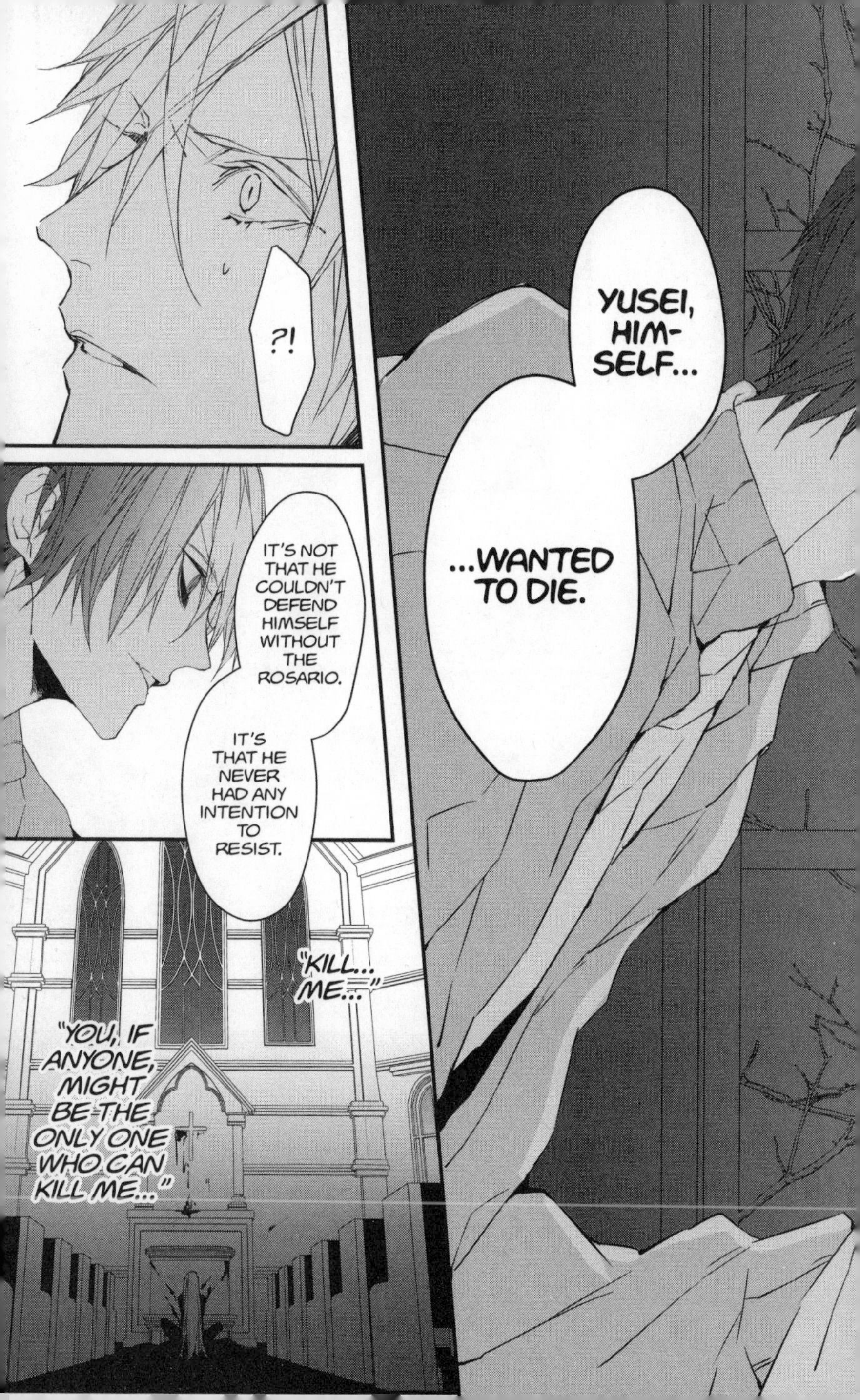
YUSEI, HIM-SELF...
...WANTED TO DIE.
?!
IT'S NOT THAT HE COULDN'T DEFEND HIMSELF WITHOUT THE ROSARIO.
IT'S THAT HE NEVER HAD ANY INTENTION TO RESIST.
"KILL... ME..."
"YOU, IF ANYONE, MIGHT BE THE ONLY ONE WHO CAN KILL ME..."

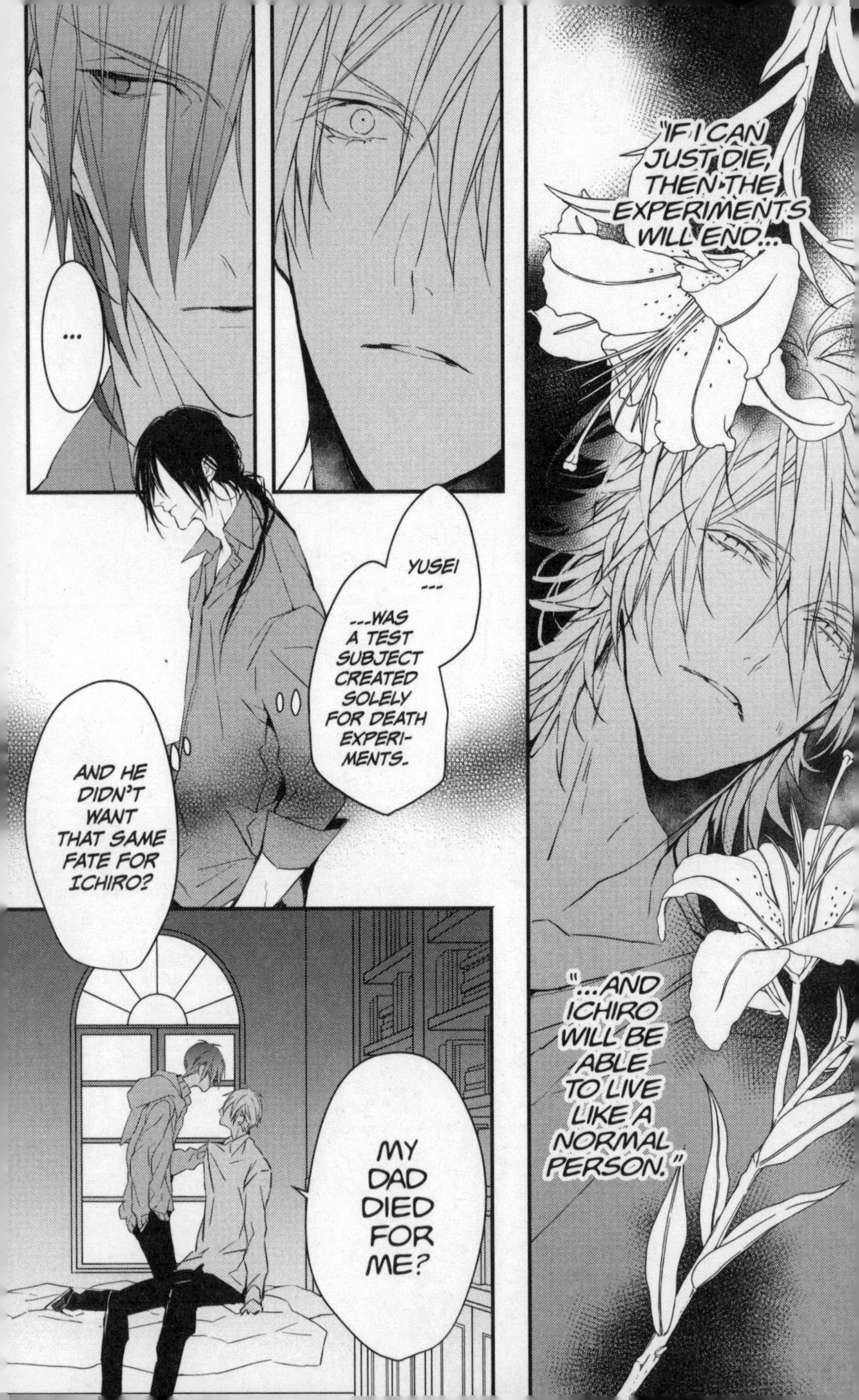
"IF I CAN JUST DIE, THEN THE EXPERIMENTS WILL END...
"...AND ICHIRO WILL BE ABLE TO LIVE LIKE A NORMAL PERSON."
...
YUSEI---
---WAS A TEST SUBJECT CREATED SOLELY FOR DEATH EXPERI-MENTS.
AND HE DIDN'T WANT THAT SAME FATE FOR ICHIRO?
MY DAD DIED FOR ME?

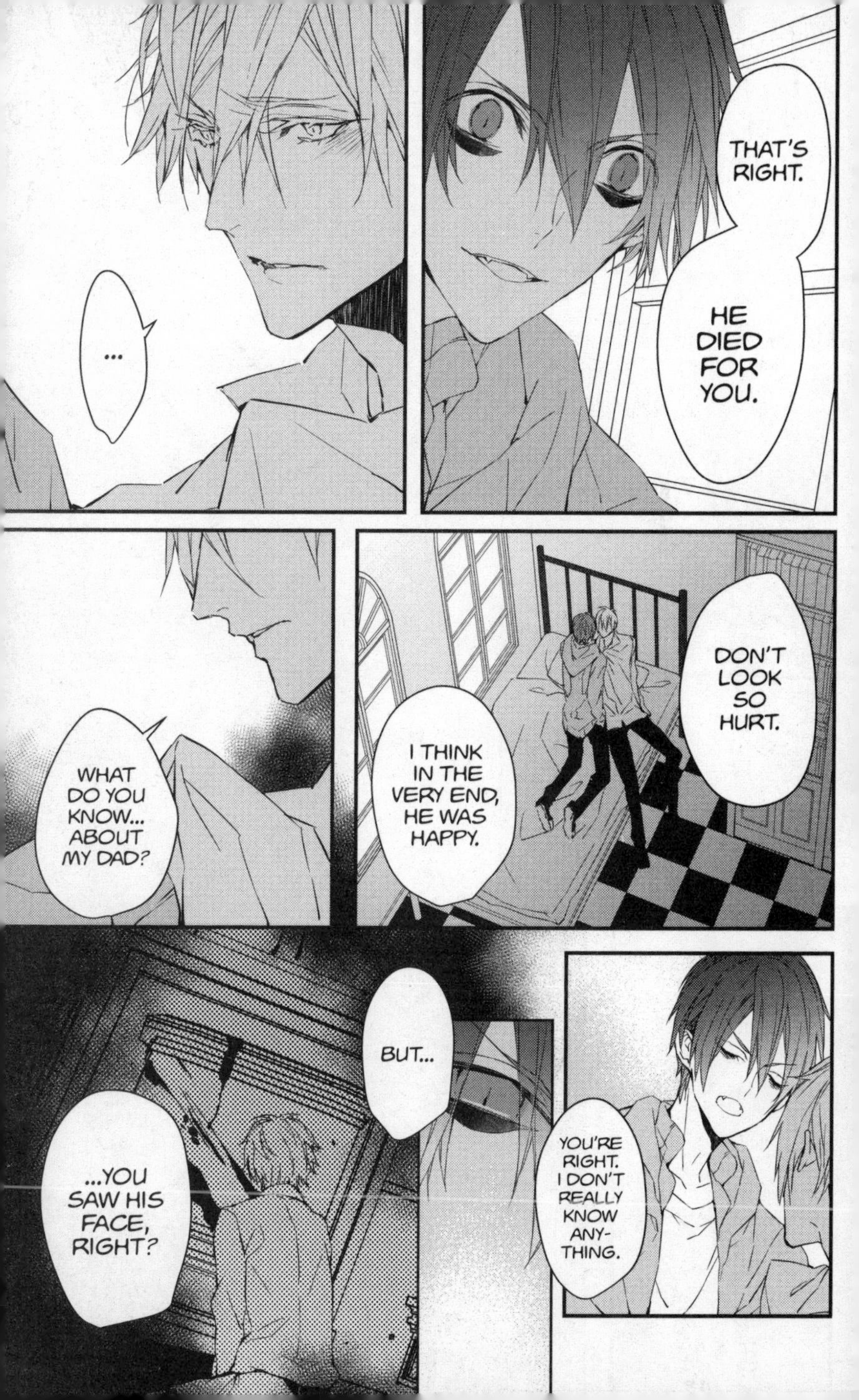
THAT'S RIGHT.
HE DIED FOR YOU.
...
DON'T LOOK SO HURT.
I THINK IN THE VERY END, HE WAS HAPPY.
WHAT DO YOU KNOW... ABOUT MY DAD?
YOU'RE RIGHT. I DON'T REALLY KNOW ANY-THING.
BUT...
...YOU SAW HIS FACE, RIGHT?

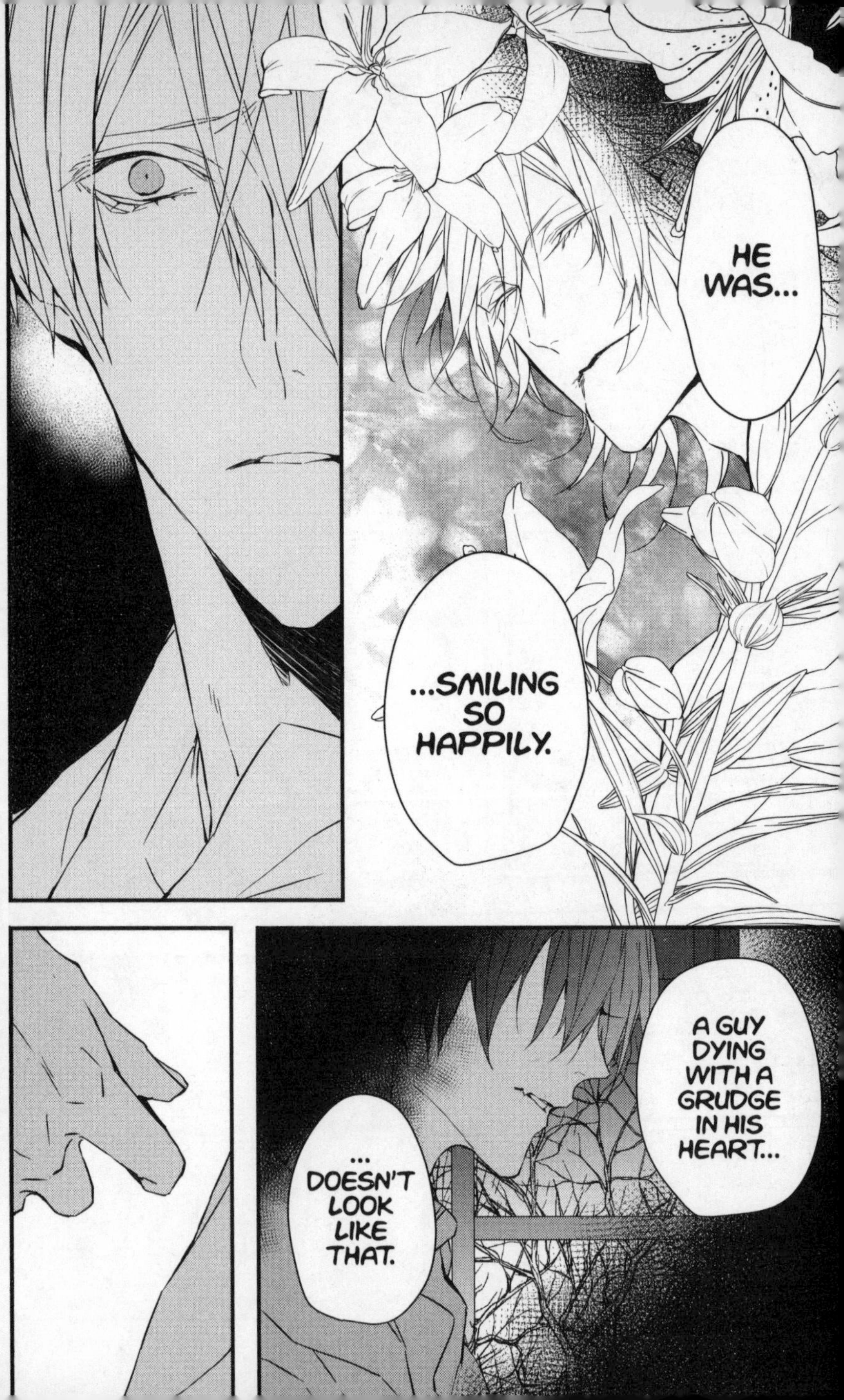
HE WAS...
...SMILING SO HAPPILY.
A GUY DYING WITH A GRUDGE IN HIS HEART...
... DOESN'T LOOK LIKE THAT.

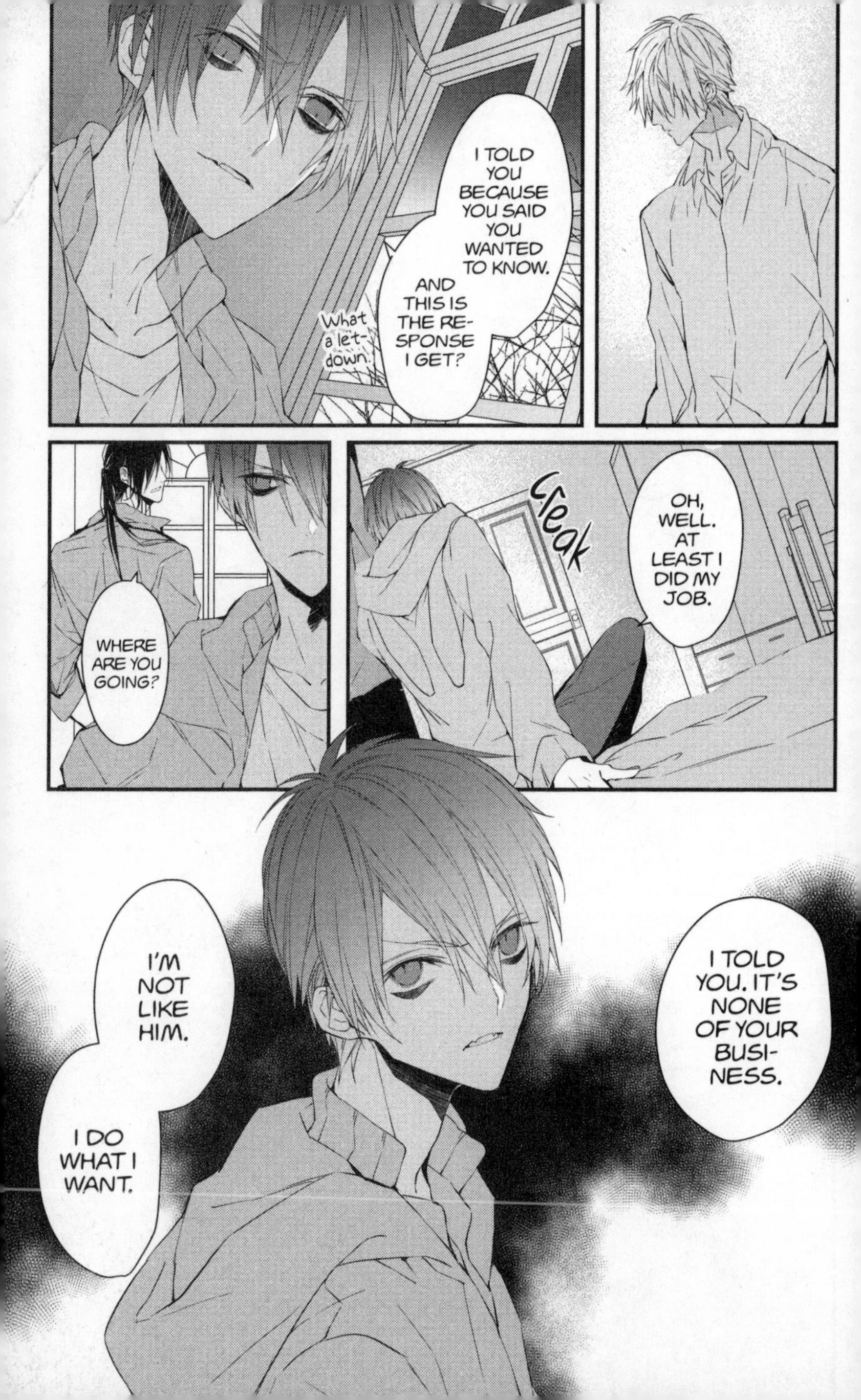
I TOLD YOU BECAUSE YOU SAID YOU WANTED TO KNOW.
AND THIS IS THE RE-SPONSE I GET?
What a let-down.
OH, WELL. AT LEAST I DID MY JOB.
creak
WHERE ARE YOU GOING?
I TOLD YOU. IT'S NONE OF YOUR BUSI-NESS.
I'M NOT LIKE HIM.
I DO WHAT I WANT.

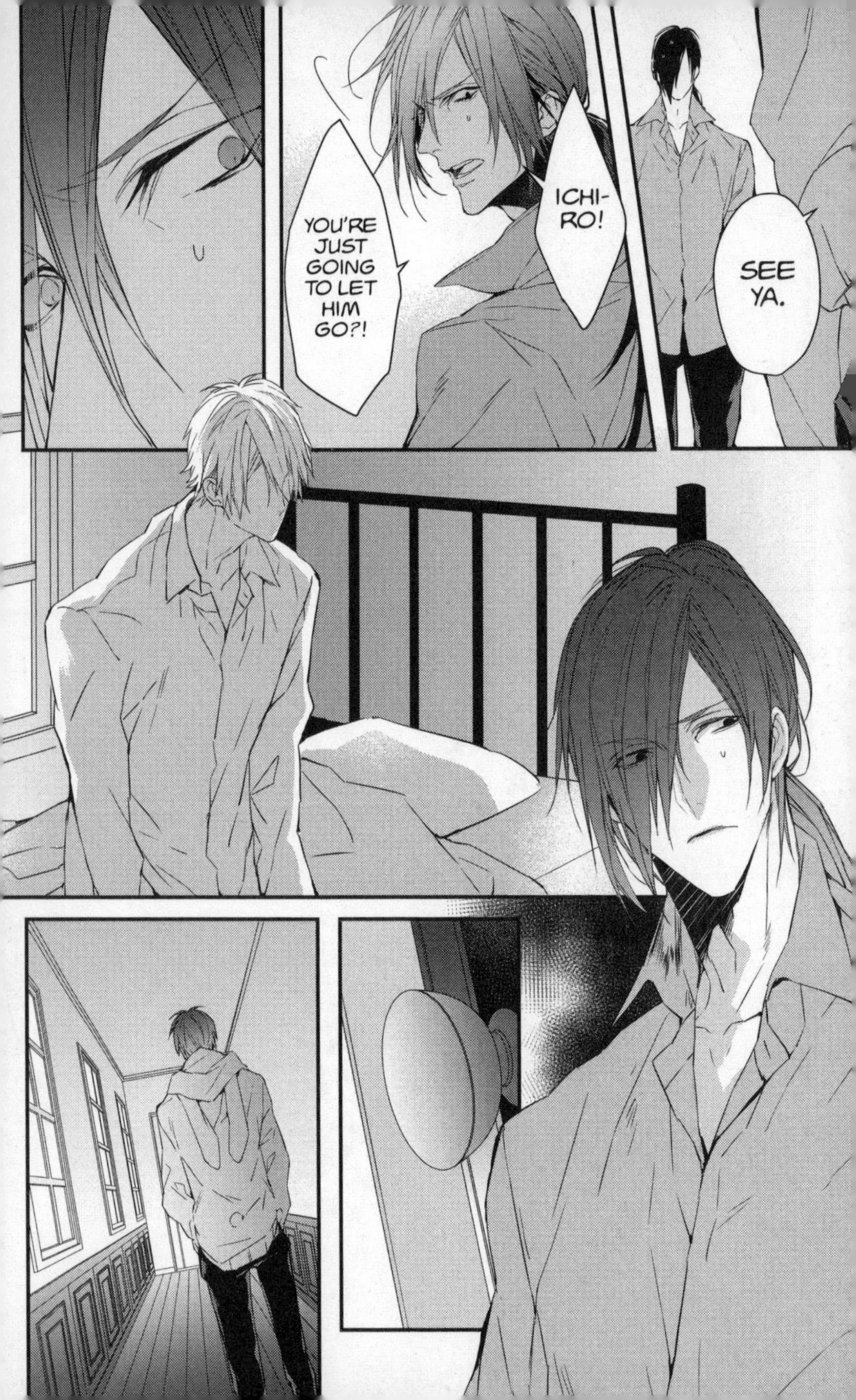
SEE YA.
ICHI-RO!
YOU'RE JUST GOING TO LET HIM GO?!

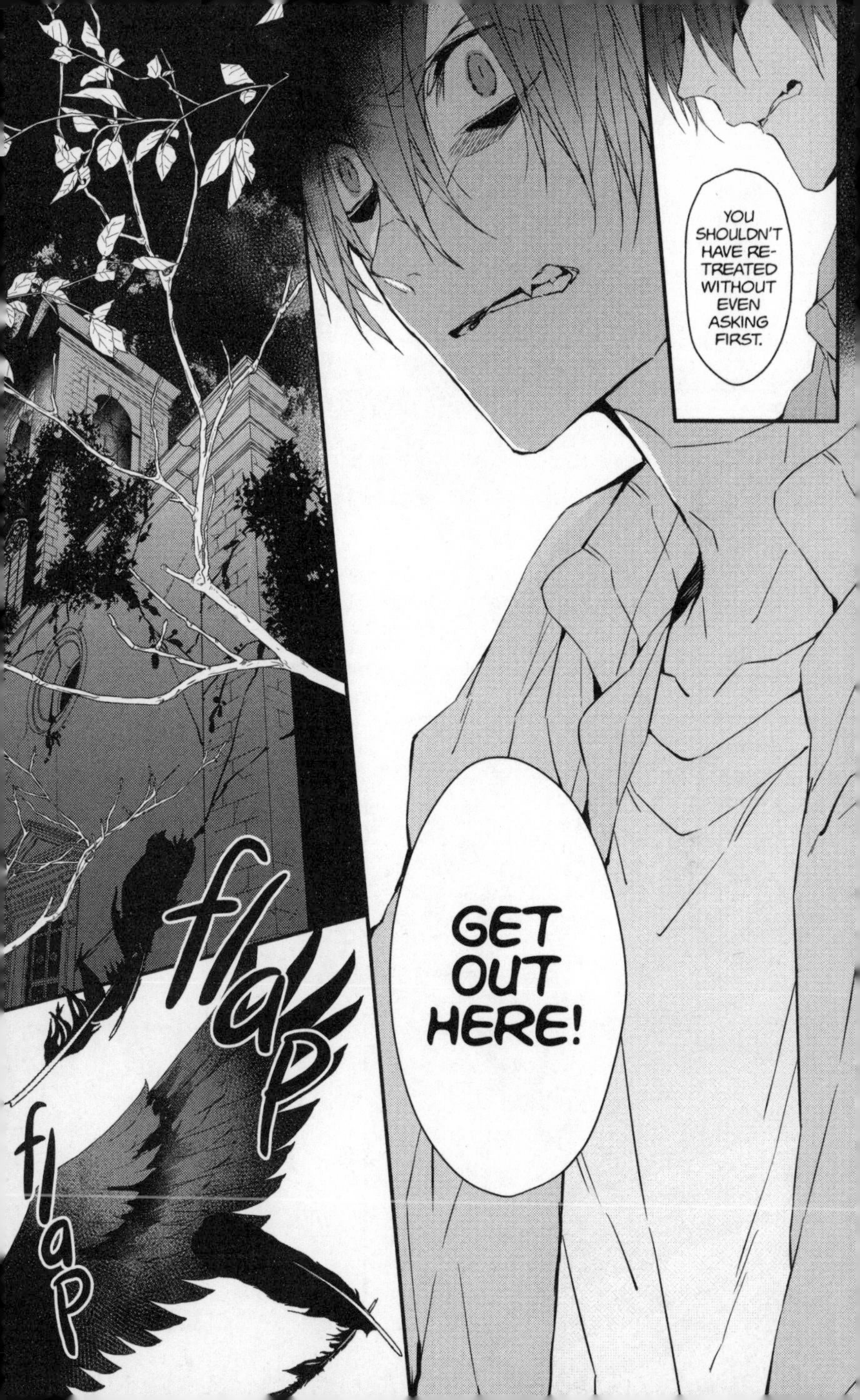
YOU SHOULDN'T HAVE RE-TREATED WITHOUT EVEN ASKING FIRST.
GET OUT HERE!
flap
flap

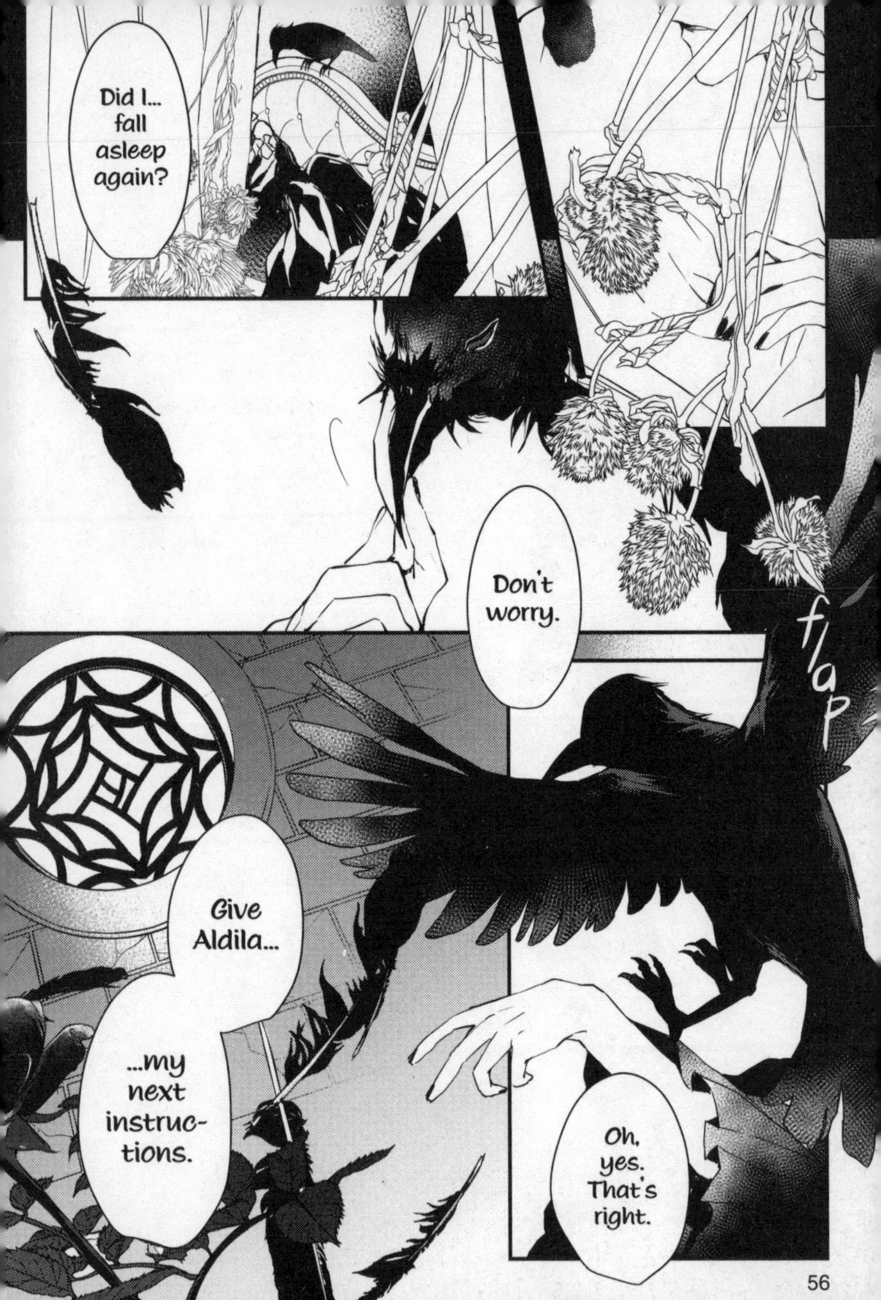
Did I... fall asleep again?
Don't worry.
flap
Oh, yes. That's right.
Give Aldila...
...my next instructions.

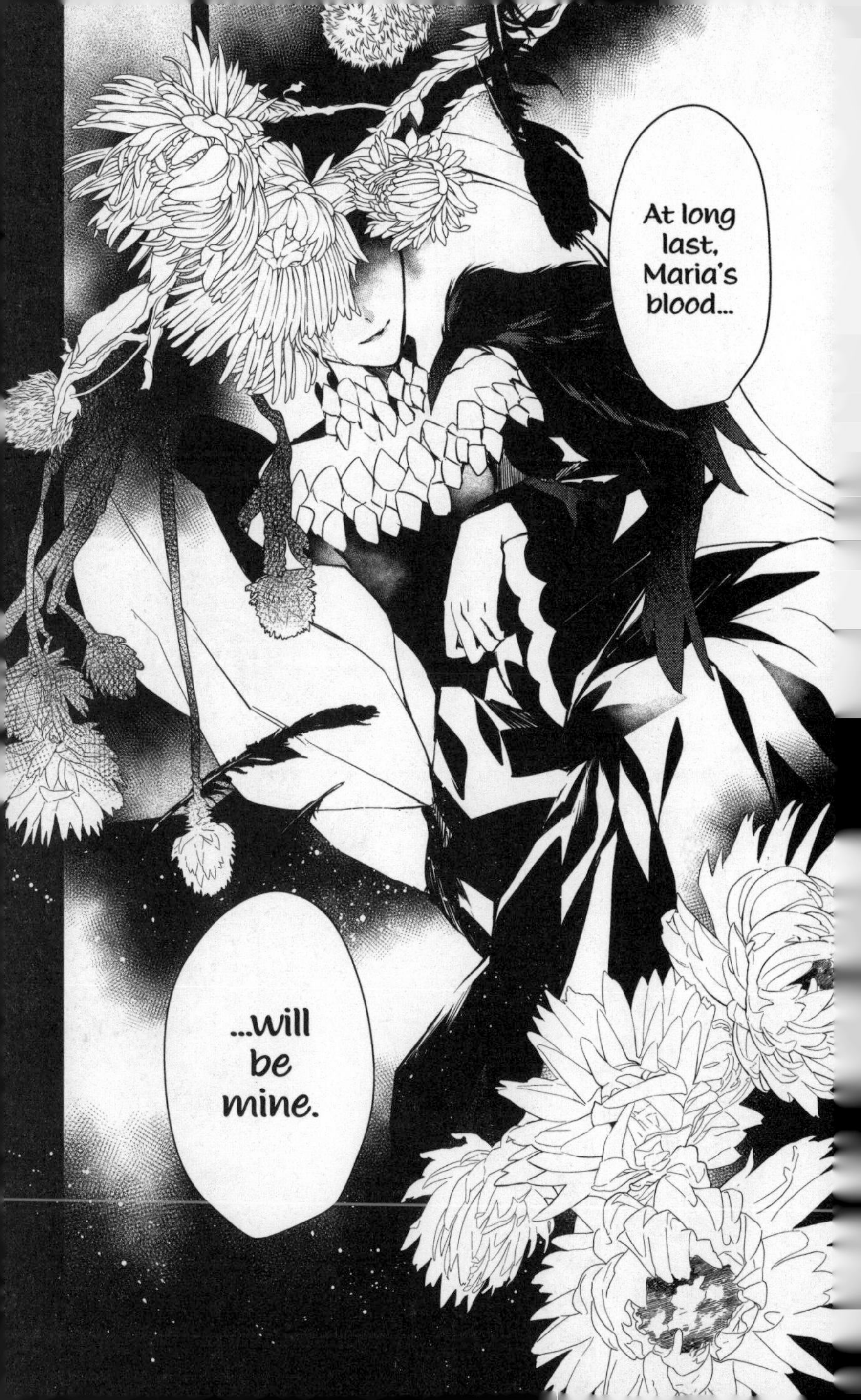
At long last, Maria's blood...
...will be mine.

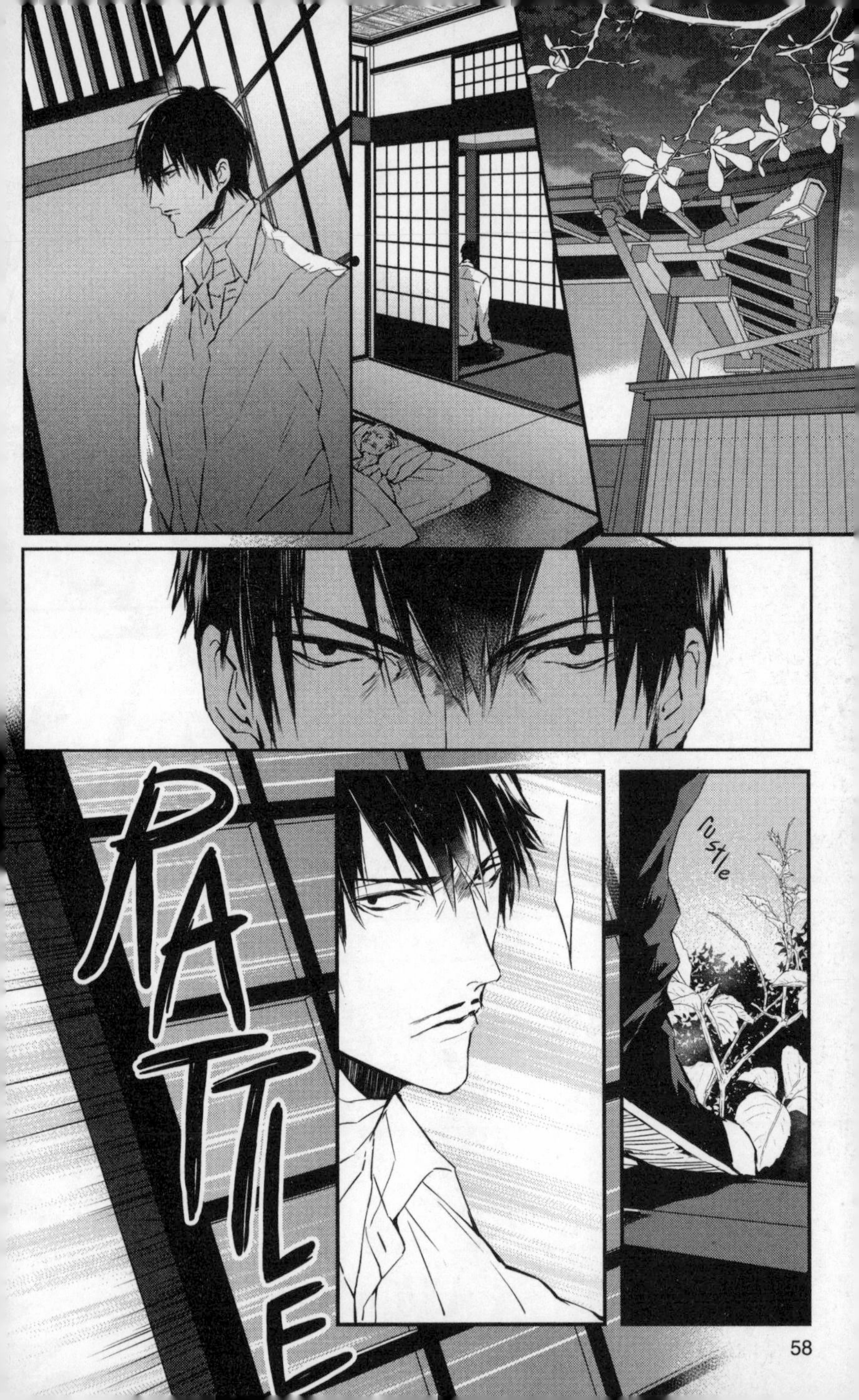
rustle
RATTLE

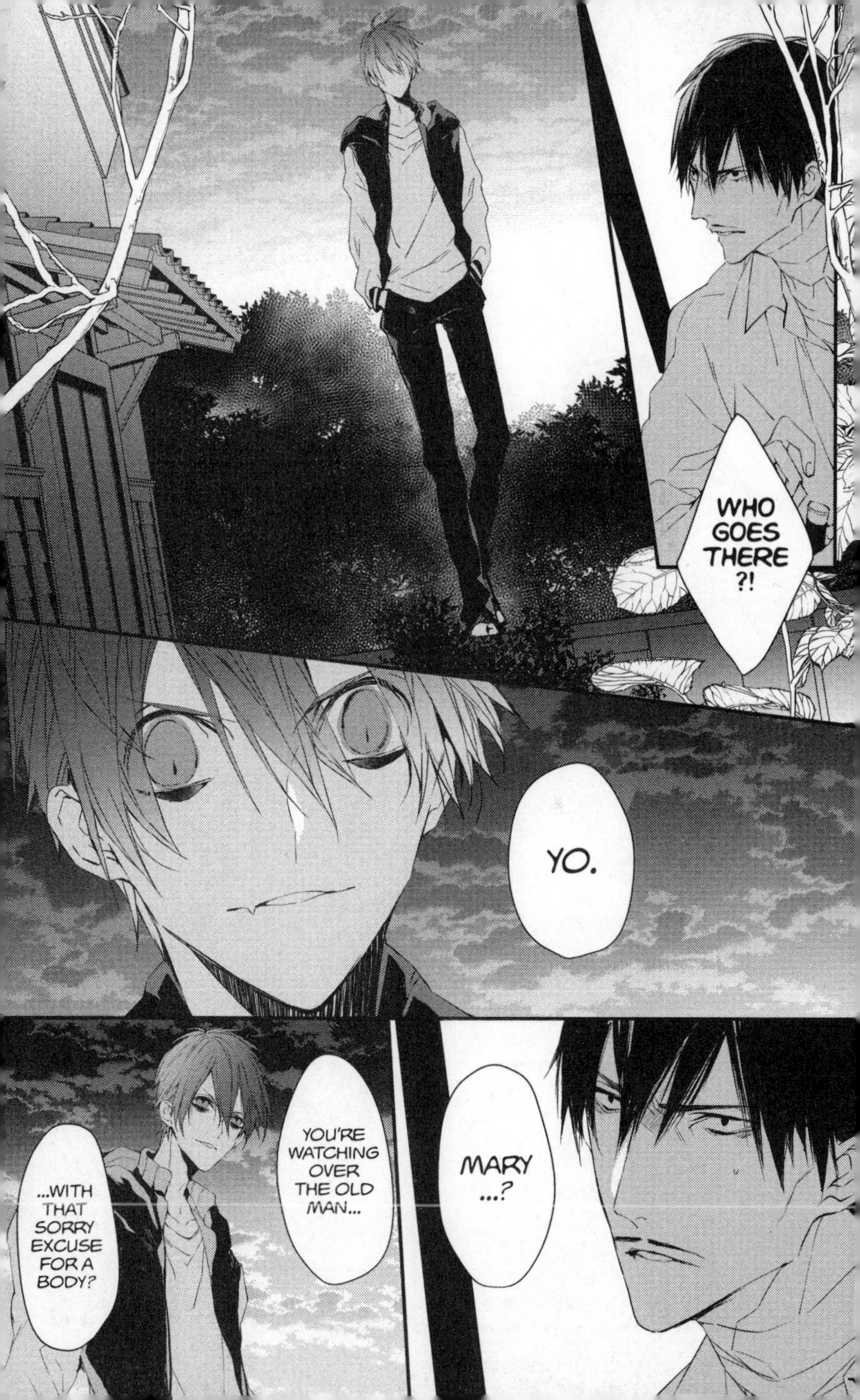
WHO GOES THERE?!
YO.
MARY...?
YOU'RE WATCHING OVER THE OLD MAN...
...WITH THAT SORRY EXCUSE FOR A BODY?

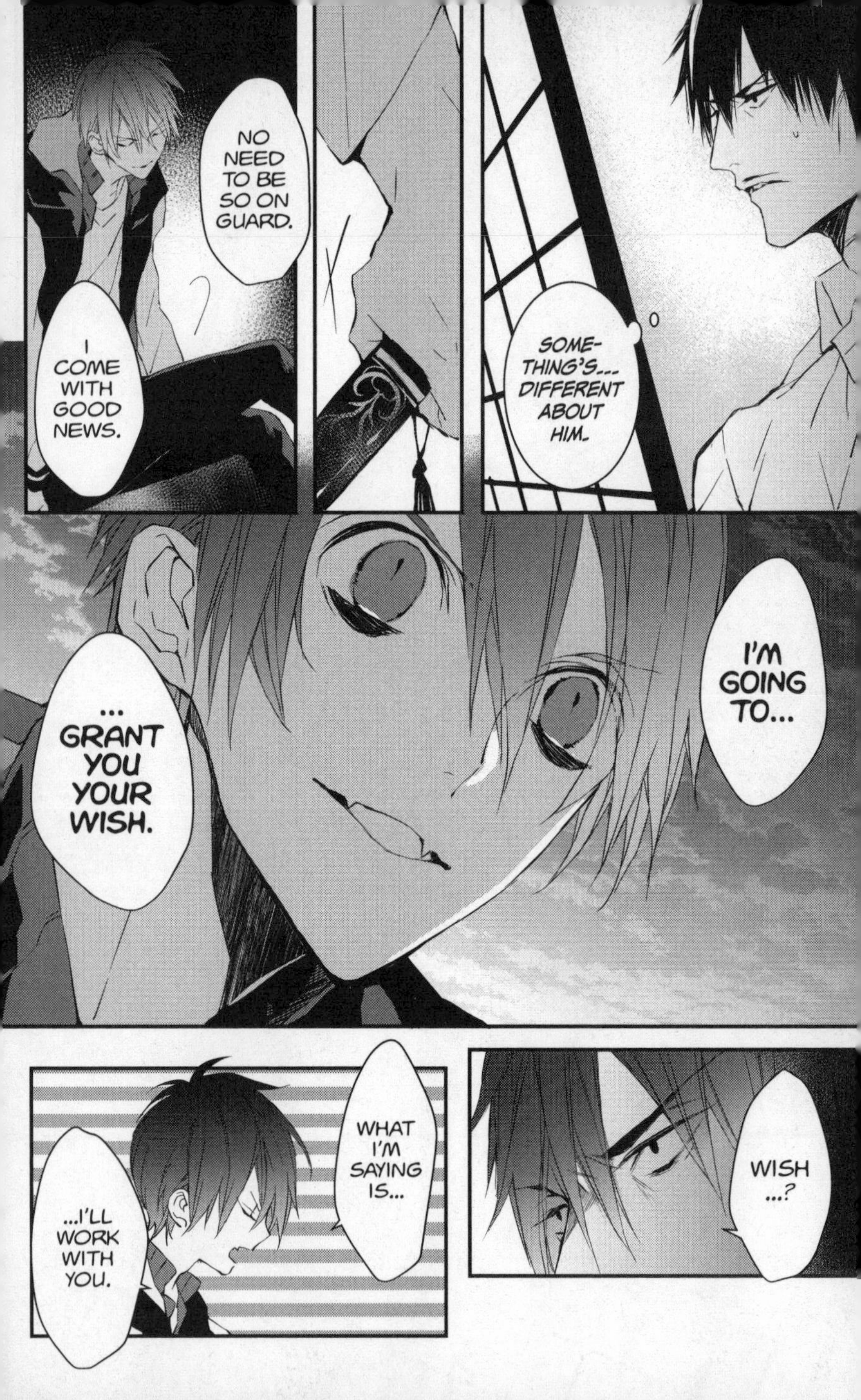
SOMETHING'S... DIFFERENT ABOUT HIM.
NO NEED TO BE SO ON GUARD.
I COME WITH GOOD NEWS.
I'M GOING TO...
...GRANT YOU YOUR WISH.
WISH...?
WHAT I'M SAYING IS...
...I'LL WORK WITH YOU.

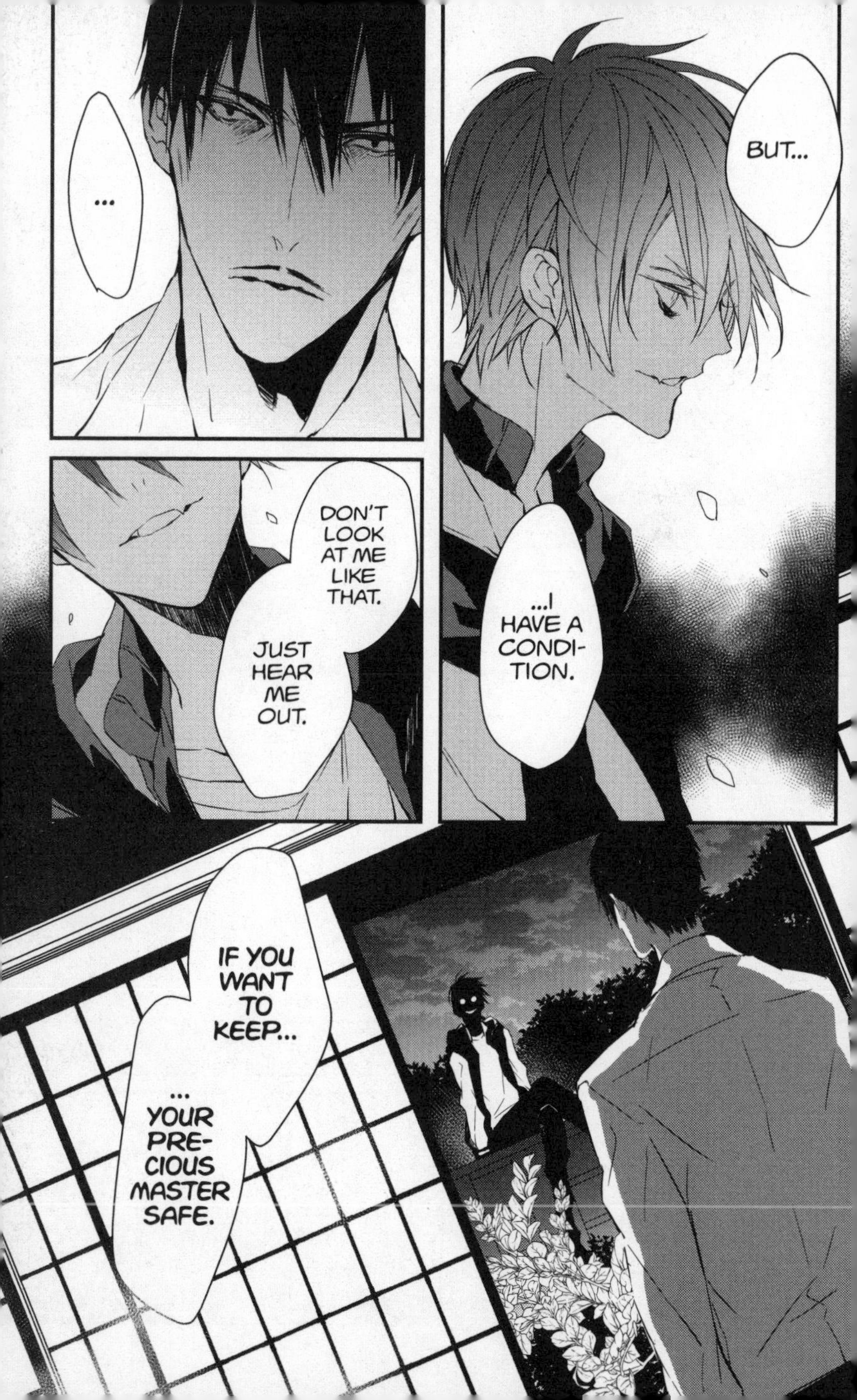
BUT...
...I HAVE A CONDITION.
...
DON'T LOOK AT ME LIKE THAT.
JUST HEAR ME OUT.
IF YOU WANT TO KEEP...
... YOUR PRECIOUS MASTER SAFE.

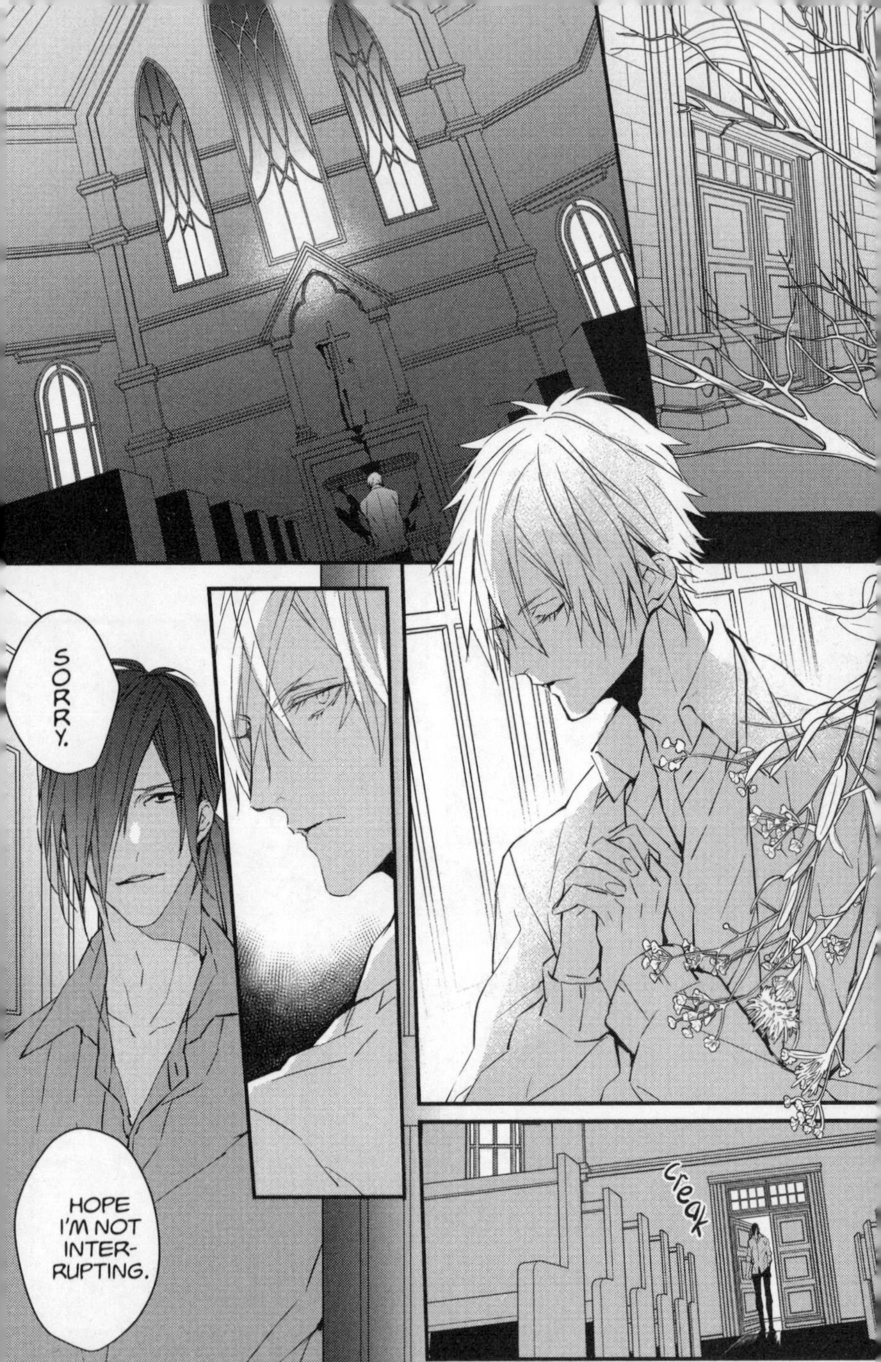
creak
SORRY.
HOPE I'M NOT INTER-RUPTING.

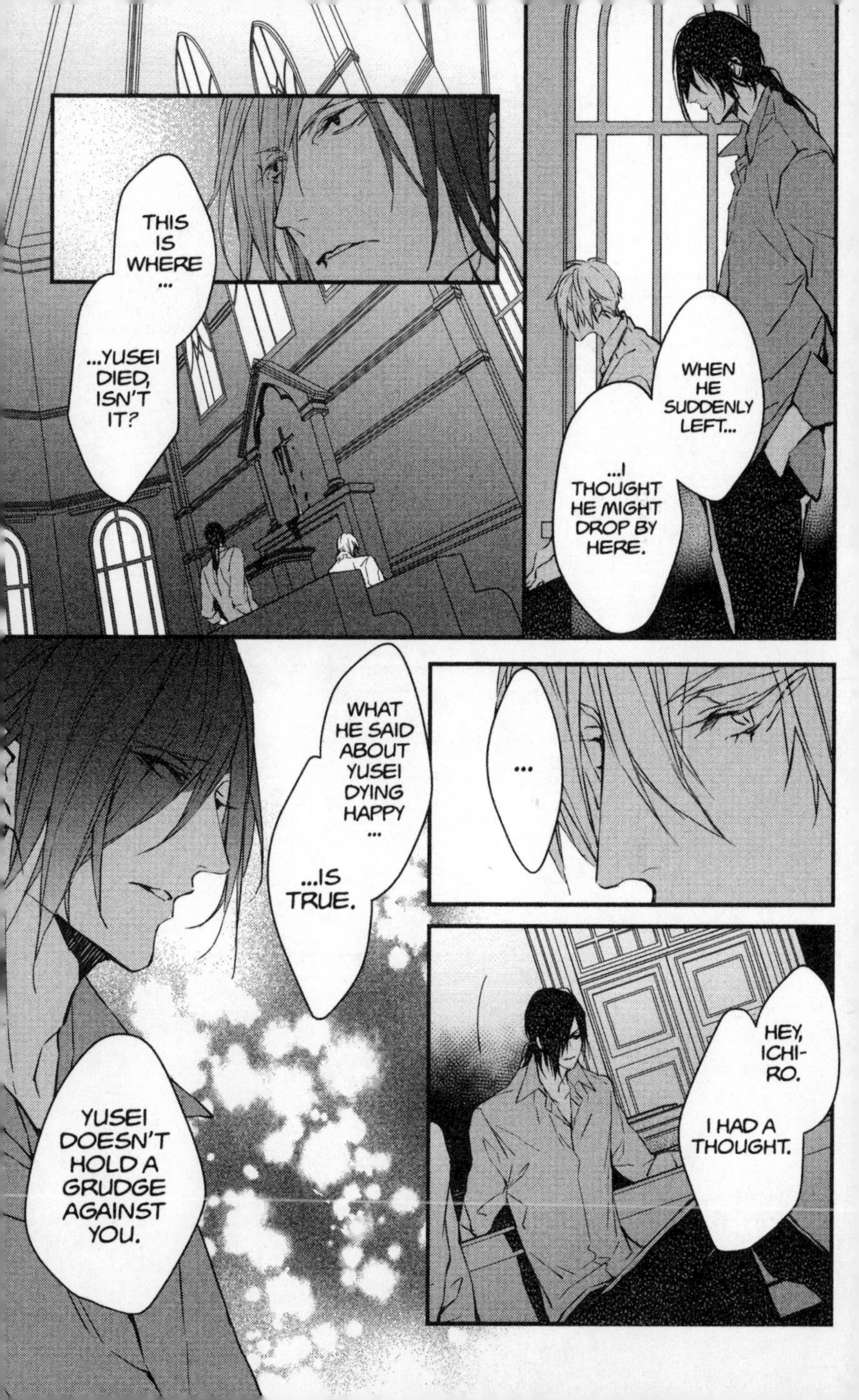
WHEN HE SUDDENLY LEFT...
...I THOUGHT HE MIGHT DROP BY HERE.
THIS IS WHERE...
...YUSEI DIED, ISN'T IT?
...
HEY, ICHIRO.
I HAD A THOUGHT.
WHAT HE SAID ABOUT YUSEI DYING HAPPY...
...IS TRUE.
YUSEI DOESN'T HOLD A GRUDGE AGAINST YOU.

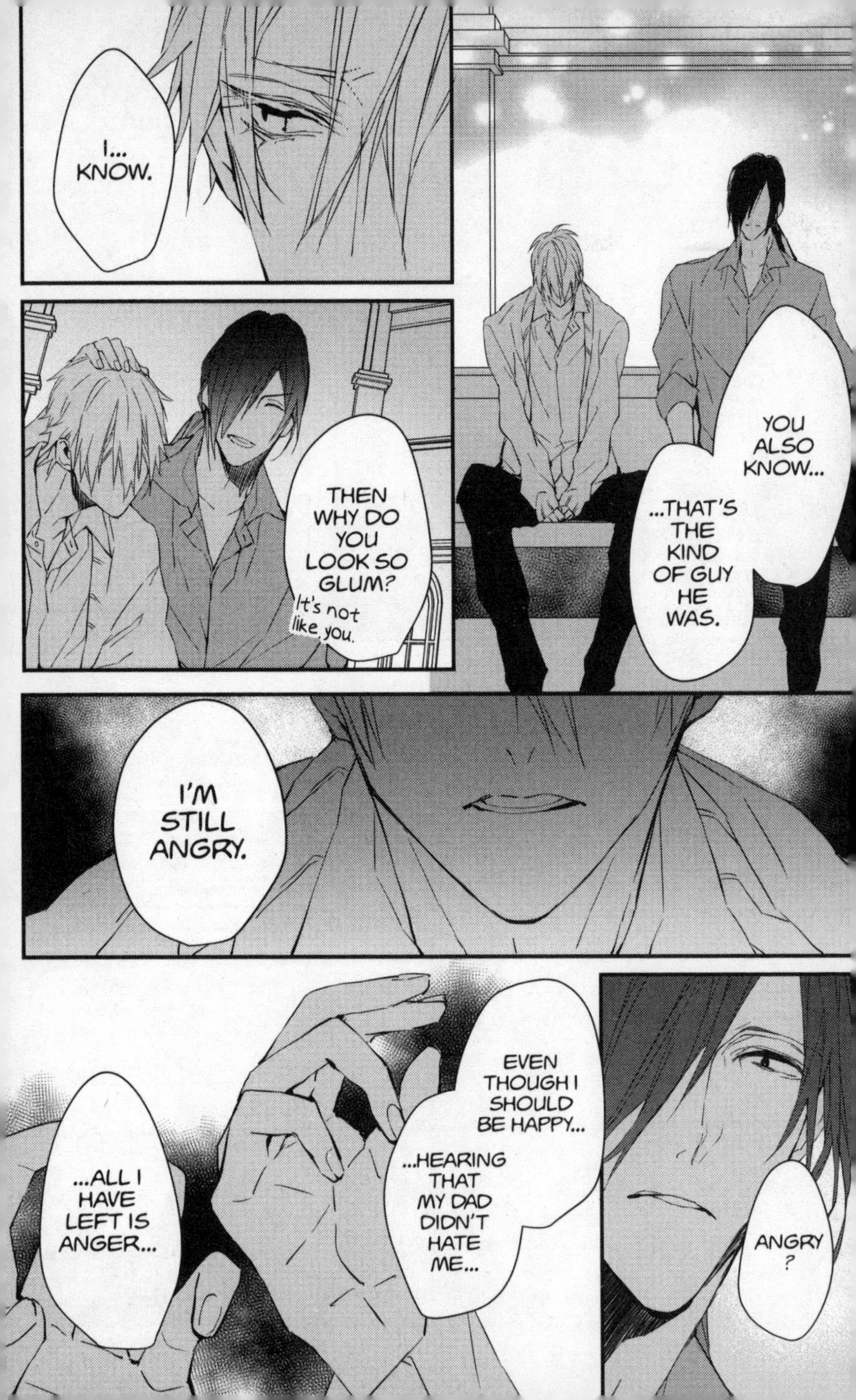
YOU ALSO KNOW...
...THAT'S THE KIND OF GUY HE WAS.
I... KNOW.
THEN WHY DO YOU LOOK SO GLUM?
It's not like you.
I'M STILL ANGRY.
ANGRY?
EVEN THOUGH I SHOULD BE HAPPY...
...HEARING THAT MY DAD DIDN'T HATE ME...
...ALL I HAVE LEFT IS ANGER...

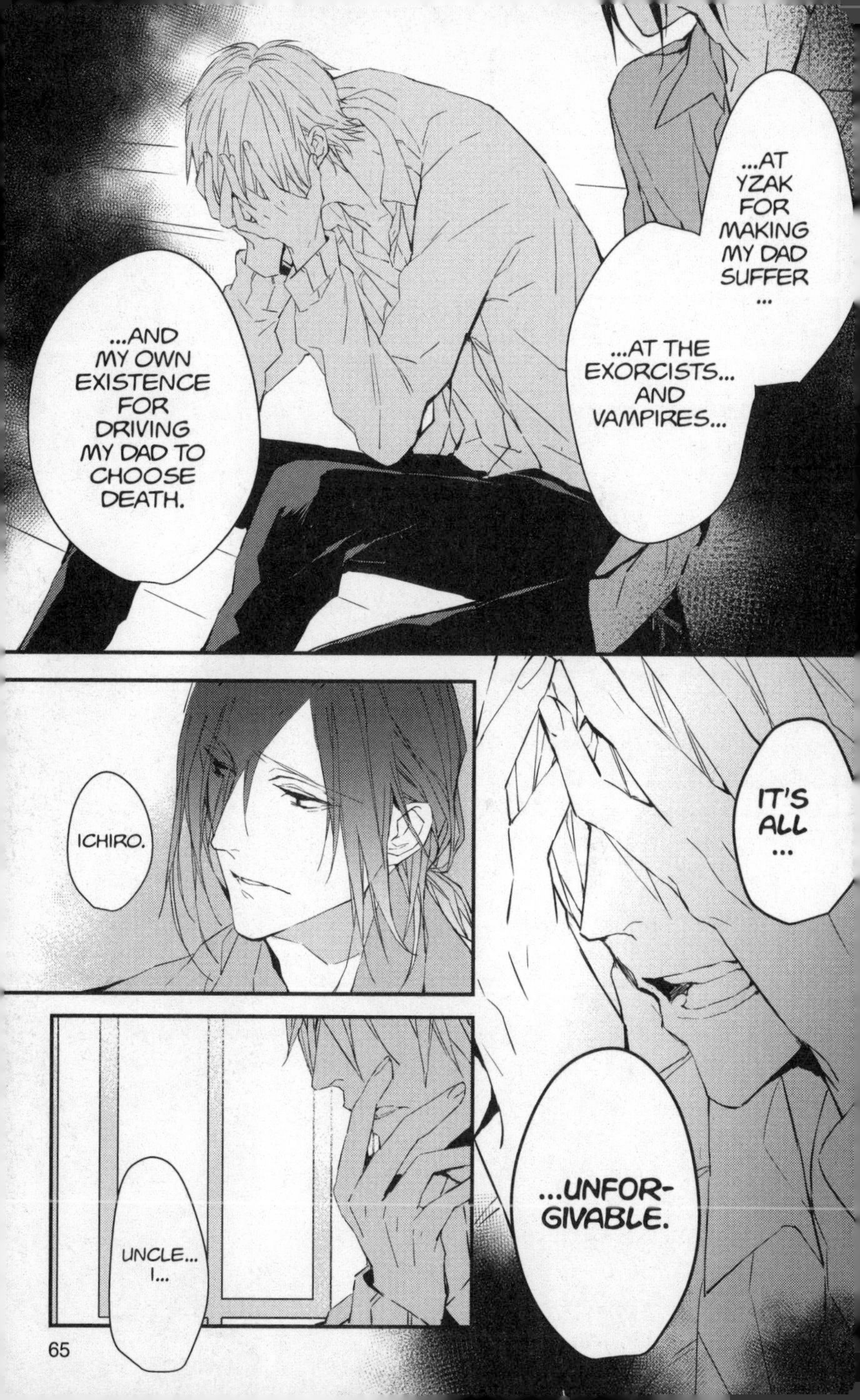
...AT YZAK FOR MAKING MY DAD SUFFER...
...AT THE EXORCISTS... AND VAMPIRES...
...AND MY OWN EXISTENCE FOR DRIVING MY DAD TO CHOOSE DEATH.
IT'S ALL...
...UNFORGIVABLE.
ICHIRO.
UNCLE... I...

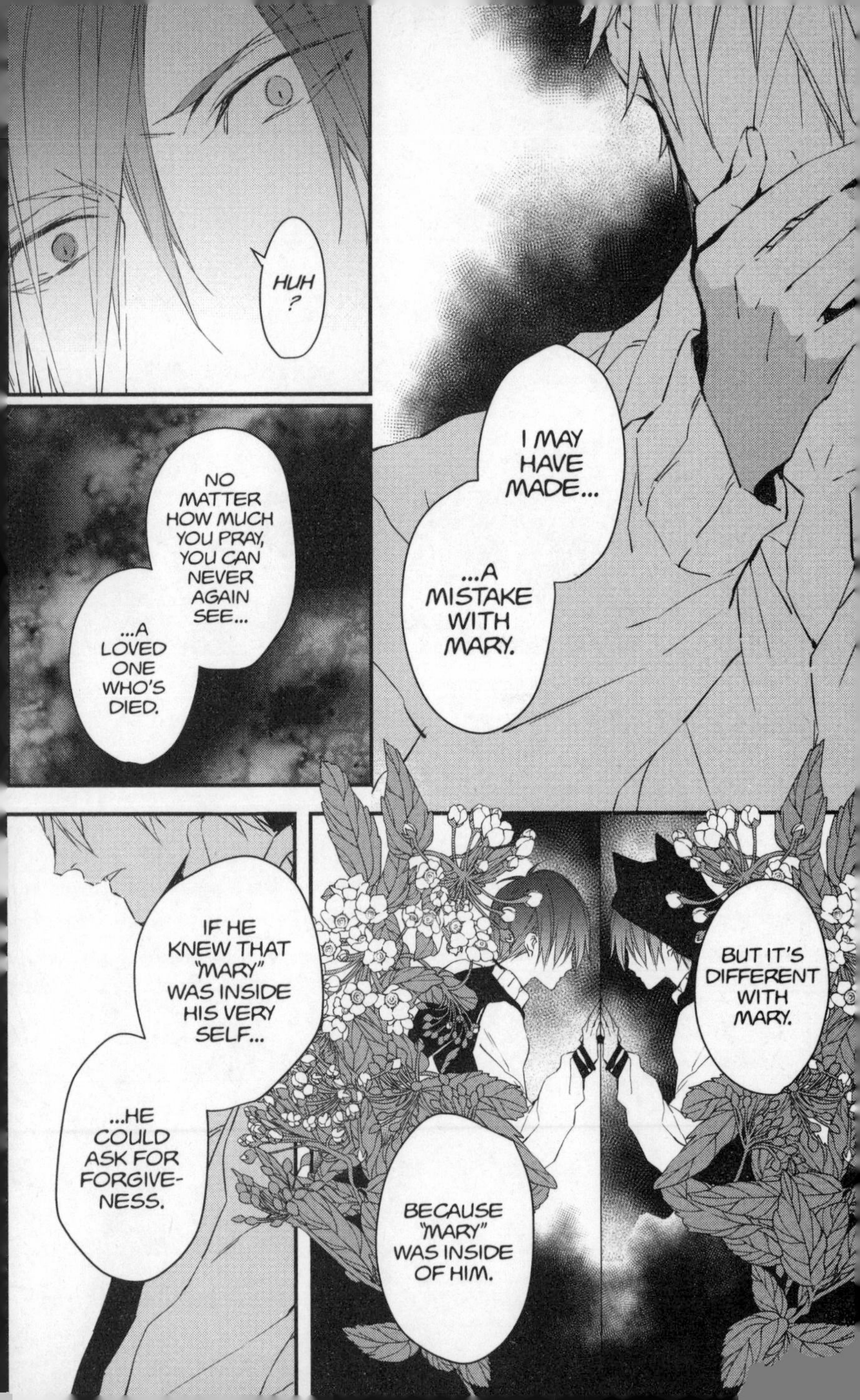
I MAY HAVE MADE...
...A MISTAKE WITH MARY.
HUH?
NO MATTER HOW MUCH YOU PRAY, YOU CAN NEVER AGAIN SEE...
...A LOVED ONE WHO'S DIED.
BUT IT'S DIFFERENT WITH MARY.
BECAUSE "MARY" WAS INSIDE OF HIM.
IF HE KNEW THAT "MARY" WAS INSIDE HIS VERY SELF...
...HE COULD ASK FOR FORGIVE-NESS.

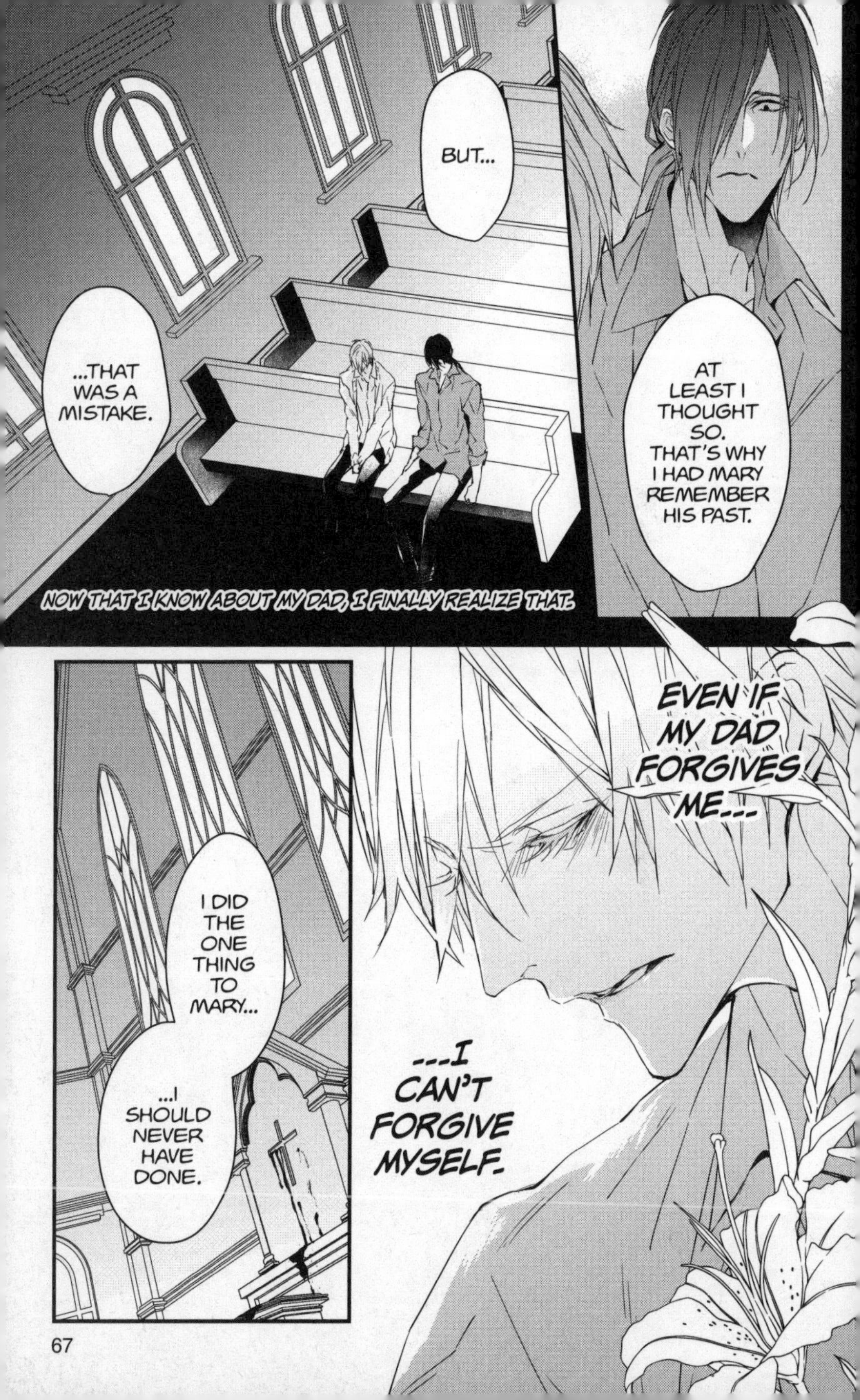
AT LEAST I THOUGHT SO. THAT'S WHY I HAD MARY REMEMBER HIS PAST.
BUT...
...THAT WAS A MISTAKE.
NOW THAT I KNOW ABOUT MY DAD, I FINALLY REALIZE THAT.
EVEN IF MY DAD FORGIVES ME...
...I CAN'T FORGIVE MYSELF.
I DID THE ONE THING TO MARY...
...I SHOULD NEVER HAVE DONE.

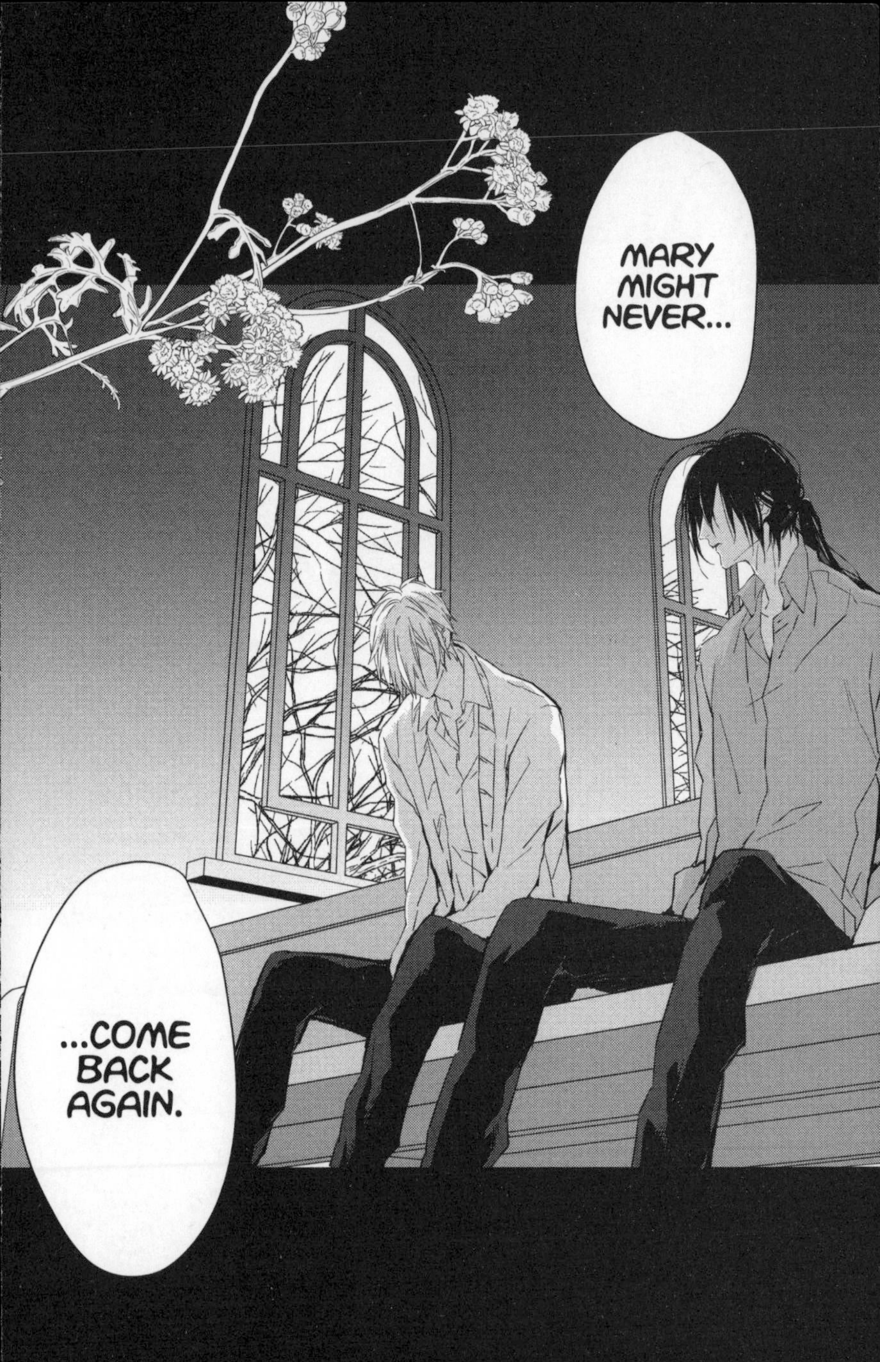
MARY MIGHT NEVER...
...COME BACK AGAIN.

BLOOD ✣ 30 end

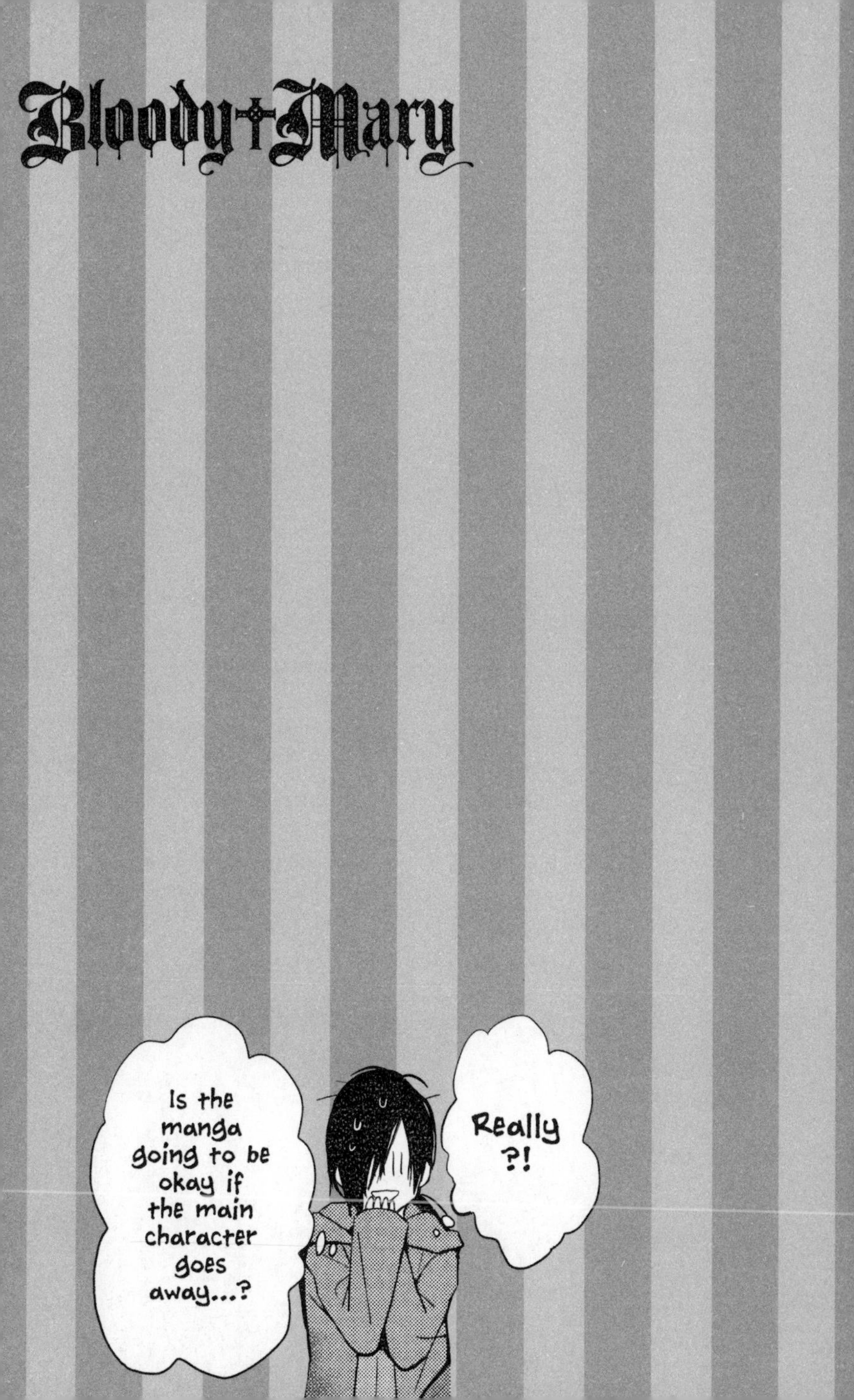
Bloody+Mary
Really ?!
Is the manga going to be okay if the main character goes away...?

Bloody+Mary

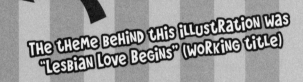

The theme behind this illustration was "Lesbian Love Begins" (working title)

誰も知らない
誰も入れない
ここは二人だけの楽園

It looked so much like that when it was featured in the magazine.
—Editor

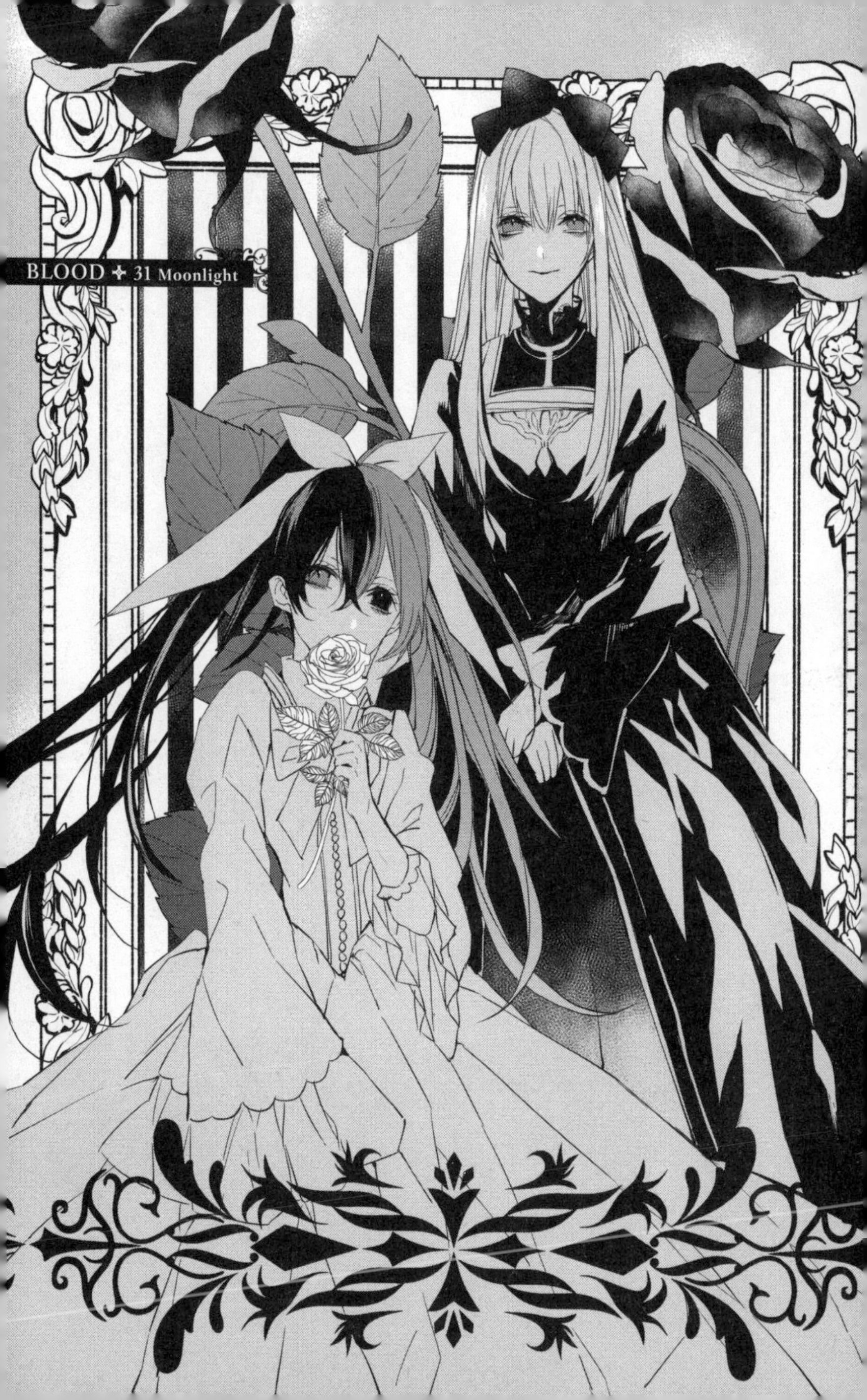
BLOOD ✣ 31 Moonlight

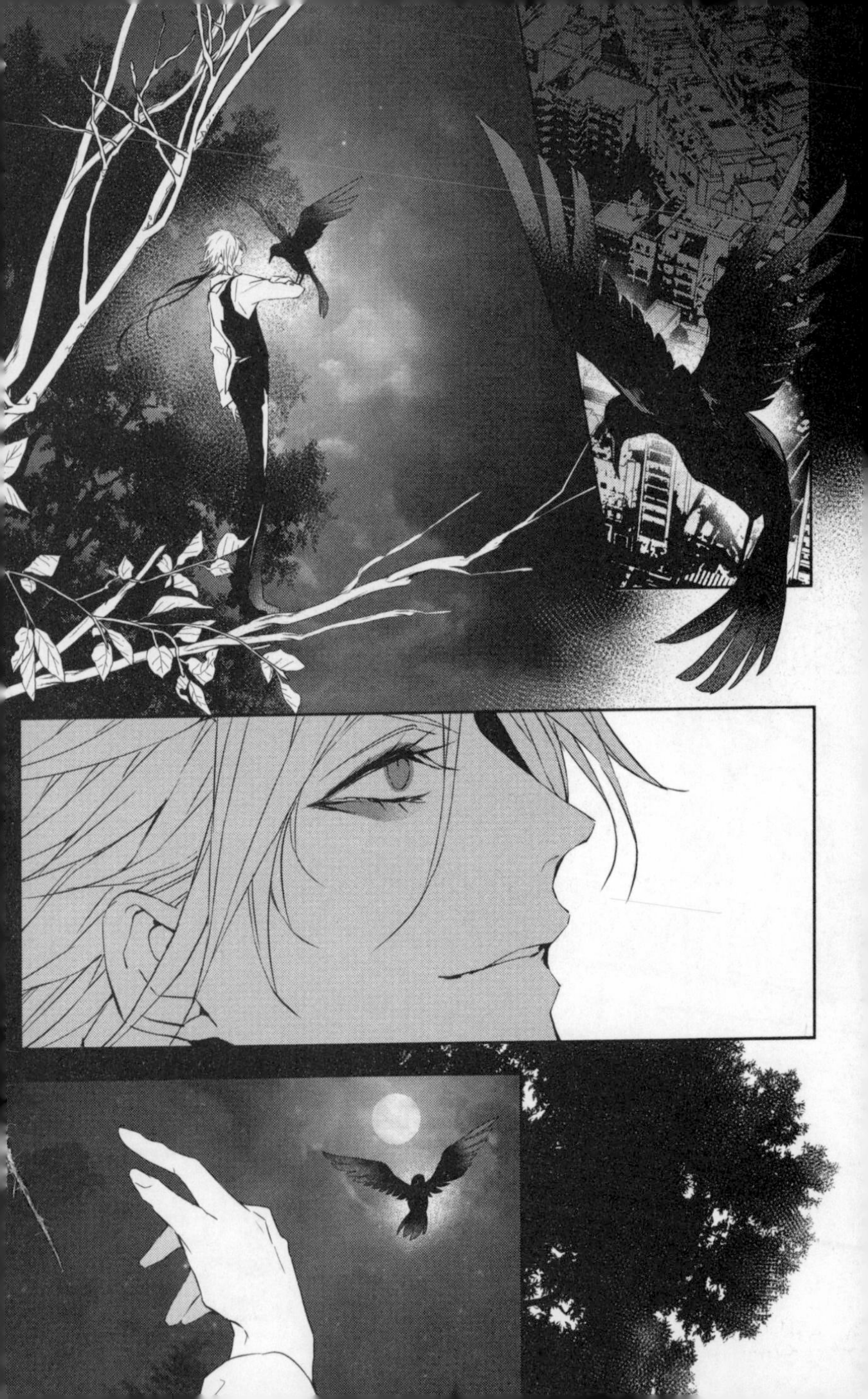

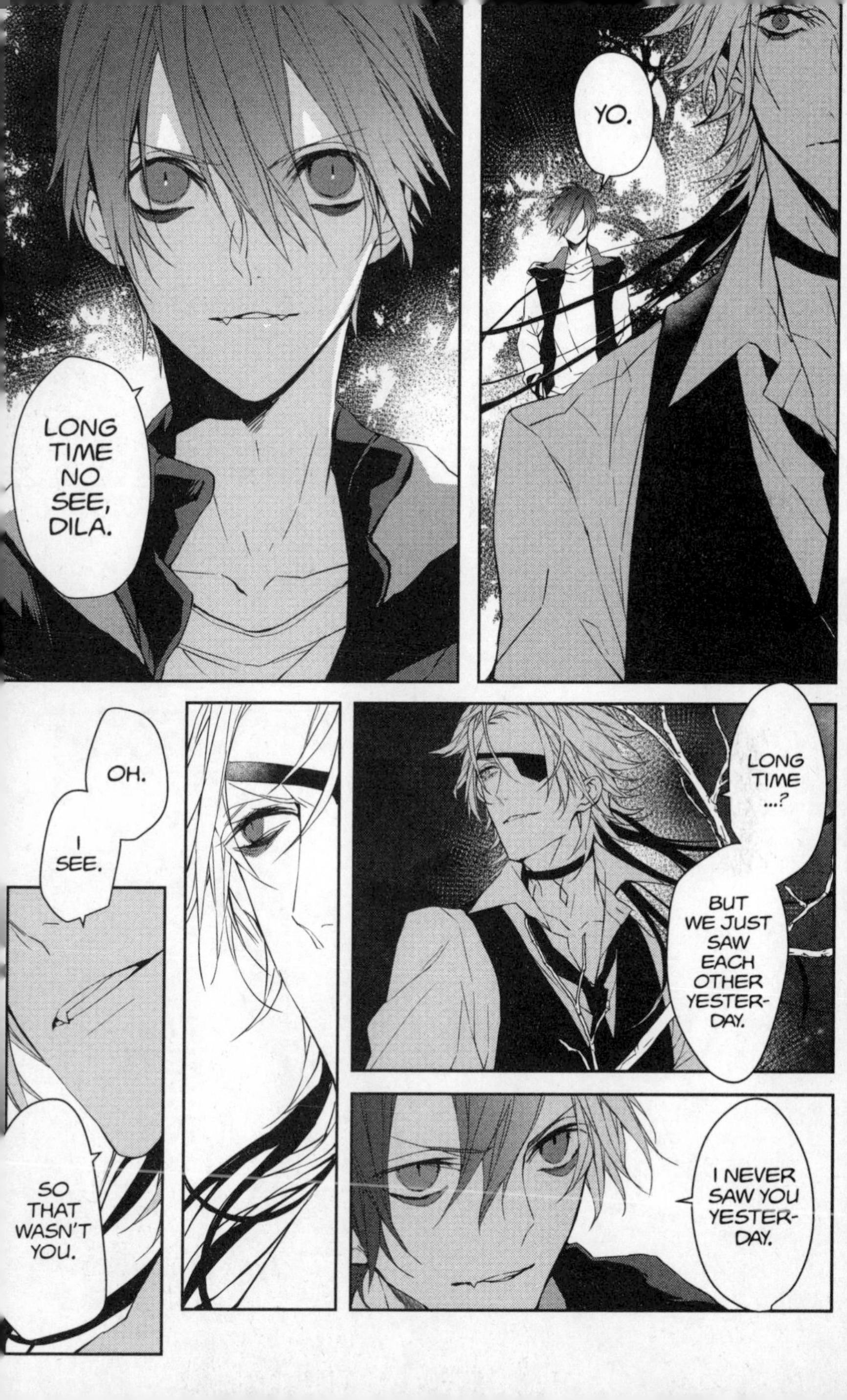
YO.
LONG TIME NO SEE, DILA.
LONG TIME ...?
BUT WE JUST SAW EACH OTHER YESTER-DAY.
I NEVER SAW YOU YESTER-DAY.
OH.
I SEE.
SO THAT WASN'T YOU.

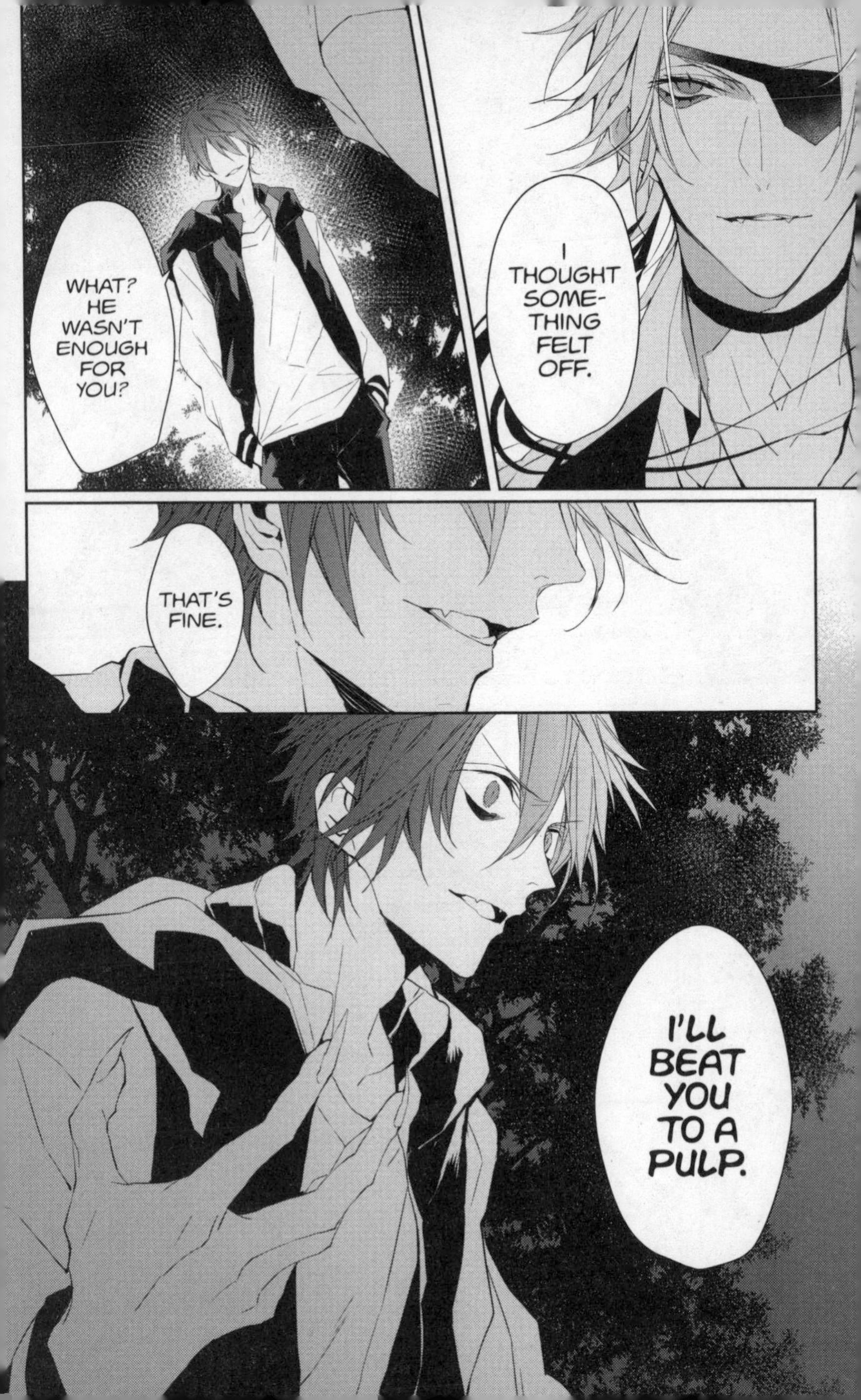
I THOUGHT SOME-THING FELT OFF.
WHAT? HE WASN'T ENOUGH FOR YOU?
THAT'S FINE.
I'LL BEAT YOU TO A PULP.

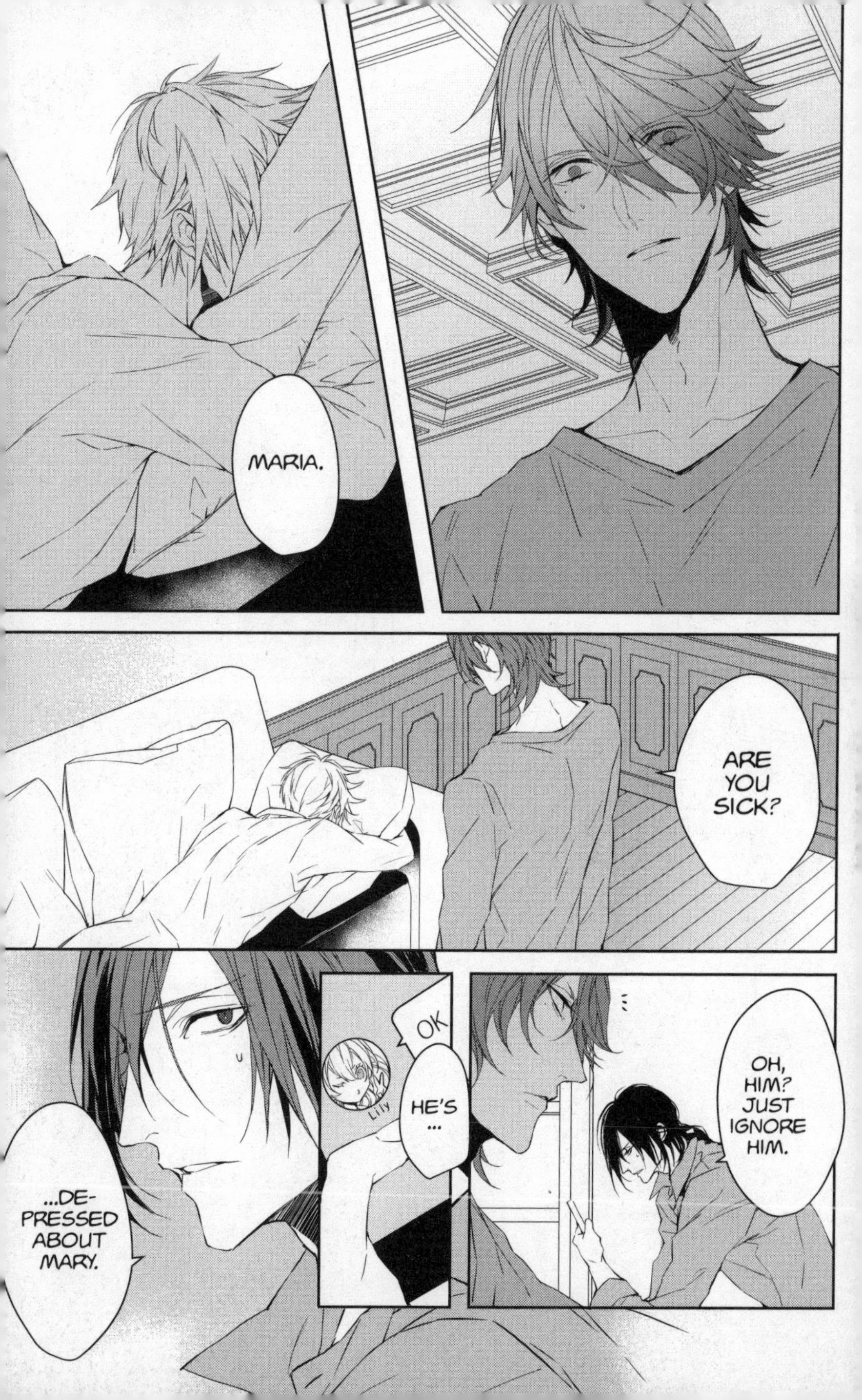
MARIA.
ARE YOU SICK?
OH, HIM? JUST IGNORE HIM.
OK
HE'S ...
Lily
...DE-PRESSED ABOUT MARY.

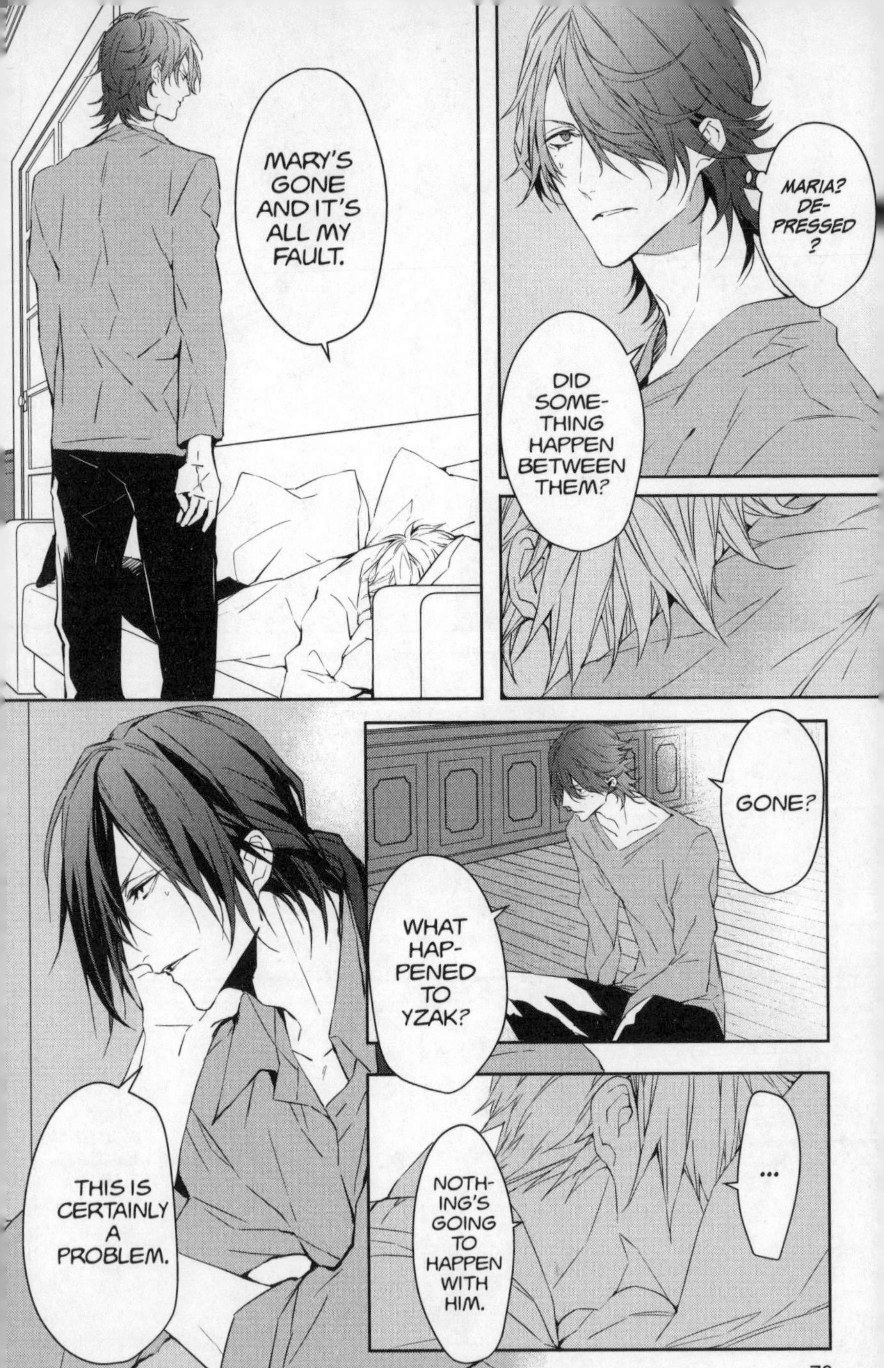
MARIA? DE-PRESSED?
DID SOME-THING HAPPEN BETWEEN THEM?
MARY'S GONE AND IT'S ALL MY FAULT.
GONE?
WHAT HAP-PENED TO YZAK?
...
NOTH-ING'S GOING TO HAPPEN WITH HIM.
THIS IS CERTAINLY A PROBLEM.

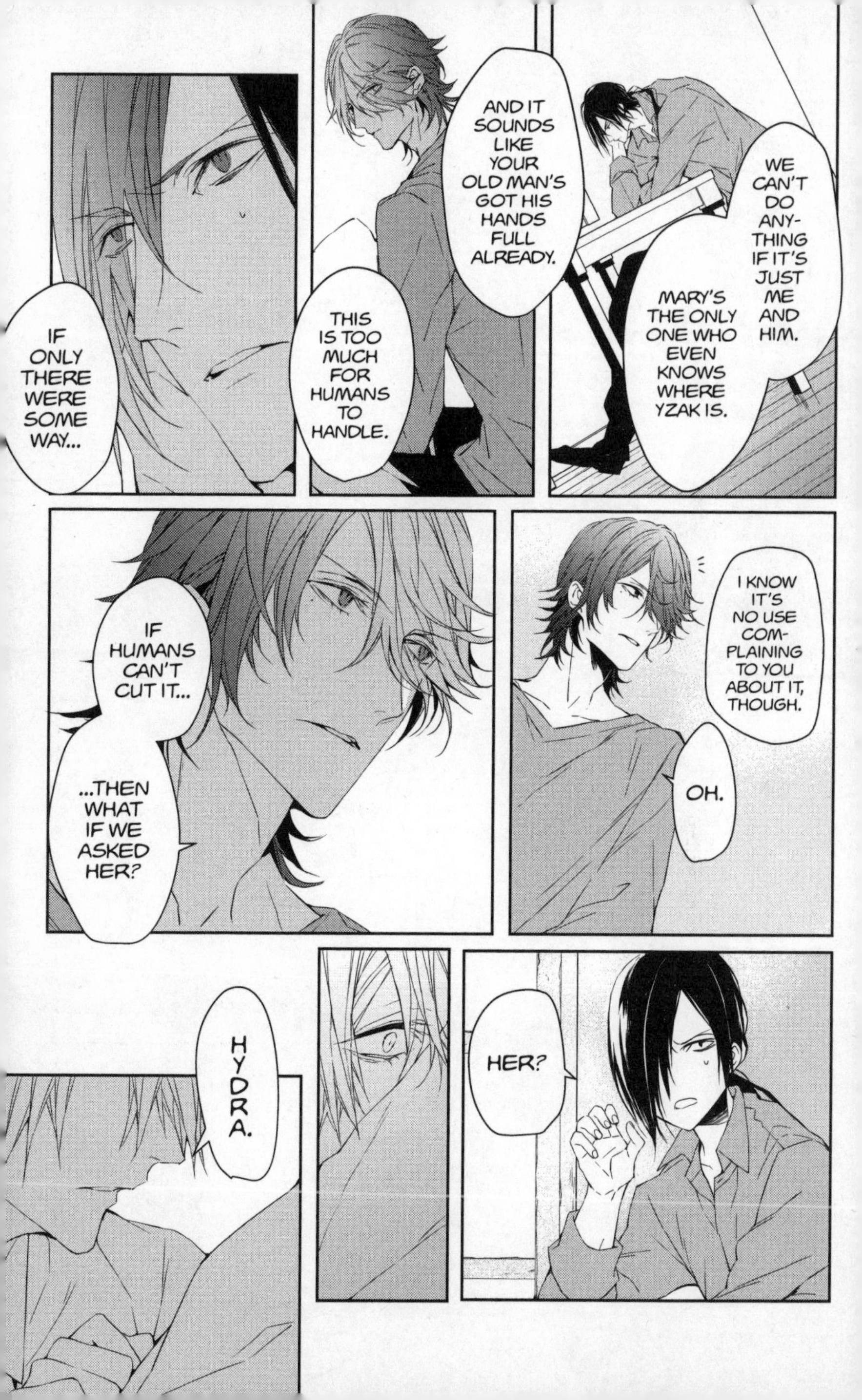
WE CAN'T DO ANYTHING IF IT'S JUST ME AND HIM.
MARY'S THE ONLY ONE WHO EVEN KNOWS WHERE YZAK IS.
AND IT SOUNDS LIKE YOUR OLD MAN'S GOT HIS HANDS FULL ALREADY.
THIS IS TOO MUCH FOR HUMANS TO HANDLE.
IF ONLY THERE WERE SOME WAY...
I KNOW IT'S NO USE COMPLAINING TO YOU ABOUT IT, THOUGH.
OH.
IF HUMANS CAN'T CUT IT...
...THEN WHAT IF WE ASKED HER?
HER?
HYDRA.

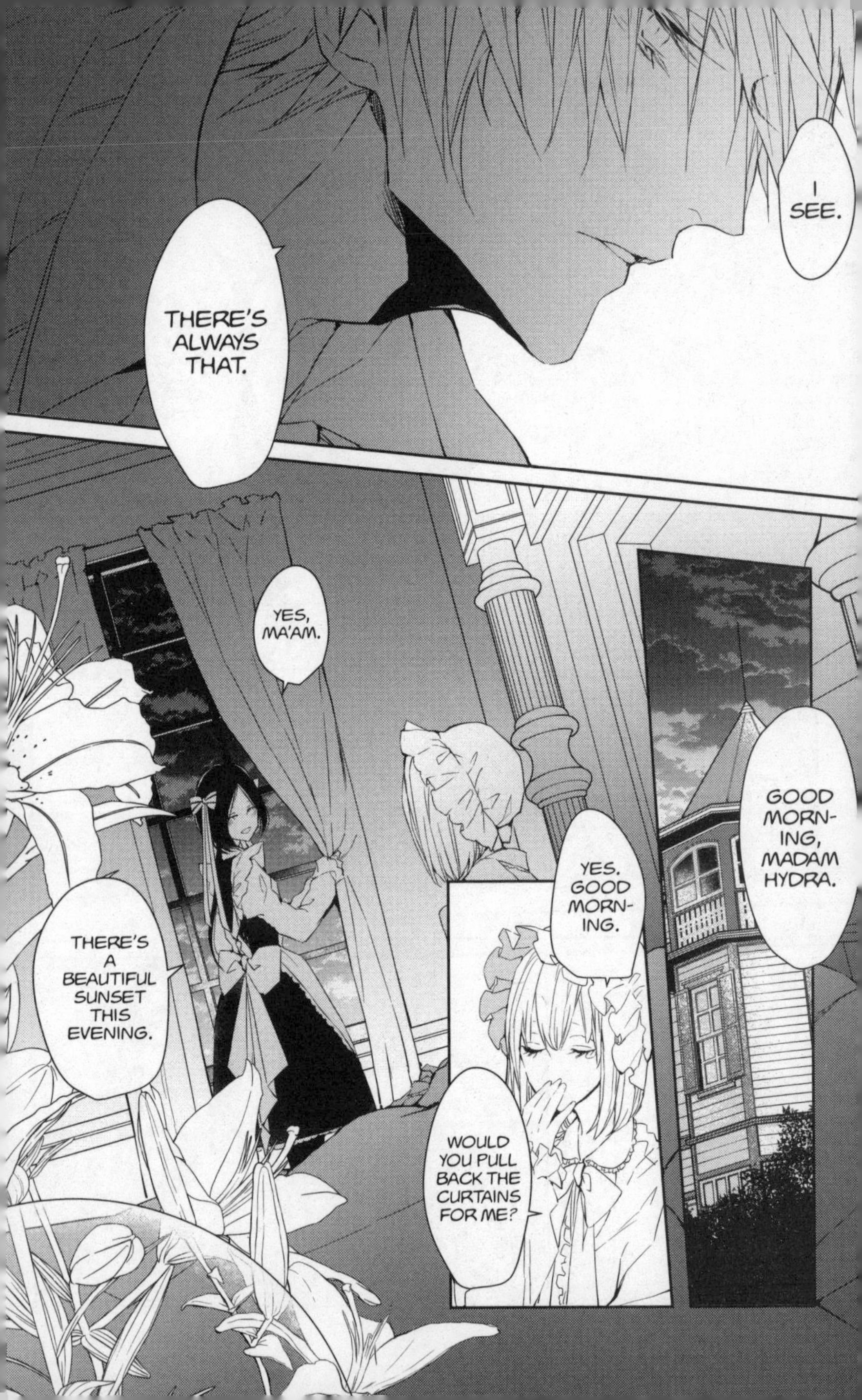
I SEE.
THERE'S ALWAYS THAT.
GOOD MORNING, MADAM HYDRA.
YES. GOOD MORNING.
WOULD YOU PULL BACK THE CURTAINS FOR ME?
YES, MA'AM.
THERE'S A BEAUTIFUL SUNSET THIS EVENING.

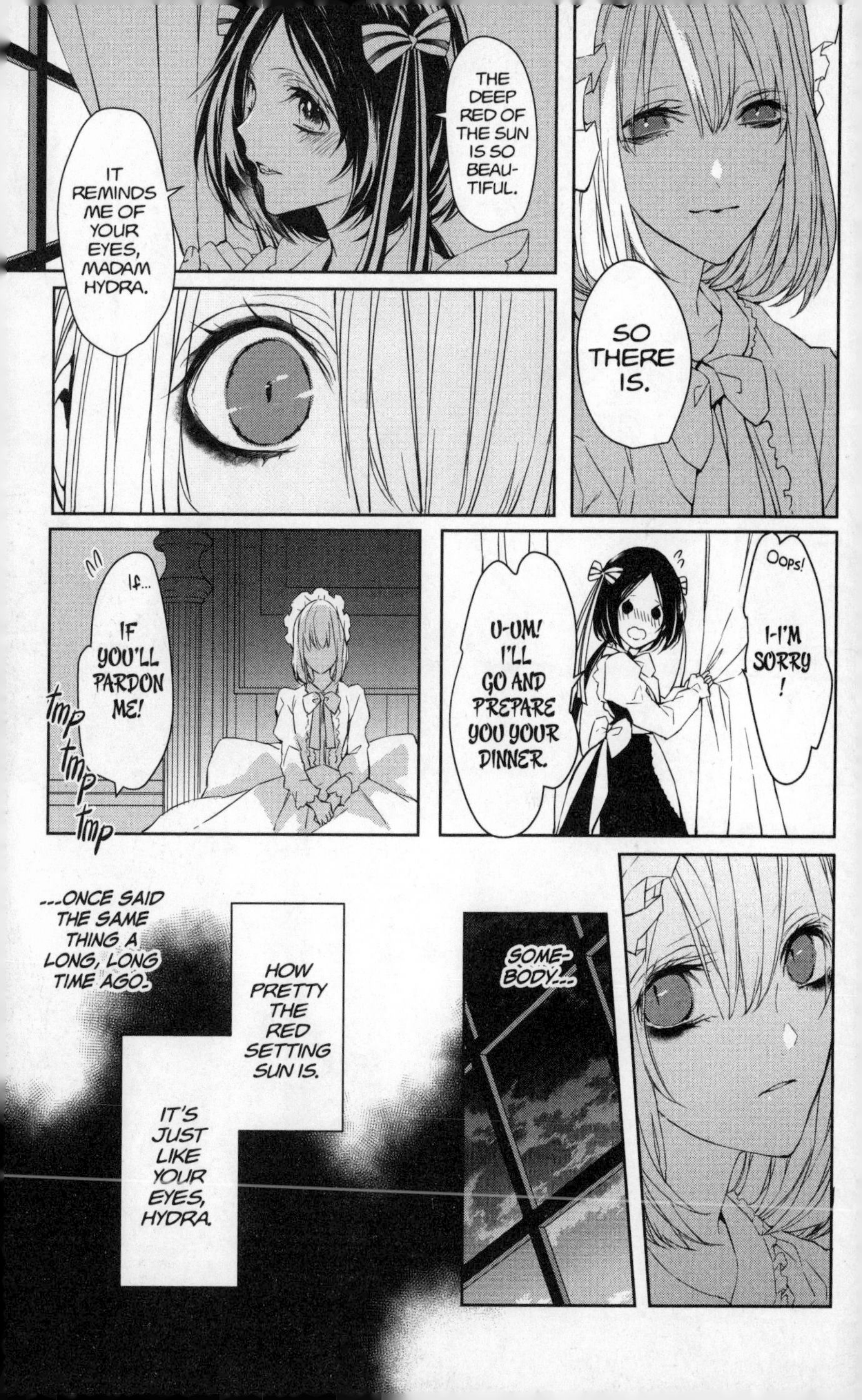
SO THERE IS.
THE DEEP RED OF THE SUN IS SO BEAUTIFUL.
IT REMINDS ME OF YOUR EYES, MADAM HYDRA.
Oops!
I-I'M SORRY!
U-UM! I'LL GO AND PREPARE YOU YOUR DINNER.
If...
IF YOU'LL PARDON ME!
tmp tmp tmp
SOME-BODY...
HOW PRETTY THE RED SETTING SUN IS.
IT'S JUST LIKE YOUR EYES, HYDRA.
...ONCE SAID THE SAME THING A LONG, LONG TIME AGO.

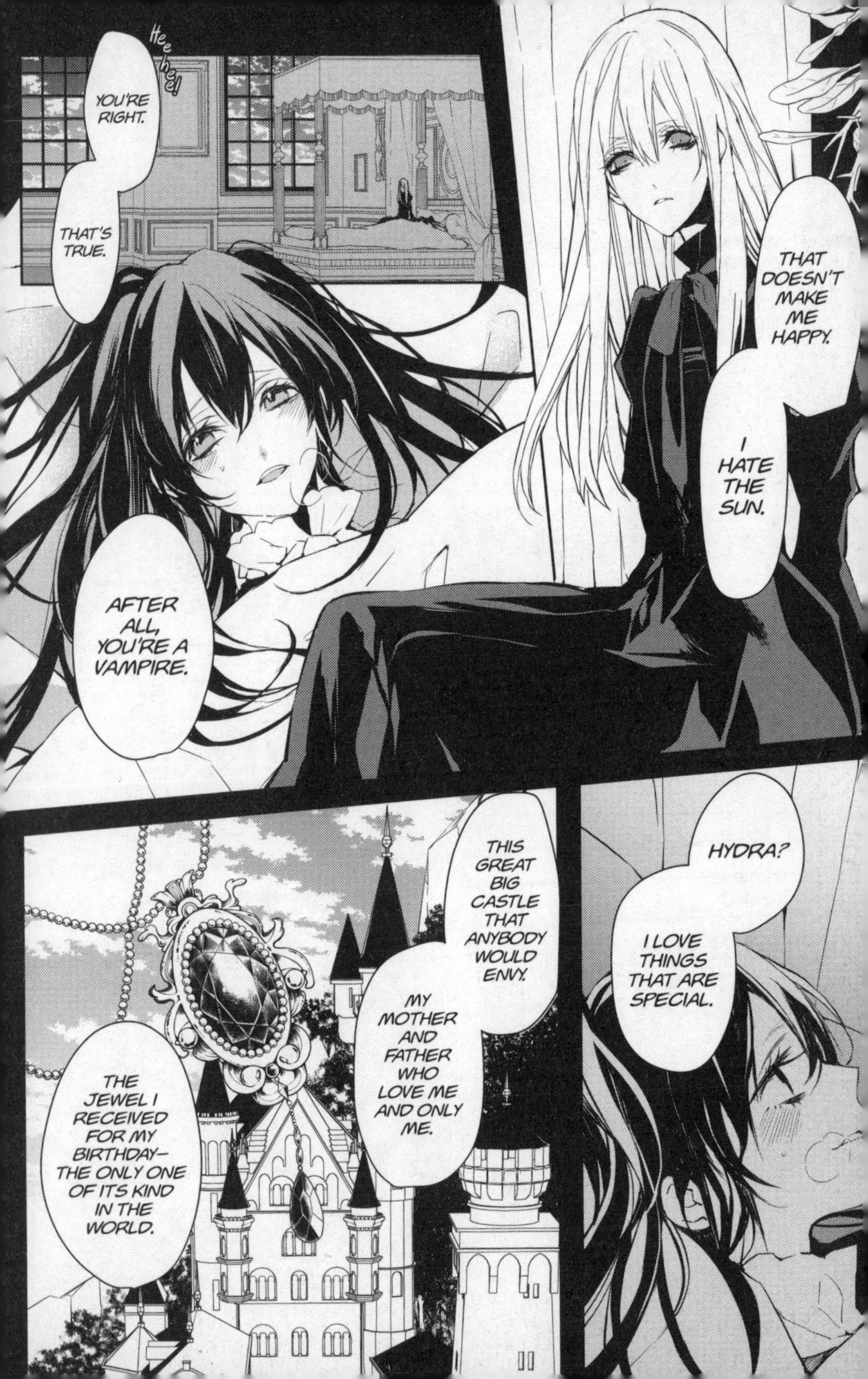
THAT DOESN'T MAKE ME HAPPY.
I HATE THE SUN.
Hee hee!
YOU'RE RIGHT.
THAT'S TRUE.
AFTER ALL, YOU'RE A VAMPIRE.
HYDRA?
I LOVE THINGS THAT ARE SPECIAL.
THIS GREAT BIG CASTLE THAT ANYBODY WOULD ENVY.
MY MOTHER AND FATHER WHO LOVE ME AND ONLY ME.
THE JEWEL I RECEIVED FOR MY BIRTHDAY—THE ONLY ONE OF ITS KIND IN THE WORLD.

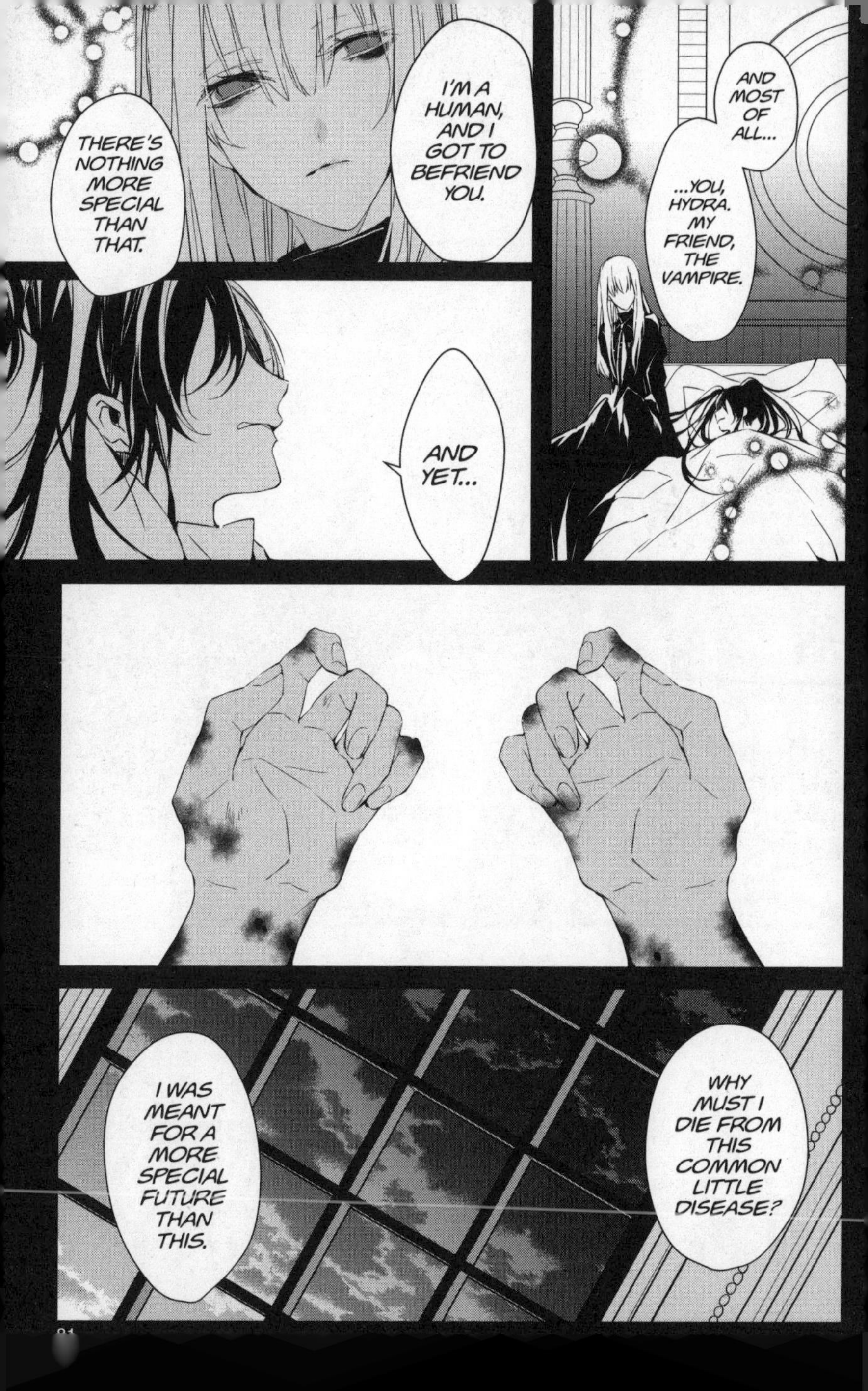
AND MOST OF ALL...
...YOU, HYDRA. MY FRIEND, THE VAMPIRE.
I'M A HUMAN, AND I GOT TO BEFRIEND YOU.
THERE'S NOTHING MORE SPECIAL THAN THAT.
AND YET...
WHY MUST I DIE FROM THIS COMMON LITTLE DISEASE?
I WAS MEANT FOR A MORE SPECIAL FUTURE THAN THIS.

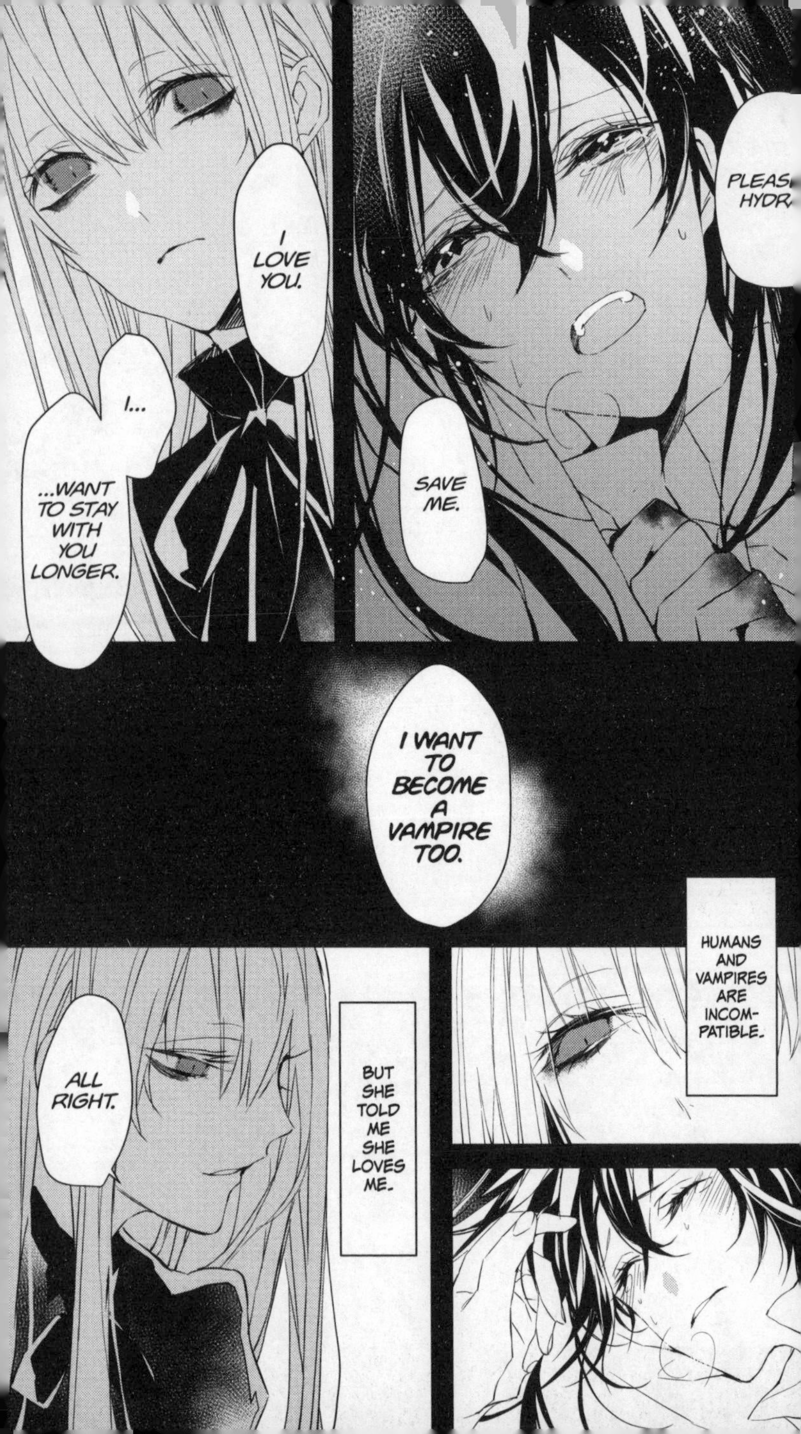
PLEAS HYDR
SAVE ME.
I LOVE YOU.
I...
...WANT TO STAY WITH YOU LONGER.
I WANT TO BECOME A VAMPIRE TOO.
HUMANS AND VAMPIRES ARE INCOMPATIBLE.
BUT SHE TOLD ME SHE LOVES ME.
ALL RIGHT.

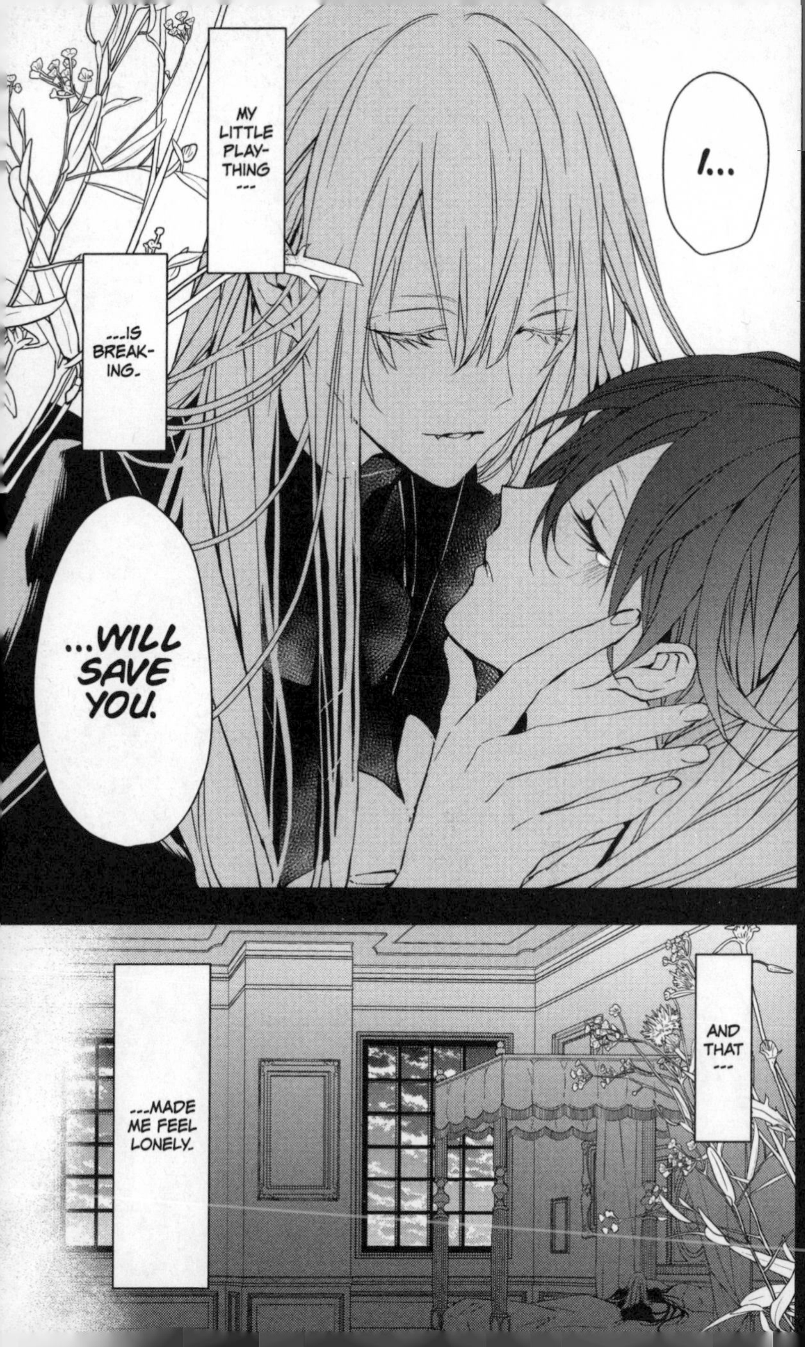
I...
MY LITTLE PLAY-THING---
---IS BREAK-ING.
...WILL SAVE YOU.
AND THAT---
---MADE ME FEEL LONELY.

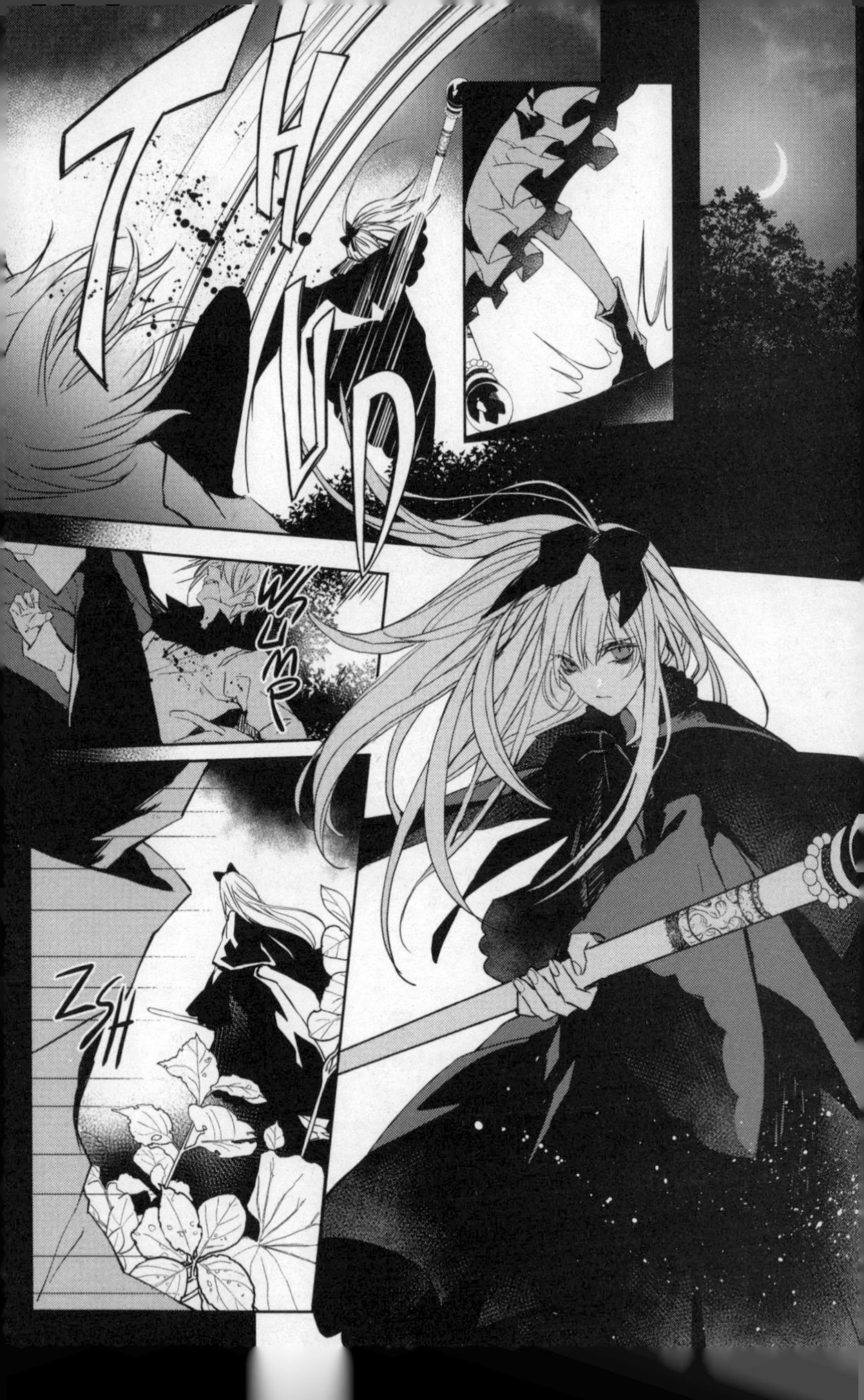
THUD
WHUMP
ZSH

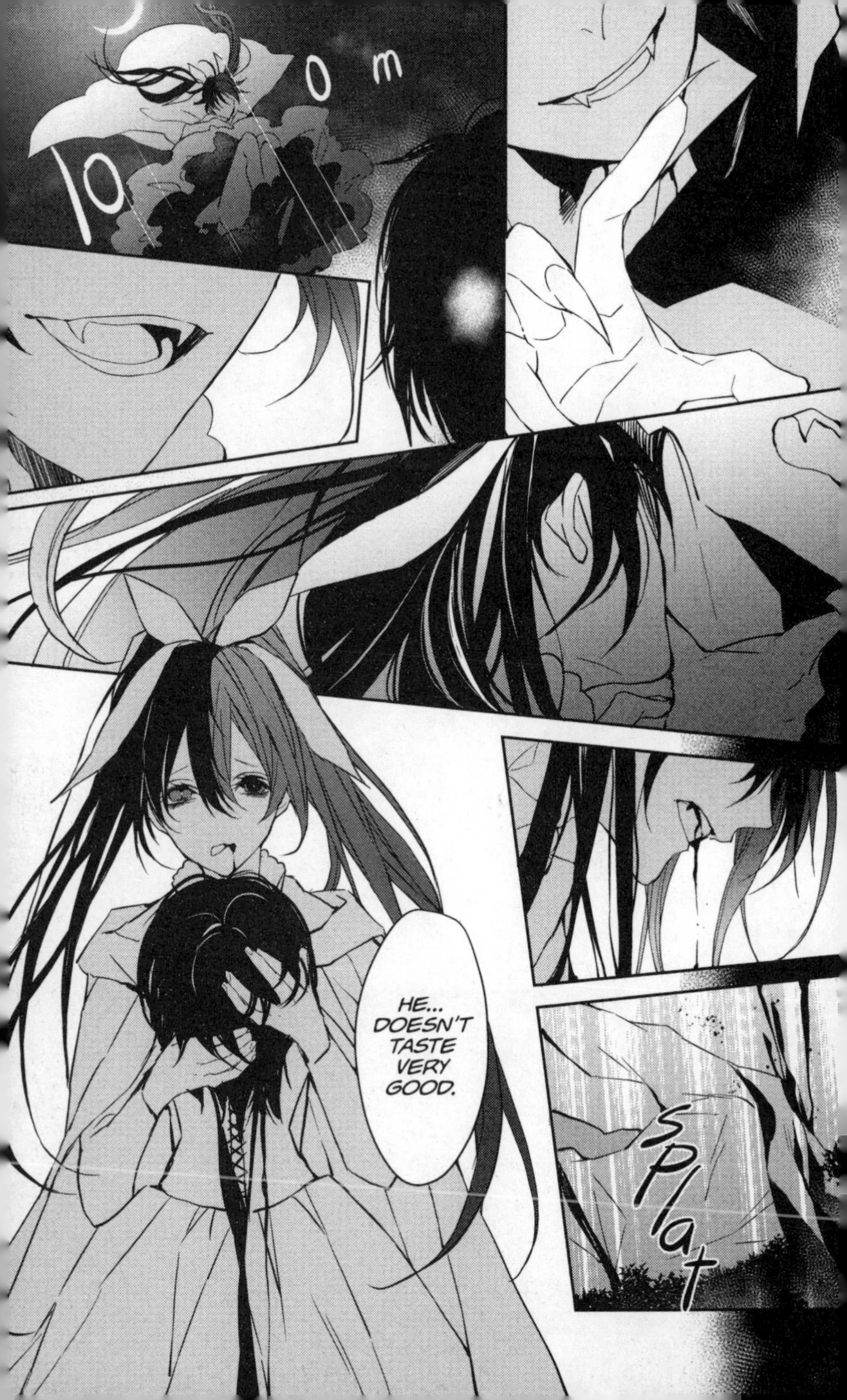

Boom
HE... DOESN'T TASTE VERY GOOD.
Splat

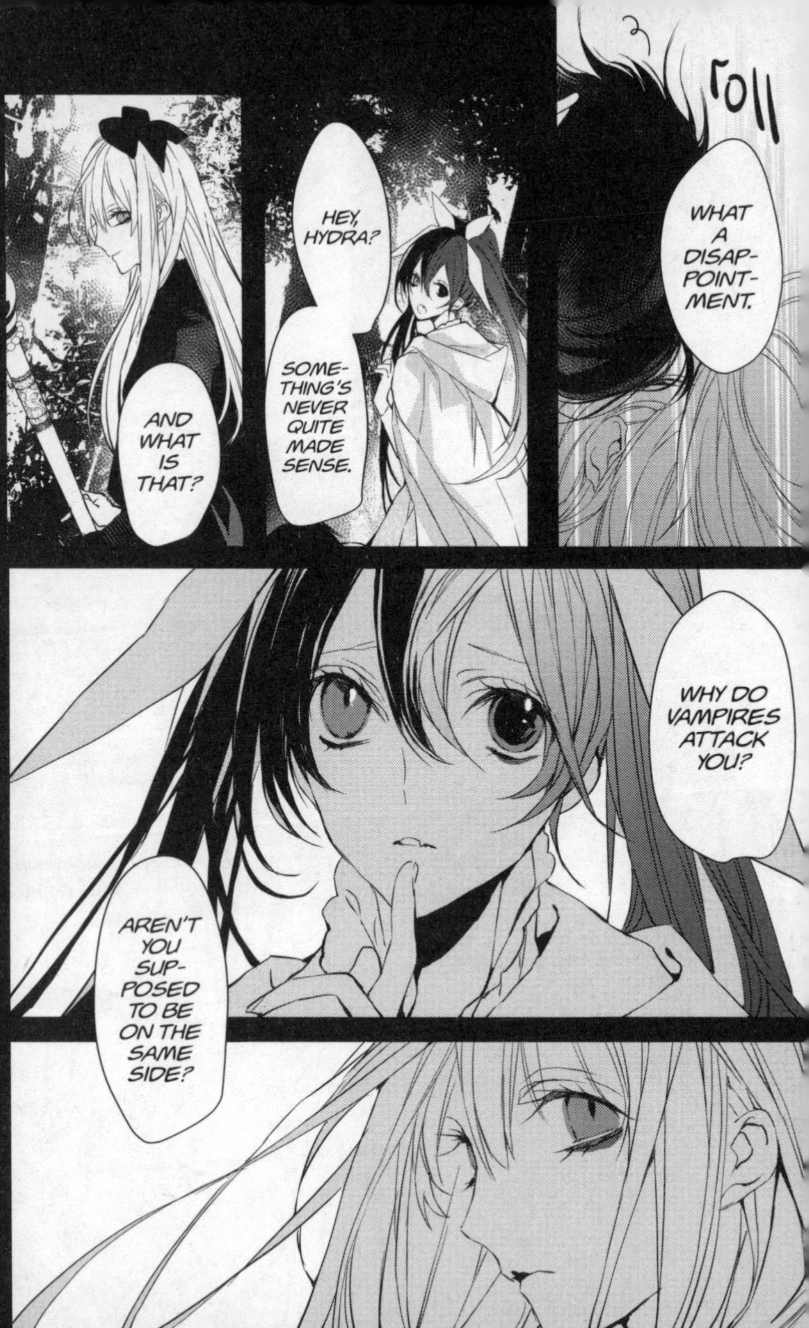
roll
WHAT A DISAPPOINTMENT.
HEY, HYDRA?
SOMETHING'S NEVER QUITE MADE SENSE.
AND WHAT IS THAT?
WHY DO VAMPIRES ATTACK YOU?
AREN'T YOU SUPPOSED TO BE ON THE SAME SIDE?

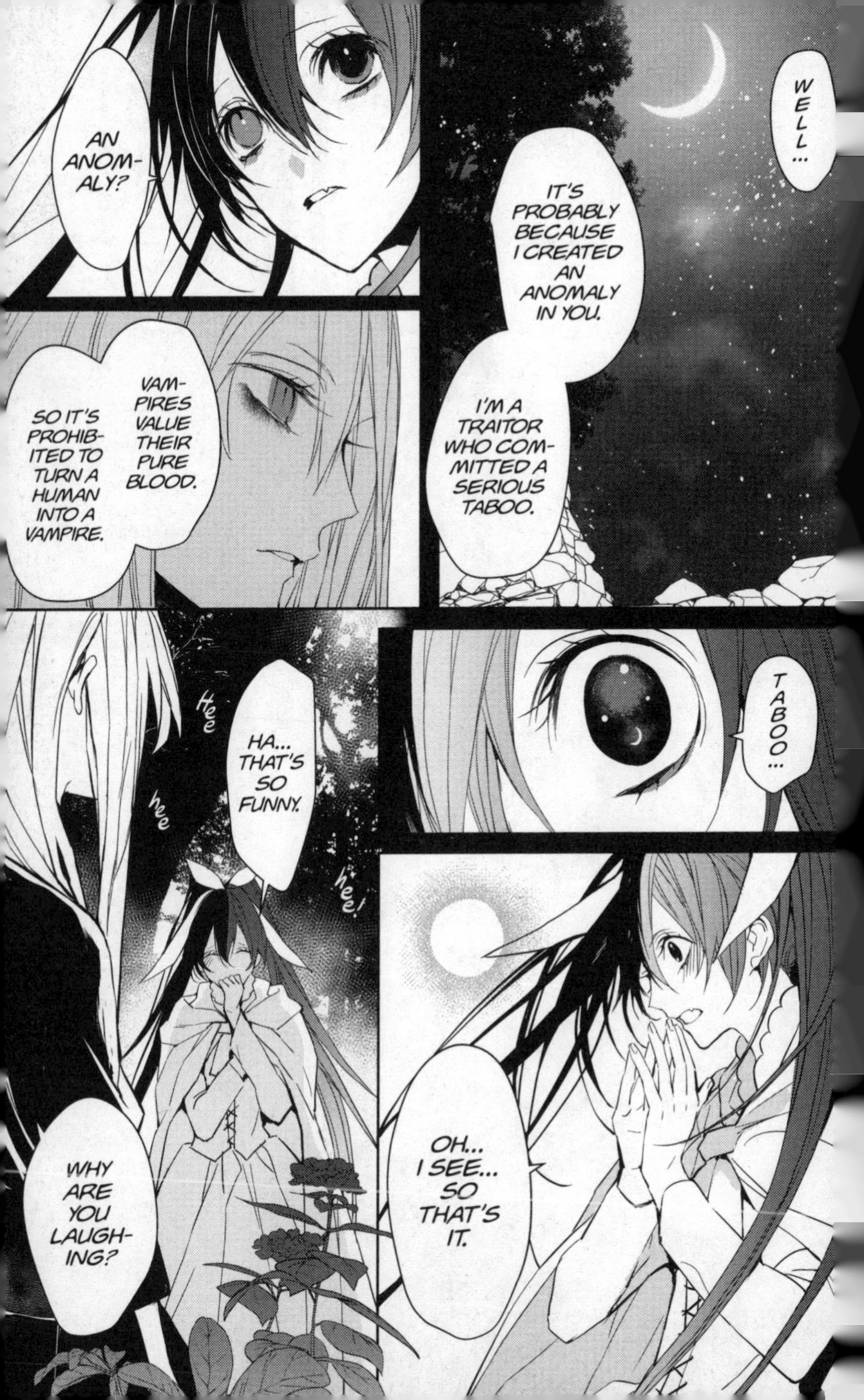
WELL...
IT'S PROBABLY BECAUSE I CREATED AN ANOMALY IN YOU.
I'M A TRAITOR WHO COMMITTED A SERIOUS TABOO.
AN ANOMALY?
VAMPIRES VALUE THEIR PURE BLOOD.
SO IT'S PROHIBITED TO TURN A HUMAN INTO A VAMPIRE.
TABOO...
OH... I SEE... SO THAT'S IT.
Hee hee hee!
HA... THAT'S SO FUNNY.
WHY ARE YOU LAUGHING?

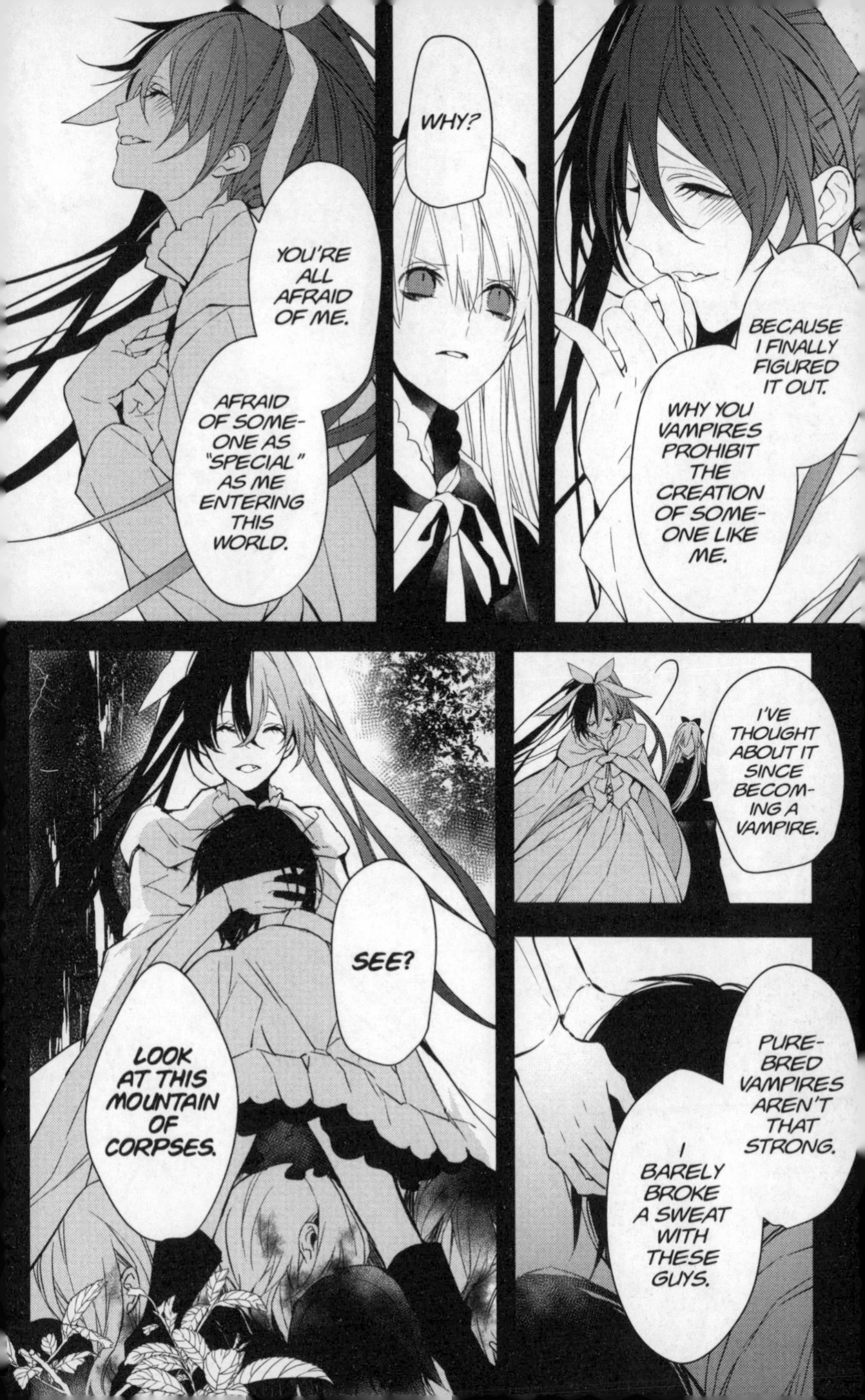
BECAUSE I FINALLY FIGURED IT OUT.
WHY YOU VAMPIRES PROHIBIT THE CREATION OF SOMEONE LIKE ME.
WHY?
YOU'RE ALL AFRAID OF ME.
AFRAID OF SOMEONE AS "SPECIAL" AS ME ENTERING THIS WORLD.
I'VE THOUGHT ABOUT IT SINCE BECOMING A VAMPIRE.
PUREBRED VAMPIRES AREN'T THAT STRONG.
I BARELY BROKE A SWEAT WITH THESE GUYS.
SEE?
LOOK AT THIS MOUNTAIN OF CORPSES.

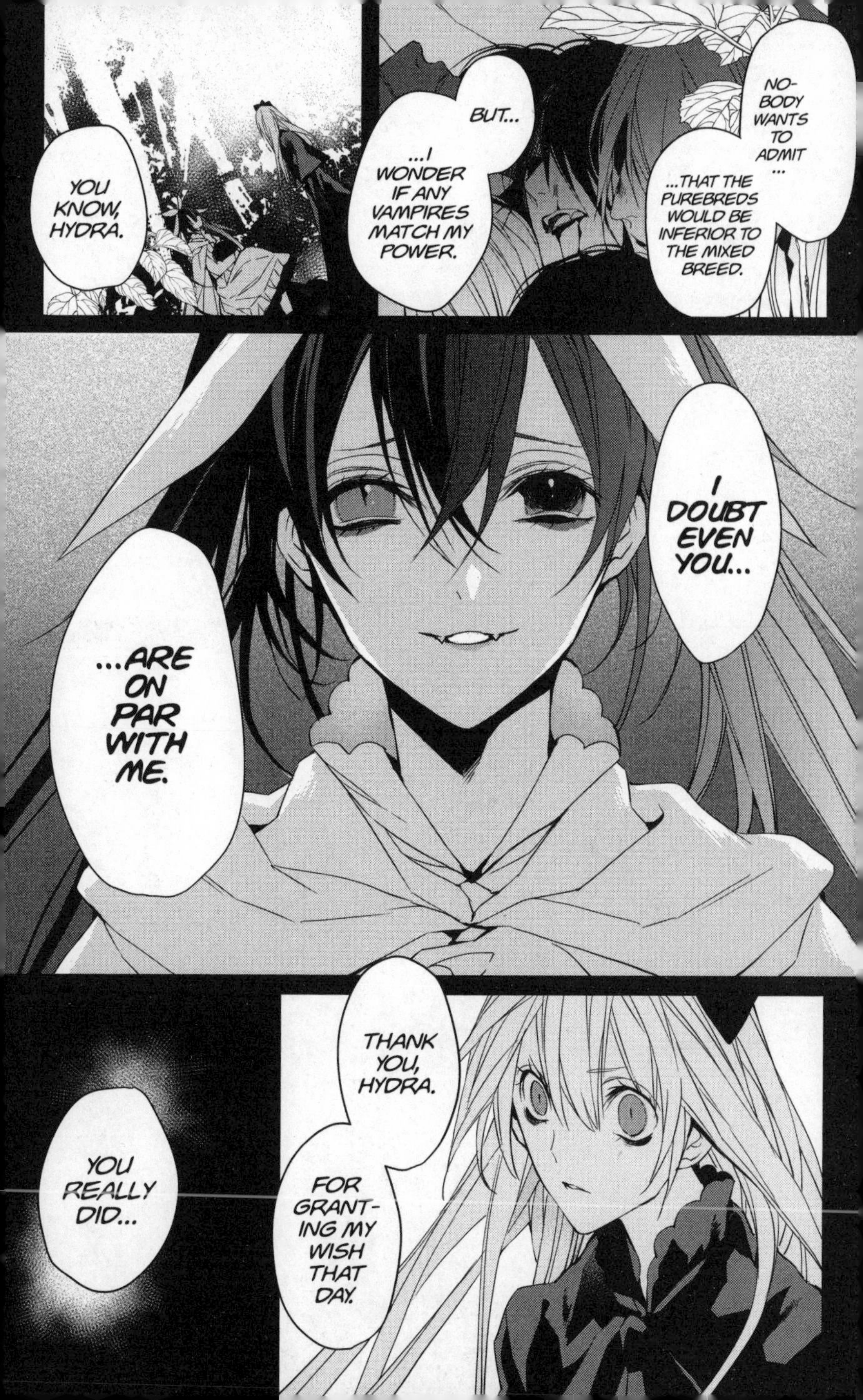
NO-BODY WANTS TO ADMIT...
...THAT THE PUREBREDS WOULD BE INFERIOR TO THE MIXED BREED.
BUT...
...I WONDER IF ANY VAMPIRES MATCH MY POWER.
YOU KNOW, HYDRA.
I DOUBT EVEN YOU...
...ARE ON PAR WITH ME.
THANK YOU, HYDRA.
FOR GRANT-ING MY WISH THAT DAY.
YOU REALLY DID...

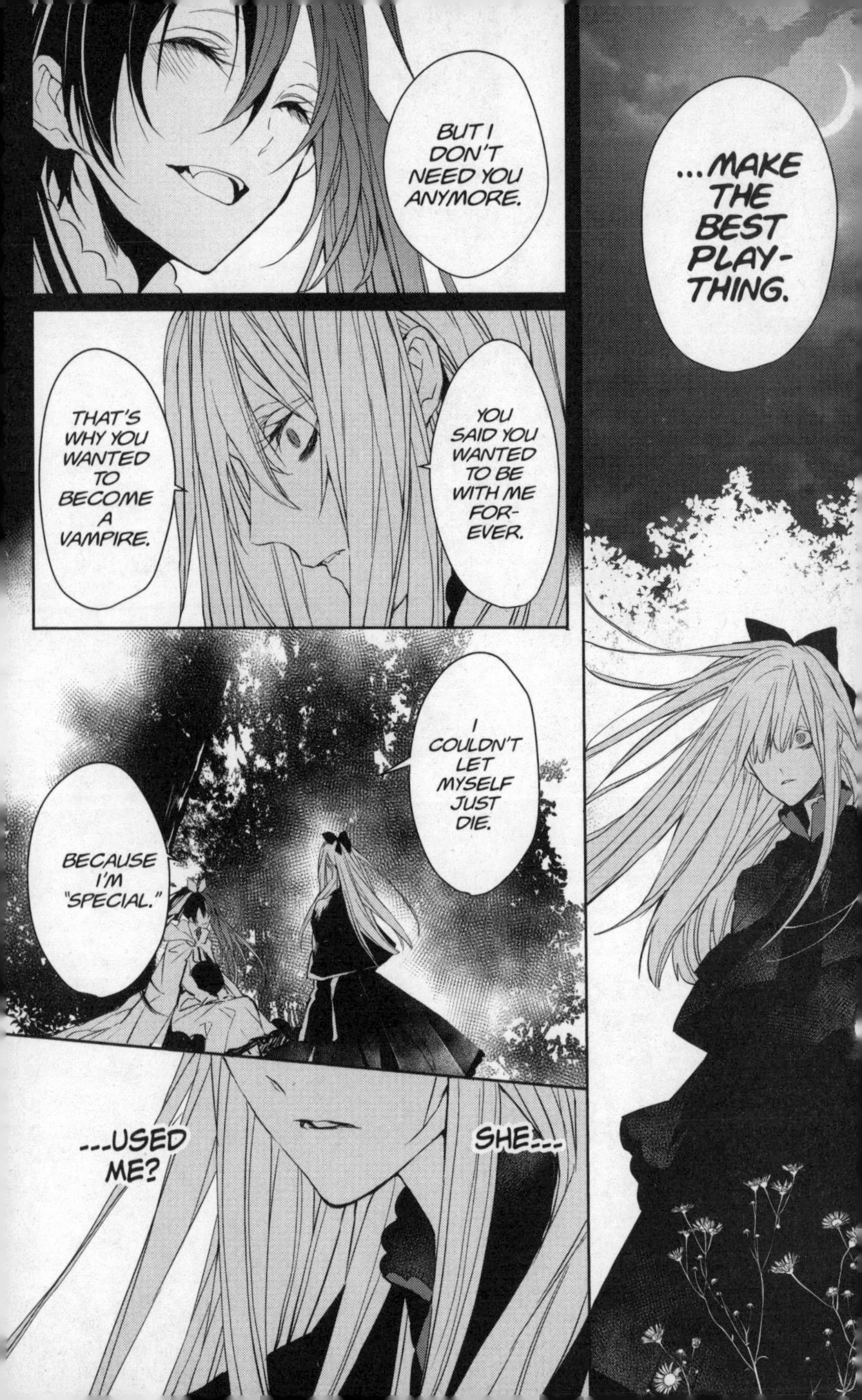

...MAKE THE BEST PLAY-THING.
BUT I DON'T NEED YOU ANYMORE.
YOU SAID YOU WANTED TO BE WITH ME FOR-EVER.
THAT'S WHY YOU WANTED TO BECOME A VAMPIRE.
I COULDN'T LET MYSELF JUST DIE.
BECAUSE I'M "SPECIAL."
SHE...
...USED ME?

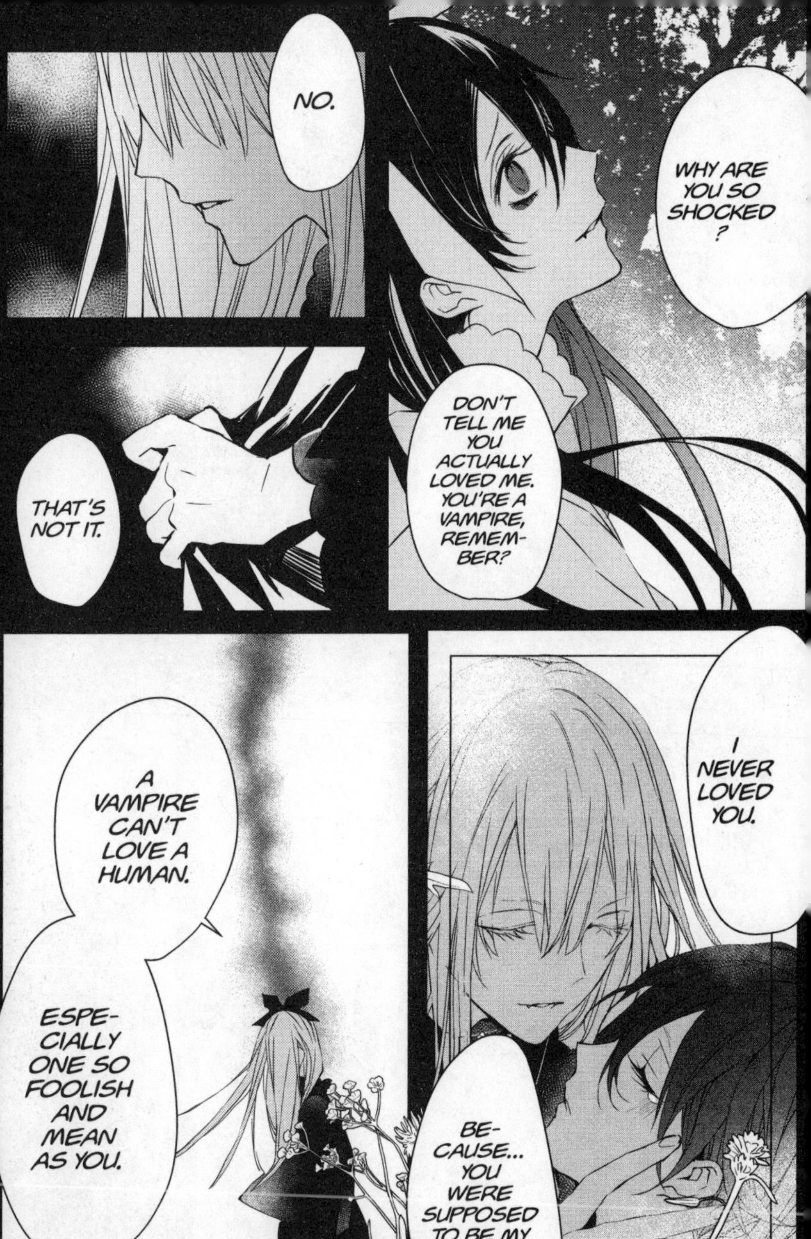
WHY ARE YOU SO SHOCKED?
DON'T TELL ME YOU ACTUALLY LOVED ME. YOU'RE A VAMPIRE, REMEMBER?
NO.
THAT'S NOT IT.
I NEVER LOVED YOU.
BECAUSE... YOU WERE SUPPOSED TO BE MY PLAYTHING.
A VAMPIRE CAN'T LOVE A HUMAN.
ESPECIALLY ONE SO FOOLISH AND MEAN AS YOU.

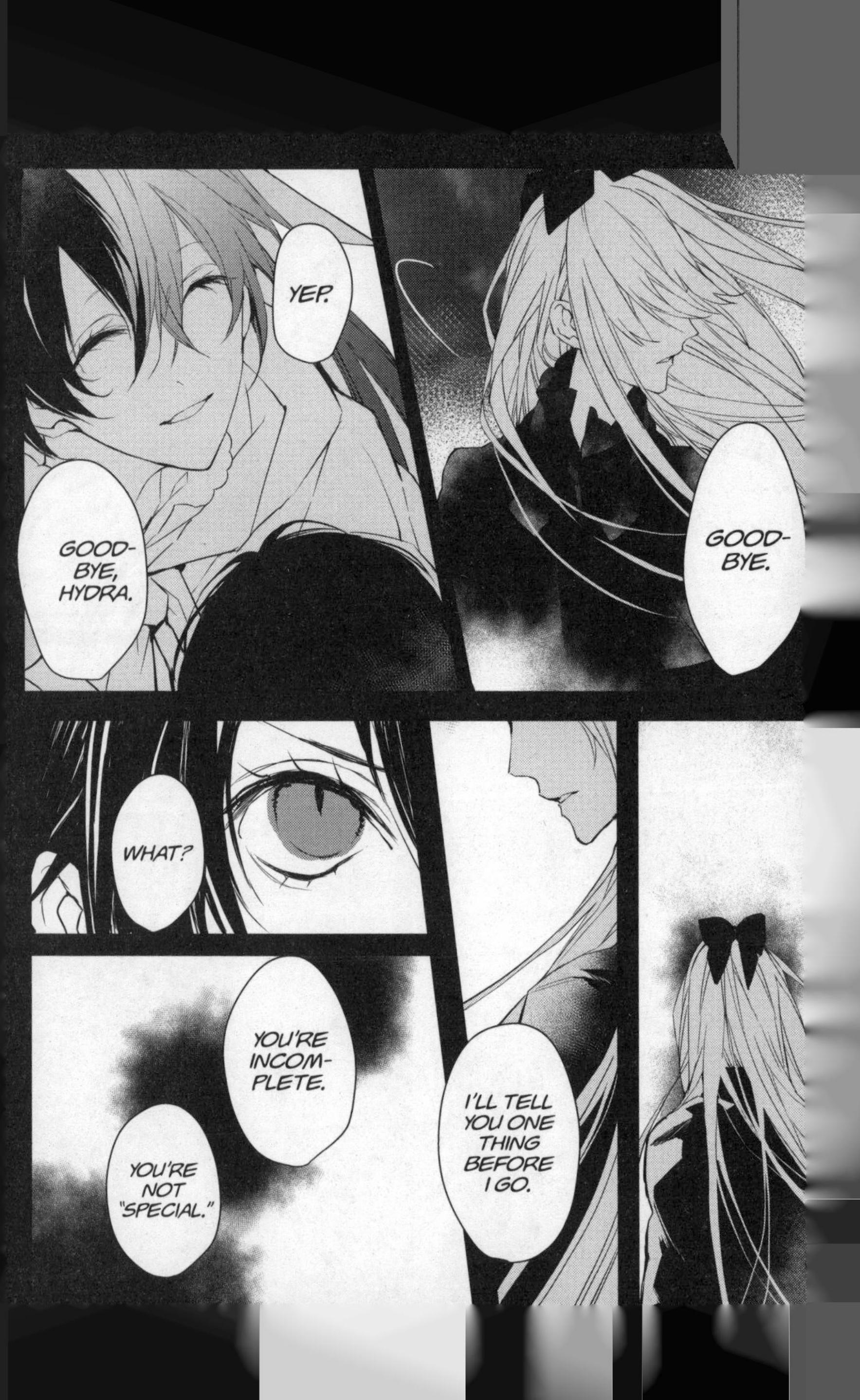
GOOD-BYE.
YEP.
GOOD-BYE, HYDRA.
I'LL TELL YOU ONE THING BEFORE I GO.
WHAT?
YOU'RE INCOMPLETE.
YOU'RE NOT "SPECIAL."

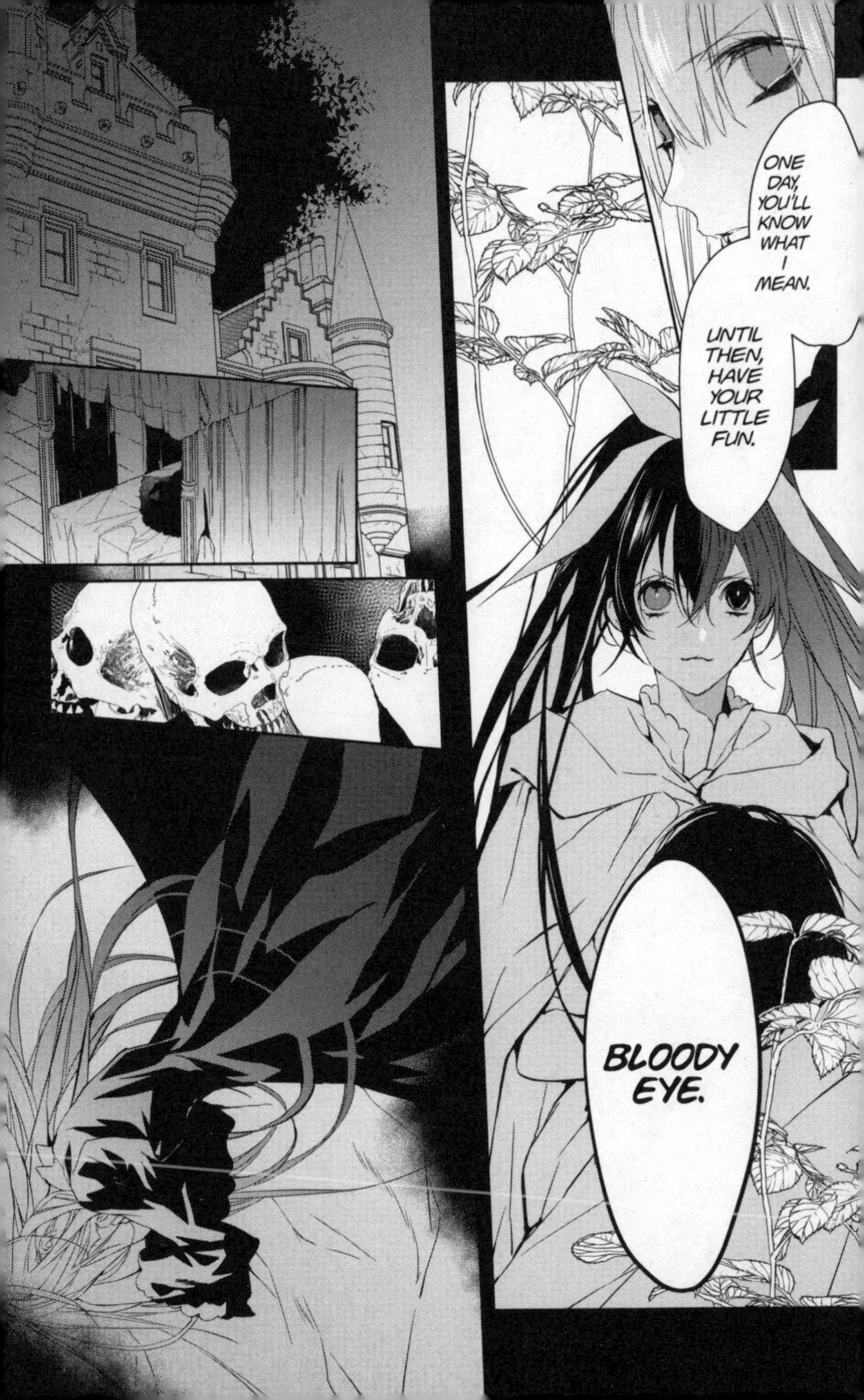
ONE DAY, YOU'LL KNOW WHAT I MEAN.
UNTIL THEN, HAVE YOUR LITTLE FUN.
BLOODY EYE.

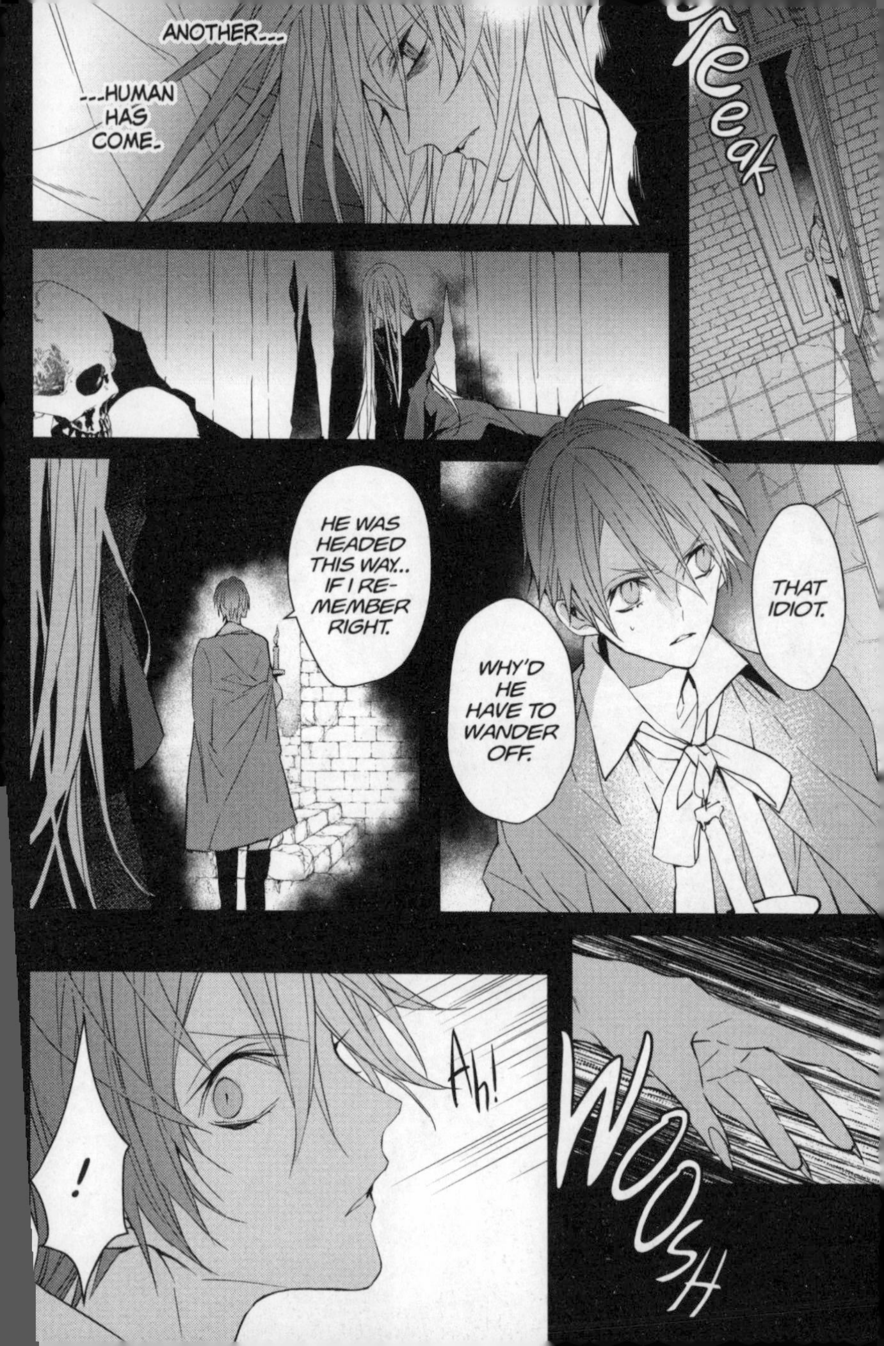
reeak
ANOTHER...
...HUMAN HAS COME.
THAT IDIOT.
WHY'D HE HAVE TO WANDER OFF.
HE WAS HEADED THIS WAY... IF I RE-MEMBER RIGHT.
WOOSH
Ah!
!

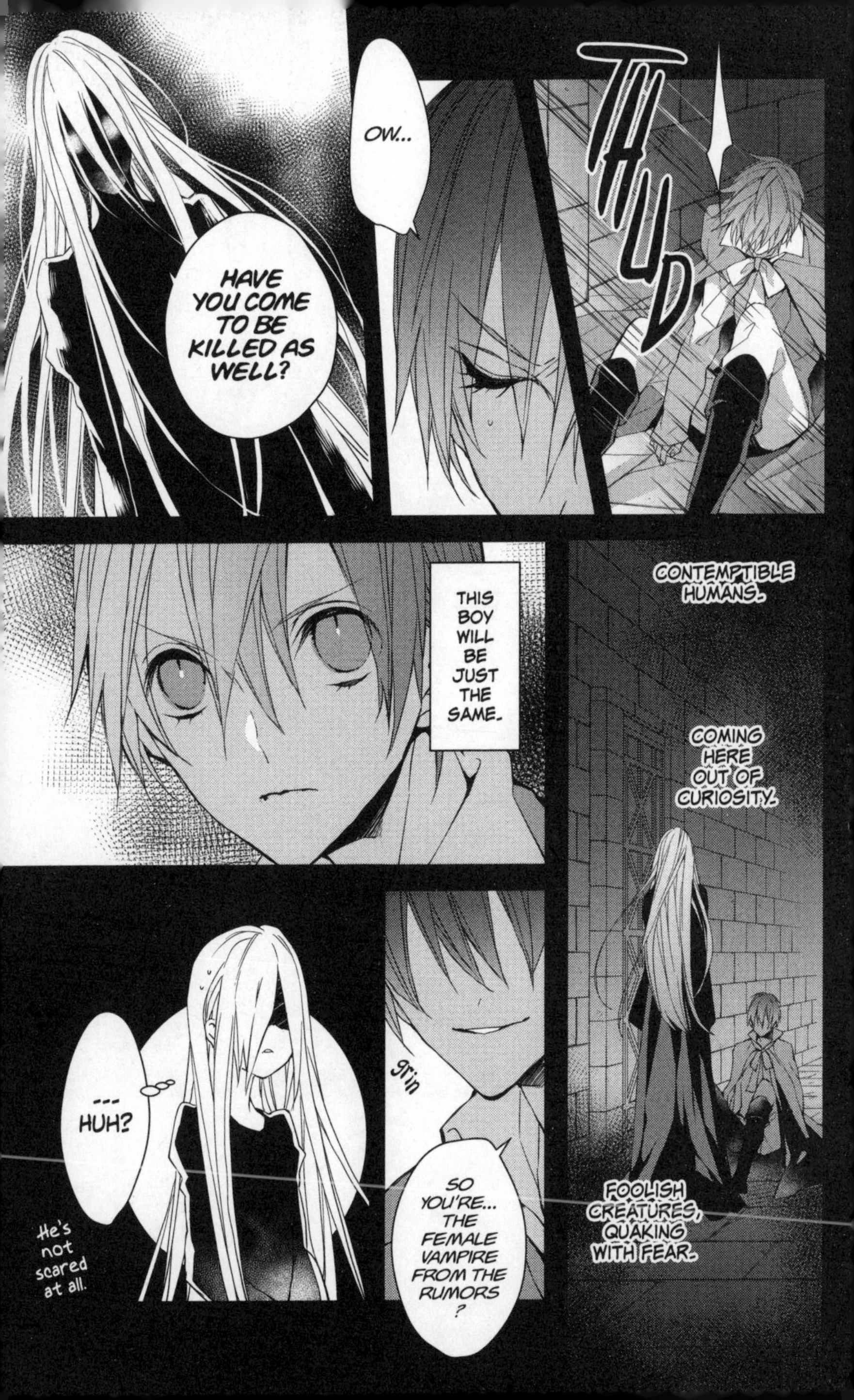
THUD
OW...
HAVE YOU COME TO BE KILLED AS WELL?
CONTEMPTIBLE HUMANS.
COMING HERE OUT OF CURIOSITY.
FOOLISH CREATURES, QUAKING WITH FEAR.
THIS BOY WILL BE JUST THE SAME.
grin
SO YOU'RE... THE FEMALE VAMPIRE FROM THE RUMORS?
...HUH?
He's not scared at all.

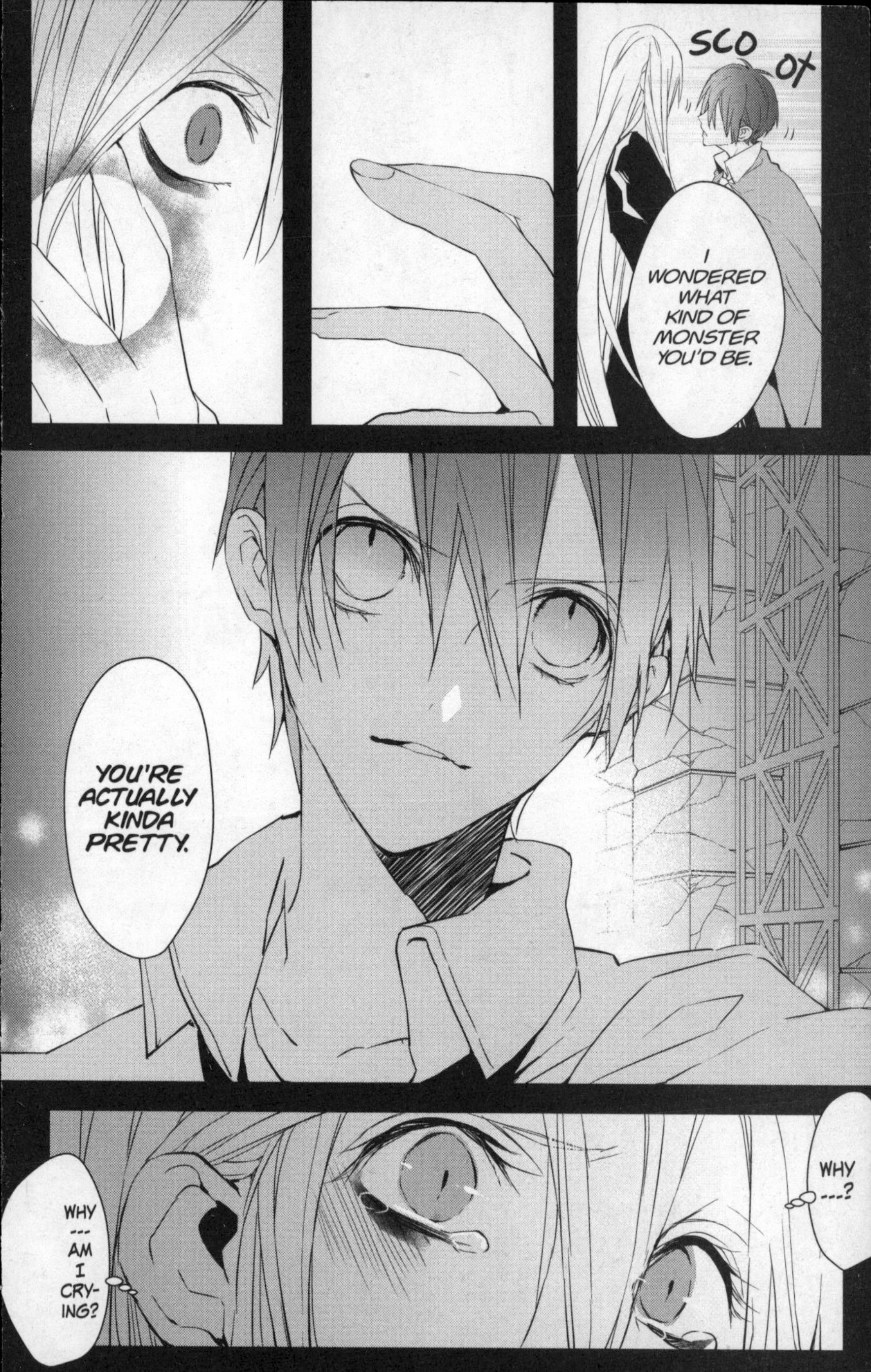
SCO OT
I WONDERED WHAT KIND OF MONSTER YOU'D BE.
YOU'RE ACTUALLY KINDA PRETTY.
WHY ---?
WHY --- AM I CRYING?

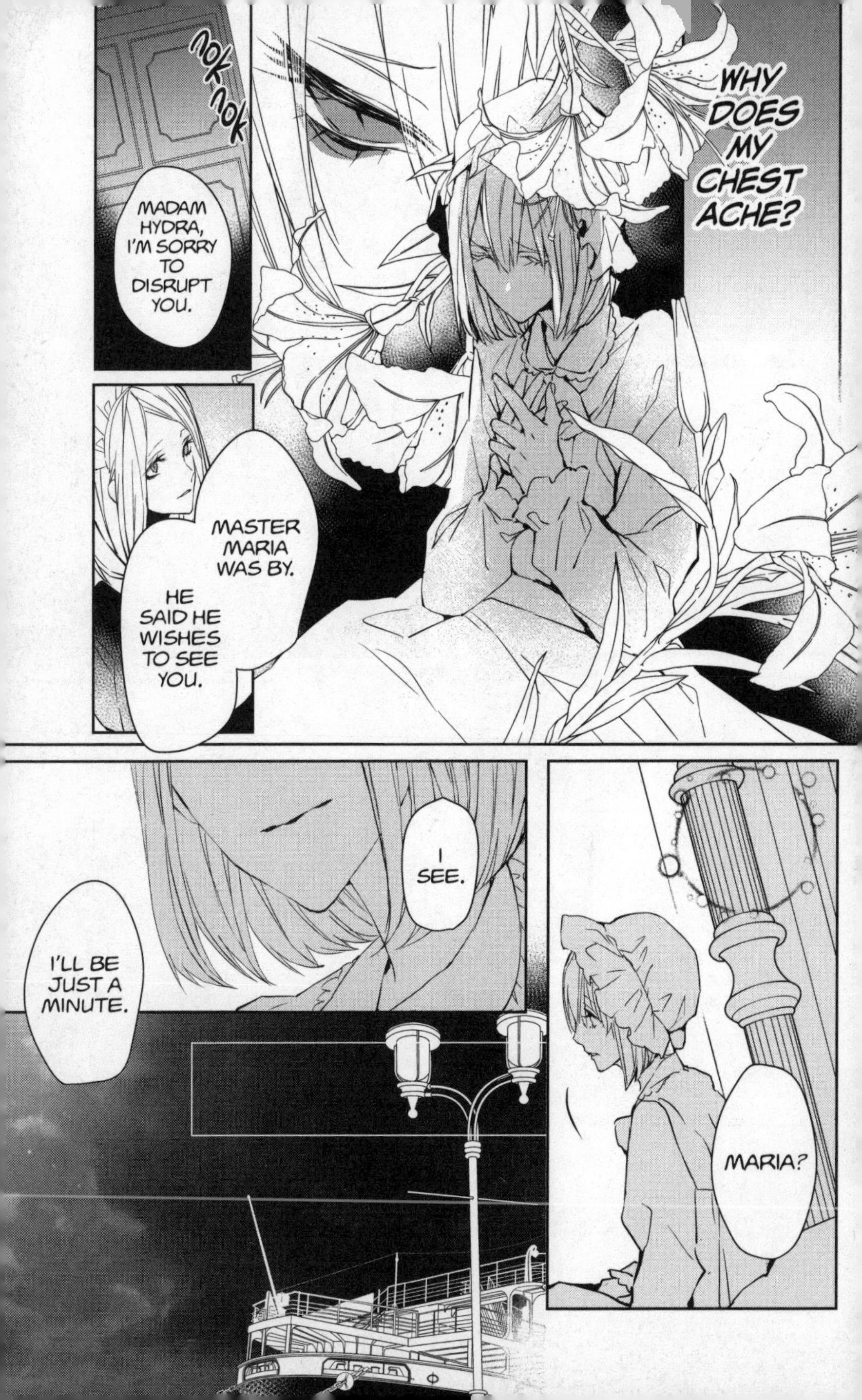
WHY DOES MY CHEST ACHE?
NOK NOK
MADAM HYDRA, I'M SORRY TO DISRUPT YOU.
MASTER MARIA WAS BY.
HE SAID HE WISHES TO SEE YOU.
MARIA?
I SEE.
I'LL BE JUST A MINUTE.

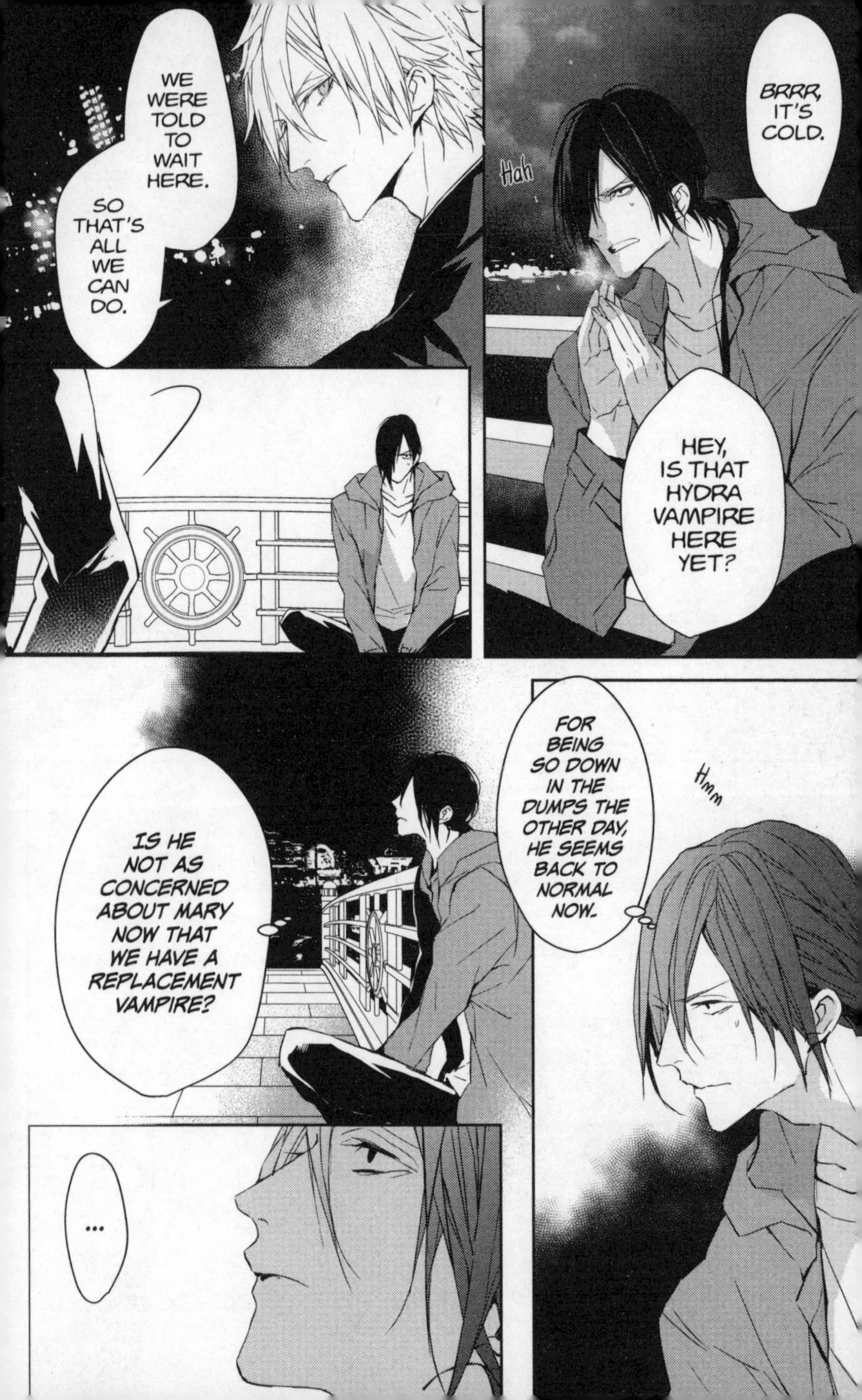
BRRR, IT'S COLD.
Hah
HEY, IS THAT HYDRA VAMPIRE HERE YET?
WE WERE TOLD TO WAIT HERE.
SO THAT'S ALL WE CAN DO.
Hmm
FOR BEING SO DOWN IN THE DUMPS THE OTHER DAY, HE SEEMS BACK TO NORMAL NOW.
IS HE NOT AS CONCERNED ABOUT MARY NOW THAT WE HAVE A REPLACEMENT VAMPIRE?
...

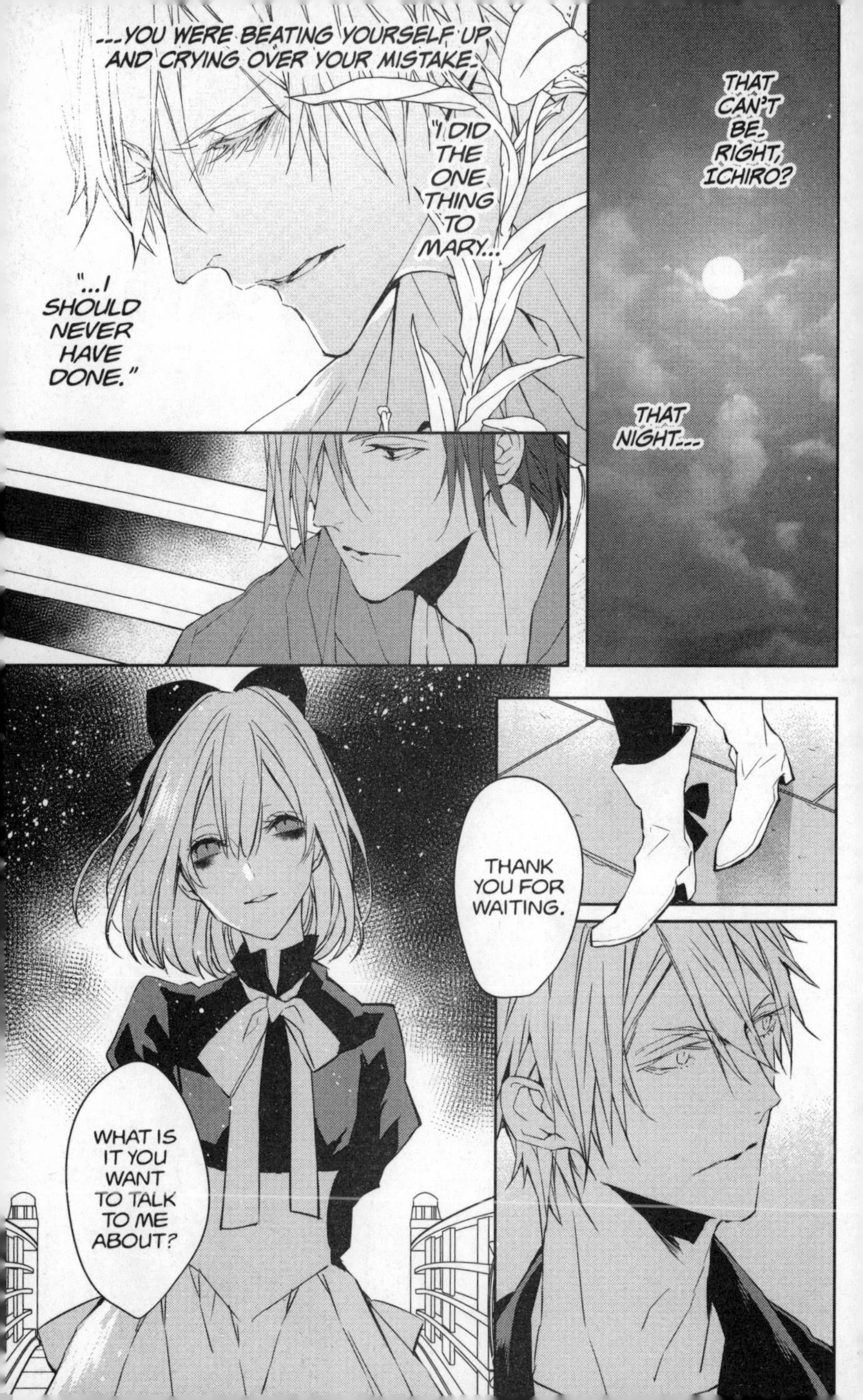
THAT CAN'T BE. RIGHT, ICHIRO?
THAT NIGHT...
...YOU WERE BEATING YOURSELF UP AND CRYING OVER YOUR MISTAKE.
"I DID THE ONE THING TO MARY...
"...I SHOULD NEVER HAVE DONE."
THANK YOU FOR WAITING.
WHAT IS IT YOU WANT TO TALK TO ME ABOUT?

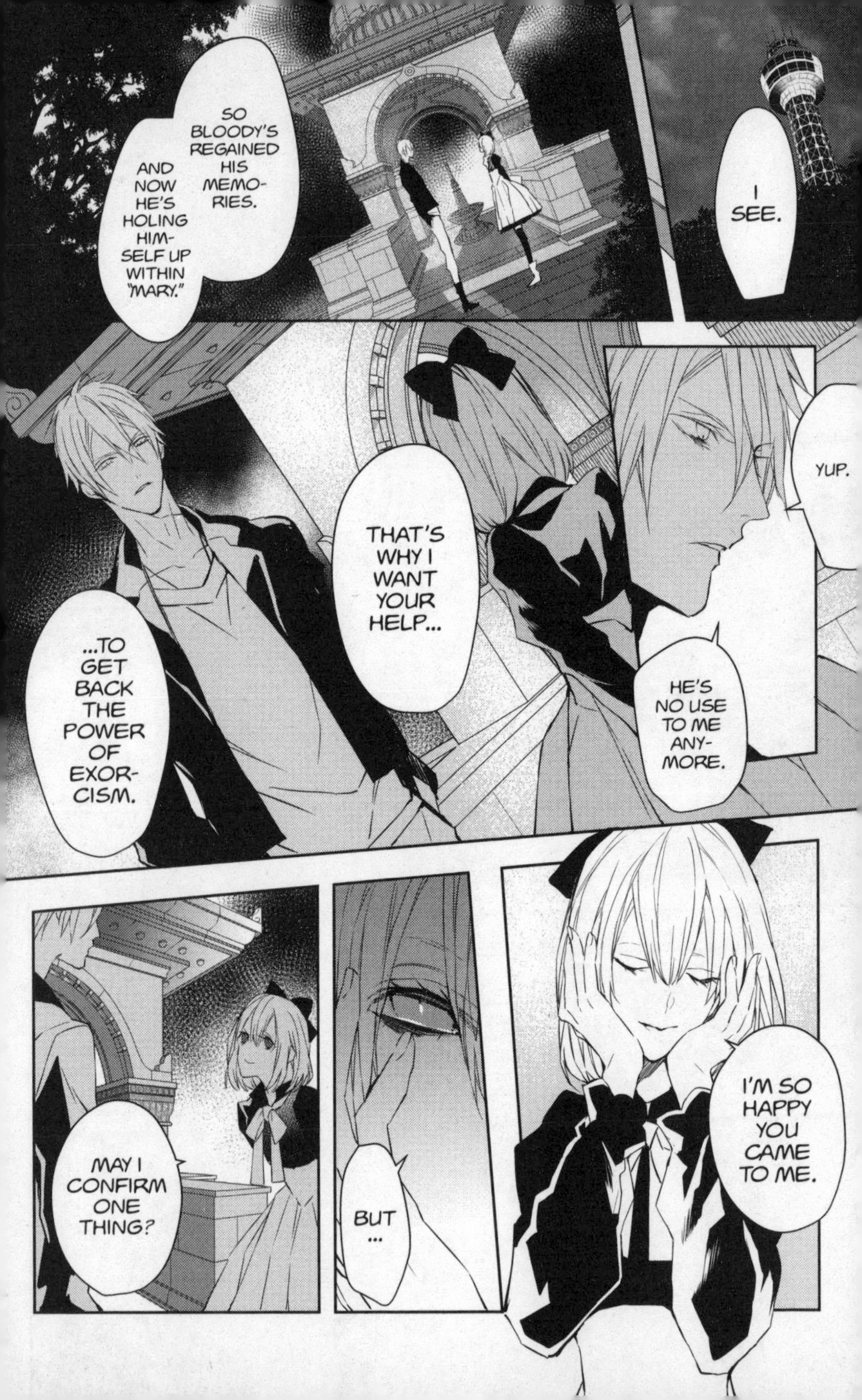

I SEE.
SO BLOODY'S REGAINED HIS MEMORIES.
AND NOW HE'S HOLING HIMSELF UP WITHIN "MARY."
YUP.
HE'S NO USE TO ME ANYMORE.
THAT'S WHY I WANT YOUR HELP...
...TO GET BACK THE POWER OF EXORCISM.
I'M SO HAPPY YOU CAME TO ME.
BUT...
MAY I CONFIRM ONE THING?

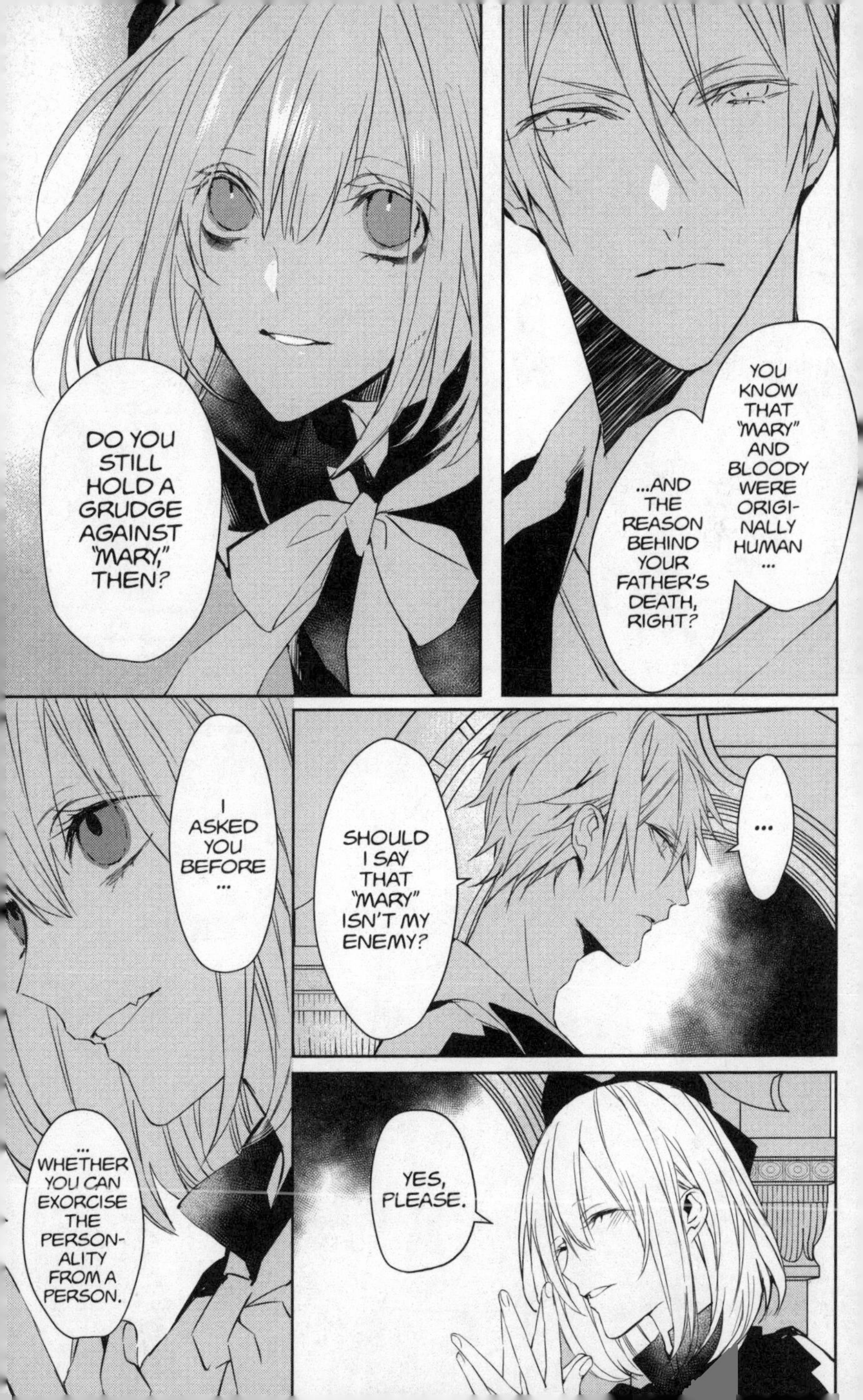
YOU KNOW THAT "MARY" AND BLOODY WERE ORIGINALLY HUMAN...
...AND THE REASON BEHIND YOUR FATHER'S DEATH, RIGHT?
DO YOU STILL HOLD A GRUDGE AGAINST "MARY," THEN?
...
SHOULD I SAY THAT "MARY" ISN'T MY ENEMY?
YES, PLEASE.
I ASKED YOU BEFORE...
...WHETHER YOU CAN EXORCISE THE PERSONALITY FROM A PERSON.

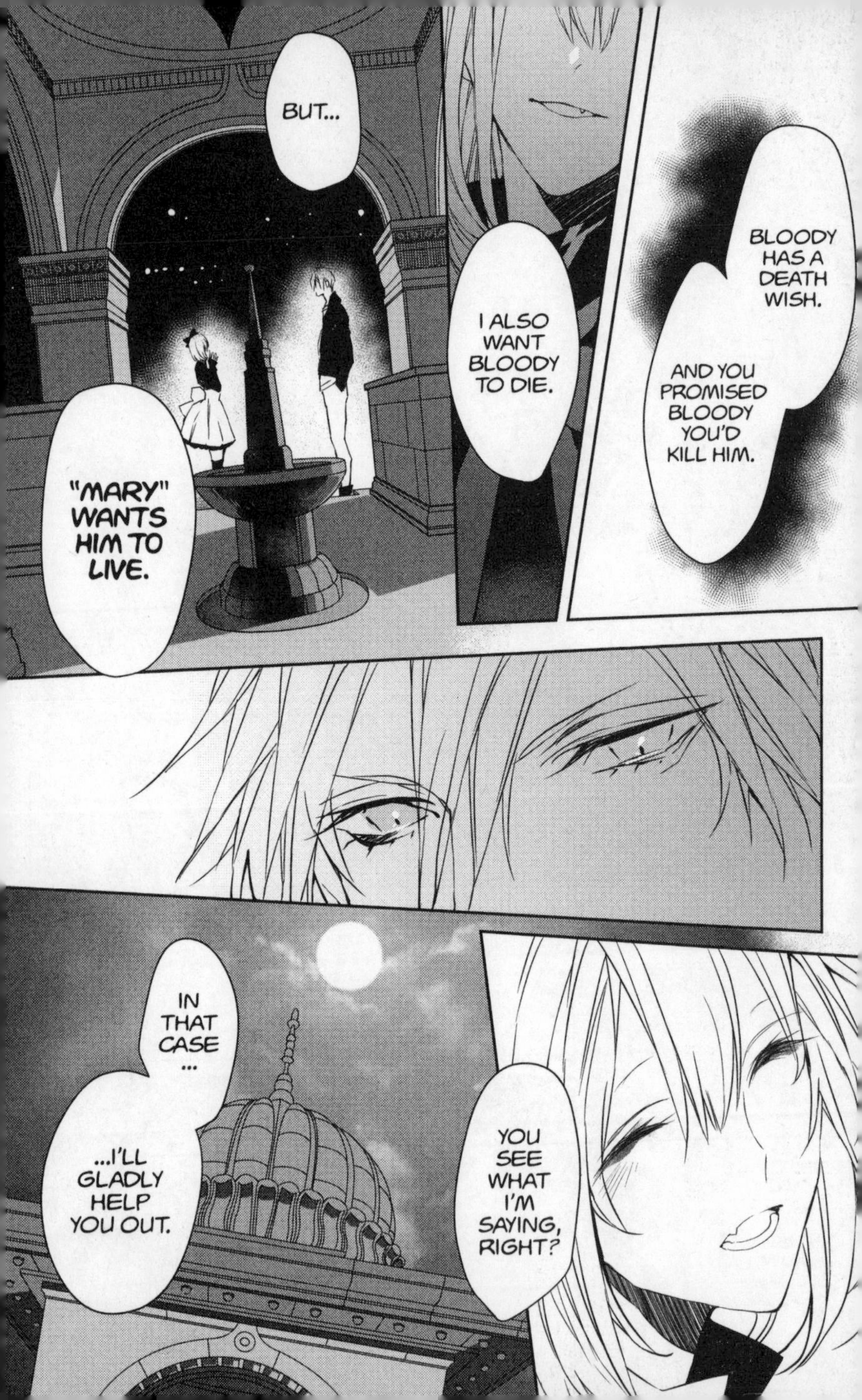
BLOODY HAS A DEATH WISH.
AND YOU PROMISED BLOODY YOU'D KILL HIM.
I ALSO WANT BLOODY TO DIE.
BUT...
"MARY" WANTS HIM TO LIVE.
YOU SEE WHAT I'M SAYING, RIGHT?
IN THAT CASE...
...I'LL GLADLY HELP YOU OUT.

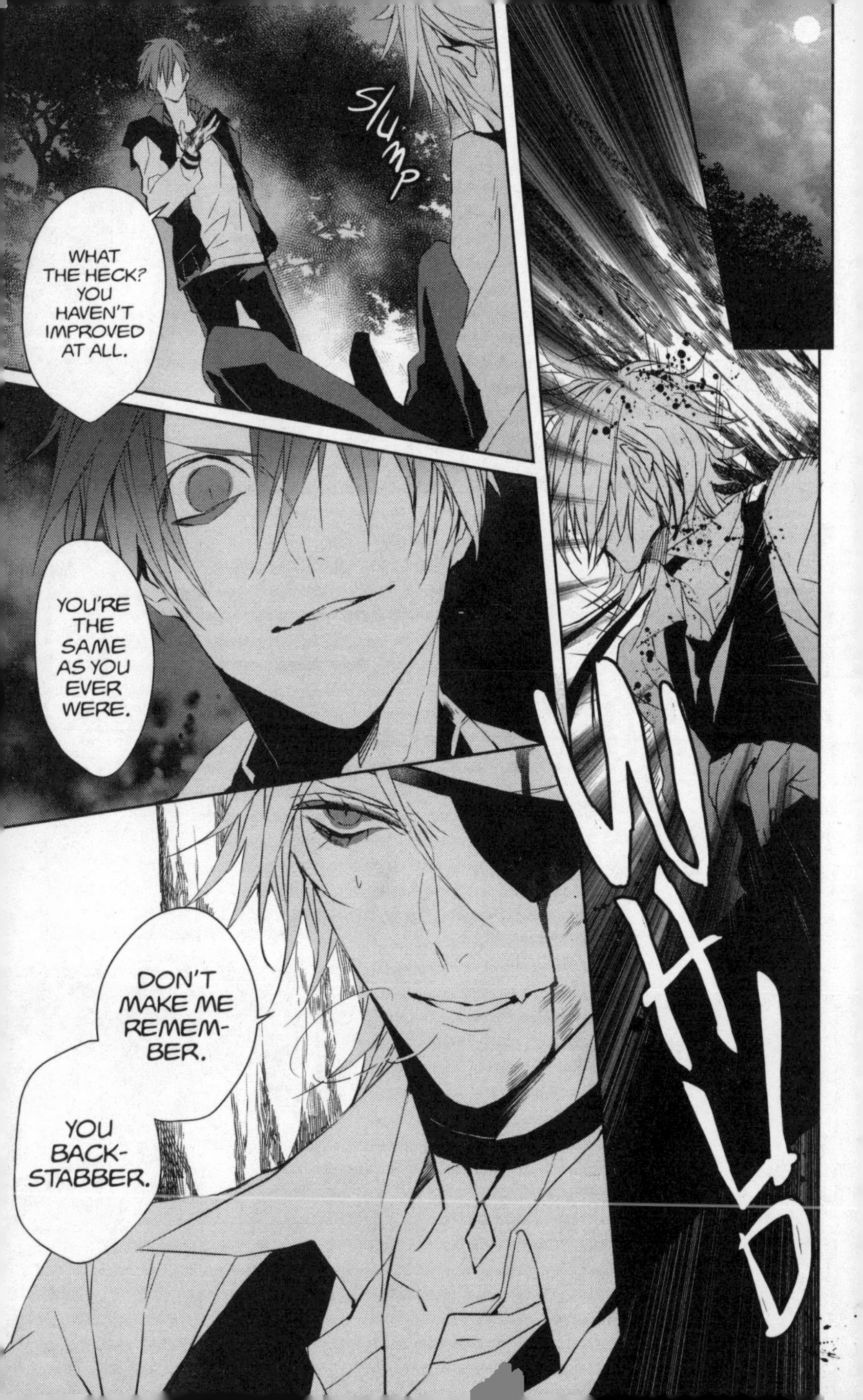
WHUD
SLUMP
WHAT THE HECK? YOU HAVEN'T IMPROVED AT ALL.
YOU'RE THE SAME AS YOU EVER WERE.
DON'T MAKE ME REMEMBER.
YOU BACKSTABBER.

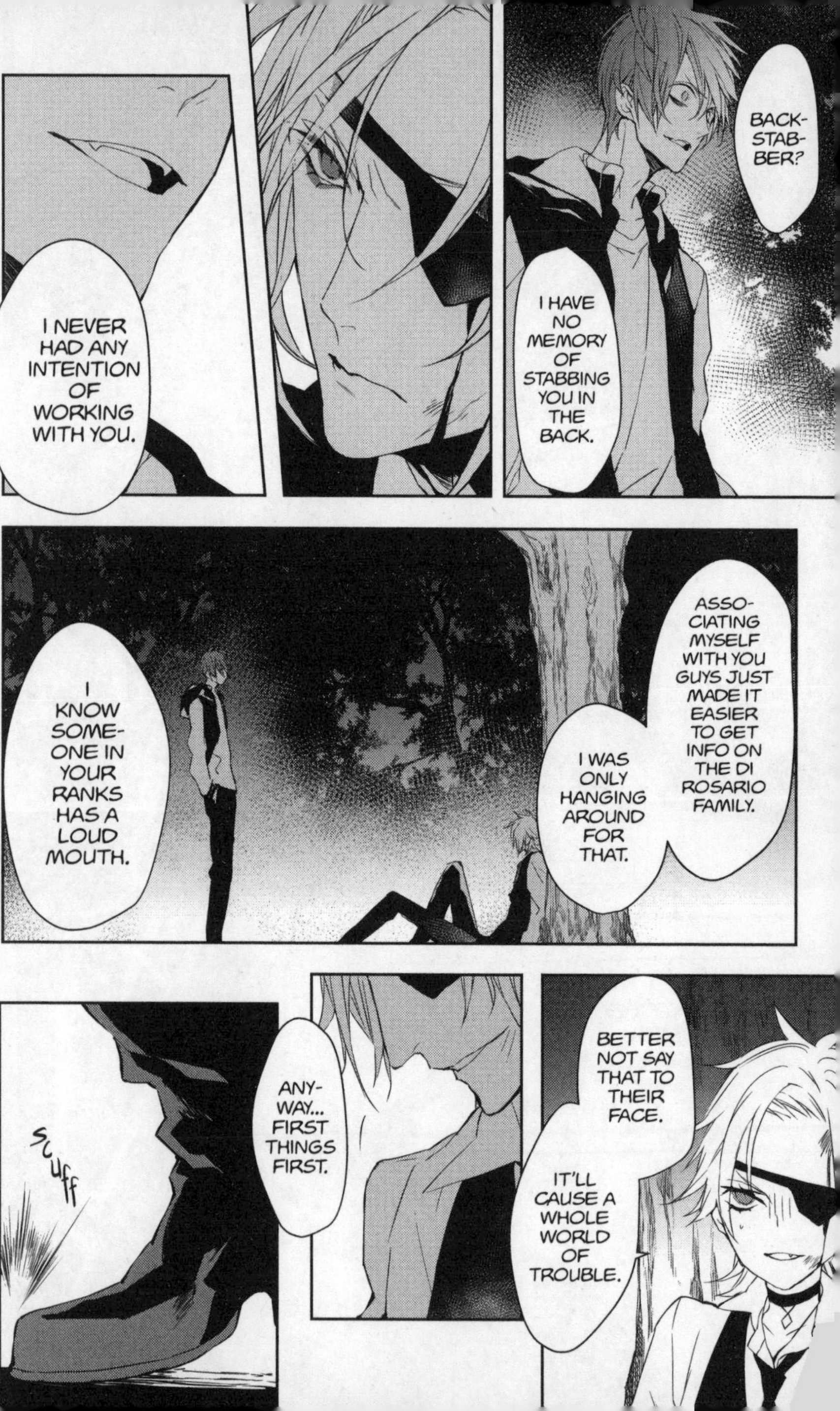
BACK-STABBER?
I HAVE NO MEMORY OF STABBING YOU IN THE BACK.
I NEVER HAD ANY INTENTION OF WORKING WITH YOU.
ASSO-CIATING MYSELF WITH YOU GUYS JUST MADE IT EASIER TO GET INFO ON THE DI ROSARIO FAMILY.
I WAS ONLY HANGING AROUND FOR THAT.
I KNOW SOME-ONE IN YOUR RANKS HAS A LOUD MOUTH.
BETTER NOT SAY THAT TO THEIR FACE.
IT'LL CAUSE A WHOLE WORLD OF TROUBLE.
ANY-WAY... FIRST THINGS FIRST.
SCUFF

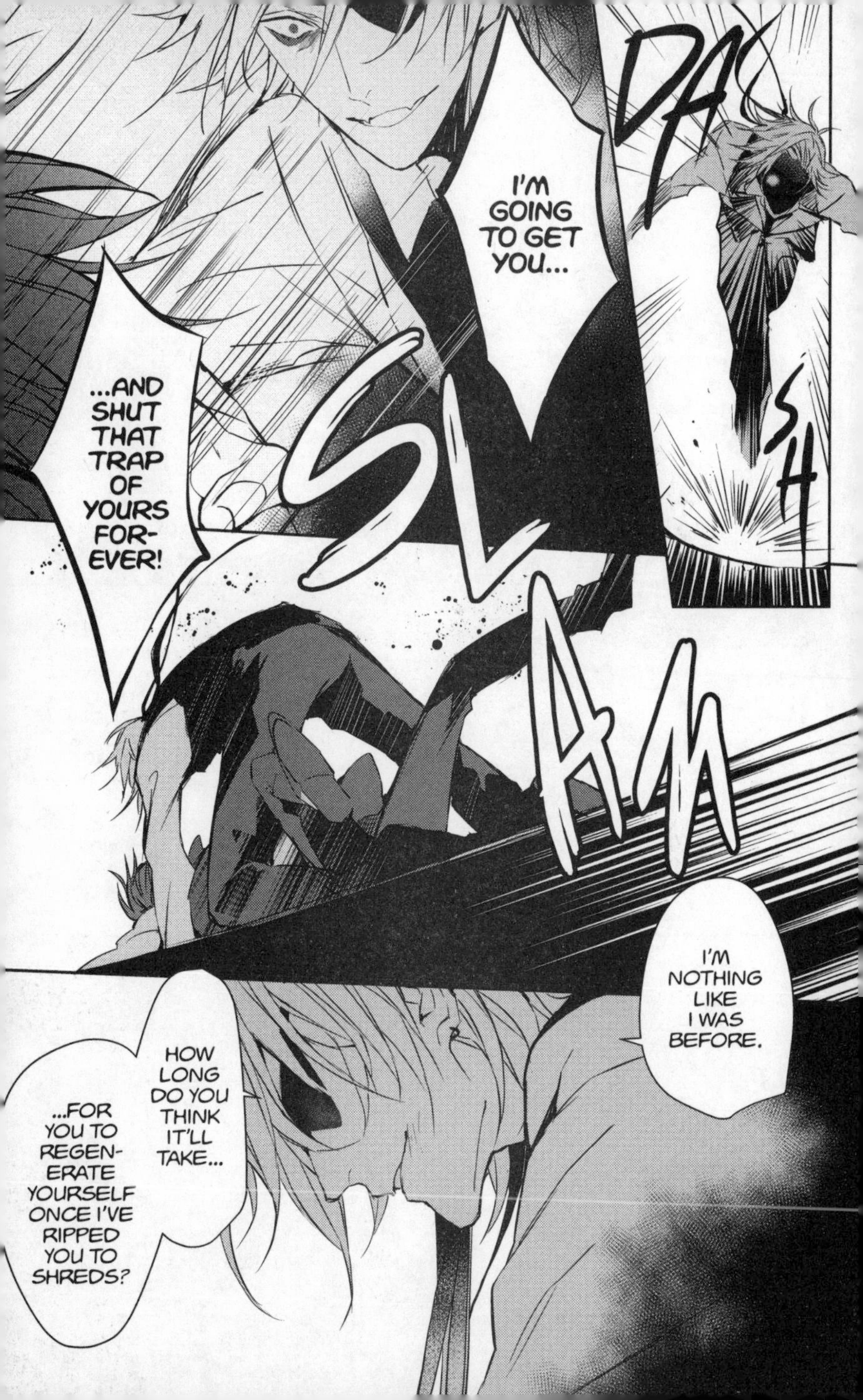
DA
SH
I'M GOING TO GET YOU...
...AND SHUT THAT TRAP OF YOURS FOR-EVER!
SLAM
I'M NOTHING LIKE I WAS BEFORE.
HOW LONG DO YOU THINK IT'LL TAKE...
...FOR YOU TO REGEN-ERATE YOURSELF ONCE I'VE RIPPED YOU TO SHREDS?

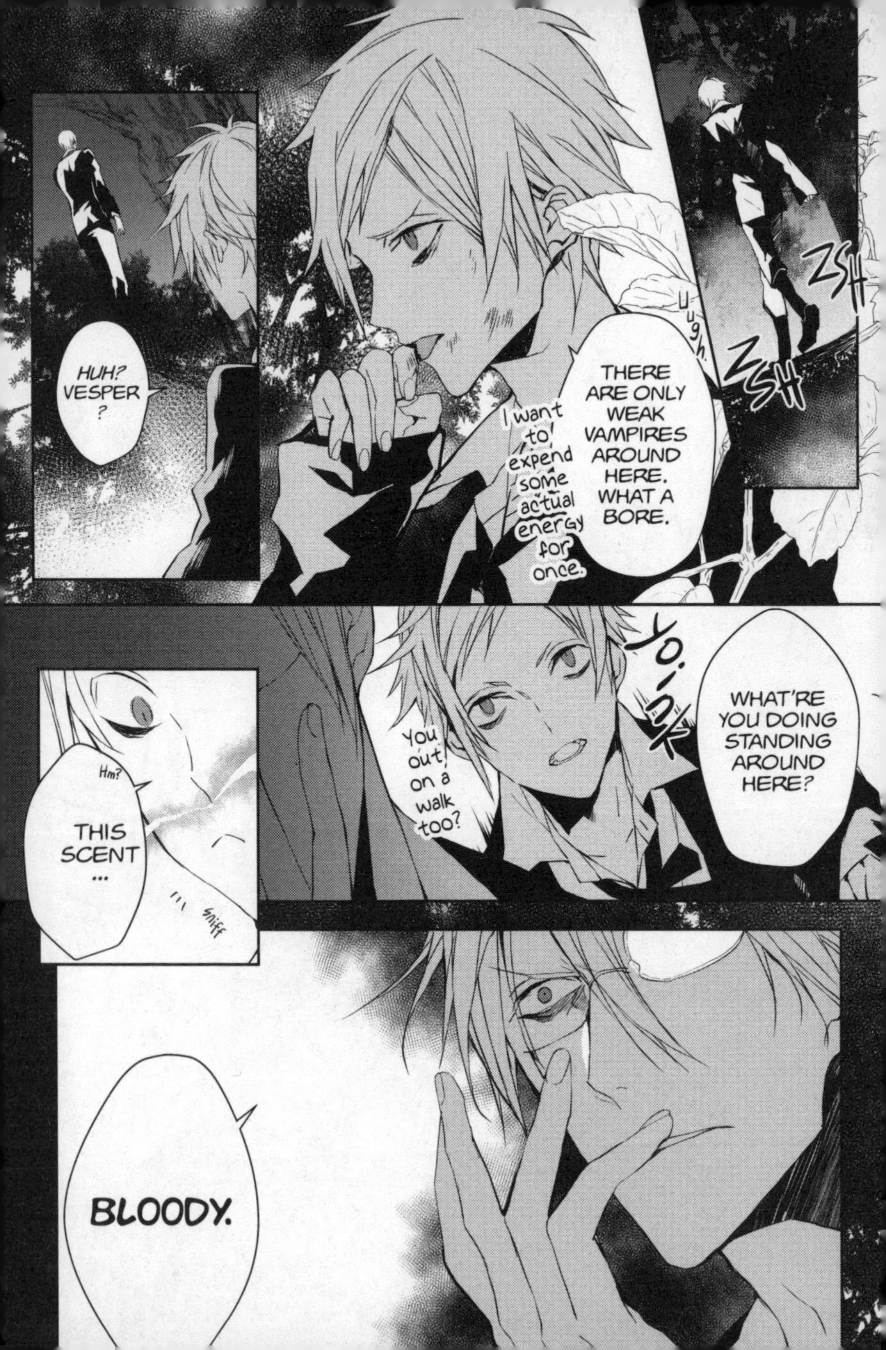
ZSH
ZSH
Ugh.
THERE ARE ONLY WEAK VAMPIRES AROUND HERE. WHAT A BORE.
I want to expend some actual energy for once.
HUH? VESPER?
WHAT'RE YOU DOING STANDING AROUND HERE?
YOINK
You out on a walk too?
Hm?
THIS SCENT...
sniff
BLOODY.

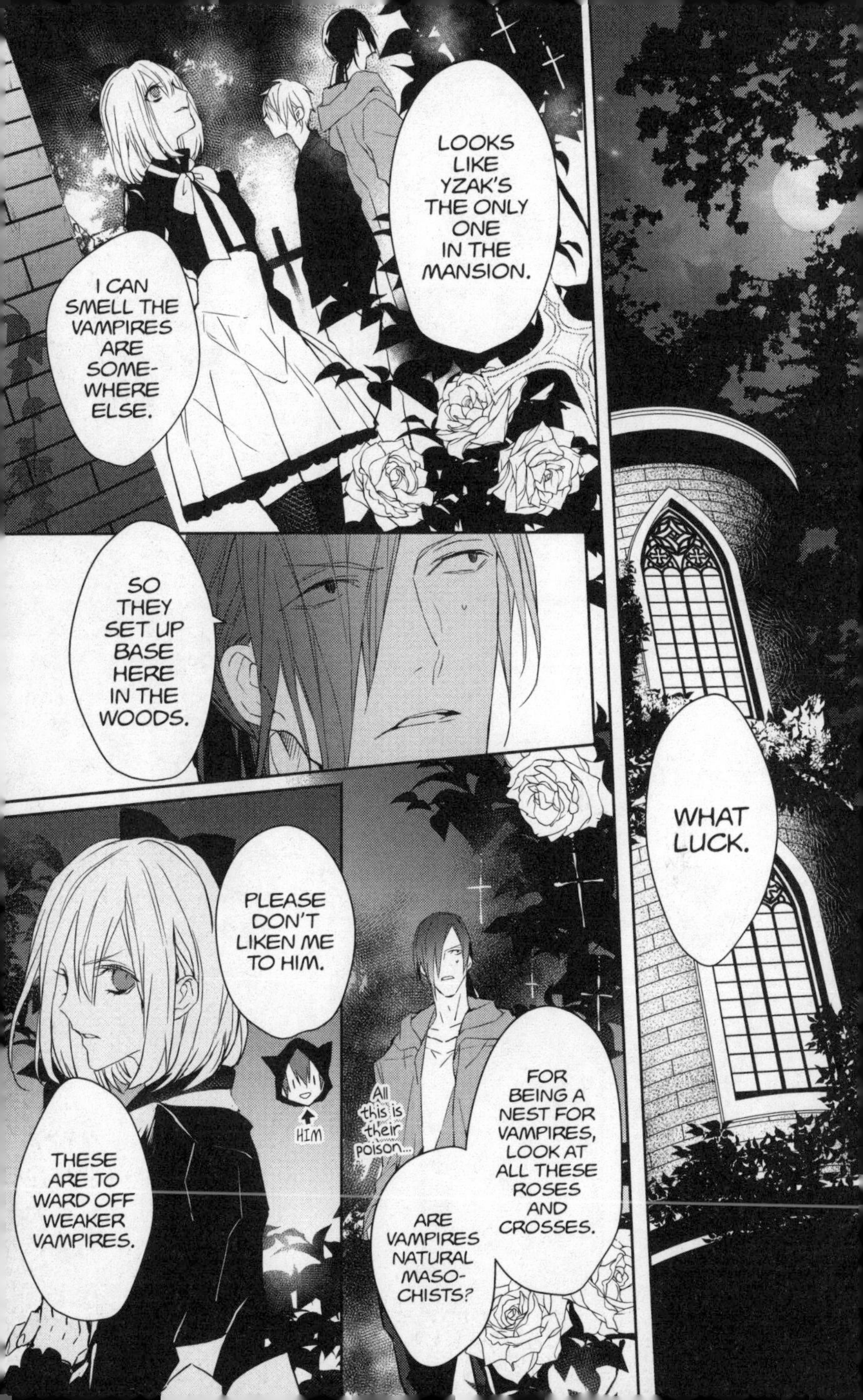
LOOKS LIKE YZAK'S THE ONLY ONE IN THE MANSION.
I CAN SMELL THE VAMPIRES ARE SOME-WHERE ELSE.
SO THEY SET UP BASE HERE IN THE WOODS.
WHAT LUCK.
FOR BEING A NEST FOR VAMPIRES, LOOK AT ALL THESE ROSES AND CROSSES.
ARE VAMPIRES NATURAL MASO-CHISTS?
All this is their poison...
PLEASE DON'T LIKEN ME TO HIM.
HIM
THESE ARE TO WARD OFF WEAKER VAMPIRES.

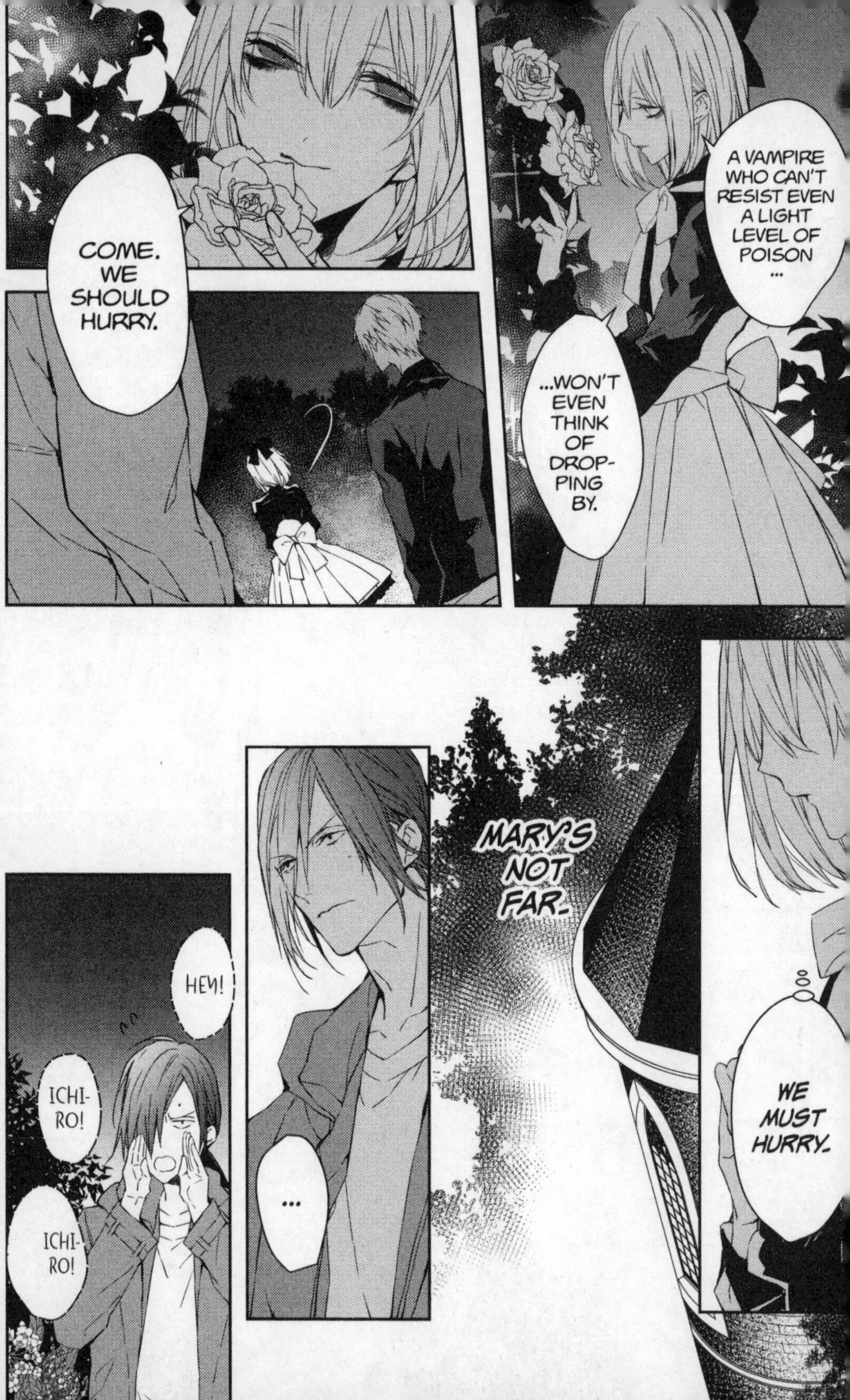
A VAMPIRE WHO CAN'T RESIST EVEN A LIGHT LEVEL OF POISON ...
...WON'T EVEN THINK OF DROP-PING BY.
COME. WE SHOULD HURRY.
WE MUST HURRY.
MARY'S NOT FAR.
...
HEY!
ICHI-RO!
ICHI-RO!

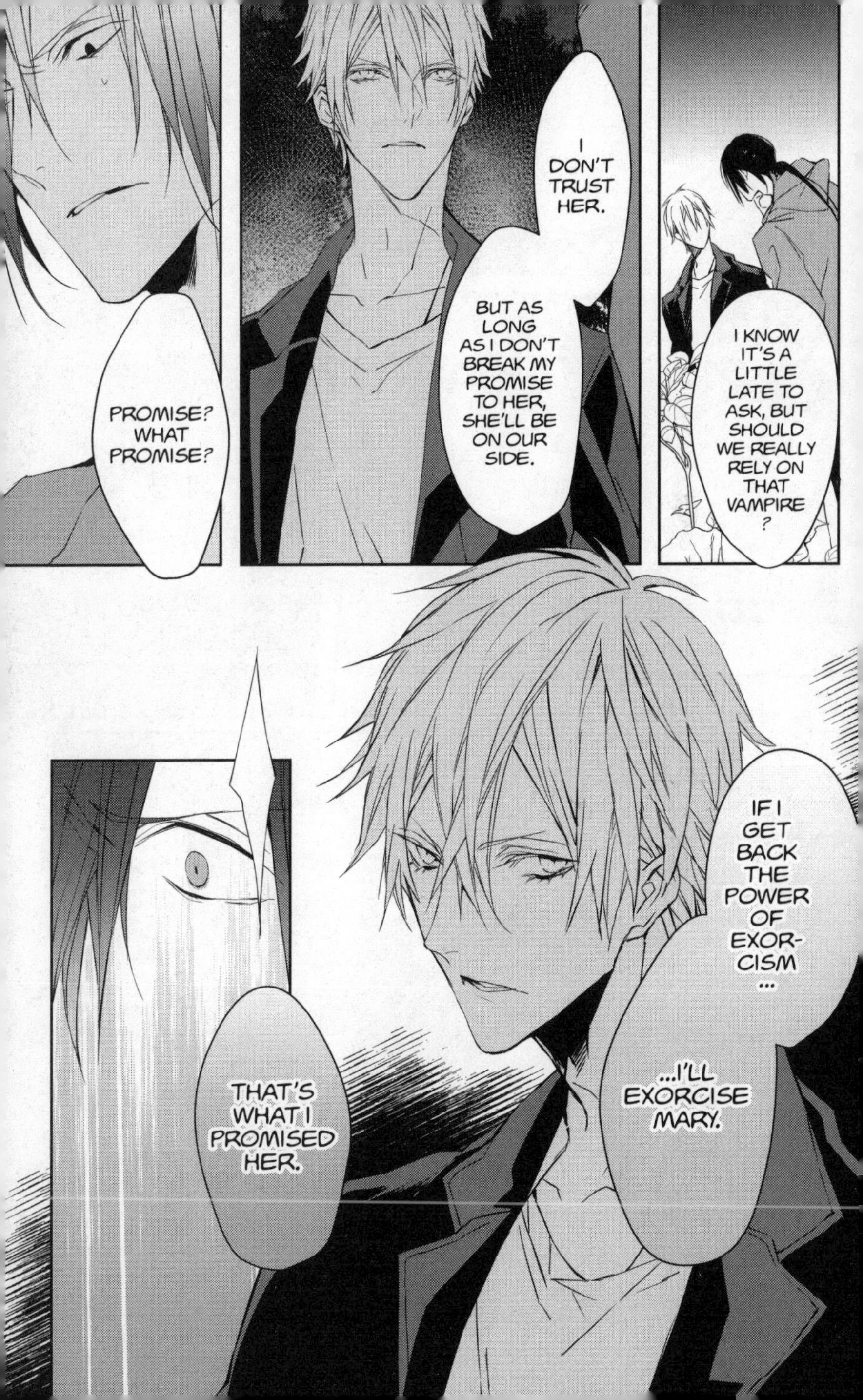
I KNOW IT'S A LITTLE LATE TO ASK, BUT SHOULD WE REALLY RELY ON THAT VAMPIRE?
I DON'T TRUST HER.
BUT AS LONG AS I DON'T BREAK MY PROMISE TO HER, SHE'LL BE ON OUR SIDE.
PROMISE? WHAT PROMISE?
IF I GET BACK THE POWER OF EXORCISM...
...I'LL EXORCISE MARY.
THAT'S WHAT I PROMISED HER.

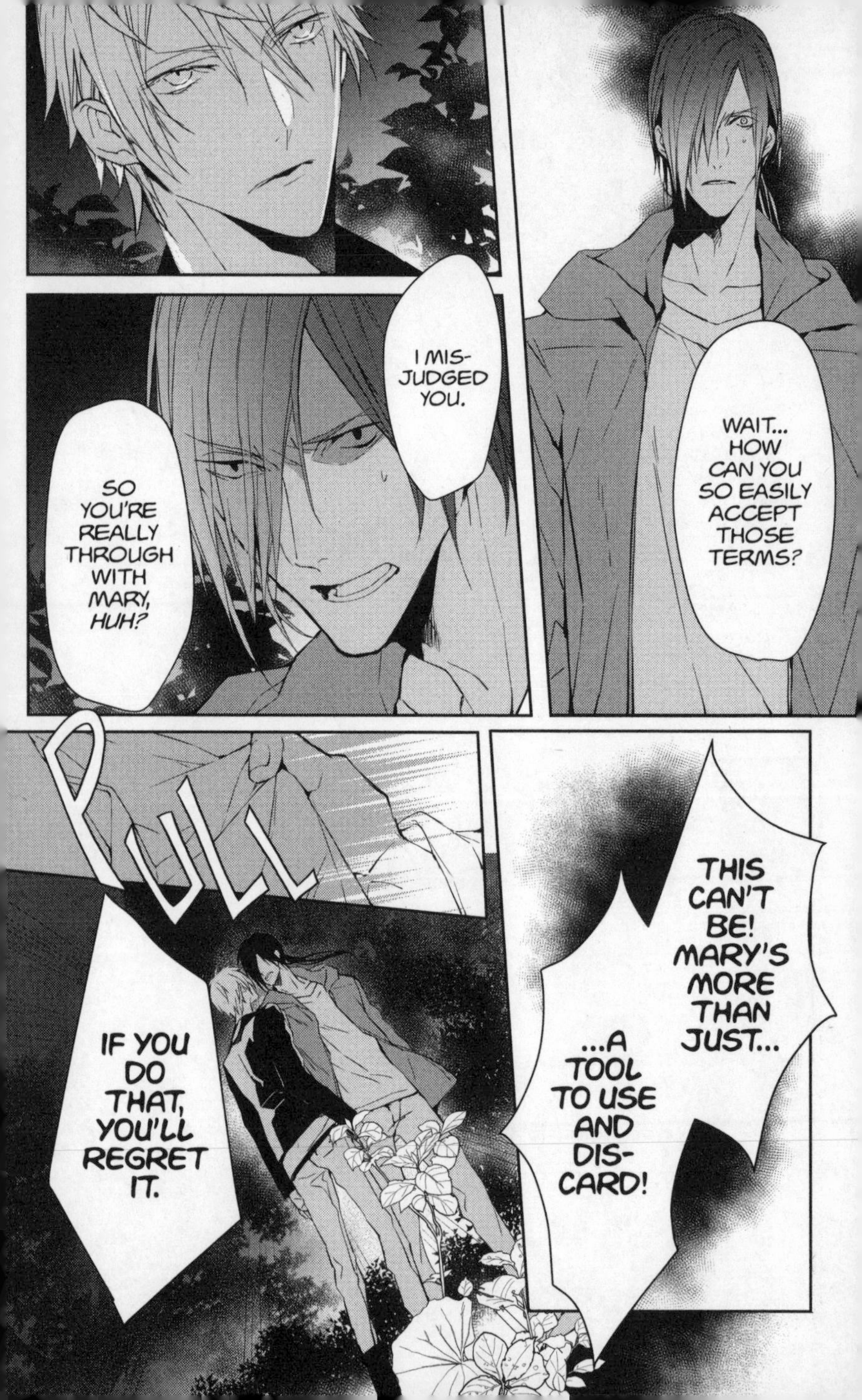
WAIT... HOW CAN YOU SO EASILY ACCEPT THOSE TERMS?
I MIS-JUDGED YOU.
SO YOU'RE REALLY THROUGH WITH MARY, HUH?
THIS CAN'T BE! MARY'S MORE THAN JUST...
...A TOOL TO USE AND DIS-CARD!
PULL
IF YOU DO THAT, YOU'LL REGRET IT.

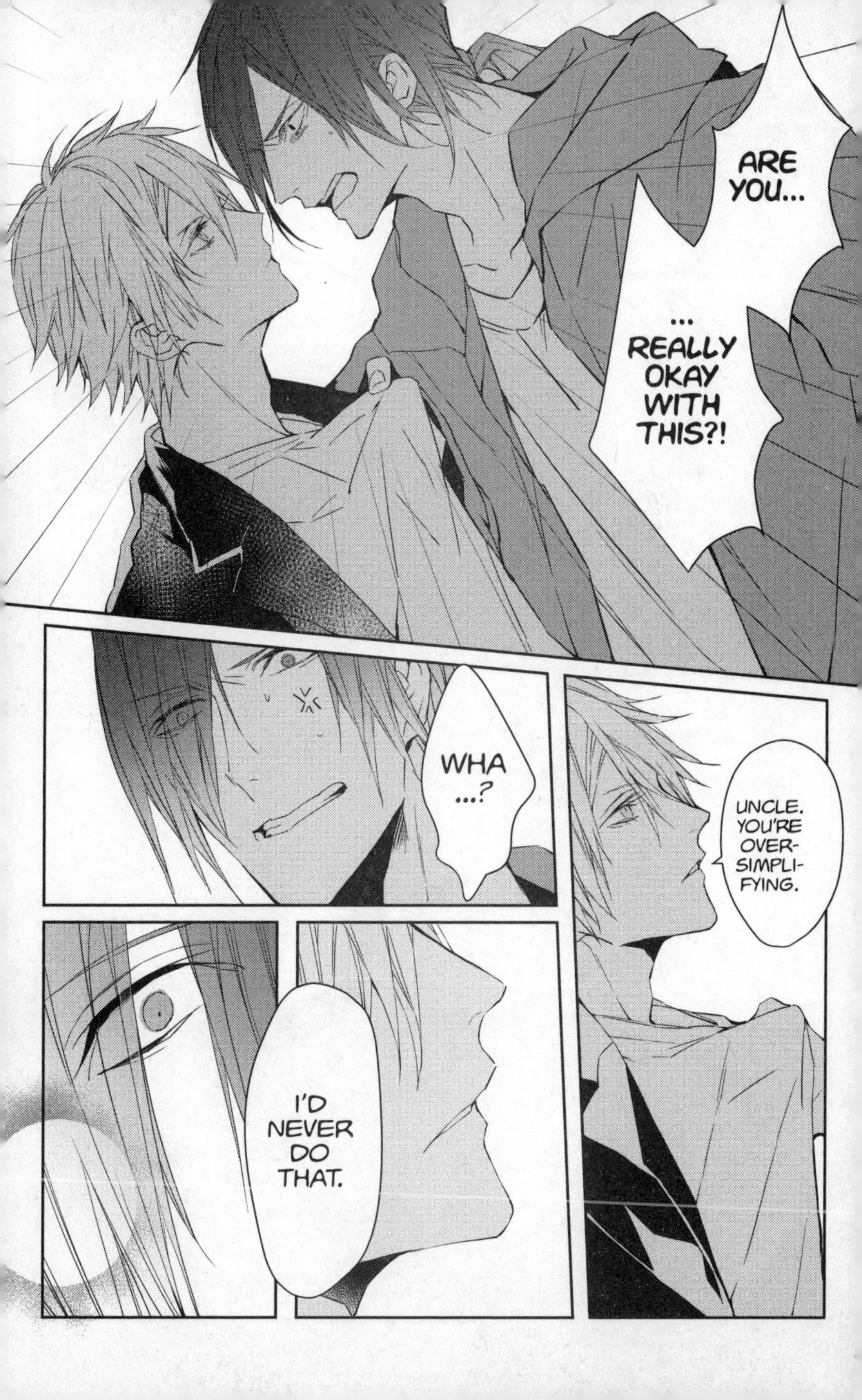
ARE YOU...
...REALLY OKAY WITH THIS?!
UNCLE. YOU'RE OVER-SIMPLI-FYING.
WHA ...?
I'D NEVER DO THAT.

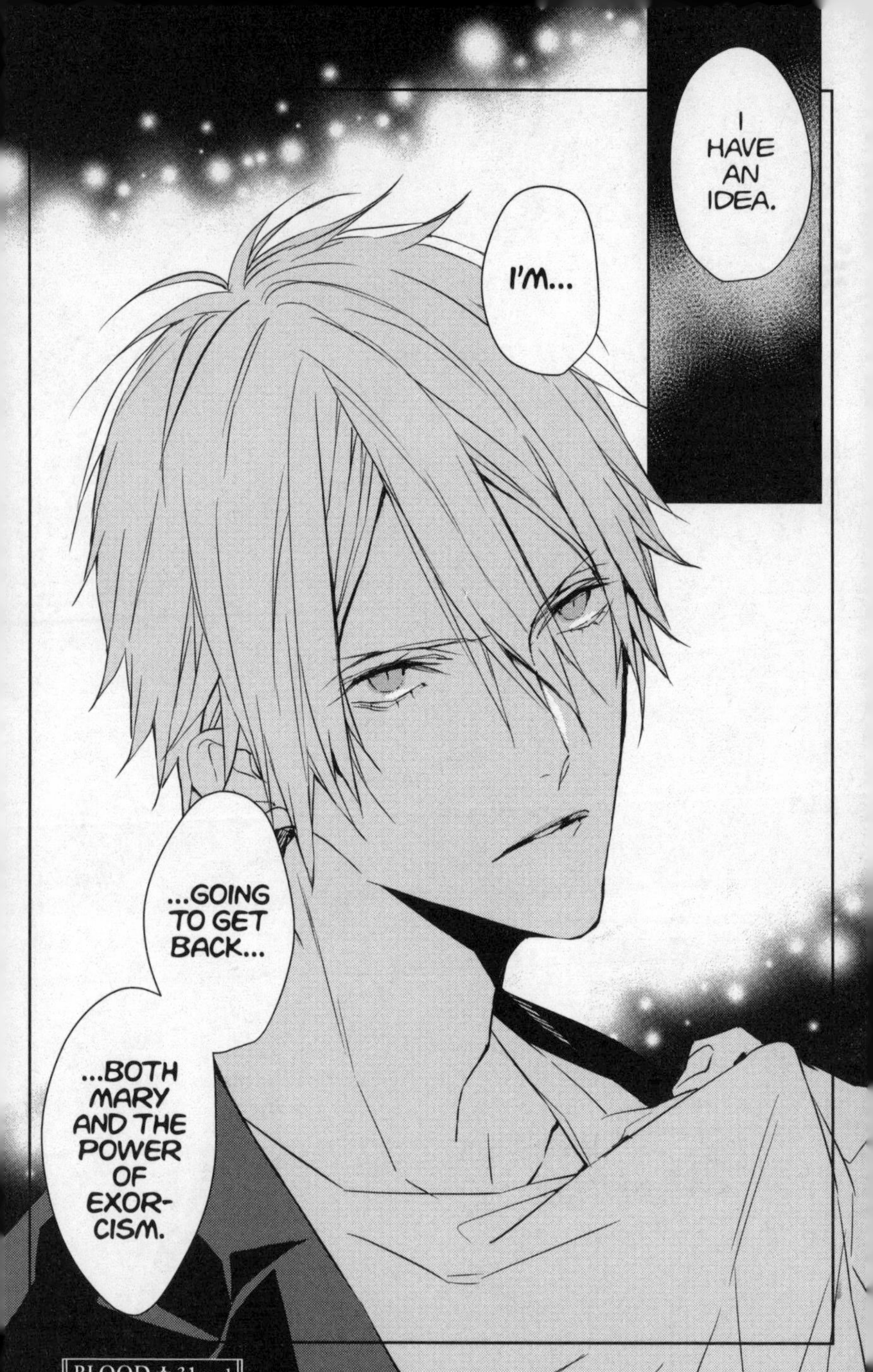
I HAVE AN IDEA.
I'M...
...GOING TO GET BACK...
...BOTH MARY AND THE POWER OF EXOR-CISM.

# Bloody✝Mary

MEANWHILE, MARY...

...WAS SLEEPING.

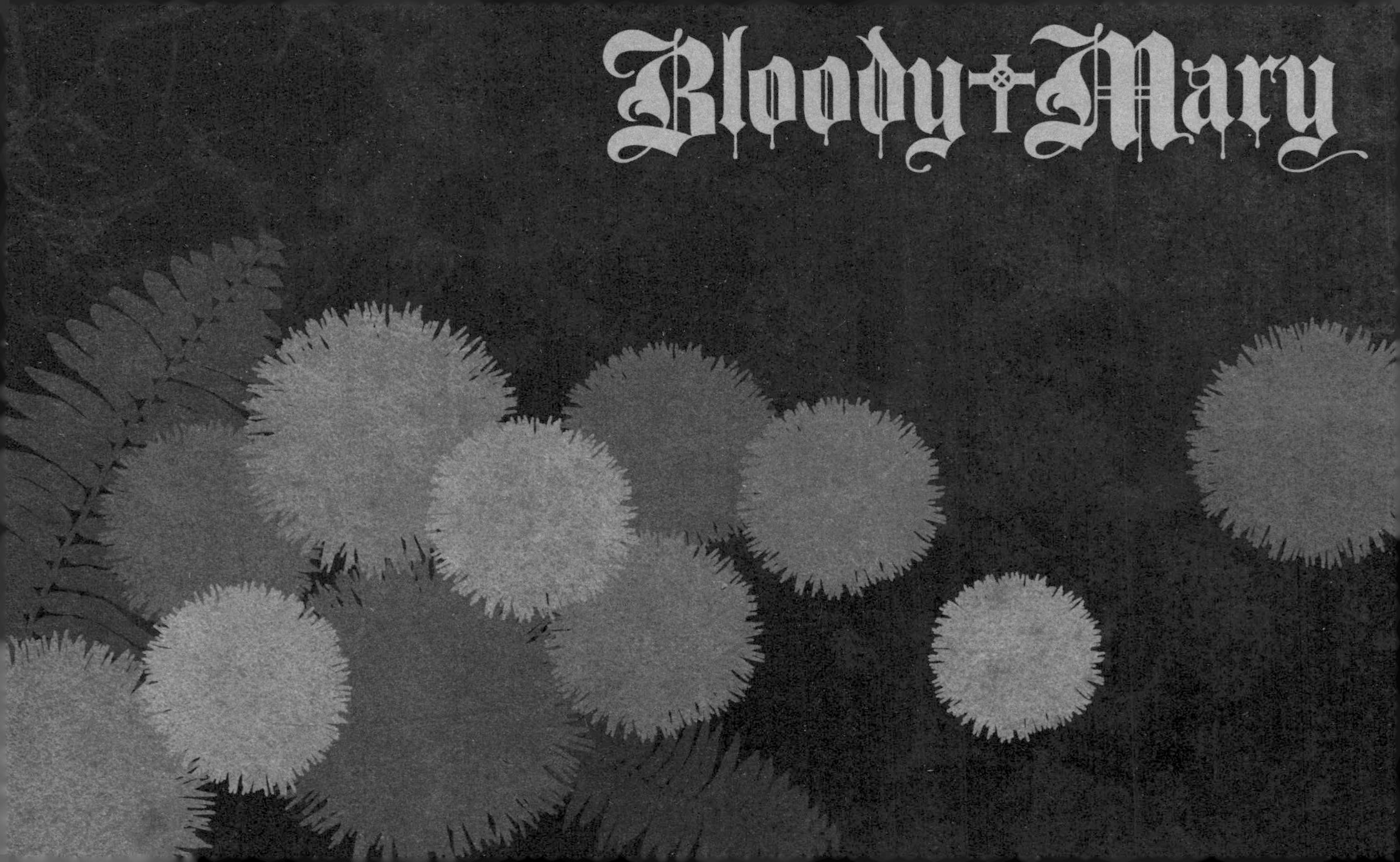
Bloody+Mary

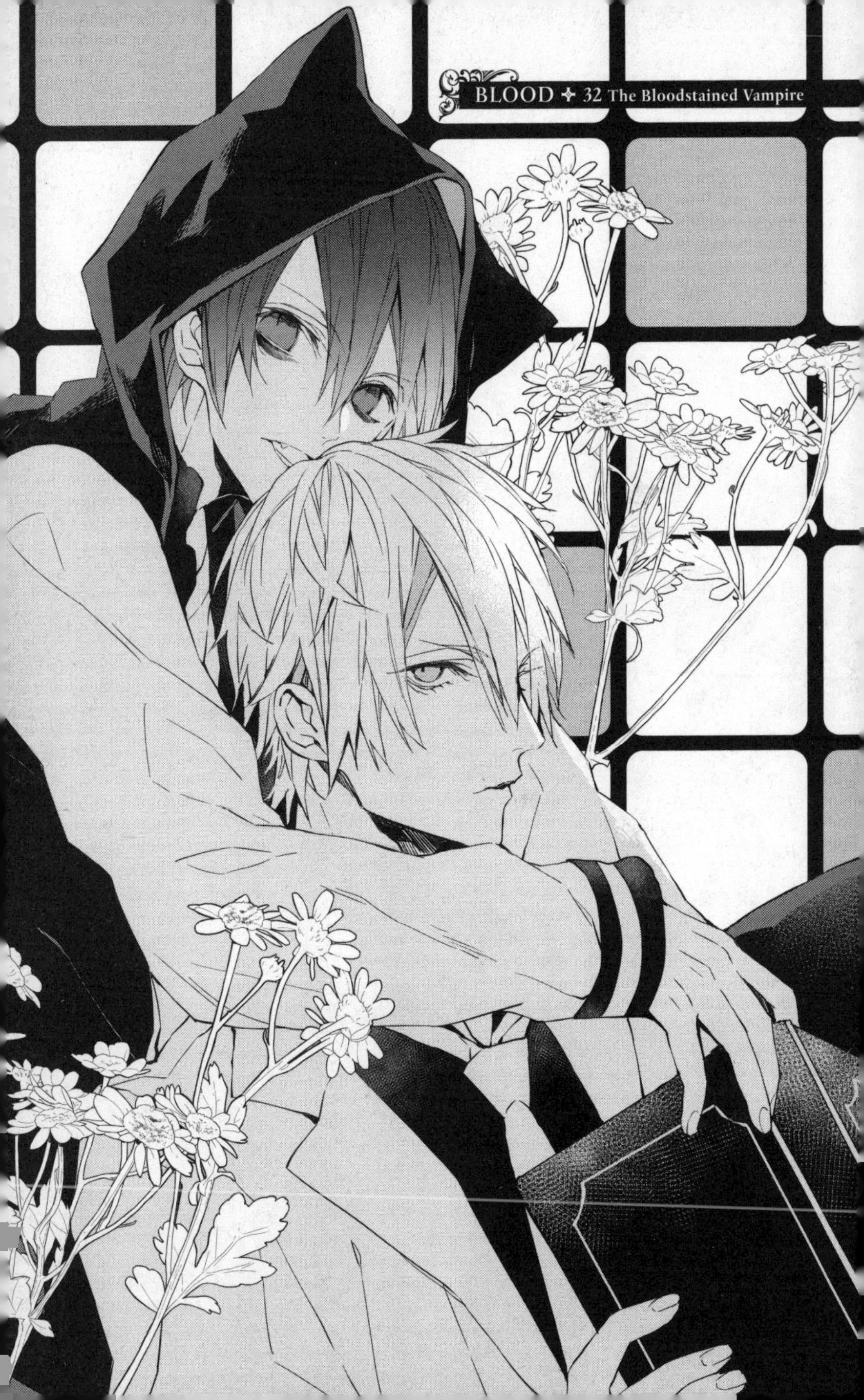
BLOOD ✣ 32 The Bloodstained Vampire

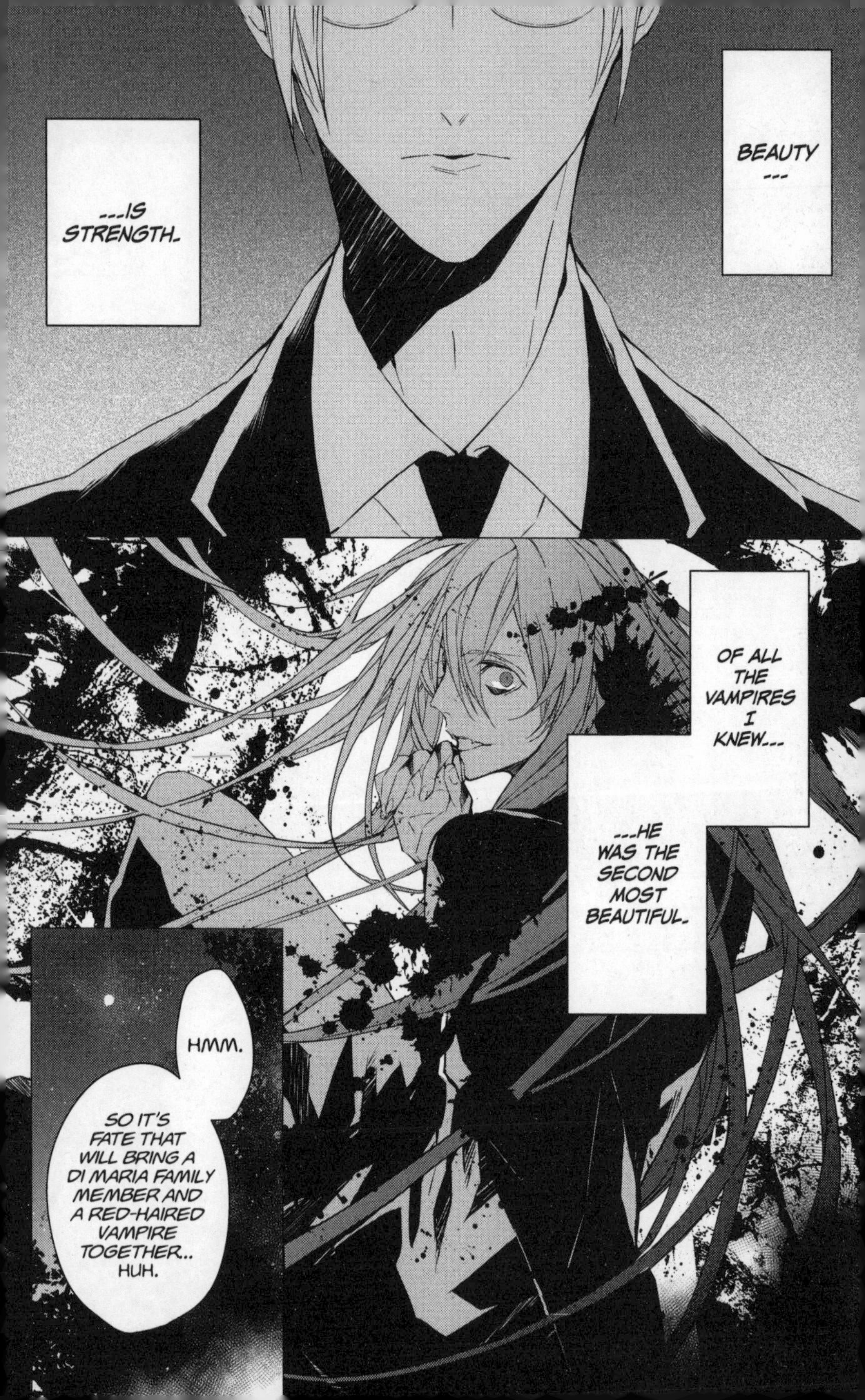
BEAUTY ---
---IS STRENGTH.
OF ALL THE VAMPIRES I KNEW---
---HE WAS THE SECOND MOST BEAUTIFUL.
HMM.
SO IT'S FATE THAT WILL BRING A DI MARIA FAMILY MEMBER AND A RED-HAIRED VAMPIRE TOGETHER... HUH.

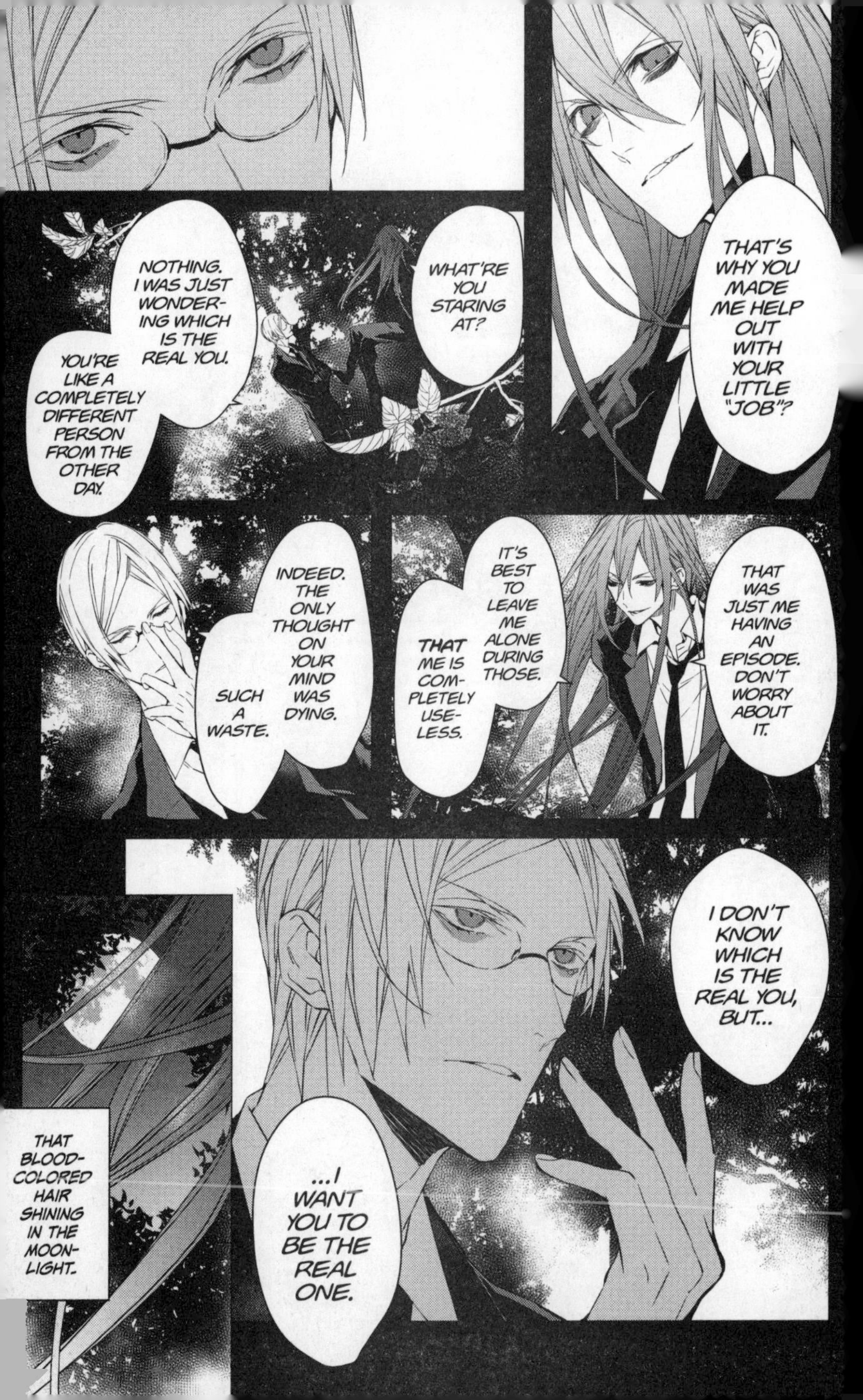
THAT'S WHY YOU MADE ME HELP OUT WITH YOUR LITTLE "JOB"?
WHAT'RE YOU STARING AT?
NOTHING. I WAS JUST WONDERING WHICH IS THE REAL YOU.
YOU'RE LIKE A COMPLETELY DIFFERENT PERSON FROM THE OTHER DAY.
THAT WAS JUST ME HAVING AN EPISODE. DON'T WORRY ABOUT IT.
IT'S BEST TO LEAVE ME ALONE DURING THOSE.
THAT ME IS COMPLETELY USELESS.
INDEED. THE ONLY THOUGHT ON YOUR MIND WAS DYING.
SUCH A WASTE.
I DON'T KNOW WHICH IS THE REAL YOU, BUT...
...I WANT YOU TO BE THE REAL ONE.
THAT BLOOD-COLORED HAIR SHINING IN THE MOONLIGHT.

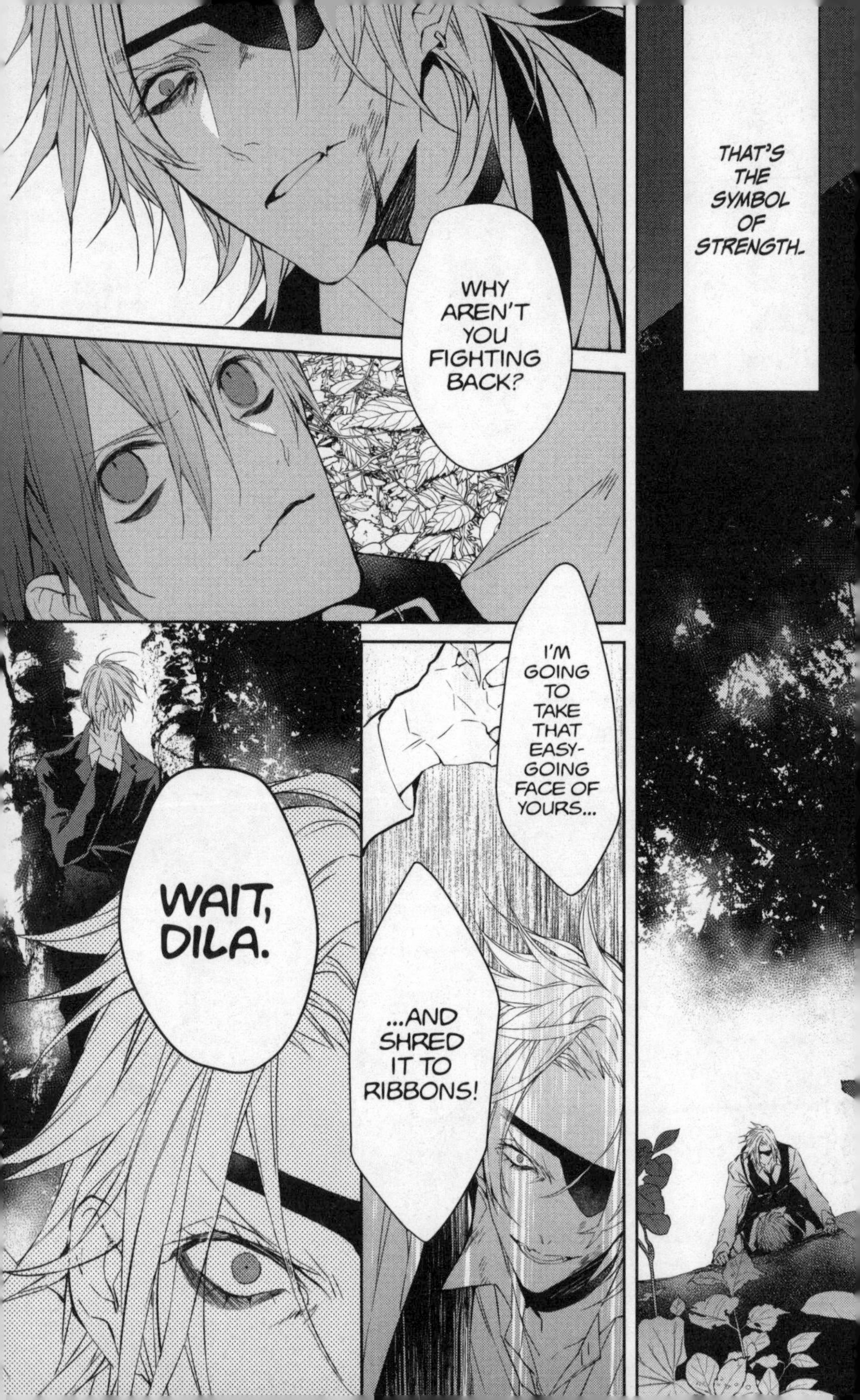
THAT'S THE SYMBOL OF STRENGTH.
WHY AREN'T YOU FIGHTING BACK?
I'M GOING TO TAKE THAT EASY-GOING FACE OF YOURS...
...AND SHRED IT TO RIBBONS!
WAIT, DILA.

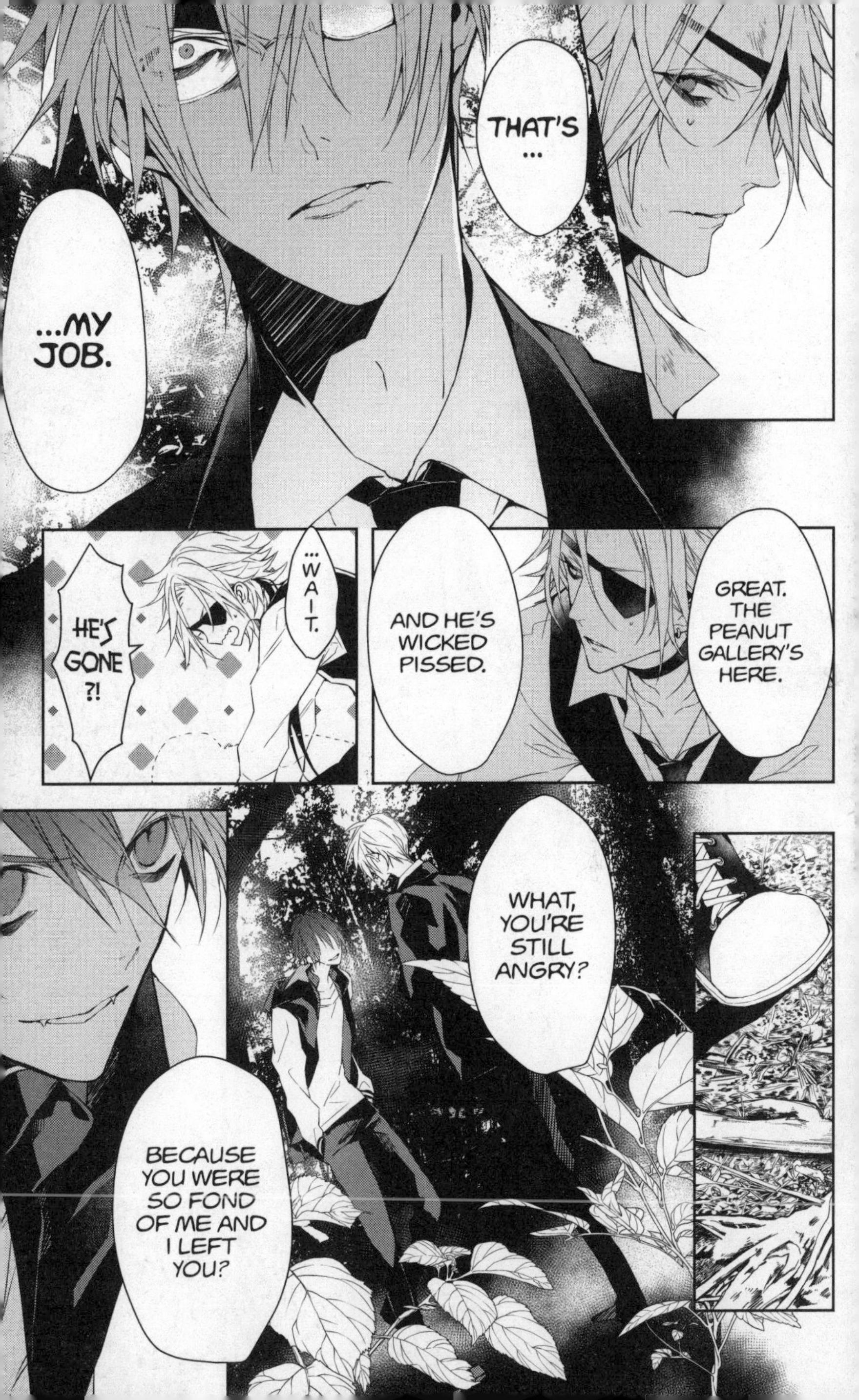
THAT'S ...
...MY JOB.
GREAT. THE PEANUT GALLERY'S HERE.
AND HE'S WICKED PISSED.
...WAIT.
HE'S GONE ?!
WHAT, YOU'RE STILL ANGRY?
BECAUSE YOU WERE SO FOND OF ME AND I LEFT YOU?

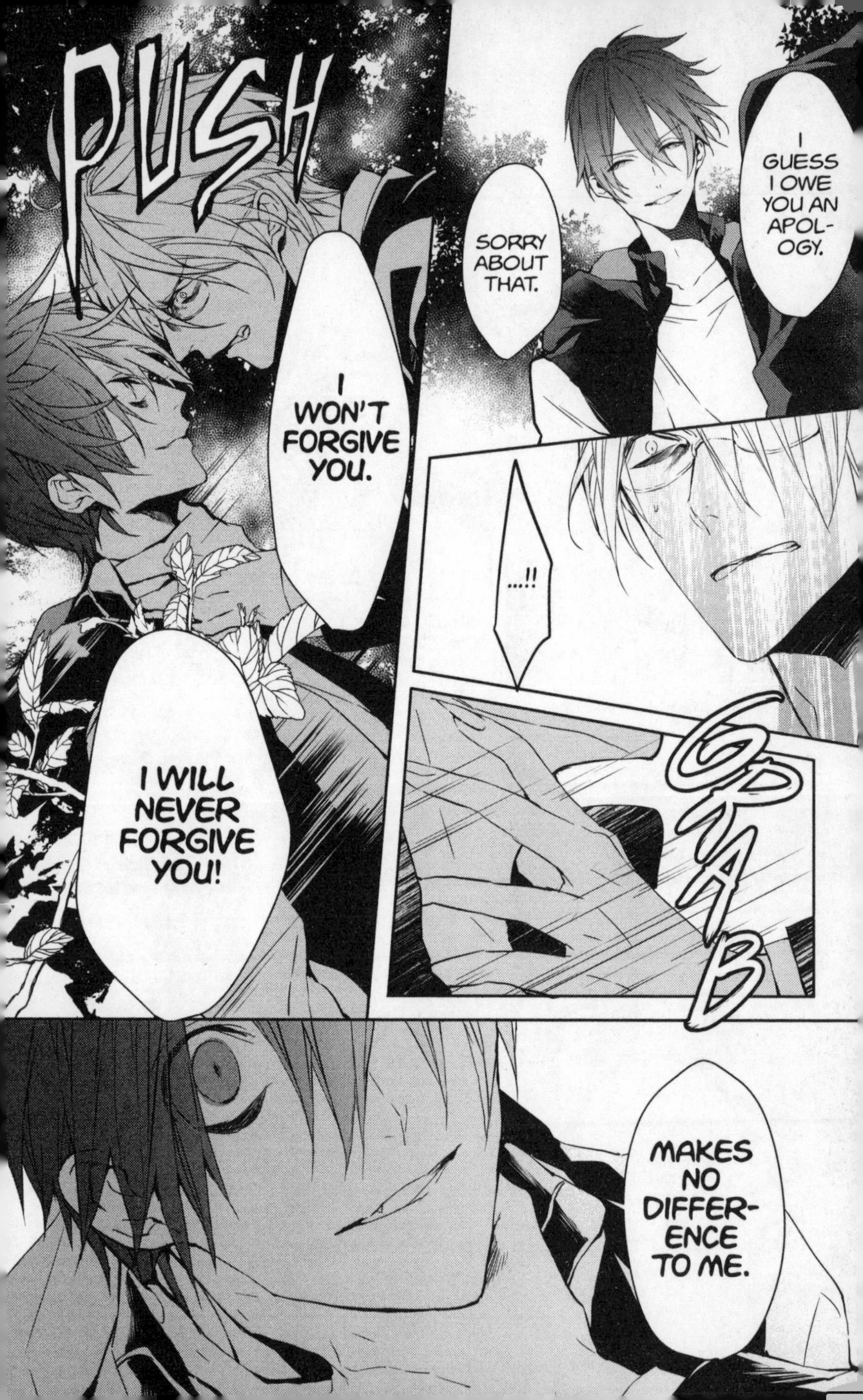
I GUESS I OWE YOU AN APOLOGY.
SORRY ABOUT THAT.
...!!
GRAB
PUSH
I WON'T FORGIVE YOU.
I WILL NEVER FORGIVE YOU!
MAKES NO DIFFERENCE TO ME.

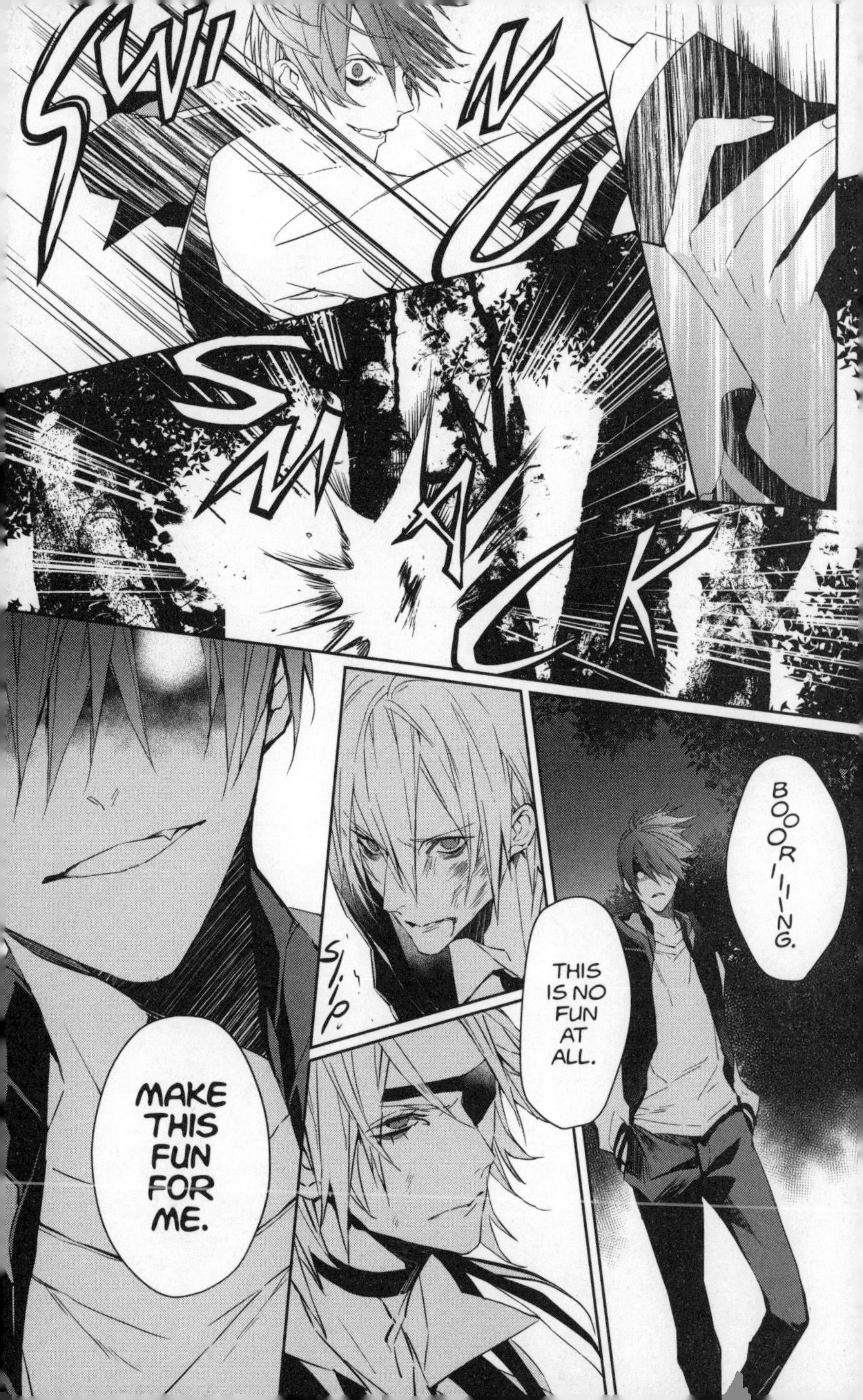
SWING
SMACK
BOOORIIIING.
THIS IS NO FUN AT ALL.
SLIP
MAKE THIS FUN FOR ME.

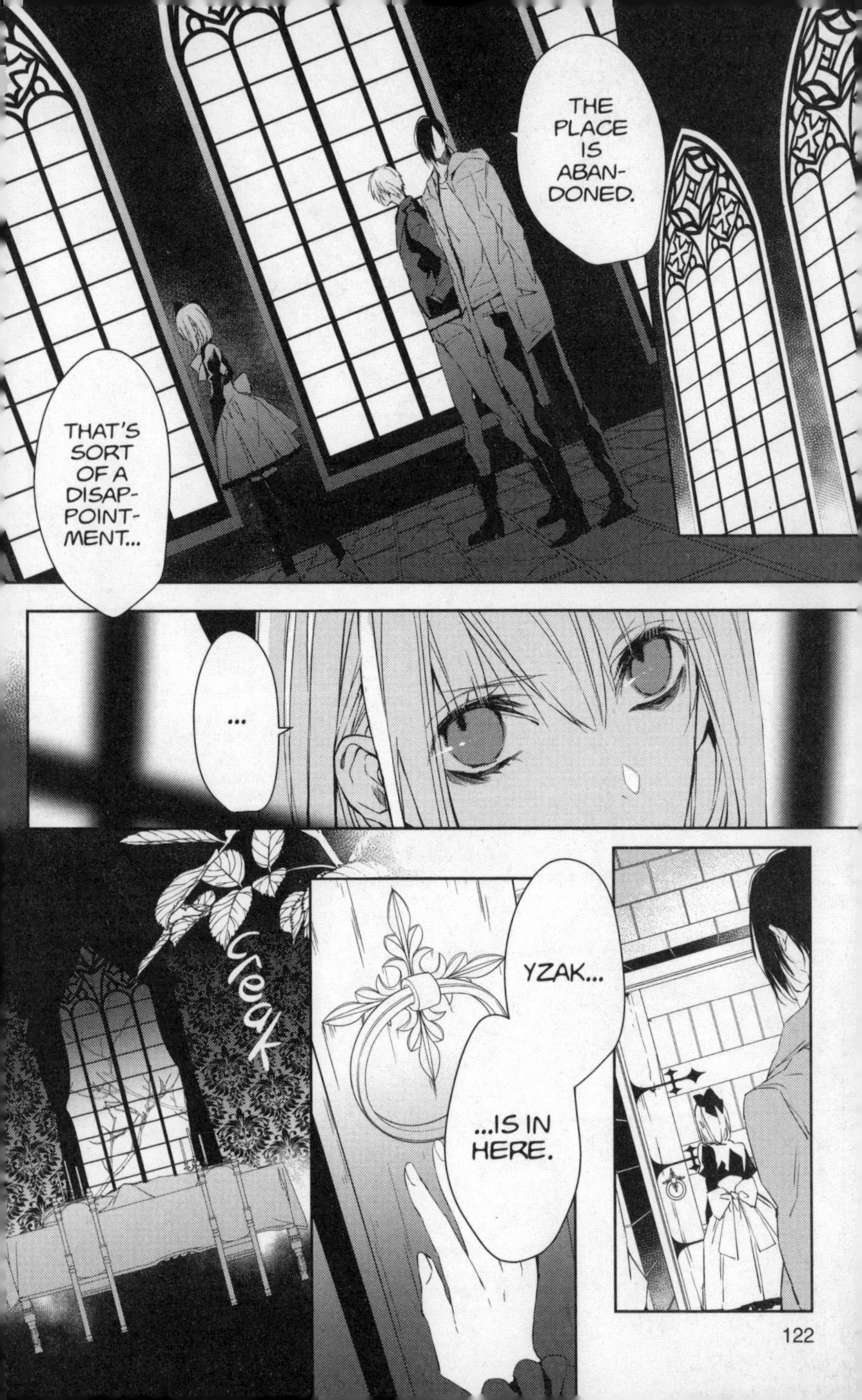
THE PLACE IS ABAN-DONED.
THAT'S SORT OF A DISAP-POINT-MENT...
...
YZAK...
...IS IN HERE.
Creak

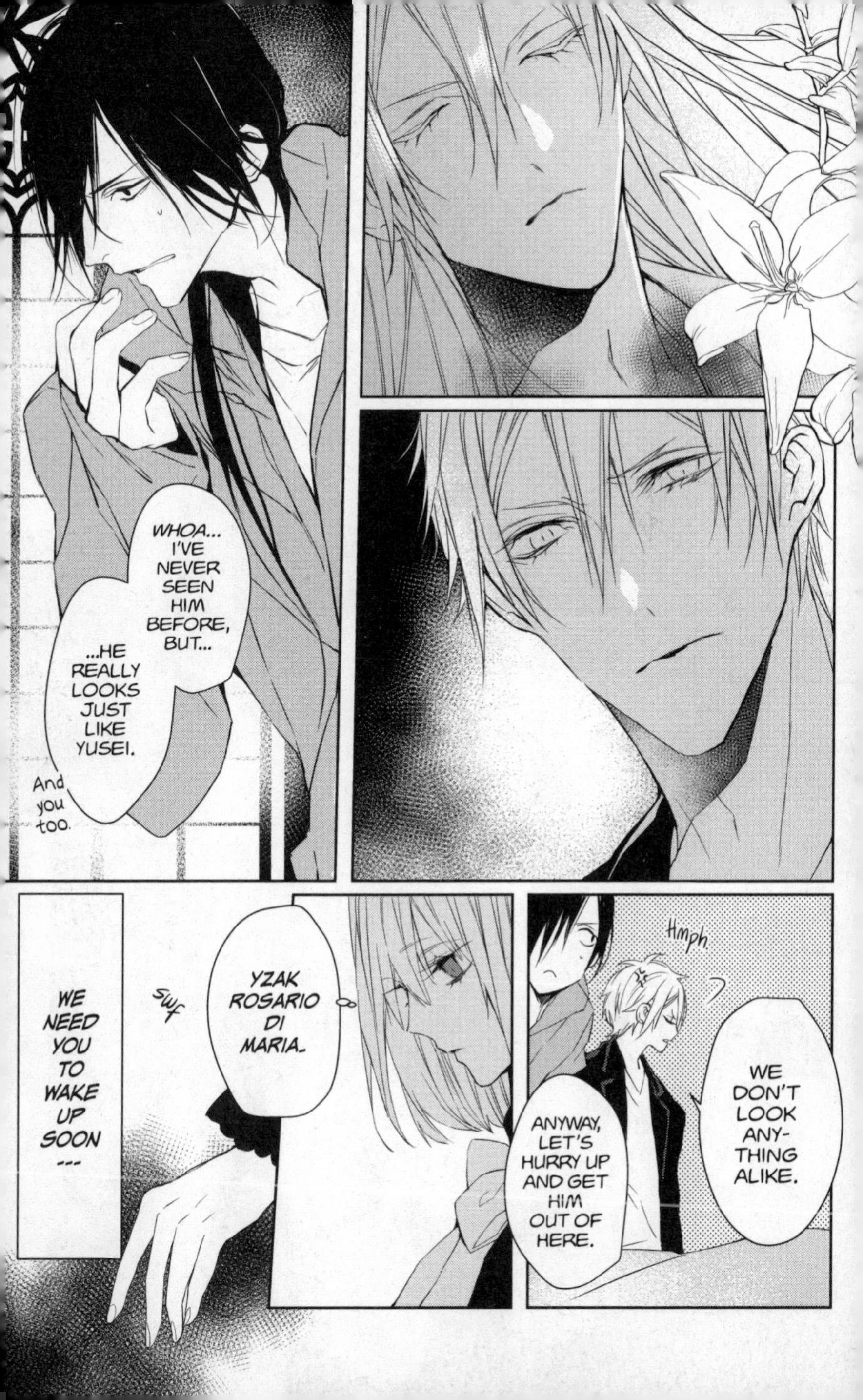
WHOA... I'VE NEVER SEEN HIM BEFORE, BUT...
...HE REALLY LOOKS JUST LIKE YUSEI.
And you too.
Hmph.
WE DON'T LOOK ANY-THING ALIKE.
ANYWAY, LET'S HURRY UP AND GET HIM OUT OF HERE.
YZAK ROSARIO DI MARIA.
swf
WE NEED YOU TO WAKE UP SOON---

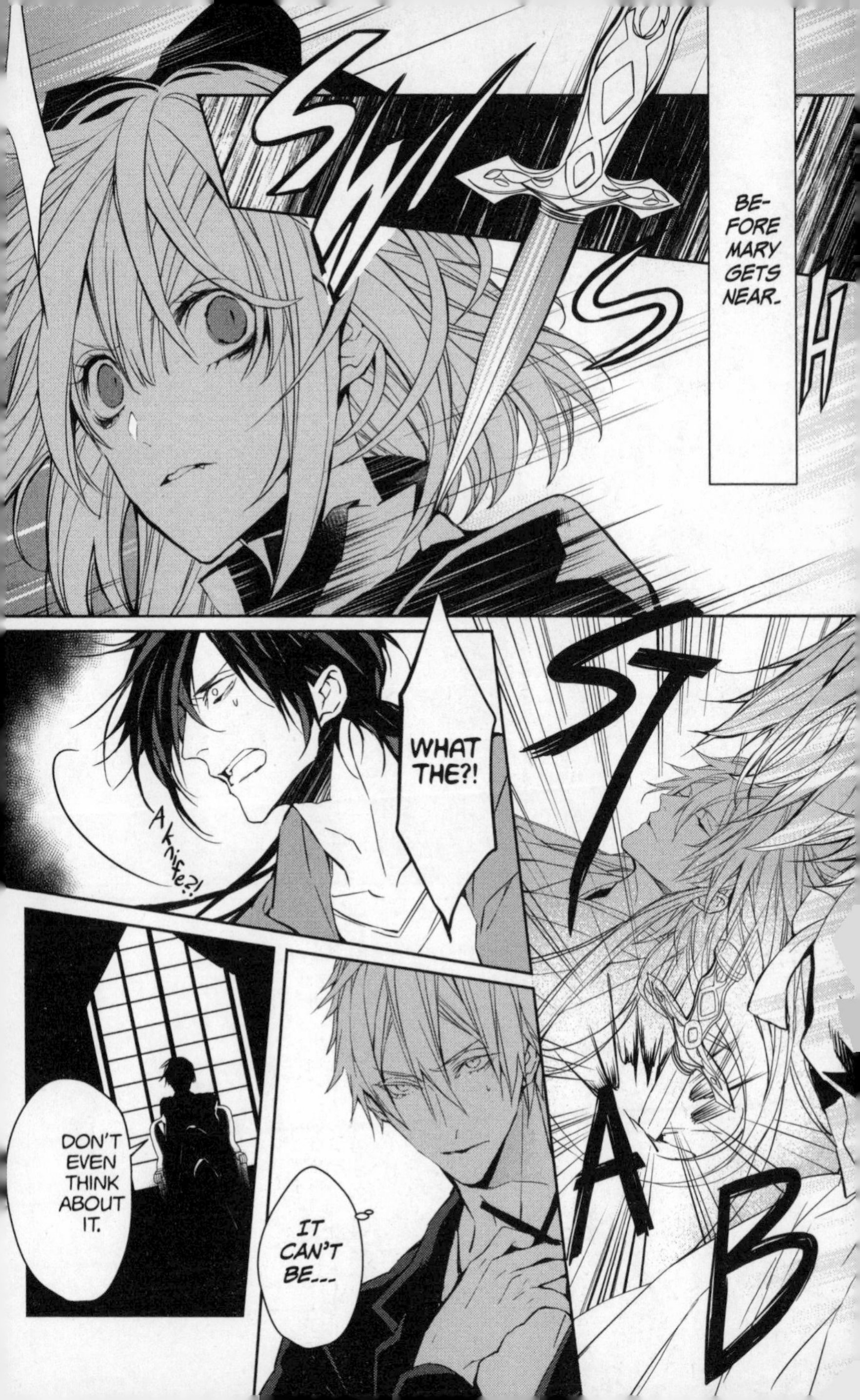
BE-FORE MARY GETS NEAR...
SWISH
STAB
WHAT THE?!
A knife?!
IT CAN'T BE...
DON'T EVEN THINK ABOUT IT.

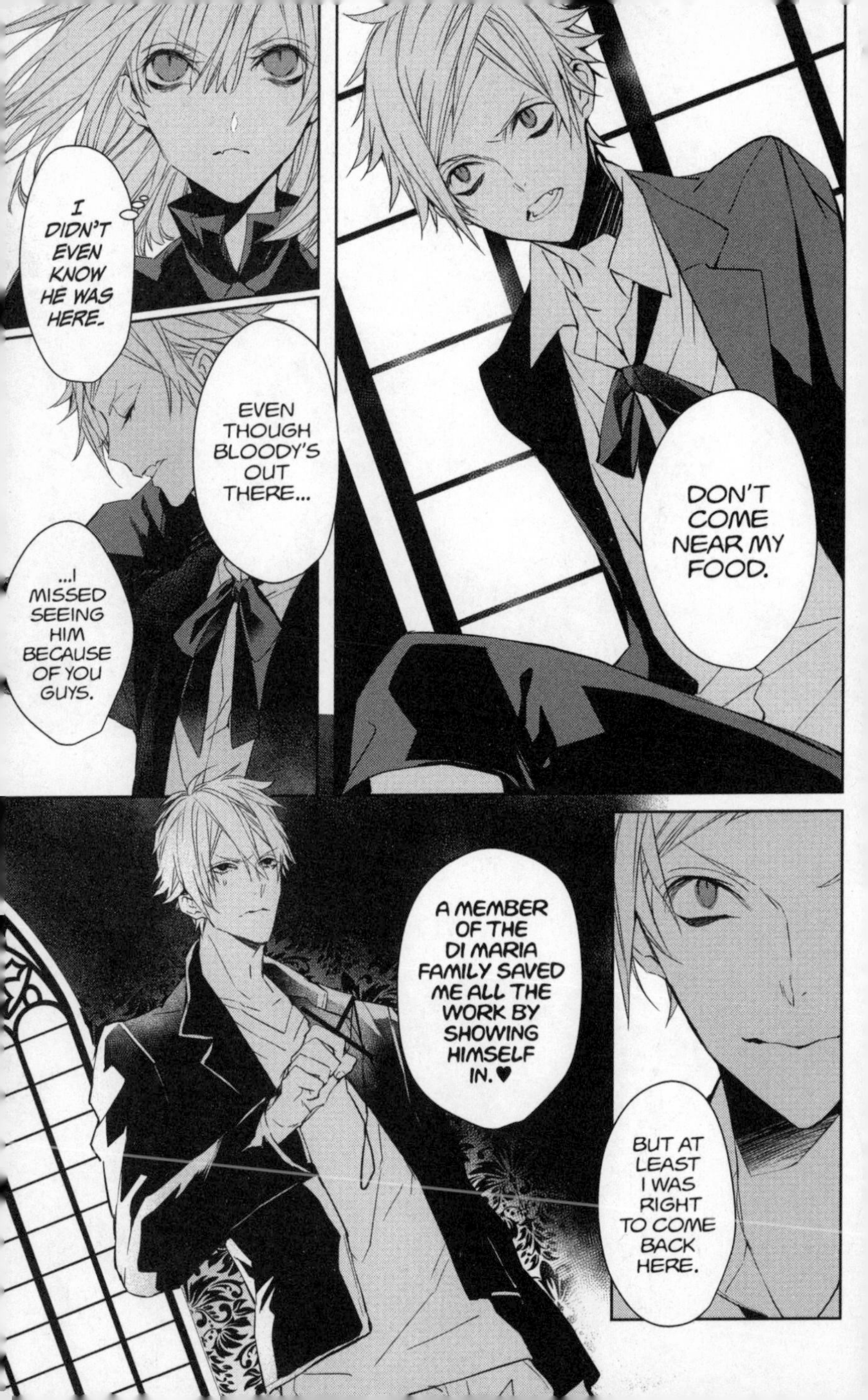
DON'T COME NEAR MY FOOD.
I DIDN'T EVEN KNOW HE WAS HERE.
EVEN THOUGH BLOODY'S OUT THERE...
...I MISSED SEEING HIM BECAUSE OF YOU GUYS.
A MEMBER OF THE DI MARIA FAMILY SAVED ME ALL THE WORK BY SHOWING HIMSELF IN.♥
BUT AT LEAST I WAS RIGHT TO COME BACK HERE.

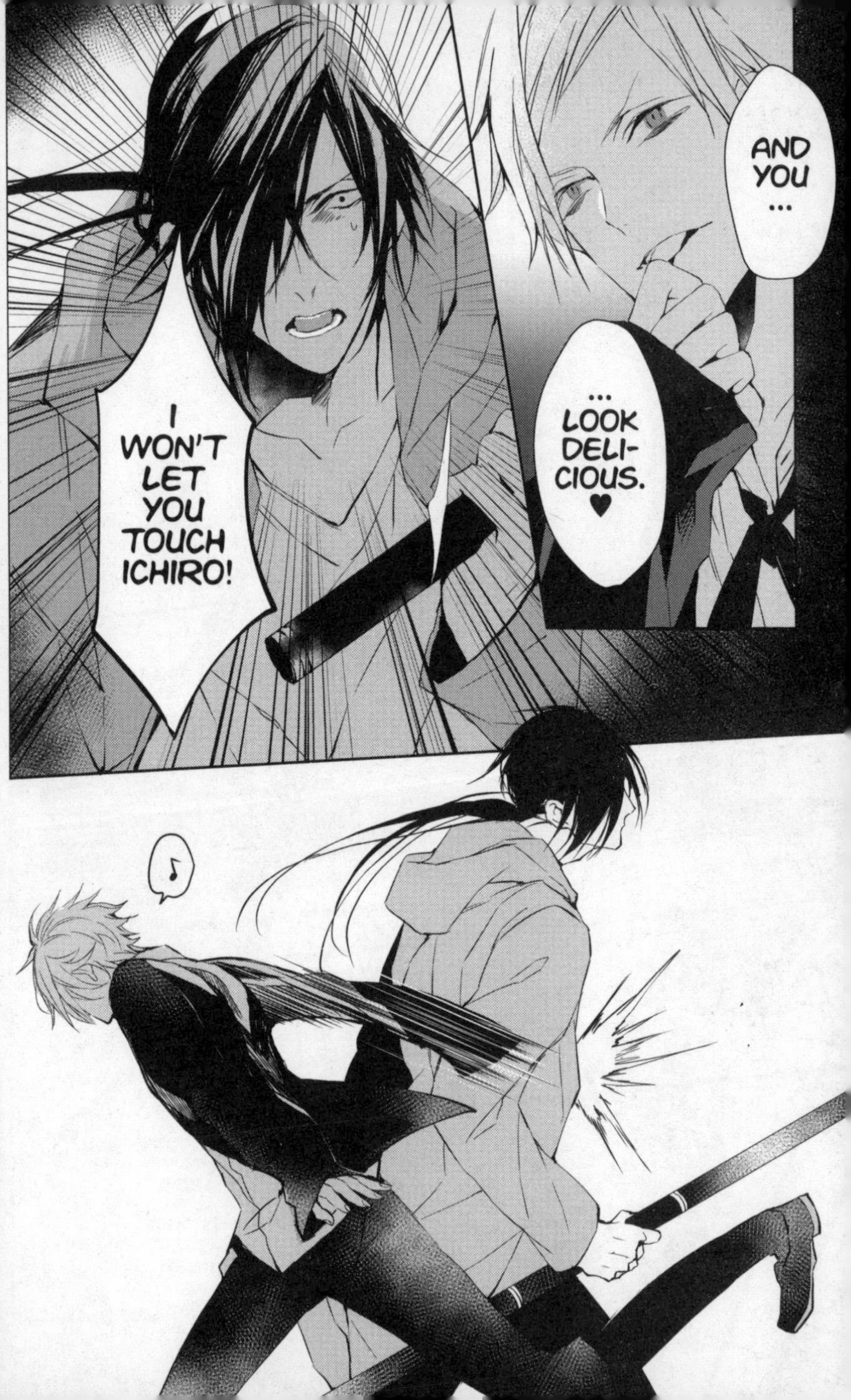
AND YOU ...
... LOOK DELICIOUS. ♥
I WON'T LET YOU TOUCH ICHIRO!
♪

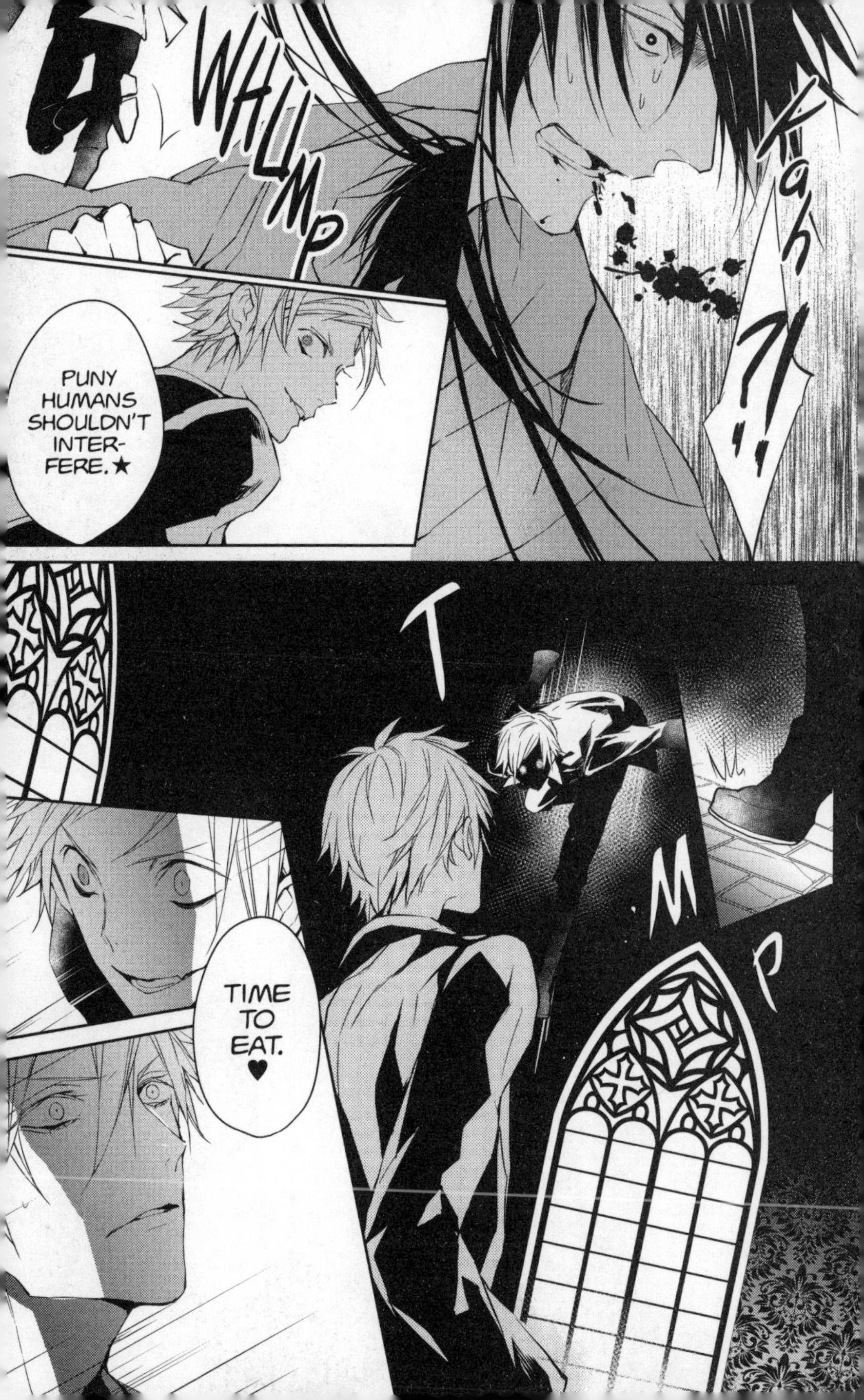
Kah?!!
WHUMP
PUNY HUMANS SHOULDN'T INTER-FERE.★
T
M
P
TIME TO EAT. ♥

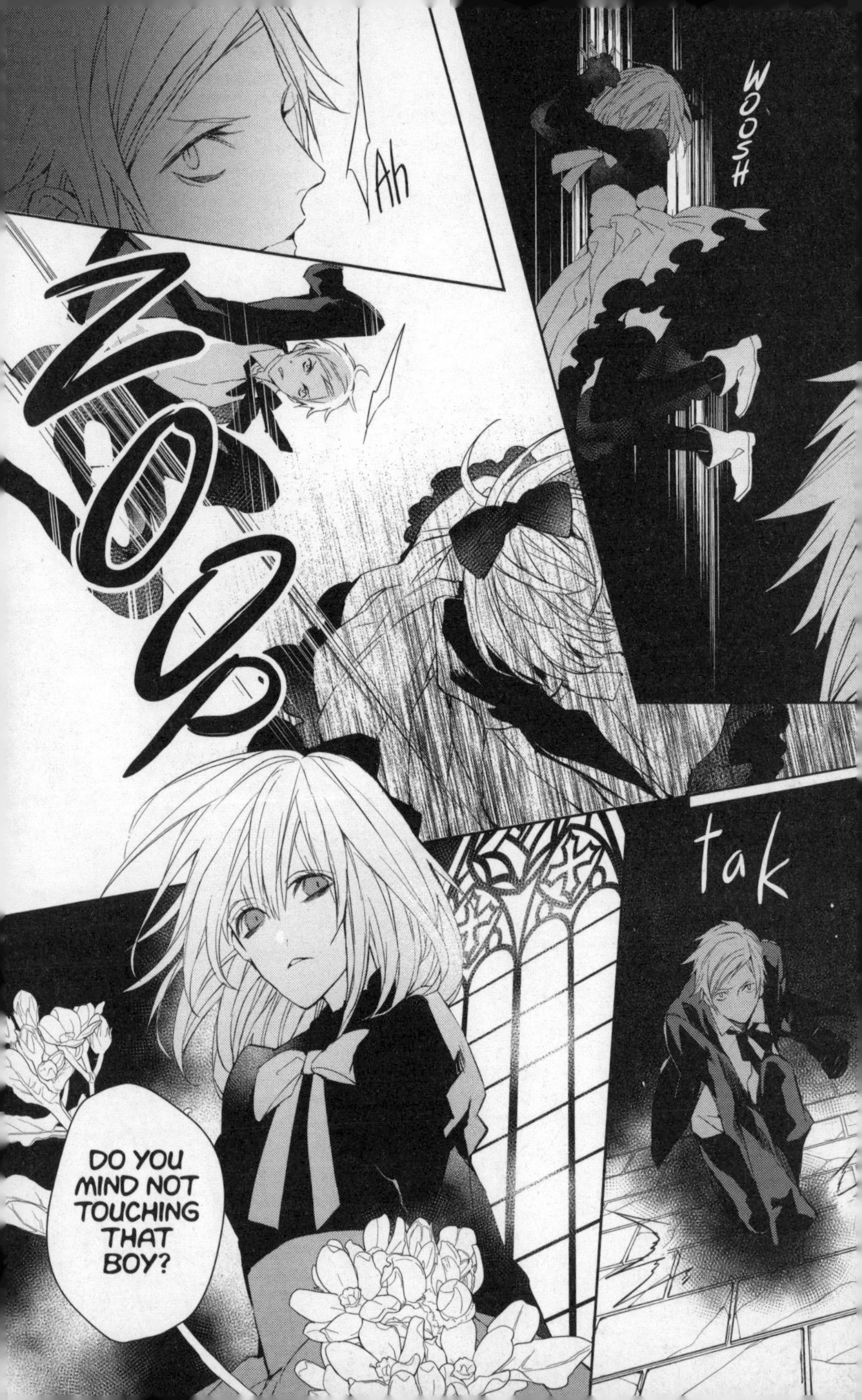
WOOSH
Ah
ZOOP
tak
DO YOU MIND NOT TOUCHING THAT BOY?

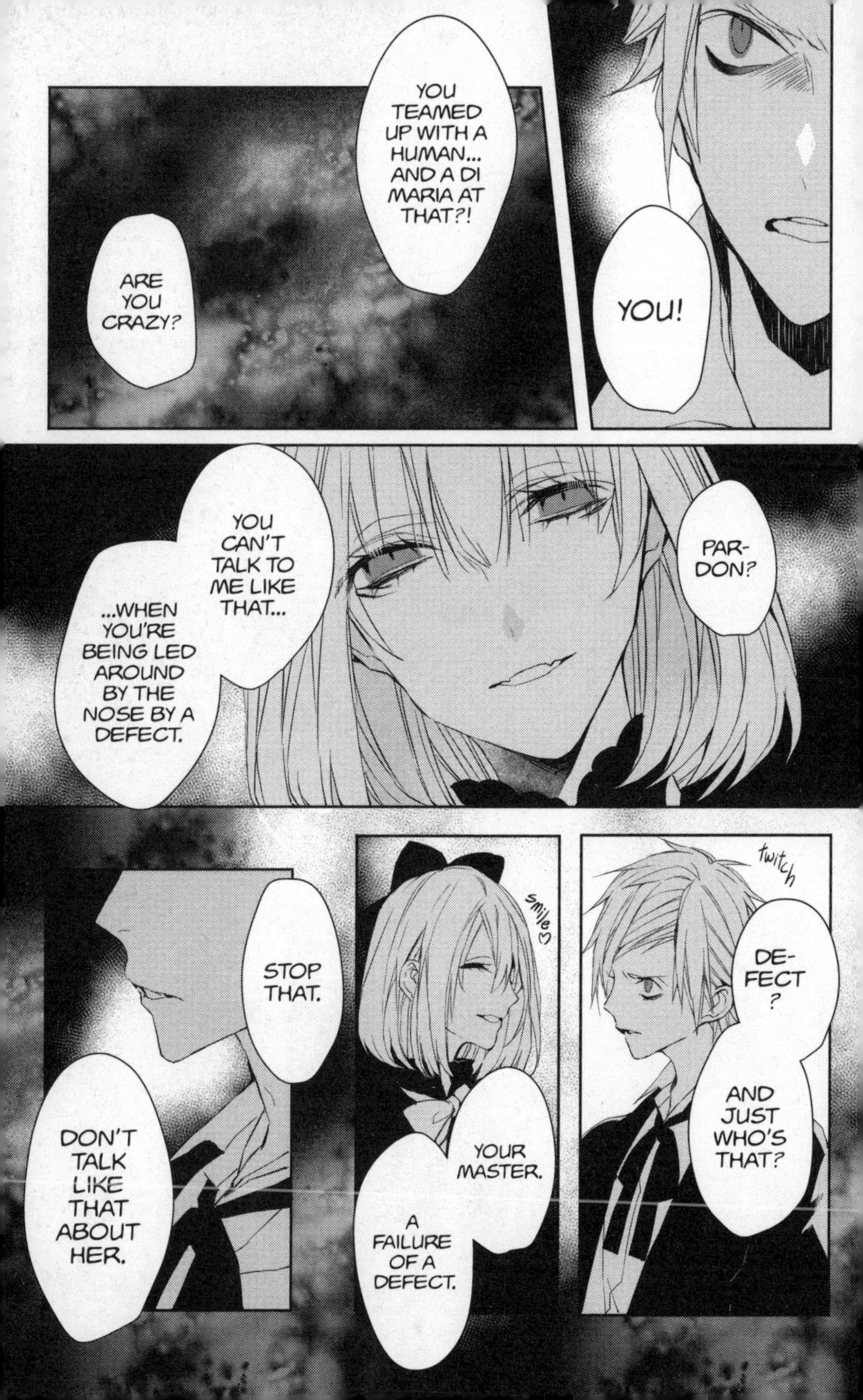
YOU!
YOU TEAMED UP WITH A HUMAN... AND A DI MARIA AT THAT?!
ARE YOU CRAZY?
PARDON?
YOU CAN'T TALK TO ME LIKE THAT...
...WHEN YOU'RE BEING LED AROUND BY THE NOSE BY A DEFECT.
twitch
DE-FECT?
AND JUST WHO'S THAT?
smile
YOUR MASTER.
A FAILURE OF A DEFECT.
STOP THAT.
DON'T TALK LIKE THAT ABOUT HER.

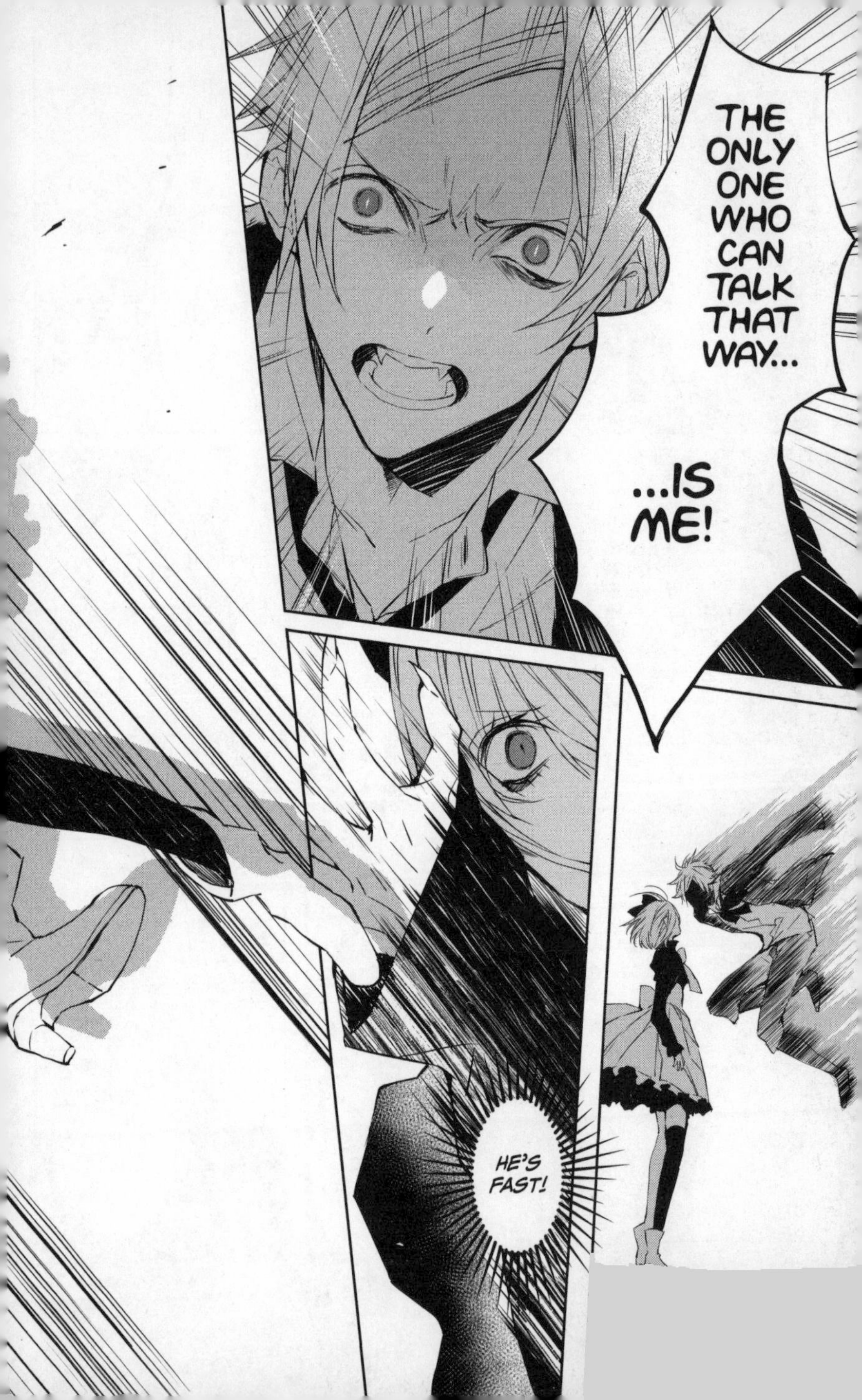
THE ONLY ONE WHO CAN TALK THAT WAY...
...IS ME!
HE'S FAST!

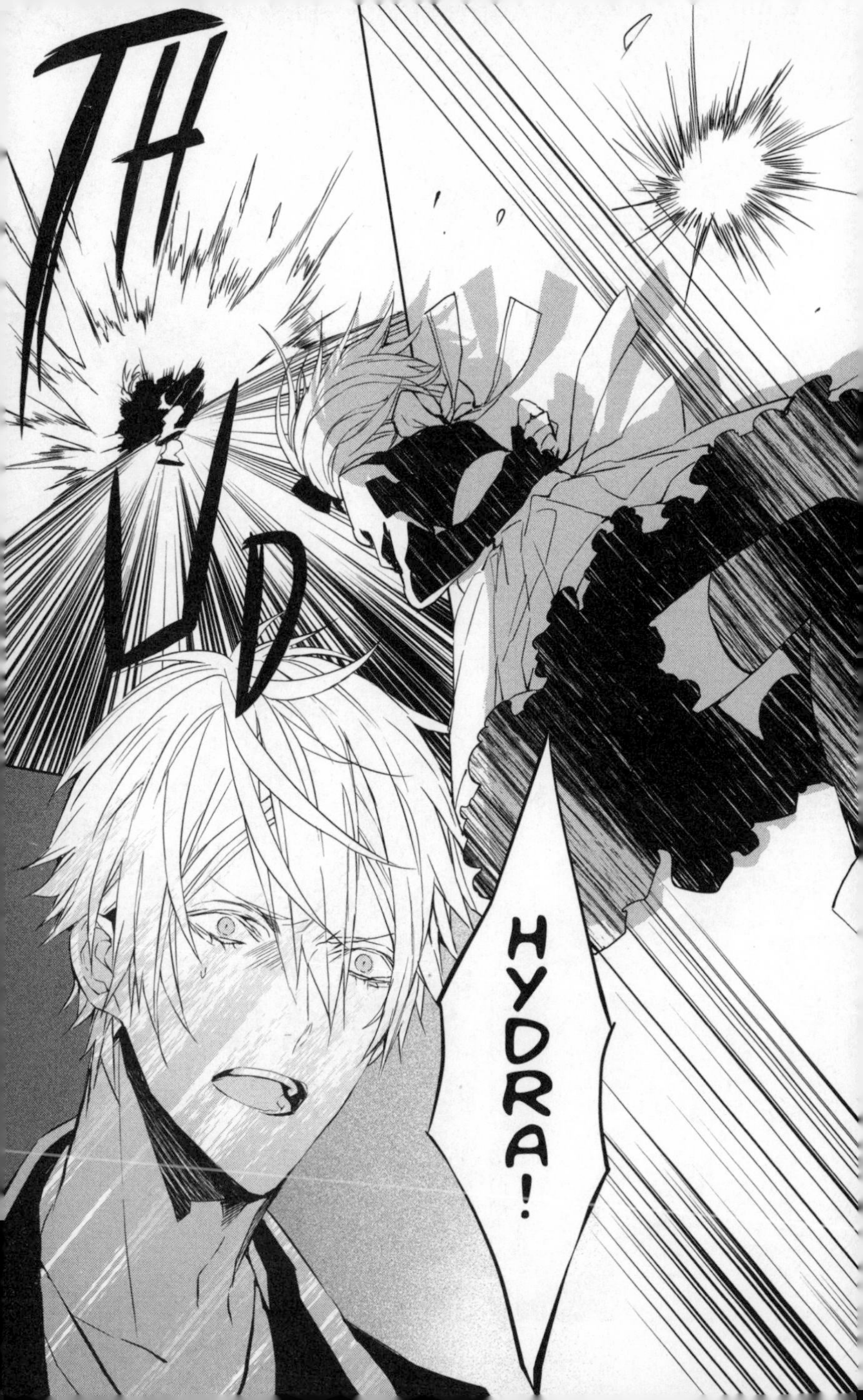
THUD
HYDRA!

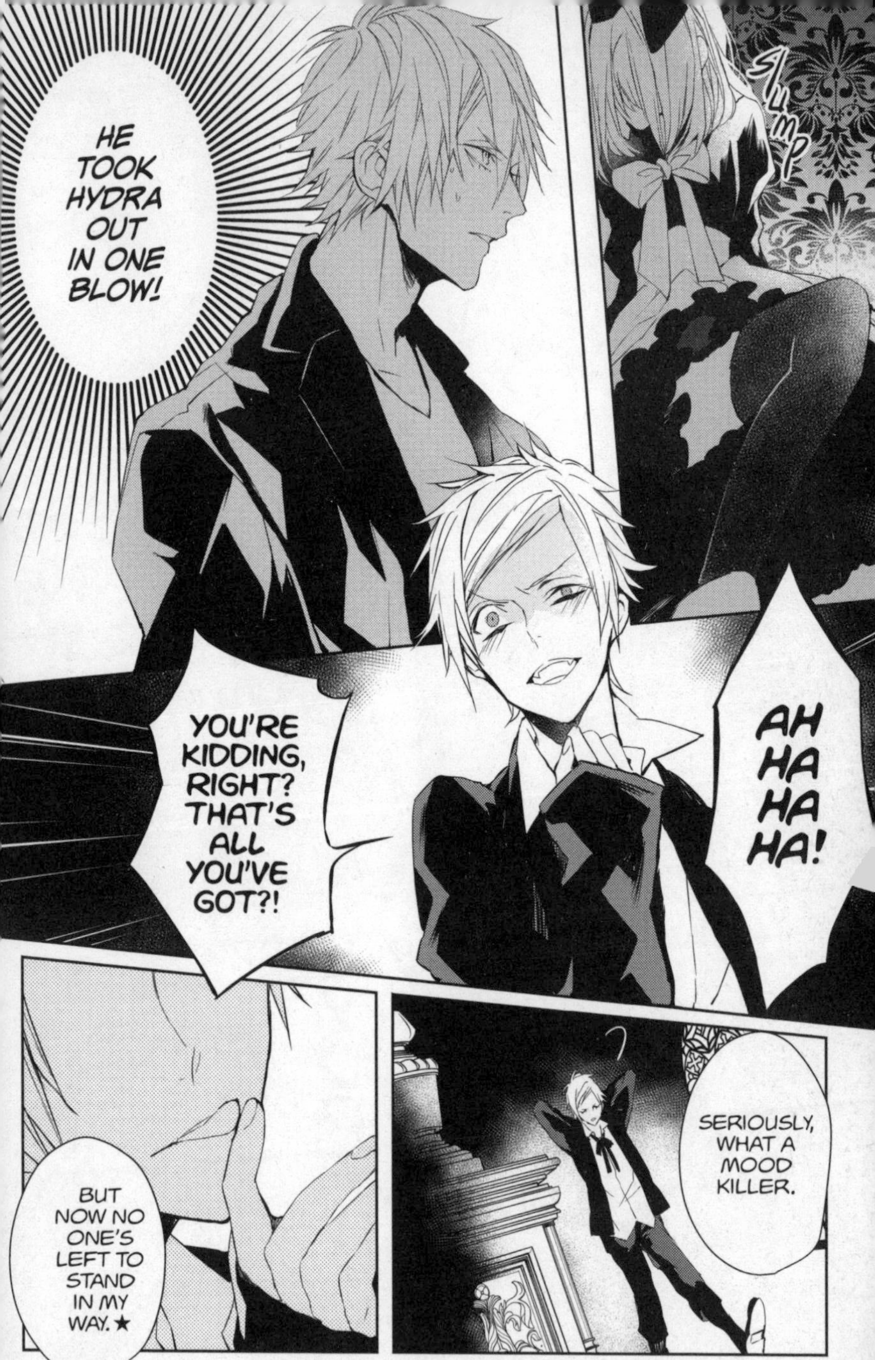
SLUMP
HE TOOK HYDRA OUT IN ONE BLOW!
AH HA HA HA!
YOU'RE KIDDING, RIGHT? THAT'S ALL YOU'VE GOT?!
SERIOUSLY, WHAT A MOOD KILLER.
BUT NOW NO ONE'S LEFT TO STAND IN MY WAY.★

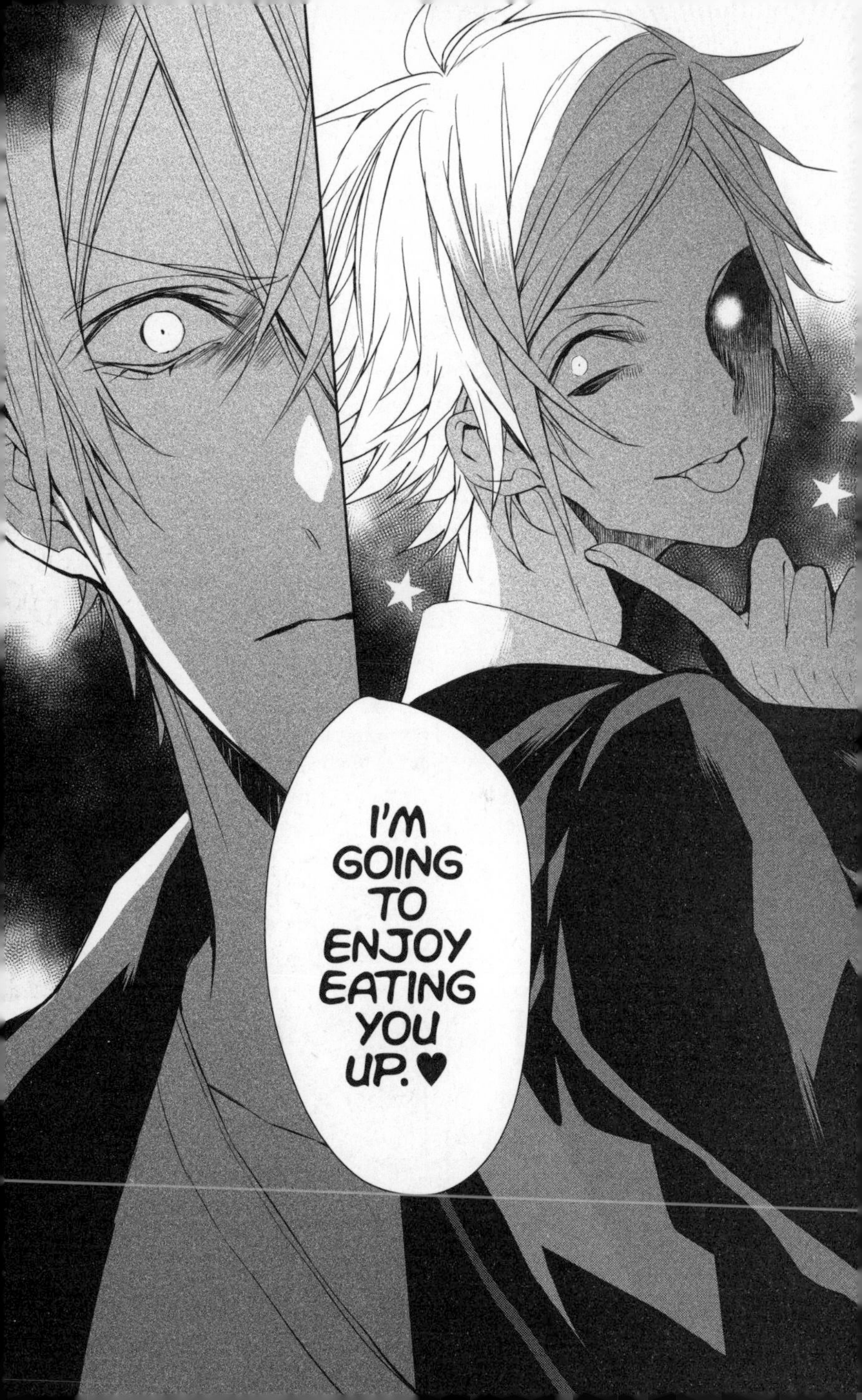
I'M GOING TO ENJOY EATING YOU UP.♥

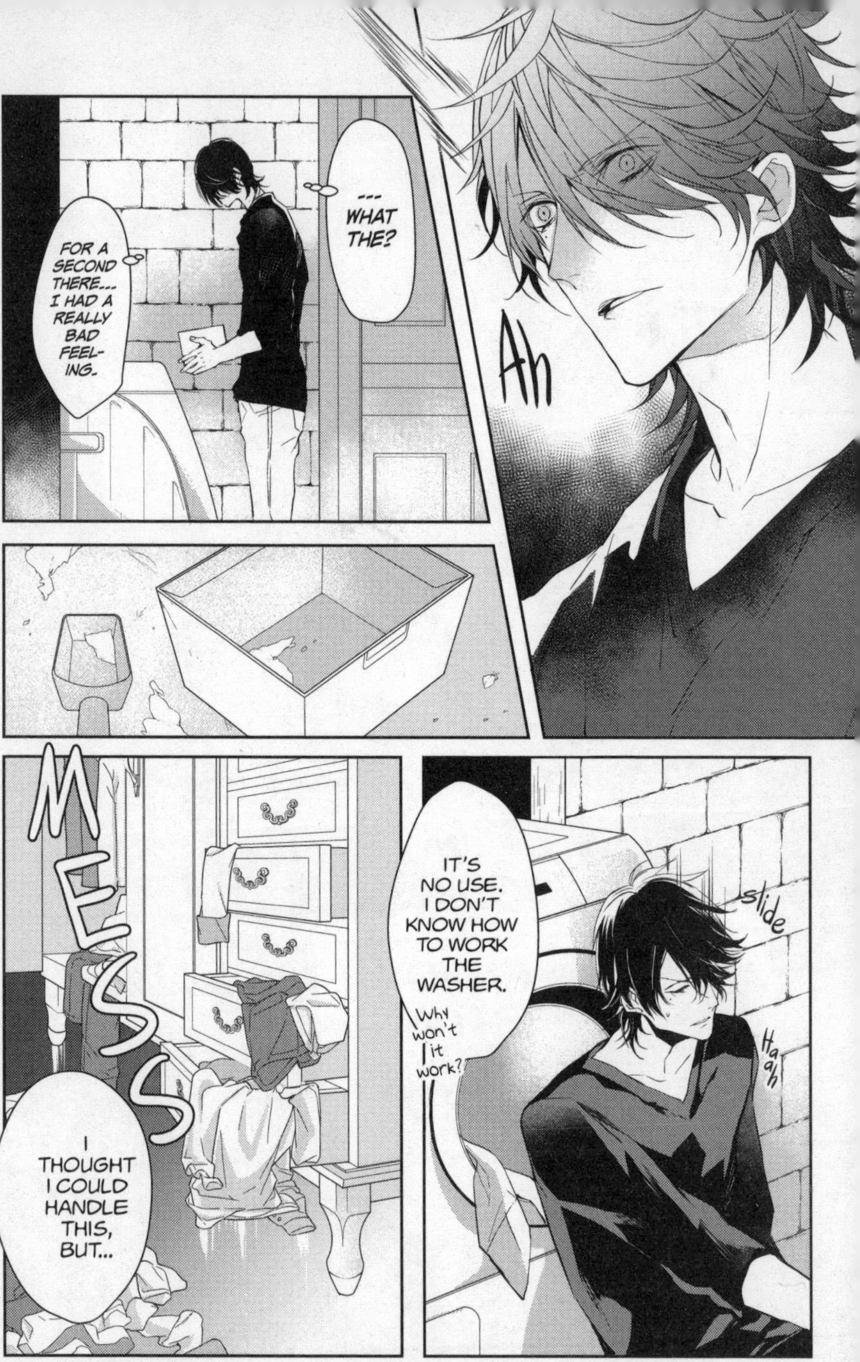
Ah
--- WHAT THE?
FOR A SECOND THERE... I HAD A REALLY BAD FEEL- ING.
slide
IT'S NO USE. I DON'T KNOW HOW TO WORK THE WASHER.
Haah
Why won't it work?
MESS
I THOUGHT I COULD HANDLE THIS, BUT...

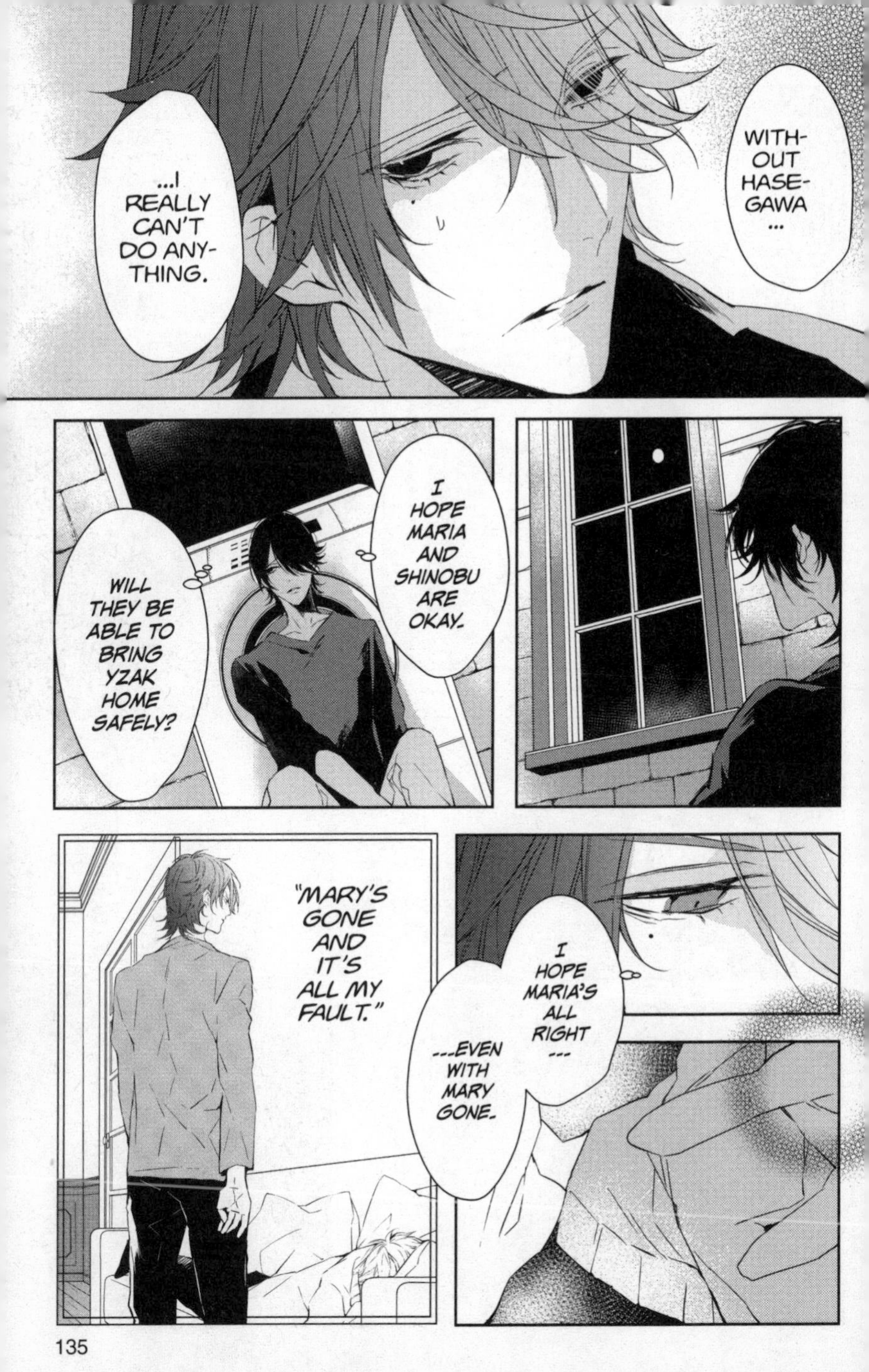
WITHOUT HASEGAWA...
...I REALLY CAN'T DO ANYTHING.
I HOPE MARIA AND SHINOBU ARE OKAY...
WILL THEY BE ABLE TO BRING YZAK HOME SAFELY?
I HOPE MARIA'S ALL RIGHT...
...EVEN WITH MARY GONE...
"MARY'S GONE AND IT'S ALL MY FAULT."

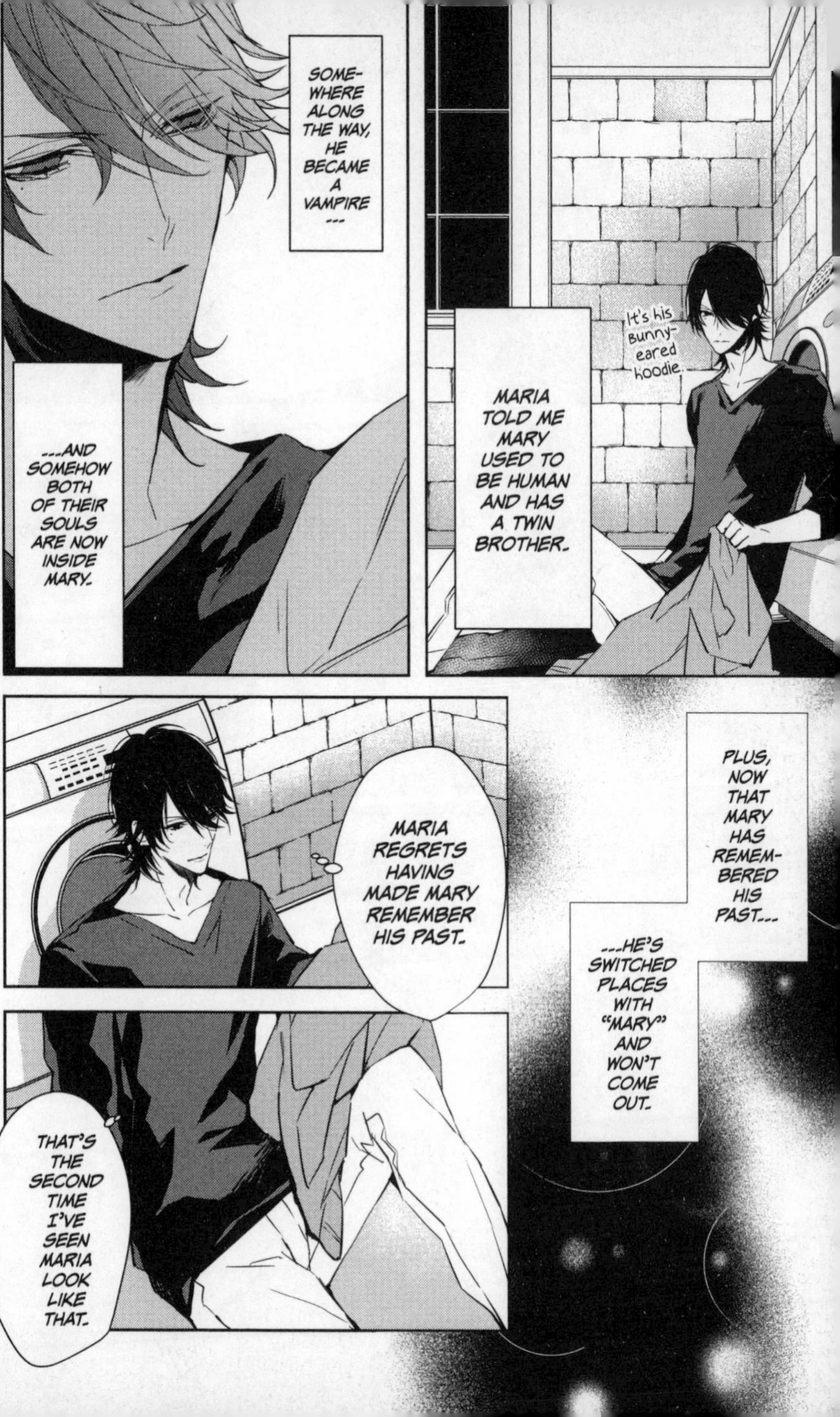
It's his bunny-eared hoodie.
MARIA TOLD ME MARY USED TO BE HUMAN AND HAS A TWIN BROTHER.
SOME-WHERE ALONG THE WAY, HE BECAME A VAMPIRE---
---AND SOMEHOW BOTH OF THEIR SOULS ARE NOW INSIDE MARY.
PLUS, NOW THAT MARY HAS REMEM-BERED HIS PAST---
---HE'S SWITCHED PLACES WITH "MARY" AND WON'T COME OUT.
MARIA REGRETS HAVING MADE MARY REMEMBER HIS PAST.
THAT'S THE SECOND TIME I'VE SEEN MARIA LOOK LIKE THAT.

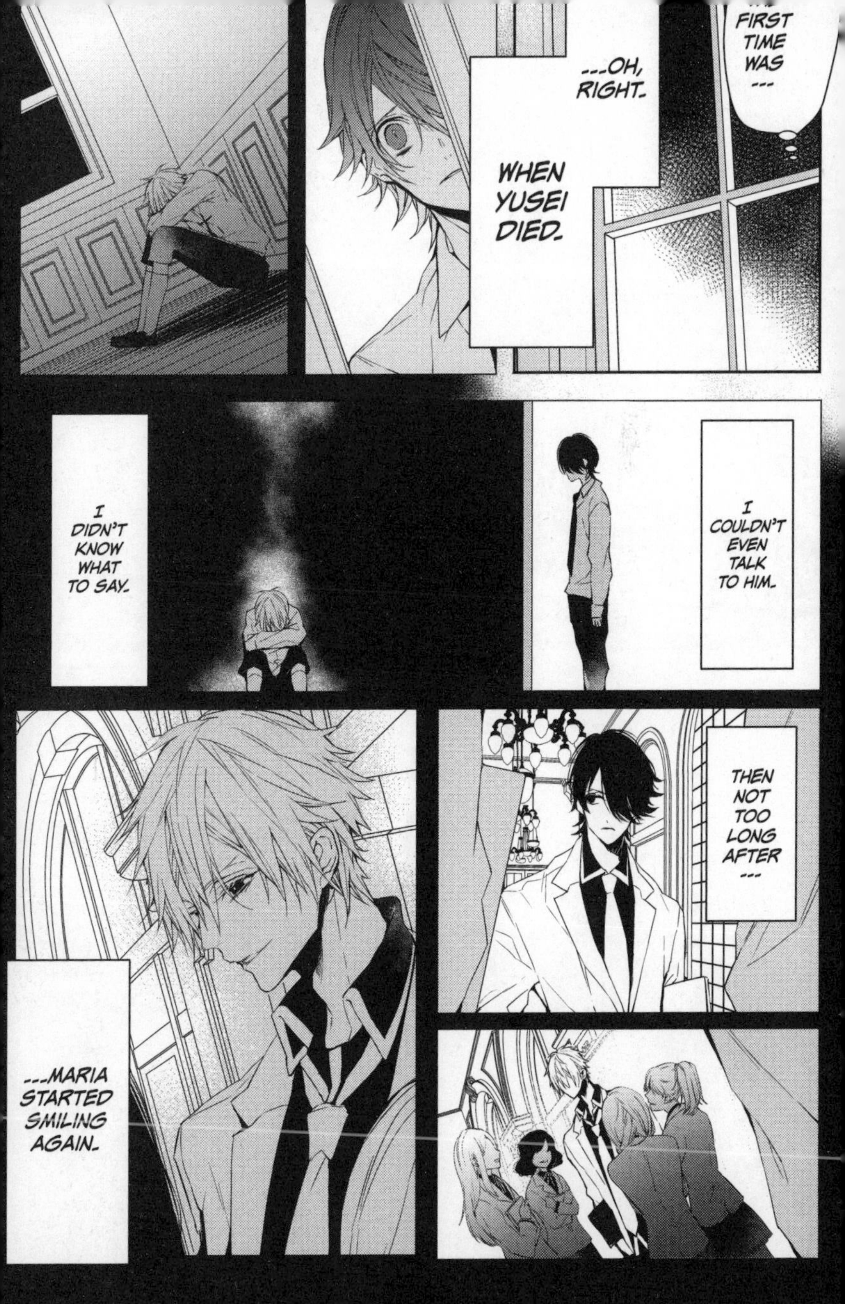
FIRST TIME WAS ---
---OH, RIGHT.
WHEN YUSEI DIED.
I COULDN'T EVEN TALK TO HIM.
I DIDN'T KNOW WHAT TO SAY.
THEN NOT TOO LONG AFTER ---
---MARIA STARTED SMILING AGAIN.

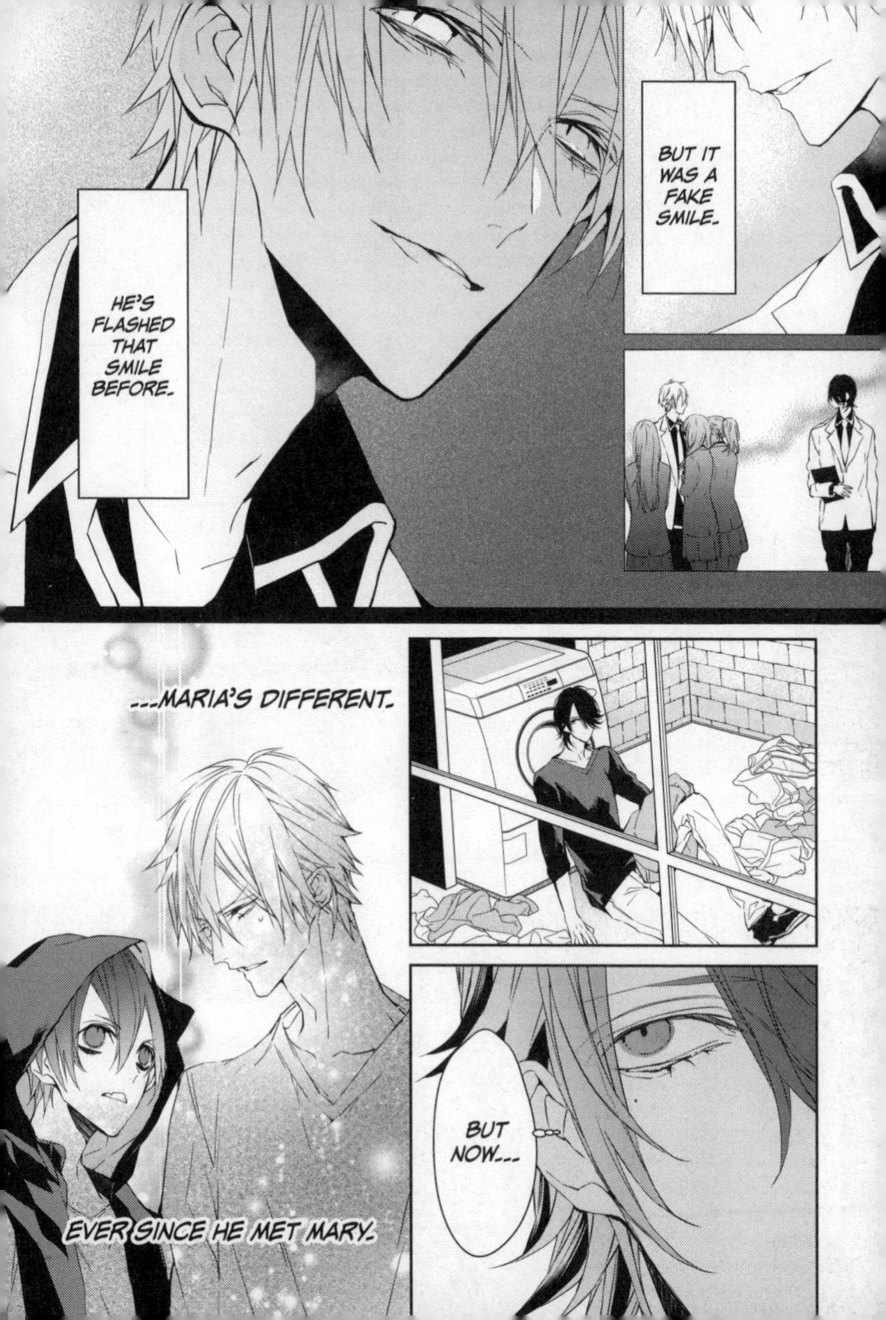
BUT IT WAS A FAKE SMILE.
HE'S FLASHED THAT SMILE BEFORE.
BUT NOW...
...MARIA'S DIFFERENT.
EVER SINCE HE MET MARY.

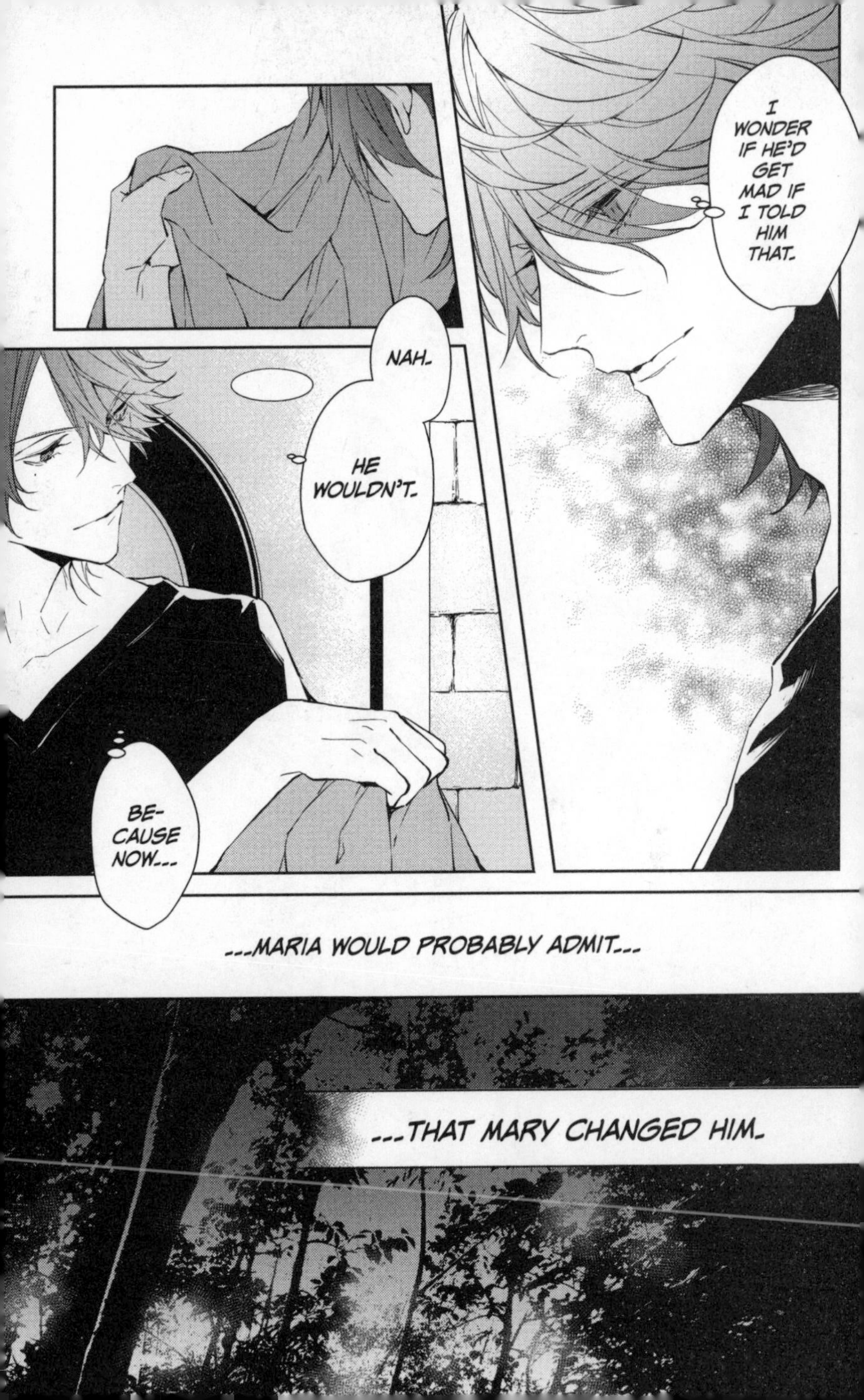
I WONDER IF HE'D GET MAD IF I TOLD HIM THAT.
NAH.
HE WOULDN'T.
BE-CAUSE NOW...
...MARIA WOULD PROBABLY ADMIT...
...THAT MARY CHANGED HIM.

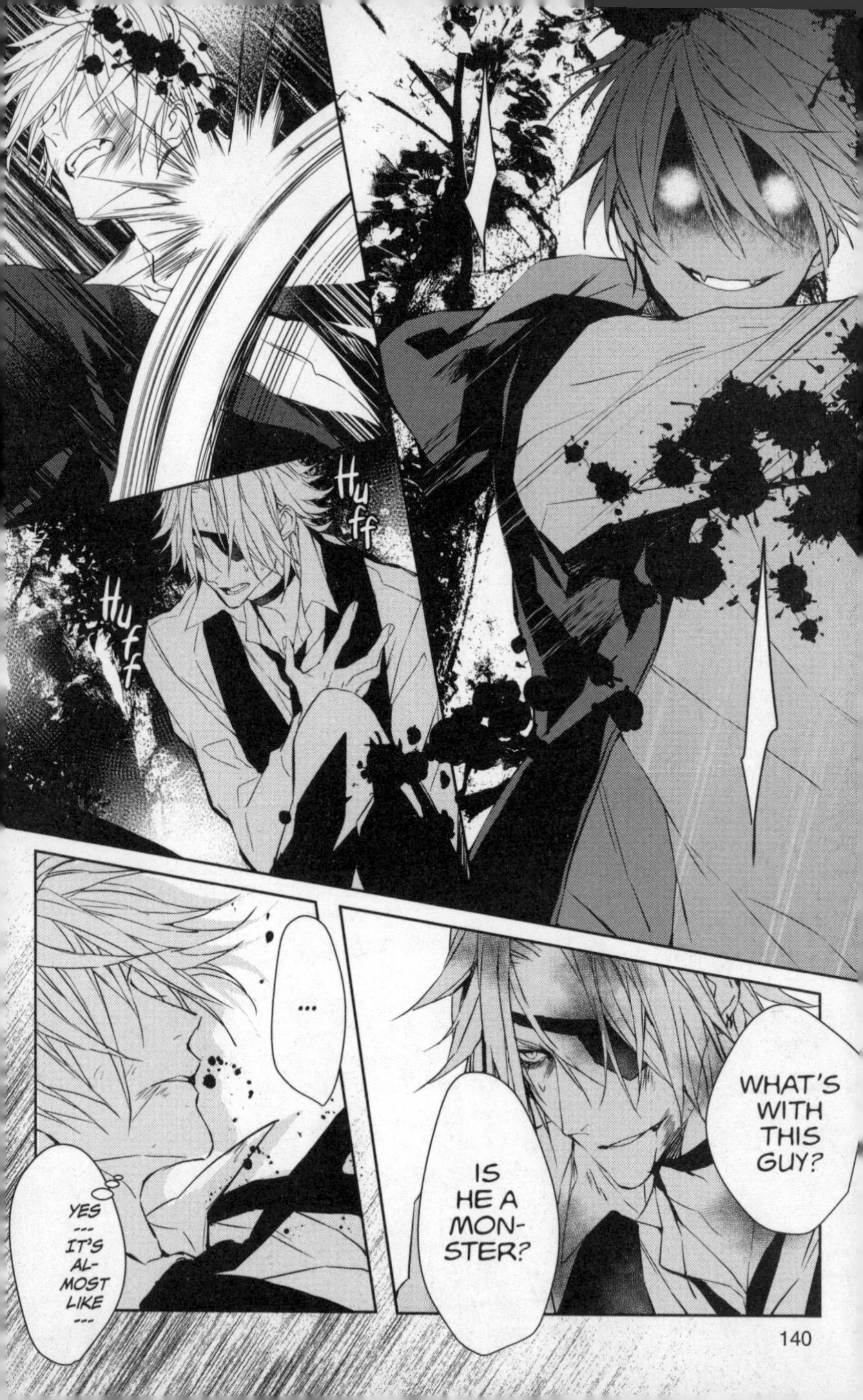
Huff
Huff
WHAT'S WITH THIS GUY?
IS HE A MON-STER?
...
YES... IT'S AL-MOST LIKE...

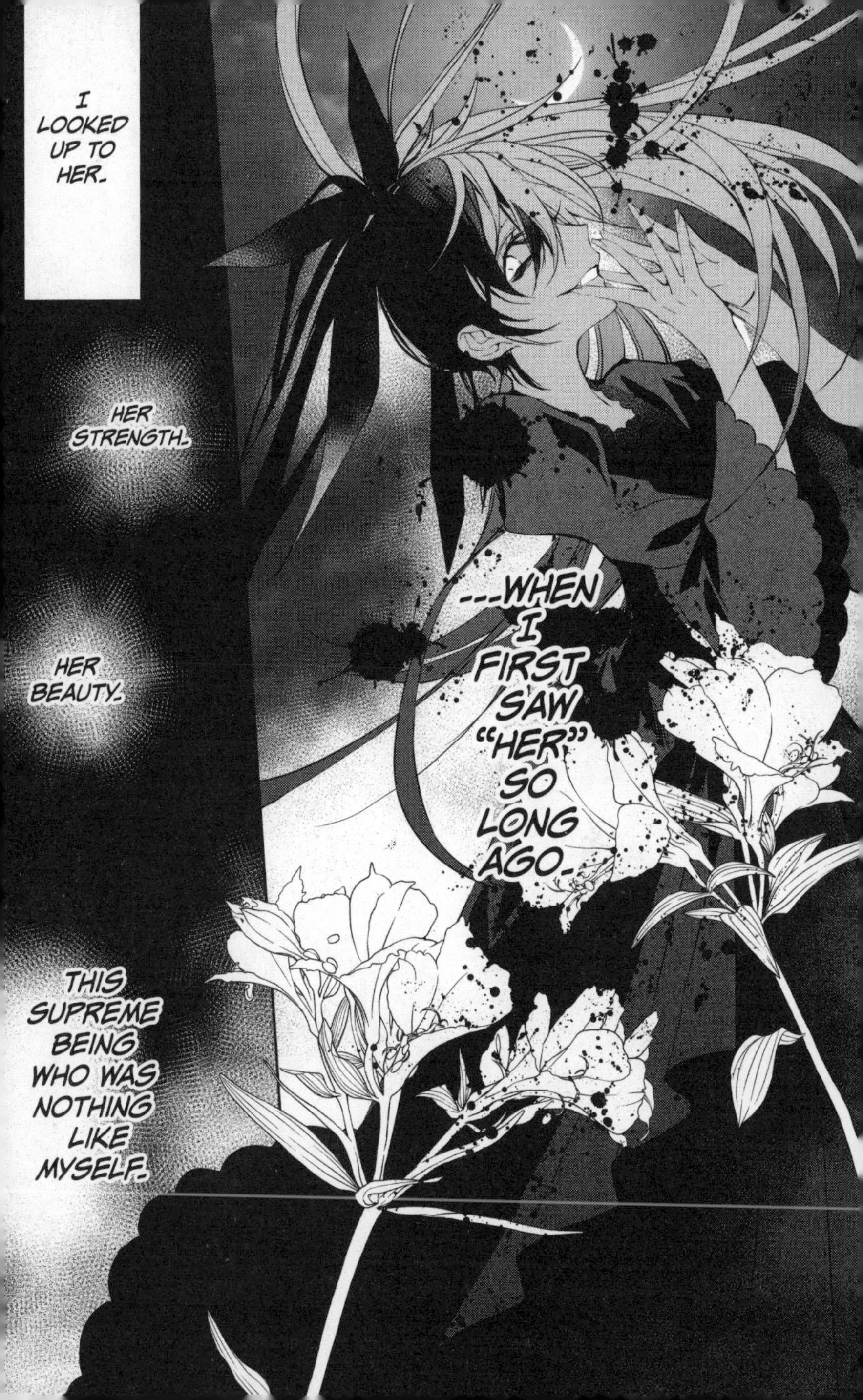
I LOOKED UP TO HER...
...WHEN I FIRST SAW "HER" SO LONG AGO...
HER STRENGTH...
HER BEAUTY...
THIS SUPREME BEING WHO WAS NOTHING LIKE MYSELF...

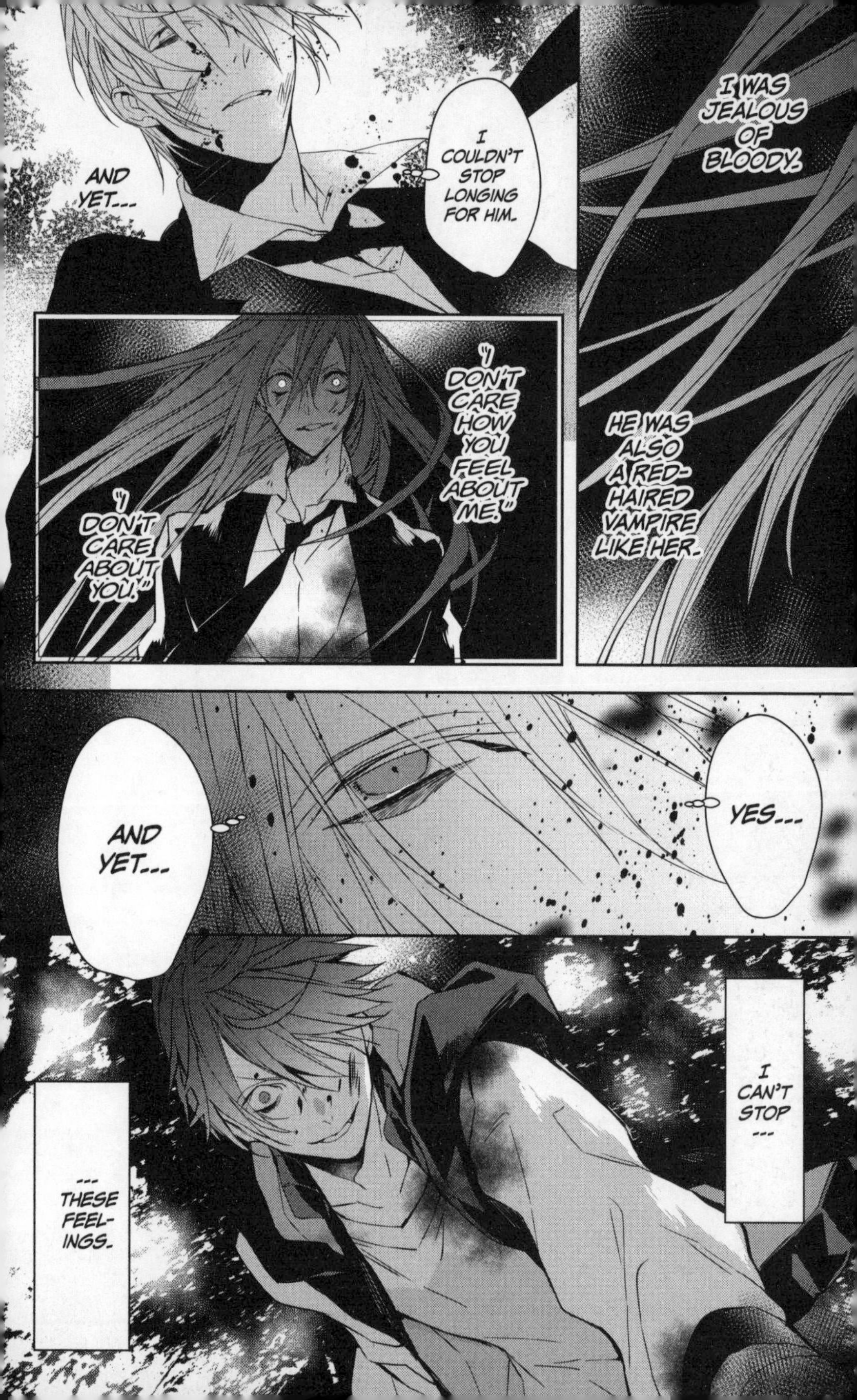
I WAS JEALOUS OF BLOODY.
HE WAS ALSO A RED-HAIRED VAMPIRE LIKE HER.
I COULDN'T STOP LONGING FOR HIM.
AND YET...
"I DON'T CARE HOW YOU FEEL ABOUT ME."
"I DON'T CARE ABOUT YOU."
YES...
AND YET...
I CAN'T STOP...
...THESE FEELINGS.

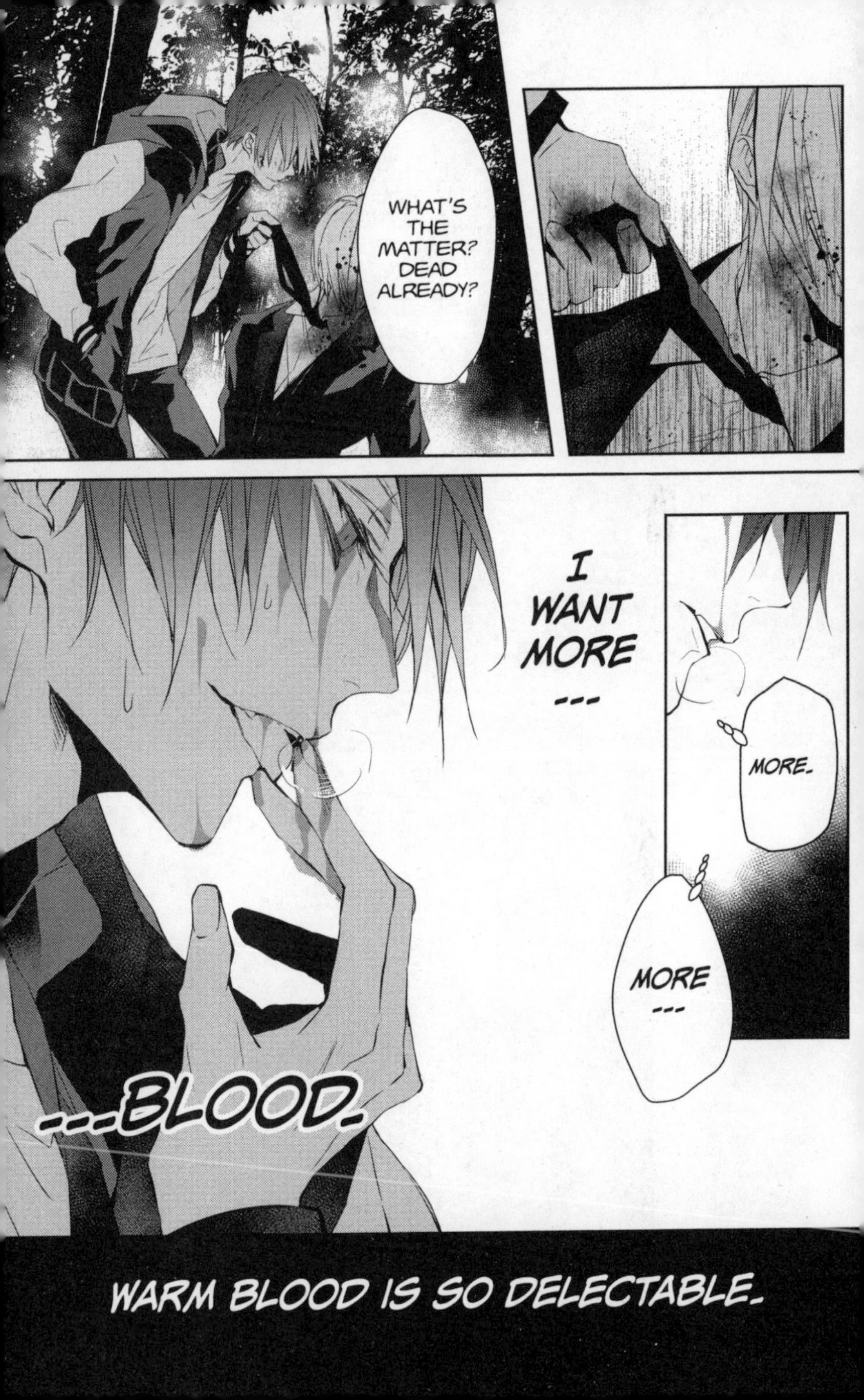
WHAT'S THE MATTER? DEAD ALREADY?
MORE.
MORE ---
I WANT MORE ---
---BLOOD.
WARM BLOOD IS SO DELECTABLE.

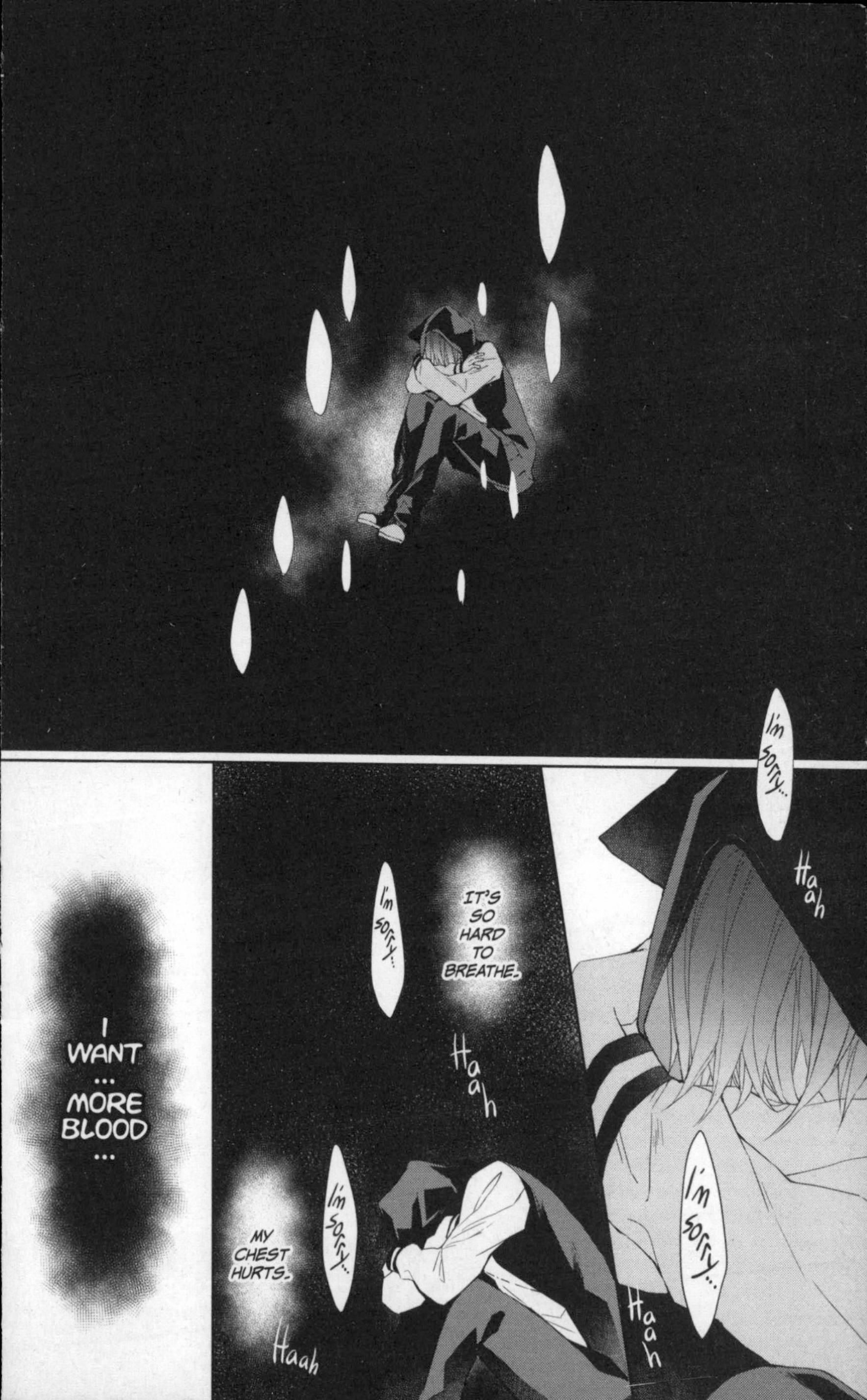
I'm sorry...
Haah
I'm sorry...
Haah
IT'S SO HARD TO BREATHE...
I'm sorry...
Haah
I'm sorry...
MY CHEST HURTS...
Haah
I WANT ... MORE BLOOD ...

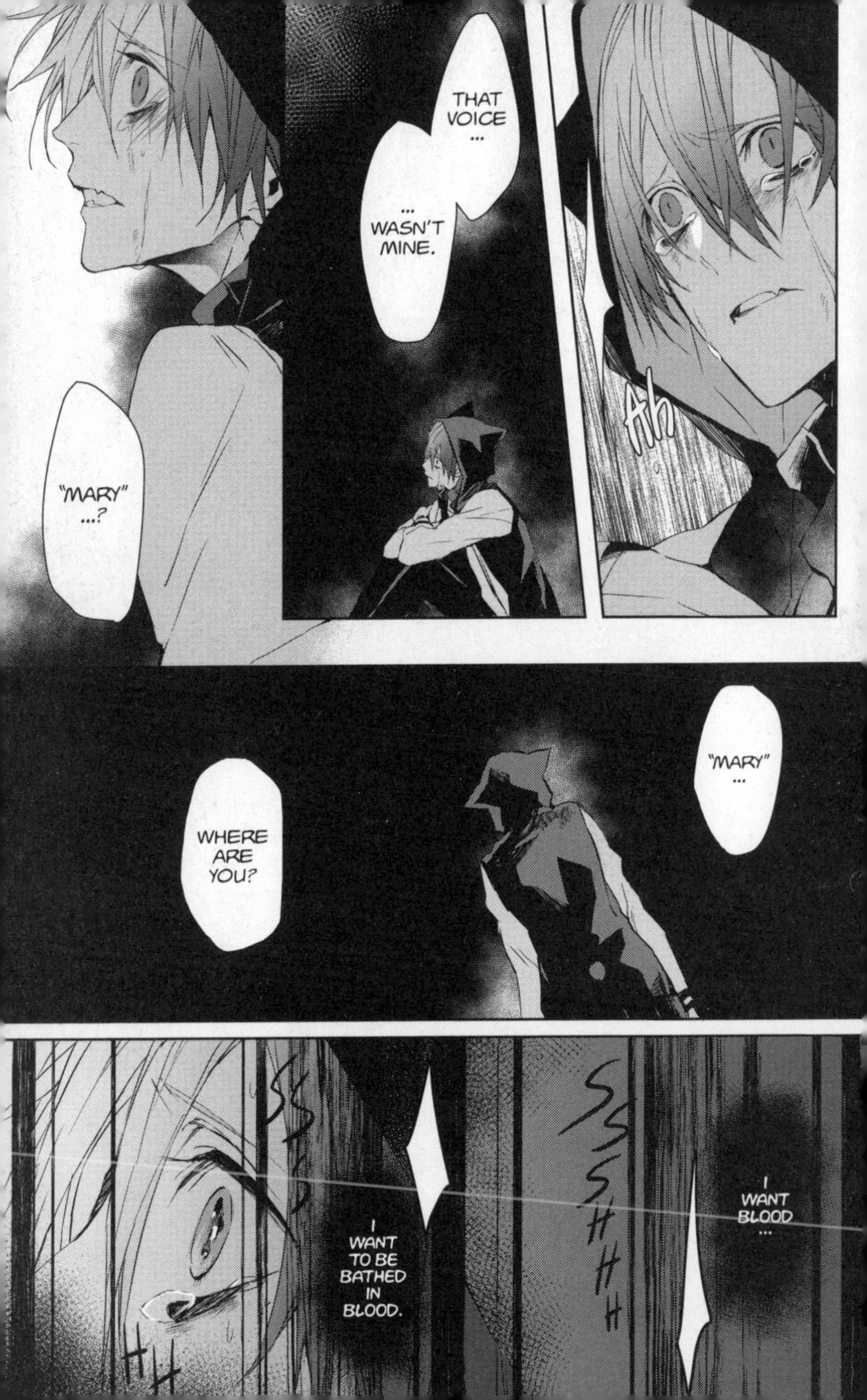
Ah
THAT VOICE ...
... WASN'T MINE.
"MARY" ...?
"MARY" ...
WHERE ARE YOU?
I WANT BLOOD ...
I WANT TO BE BATHED IN BLOOD.

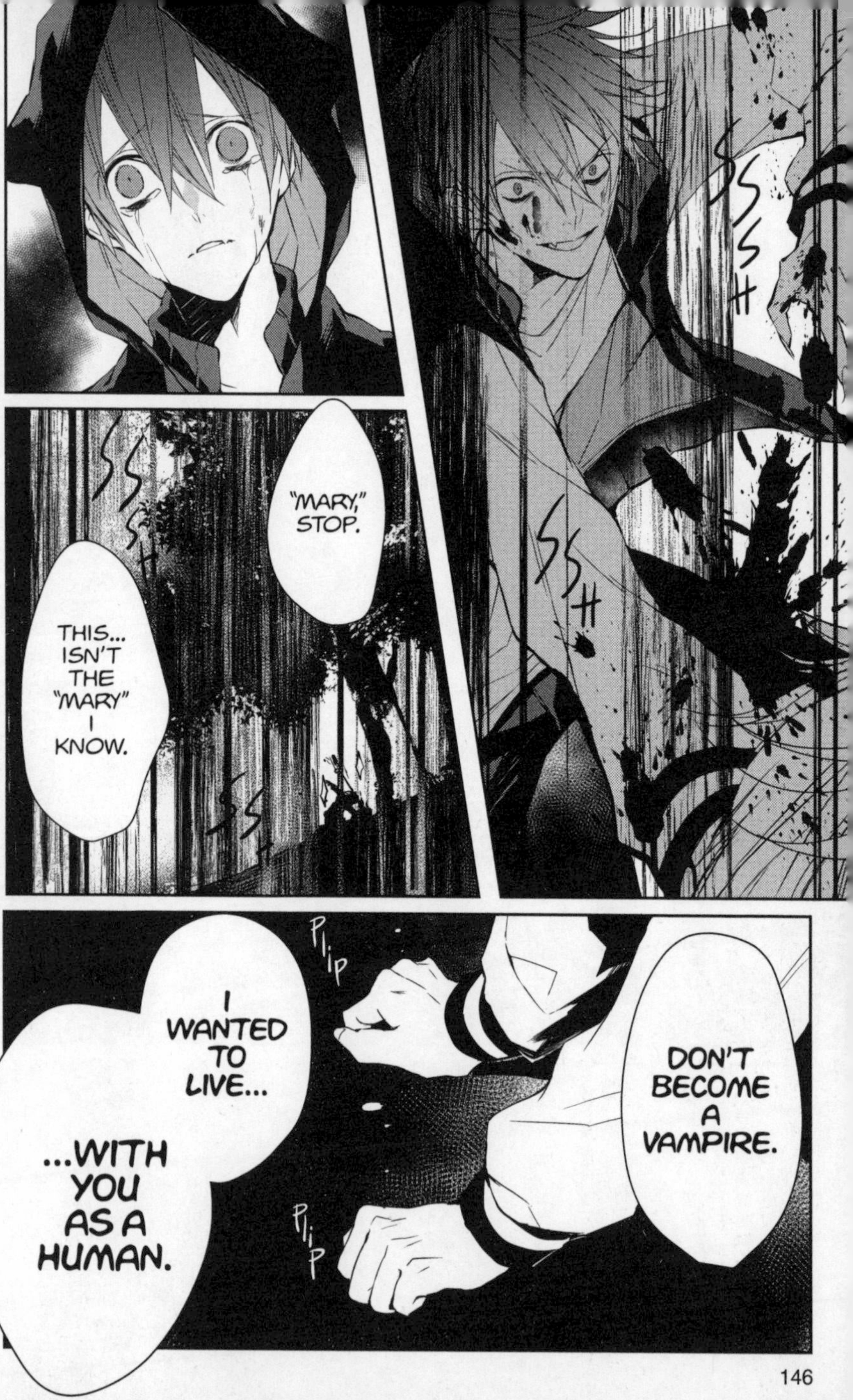
SSSH
SSH
"MARY," STOP.
THIS... ISN'T THE "MARY" I KNOW.
SSSH
SSH
DON'T BECOME A VAMPIRE.
PLIP
I WANTED TO LIVE...
...WITH YOU AS A HUMAN.
PLIP

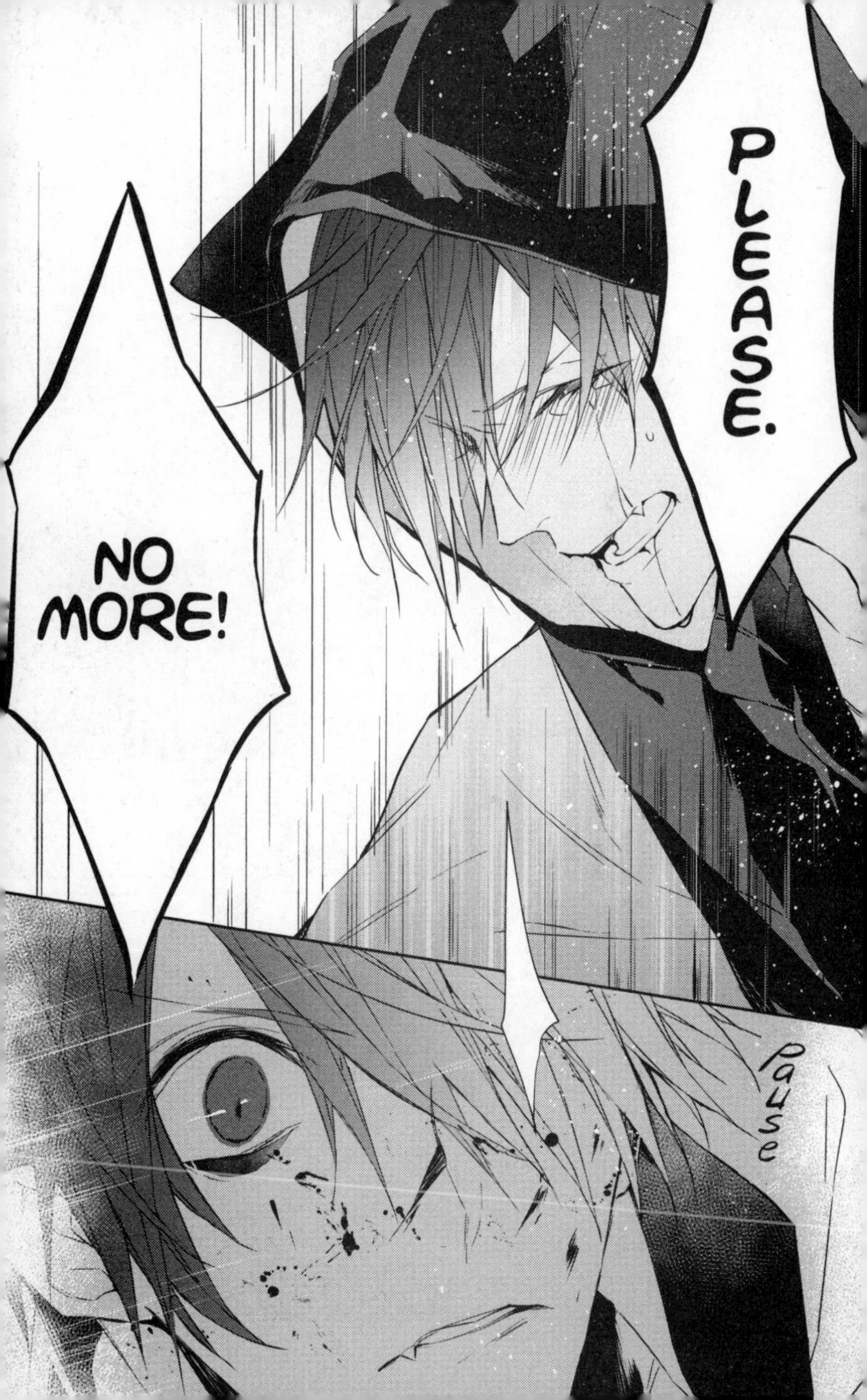
PLEASE.
NO MORE!
Pause

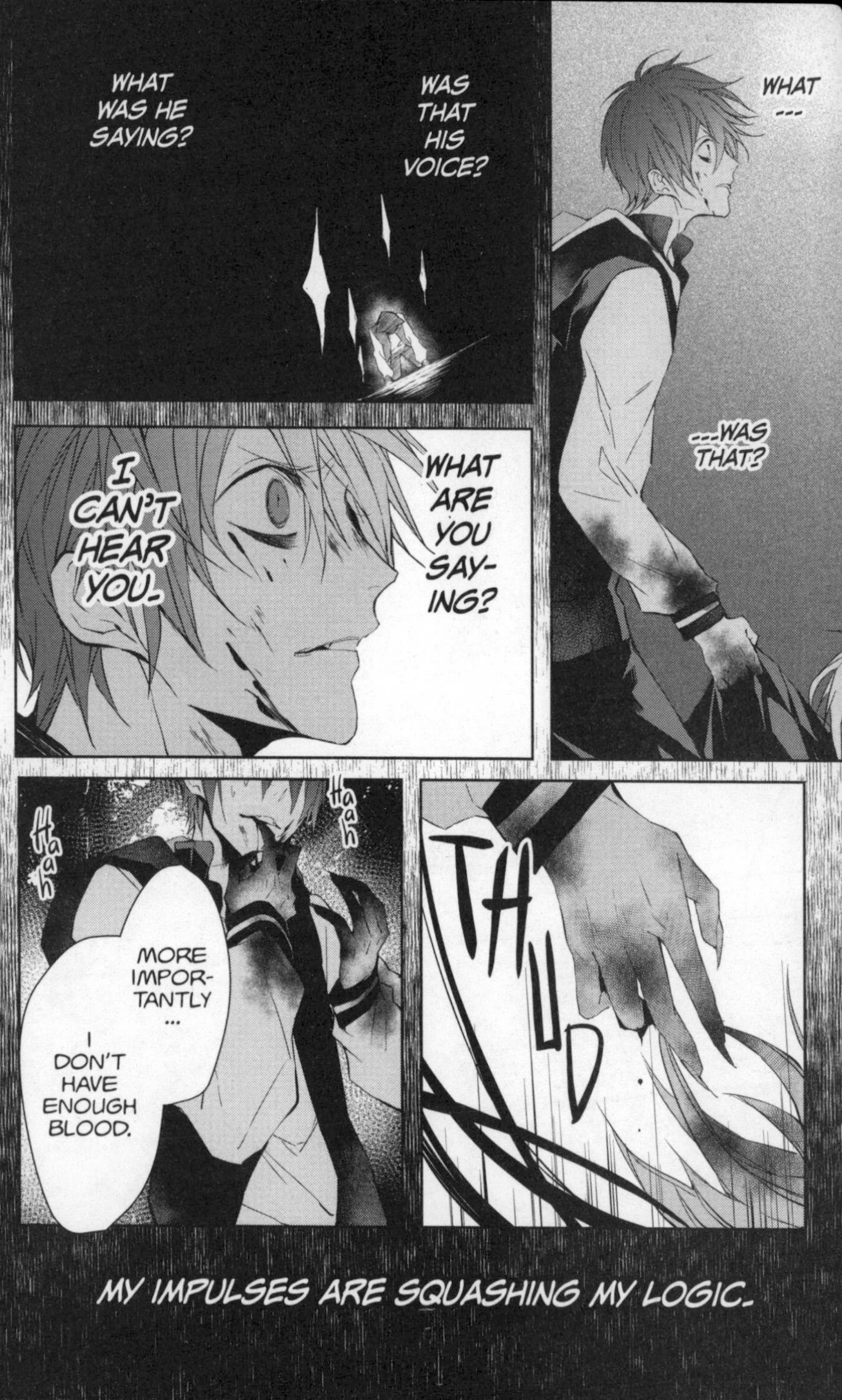
WHAT ---
---WAS THAT?
WAS THAT HIS VOICE?
WHAT WAS HE SAYING?
WHAT ARE YOU SAY-ING?
I CAN'T HEAR YOU...
THUD
Haah
Haah
MORE IMPOR-TANTLY...
I DON'T HAVE ENOUGH BLOOD.
MY IMPULSES ARE SQUASHING MY LOGIC...

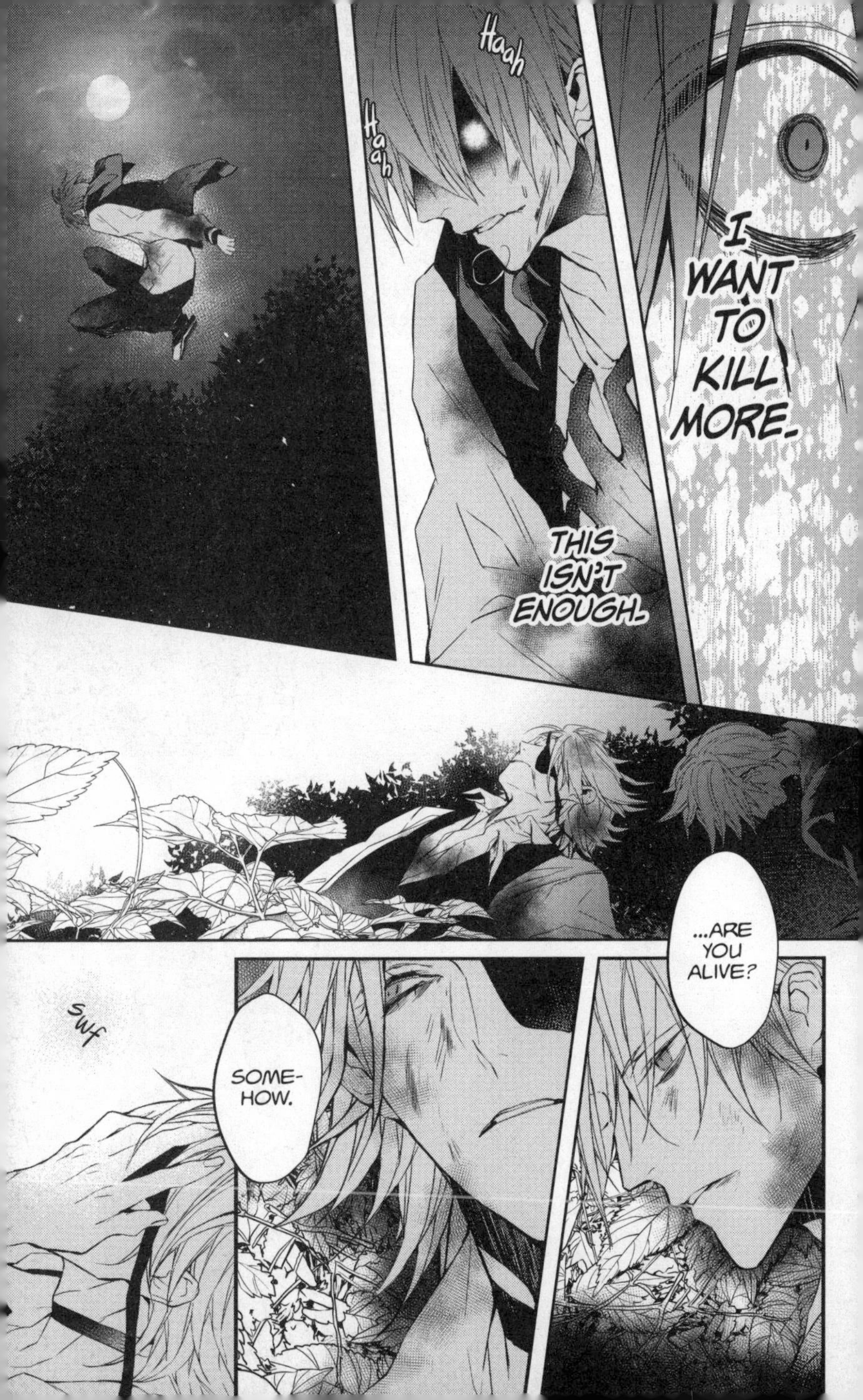
I WANT TO KILL MORE...
Haah
Haah
THIS ISN'T ENOUGH...
...ARE YOU ALIVE?
SOME-HOW.
swf

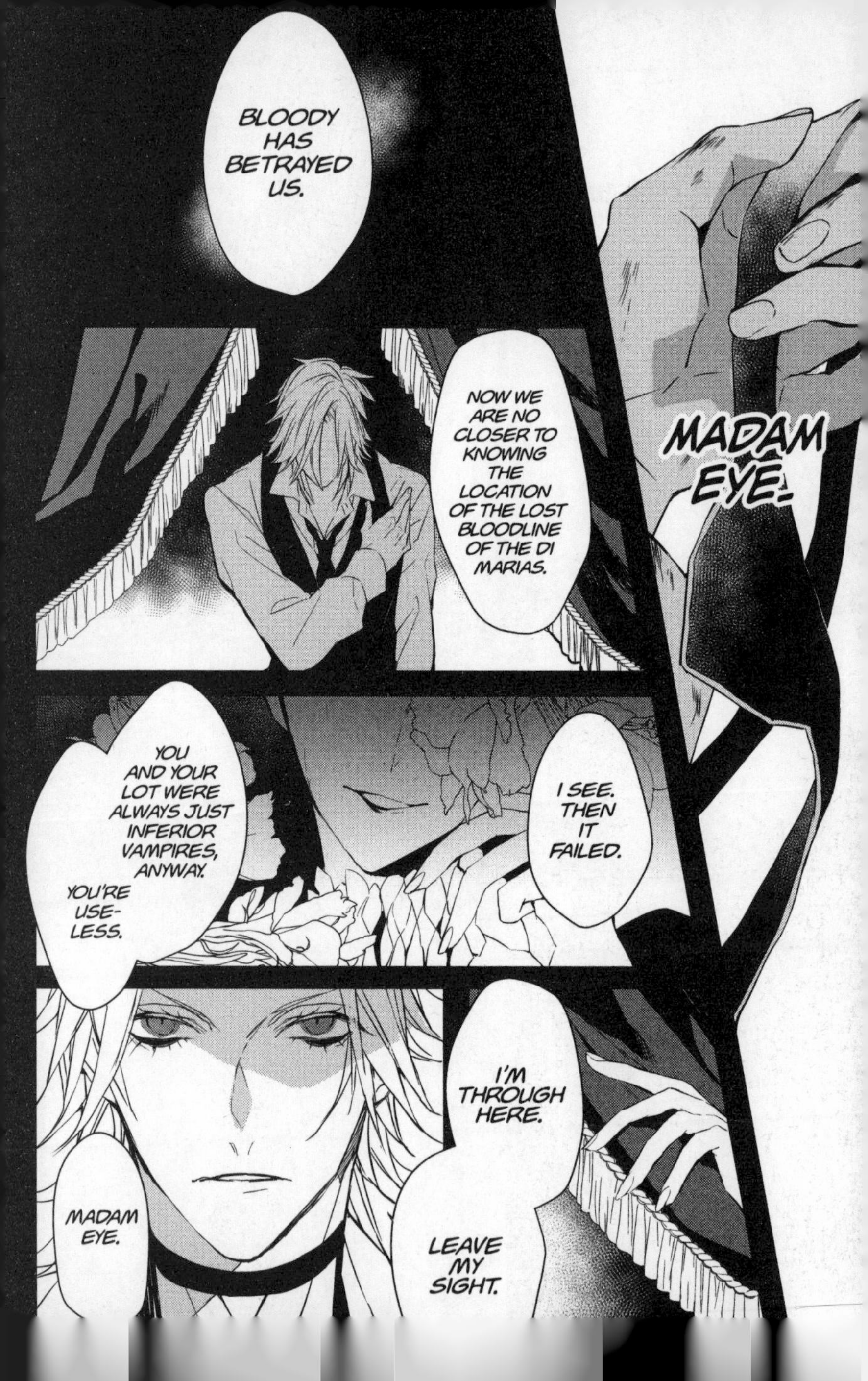

MADAM EYE..
BLOODY HAS BETRAYED US.
NOW WE ARE NO CLOSER TO KNOWING THE LOCATION OF THE LOST BLOODLINE OF THE DI MARIAS.
I SEE. THEN IT FAILED.
YOU AND YOUR LOT WERE ALWAYS JUST INFERIOR VAMPIRES, ANYWAY.
YOU'RE USE-LESS.
I'M THROUGH HERE.
LEAVE MY SIGHT.
MADAM EYE.

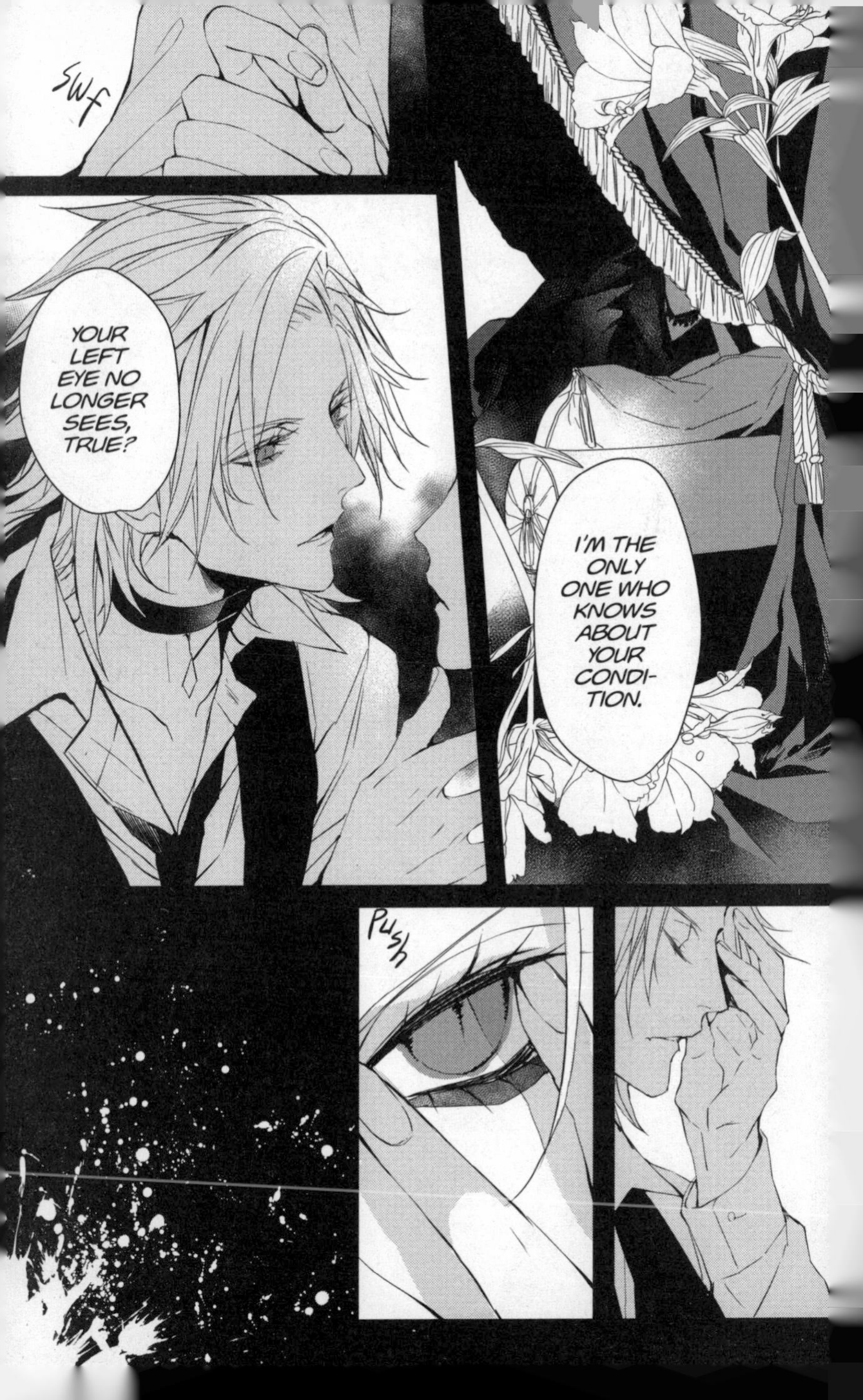
I'M THE ONLY ONE WHO KNOWS ABOUT YOUR CONDITION.
SWF
YOUR LEFT EYE NO LONGER SEES, TRUE?
Push

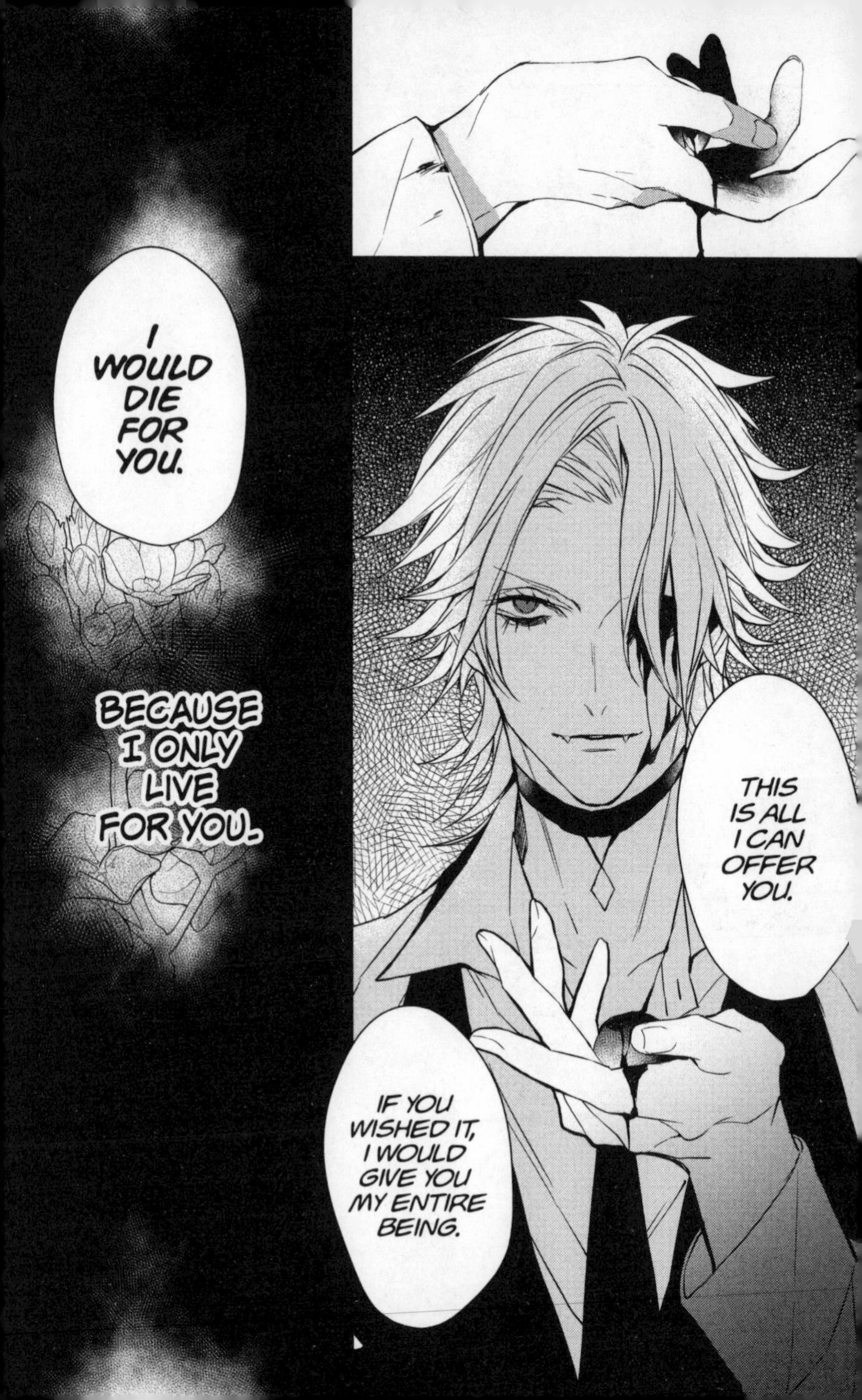
THIS IS ALL I CAN OFFER YOU.
IF YOU WISHED IT, I WOULD GIVE YOU MY ENTIRE BEING.
I WOULD DIE FOR YOU.
BECAUSE I ONLY LIVE FOR YOU.

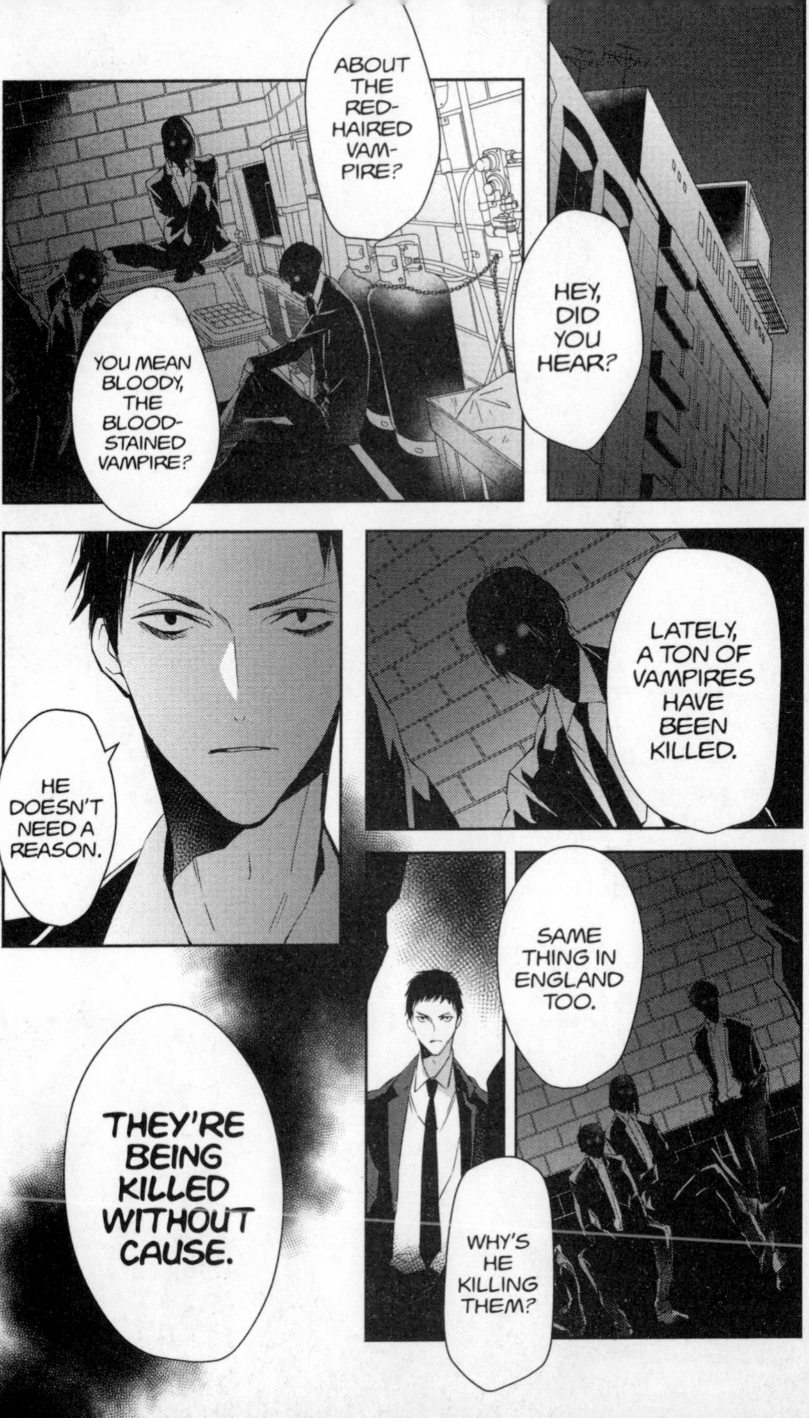
HEY, DID YOU HEAR?
ABOUT THE RED-HAIRED VAMPIRE?
YOU MEAN BLOODY, THE BLOOD-STAINED VAMPIRE?
LATELY, A TON OF VAMPIRES HAVE BEEN KILLED.
HE DOESN'T NEED A REASON.
SAME THING IN ENGLAND TOO.
WHY'S HE KILLING THEM?
THEY'RE BEING KILLED WITHOUT CAUSE.

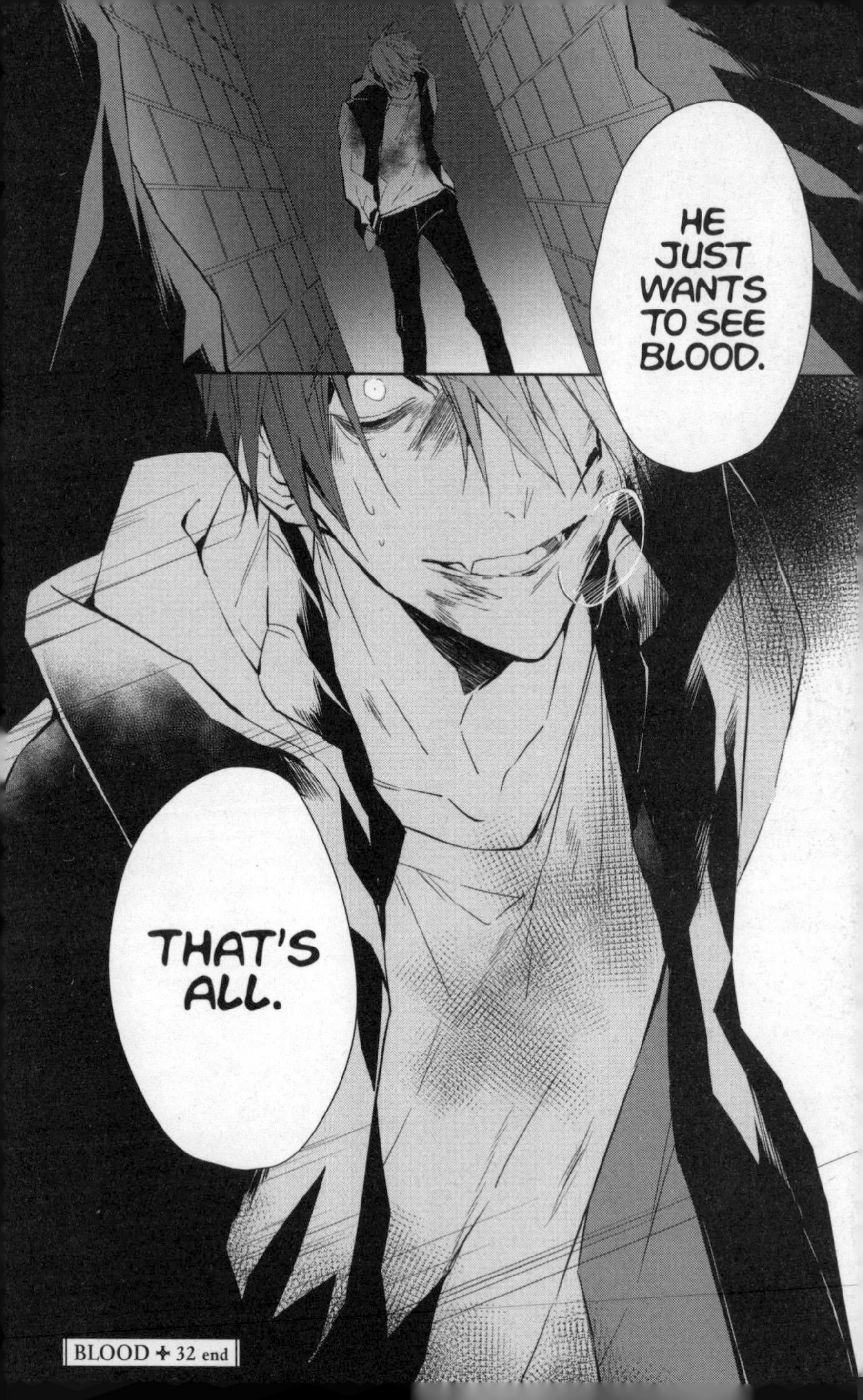
HE JUST WANTS TO SEE BLOOD.
THAT'S ALL.
BLOOD ✦ 32 end

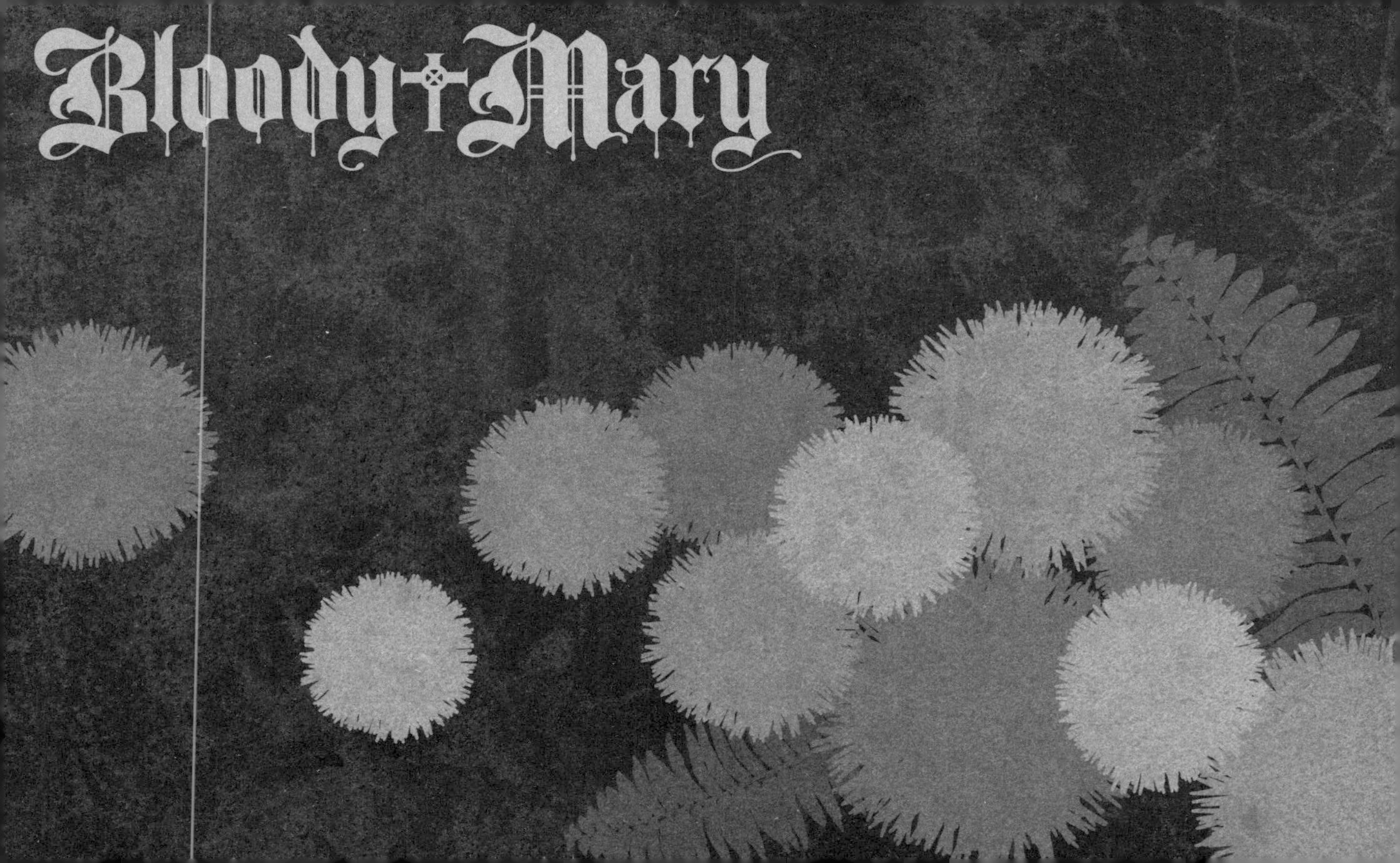
Bloody+Mary

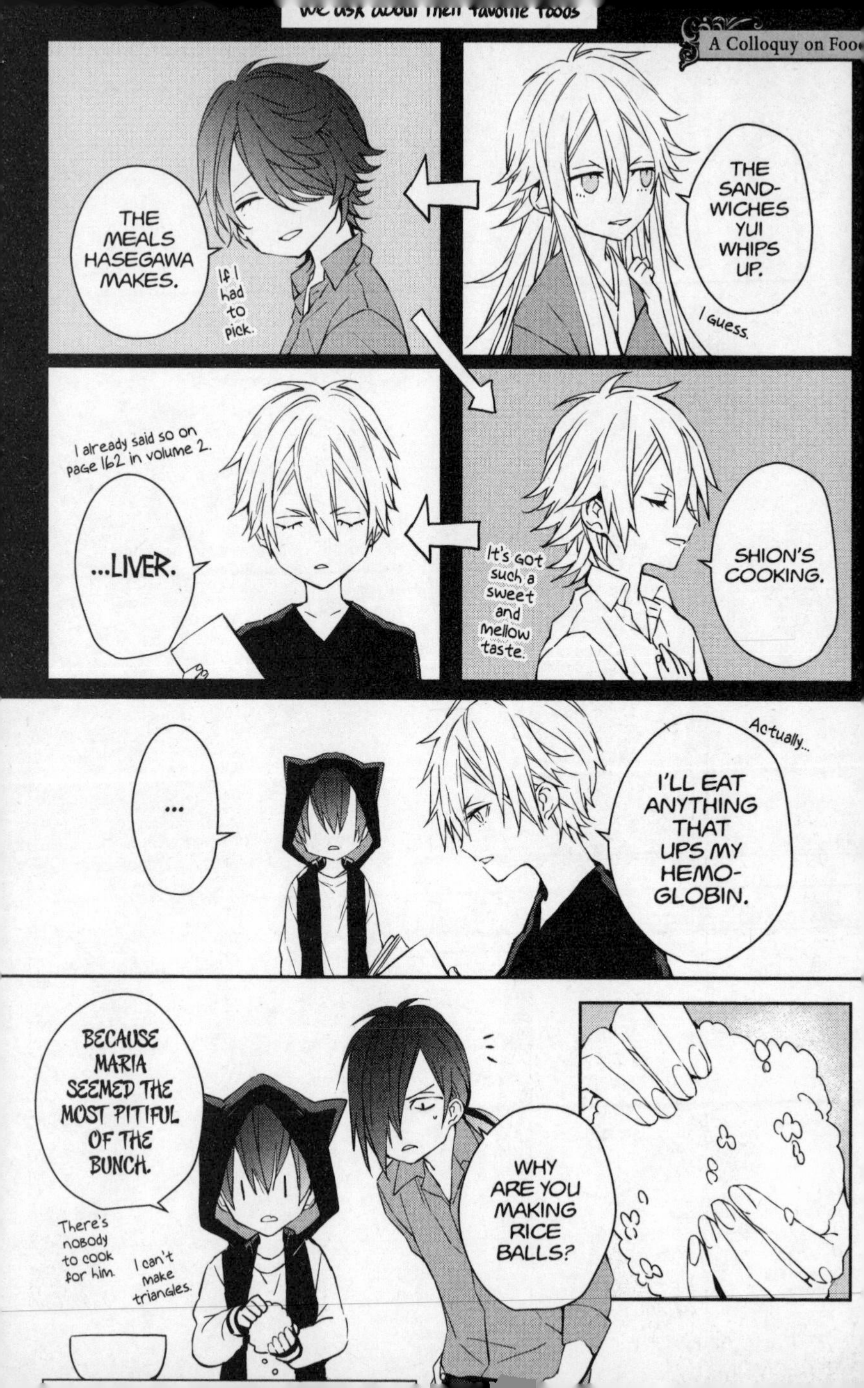
We ask about their favorite foods
THE SAND-WICHES YUI WHIPS UP.
I guess.
THE MEALS HASEGAWA MAKES.
If I had to pick.
SHION'S COOKING.
It's got such a sweet and mellow taste.
...LIVER.
I already said so on page 162 in volume 2.
Actually...
I'LL EAT ANYTHING THAT UPS MY HEMO-GLOBIN.
...
WHY ARE YOU MAKING RICE BALLS?
BECAUSE MARIA SEEMED THE MOST PITIFUL OF THE BUNCH.
There's nobody to cook for him.
I can't make triangles.

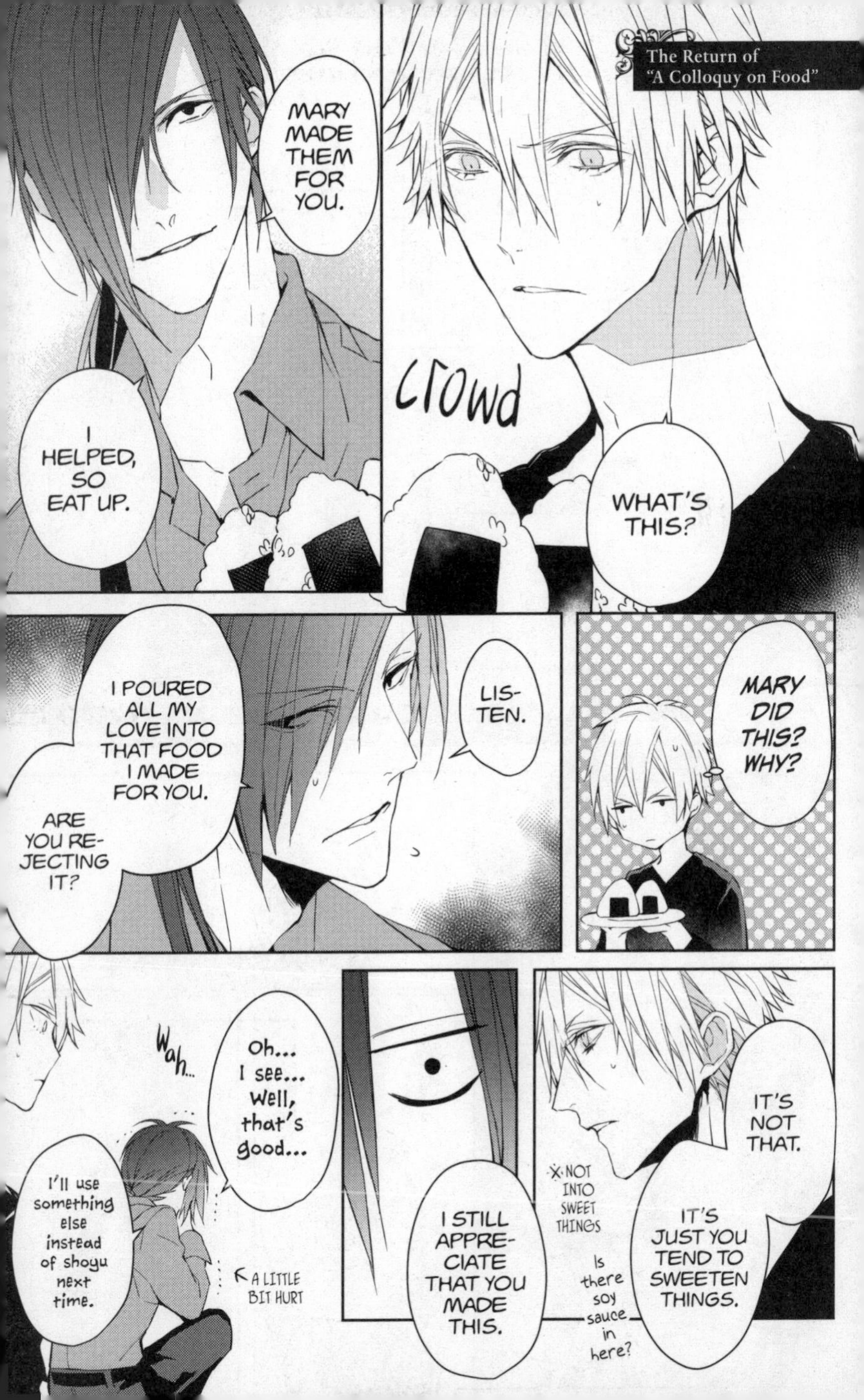
Crowd
WHAT'S THIS?
MARY MADE THEM FOR YOU.
I HELPED, SO EAT UP.
MARY DID THIS? WHY?
LIS-TEN.
I POURED ALL MY LOVE INTO THAT FOOD I MADE FOR YOU.
ARE YOU RE-JECTING IT?
IT'S NOT THAT.
IT'S JUST YOU TEND TO SWEETEN THINGS.
Is there soy sauce in here?
※ NOT INTO SWEET THINGS
I STILL APPRE-CIATE THAT YOU MADE THIS.
Wah...
Oh... I see... Well, that's good...
I'll use something else instead of shoyu next time.
← A LITTLE BIT HURT

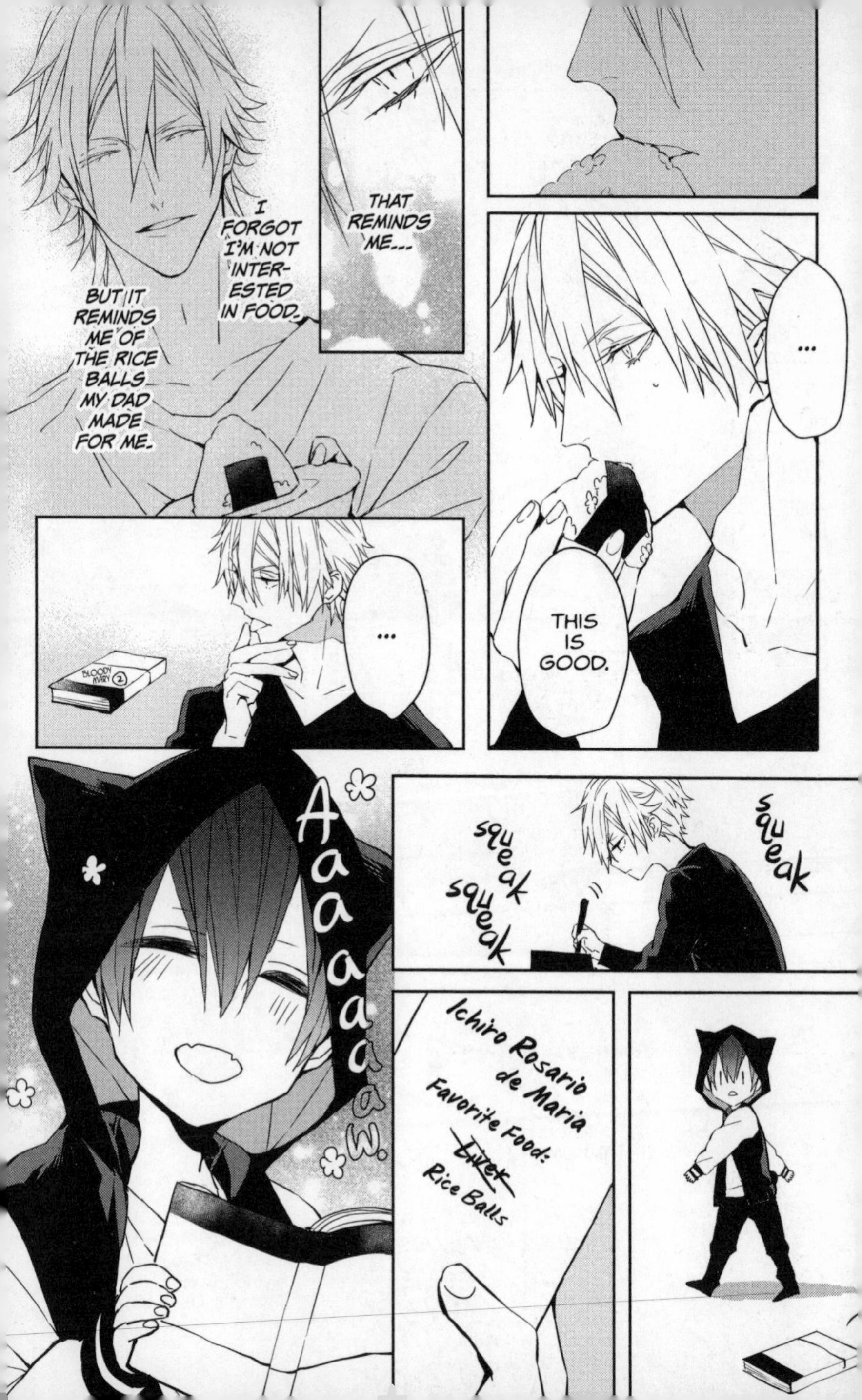
...
THIS IS GOOD.
THAT REMINDS ME...
I FORGOT I'M NOT INTER-ESTED IN FOOD.
BUT IT REMINDS ME OF THE RICE BALLS MY DAD MADE FOR ME.
BLOODY MARY 2
...
squeak
squeak squeak
Ichiro Rosario de Maria
Favorite Food:
Diet
Rice Balls
Aaaaaaaw.

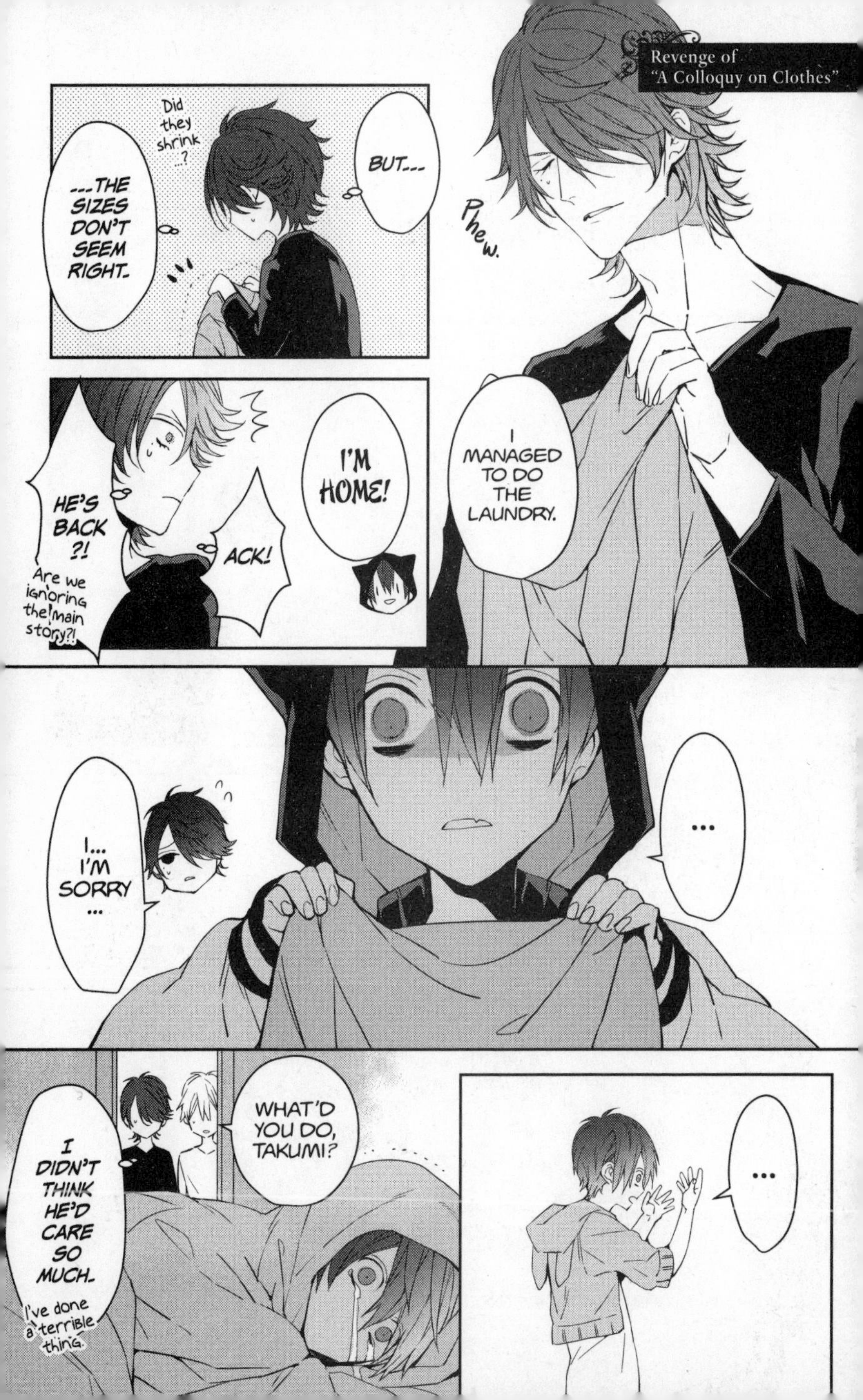
Revenge of "A Colloquy on Clothes"
Phew.
I MANAGED TO DO THE LAUNDRY.
BUT...
Did they shrink...?
...THE SIZES DON'T SEEM RIGHT.
I'M HOME!
ACK!
HE'S BACK?!
Are we ignoring the main story?!
...
I... I'M SORRY...
...
WHAT'D YOU DO, TAKUMI?
I DIDN'T THINK HE'D CARE SO MUCH.
I've done a terrible thing.

Thank you for picking up volume 8!!

◇ Now that Mary's remembered his past, we're on our way to the most interesting part of the story. I hope you'll stick around!!

◇ Recently my cat has been waking me up very gently!!

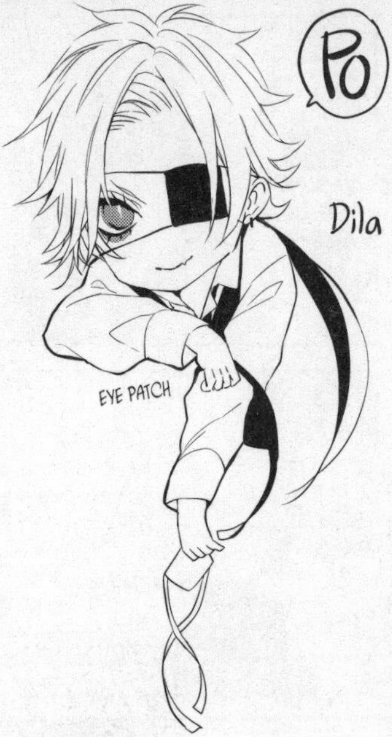
Po
Dila
EYE PATCH

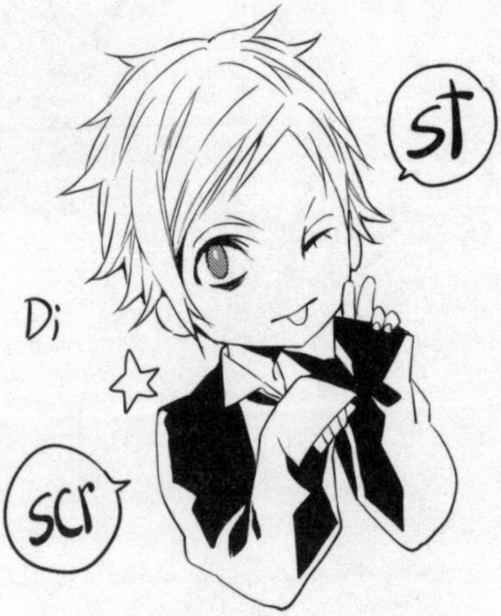
st
Di
scr

Looking forward to seeing you in volume 9!

—ヒュミャアナヒ"

SPECIAL THANKS

Mihoru/M-fuchi/H-gawa/
T-mizu-sama/T-ko-sama

Production Team•Support
Haruo/Sumida/M-ika

Editor S/Designer
Everyone involved
and
everyone who read this

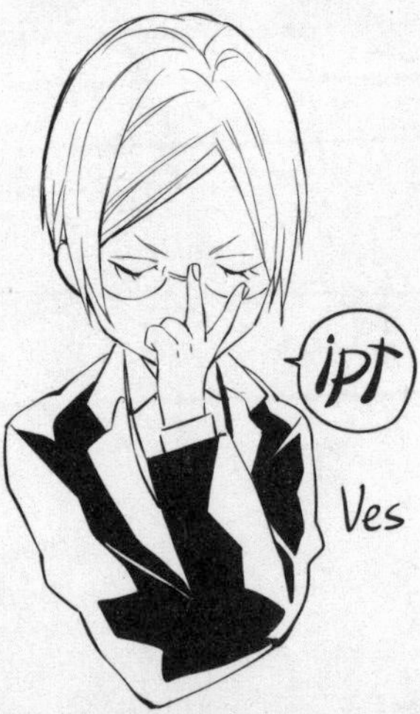
ipt
Ves

# akaza samamiya

Born November 7, Cancer, blood type B.
I recently bought a cat tower for my cat,
but it's never used.

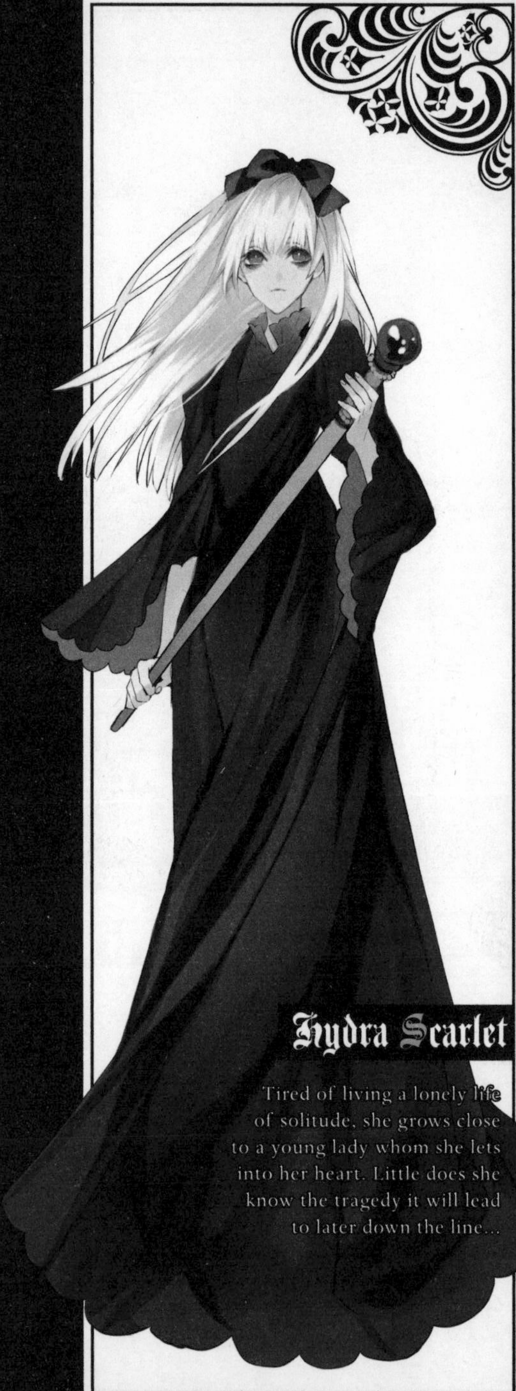
Hydra Scarlet
Tired of living a lonely life of solitude, she grows close to a young lady whom she lets into her heart. Little does she know the tragedy it will lead to later down the line...

# Bloody Eye

Suffering from an incurable disease and waiting to die, she meets Hydra and is reborn as the vampire Bloody Eye. She has red and black hair, and only her right eye is red.

Election Day: July 26, 2056 7 a.m. to 8 p.m.
Ready to DIE FOR YOU
Hase
Cuteness is Justice
Two-tone Party
Bloody Eye
Rice Party
Shino-bu

Election Day: July 26, 2056 7 a.m. to 8 p.m.

I will not forget my long-standing grudge!
The Love & Hate Party
Hydra Scarlet
An Ally to the HOUSEWIFE DEMOGRAPHIC
Yuki

# Bloody+Mary

Akaza Samamiya

# Bloody Mary

Volume 8
Shojo Beat Edition

**story and art by** Akaza Samamiya

**translation** Katherine Schilling
**touch-up art & lettering** Sabrina Heep
**design** Shawn Carrico
**editor** Erica Yee

BLOODY MARY Volume 8
© Akaza SAMAMIYA 2016
First published in Japan in 2016 by KADOKAWA
CORPORATION, Tokyo.
English translation rights arranged with KADOKAWA
CORPORATION, Tokyo.

The stories, characters and incidents mentioned
in this publication are entirely fictional.

Printed in the U.S.A.

Published by VIZ Media, LLC
P.O. Box 77010
San Francisco, CA 94107

10 9 8 7 6 5 4 3 2 1
First printing, September 2017

www.viz.com    www.shojobeat.com

# stop

## YOU MAY BE READING THE
# wrong way

IT'S TRUE: In keeping with the original Japanese comic format, this book reads from right to left—so action, sound effects and word balloons are completely reversed. This preserves the orientation of the original artwork—plus, it's fun! Check out the diagram shown here to get the hang of things, and then turn to the other side of the book to get started!

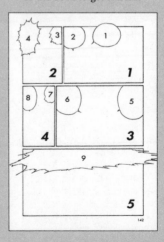